D1713071

SHAKESPEARE
STUDIES

SHAKESPEARE STUDIES VOLUME XXXI

EDITED BY
LEEDS BARROLL

BOOK REVIEW EDITOR

Susan Zimmerman

Queens College
City University of New York

Madison • Teaneck
Fairleigh Dickinson University Press
London: Associated University Presses

Associated University Presses
2010 Eastpark Boulevard
Cranbury, NJ 08512

Associated University Presses
Unit 304
The Chandlery
50 Westminster Bridge Road
London SE1 7QY, England

Associated University Presses
P.O. Box 338, Port Credit
Mississauga, Ontario
Canada L5G 4L8

The paper used in this publication meets the requirements of the American National Standard for Permanence of Paper for Printed Library Materials Z39.48-1984.

International Standard Book Number: 0-8386-3999-2 (vol. XXXI)
International Standard Serial Number: 0-0582-9399

All editorial correspondence concerning *Shakespeare Studies* should be addressed to the Editorial Office, *Shakespeare Studies,* English Dept., Fine Arts, University of Maryland (Baltimore County), Baltimore, Maryland 21250. Manuscripts submitted without appropriate postage will not be returned. Orders and subscriptions should be directed to Associated University Presses, 2010 Eastpark Boulevard, Cranbury, New Jersey 08512.

Shakespeare Studies disclaims responsibility for statements, either of fact or opinion, made by contributors.

PRINTED IN THE UNITED STATES OF AMERICA

Contents

6   *Contents*

                               Reviews

Foreword

SHAKESPEARE STUDIES is very pleased to offer in Volume XXXI a new feature, the first in an annual series of articles on "Early Modern Drama around the World." In this series, specialists in drama performed in other areas of the globe during Shakespeare's time will discuss the state of scholarly study for each of these regions. Thus, in the present volume, Grant Shen discusses the study of late Ming theatrical activity in China, while Richard Pym views the state of scholarship on drama in Golden-Age Spain. Volume XXXII will present similar approaches to French and to Japanese dramatic activity in the same period while succeeding volumes will, among other topics, deal with theatrical studies of Mughul India and of the Ottoman Empire in the early modern period of Europe.

Volume XXXI also includes two review articles: "Imagination in History" by David Harris Sacks, on the recent work of Stephen Greenblatt, and an essay by Raphael Falco, "Is the Renaissance an Aesthetic Category?" based on *The Waning of the Renaissance* by William J. Bouwsma and *Cosmopoiesis* by Giuseppe Mazzotta. Like several of the reviews in this volume (such as Stuart Clark's, for example), Falco's essay supports the aim in *Shakespeare Studies* of extending its intellectual reach to include relevant historical, philosophical, and theoretical works that are not directly related to the theatre. Four full-length articles by Gustav Ungerer, Patricia Parker, Thomas Moisan, and Jennifer Lewin deal with *The Merchant of Venice, Hamlet, Much Ado about Nothing*, and Shakespeare's final plays, respectively. Finally, our review section includes twenty-one reviews of books on varied topics such as witchcraft, vagrancy, and public devotion in early modern England, as well as on editions of the collected works of Elizabeth I and of writings by other early modern women.

LEEDS BARROLL

Contributors

REID BARBOUR is Professor of English at the University of North Carolina, Chapel Hill. He is the author of *Deciphering Elizabethan Fiction* (1993); *English Epicures and Stoics: Ancient Legacies in Early Stuart Culture* (1998); *Literature and Religious Culture in Seventeenth-Century England* (2002); and *John Selden: Measures of the Holy Commonwealth in Seventeenth-Century England* (forthcoming, 2003). He is currently at work on the Oxford edition of Lucy Hutchinson (under the general editorship of David Norbrook).

STUART CLARK is Professor of History at the University of Wales Swansea. He has published *Thinking with Demons: The Idea of Witchcraft in Early Modern Europe* (1997) and is currently at work on a book on visual reality and visual paradox in the sixteenth and seventeenth centuries.

PETER S. DONALDSON is Professor of Literature at MIT. He is the author of *Machiavelli and Mystery of State* (1988), *Shakespearean Films/Shakespearean Directors* (1990), and of numerous articles on Shakespeare on film. He is currently working on a book on Shakespeare on film in the digital age.

RAPHAEL FALCO is Professor of English at the University of Maryland, Baltimore County. His most recent book is *Charismatic Authority in Early Modern English Tragedy* (2000). He is currently at work on a comparative study of early modern intellectual descent, tentatively titled *The Institution of Myth*.

SUSAN FRYE is Professor of English at the University of Wyoming. She is author of *Elizabeth I: The Competition for Representation* (1993), and has edited (with Karen Robertson) *Maids and Mistresses, Cousins and Queens: Women's Alliances in Early Modern England* (1998).

TIMOTHY HAMPTON is Professor of Comparative Literature, French, and Italian Studies at the University of California at Berkeley. His most recent book is *Literature and Nation: Inventing Renaissance France* (2000). He is currently completing a book on diplomacy and culture from Machiavelli to Leibniz.

CYNTHIA HERRUP is William K. Boyd Professor of History at Duke University. Her most recent book is *A House in Gross Disorder: Sex, Law, and the 2nd Earl of Castlehaven* (1999). She is currently working on a study of pardoning in seventeenth-century England.

HEATHER HIRSCHFELD is Assistant Professor of English at the University of Tennessee. Her book *Joint Enterprises: Collaborative Drama and the Institutionalization of the English Renaissance Theater* is forthcoming. She has published essays on various aspects of early modern drama and authorship in *PMLA, Genre, Renaissance Drama, Journal of Medieval and Early Modern Studies*, and *Shakespeare Quarterly* (forthcoming).

JEAN E. HOWARD is Professor of English at Columbia University. Her books include *Shakespeare's Art of Orchestration: Stage Technique and Audience Response, The Stage and Social Struggle in Early Modern England,* and, with Phyllis Rackin, *Engendering a Nation: A Feminist Account of Shakespeare's English Histories.* She is also one of the four coeditors of *The Norton Shakespeare* and General Editor of the Bedford Contextual Editions of Shakespeare. She is currently completing *Theater of a City: Social Change and Generic Innovation on the Early Modern Stage.*

ANN ROSALIND JONES is Esther Cloudman Dunn Professor of Comparative Literature at Smith College. She is the author (with Peter Stallybrass) of *Renaissance Clothing and the Materials of Memory* (2000); and of *Currency of Eros: Women's Love Lyric in Europe, 1540–1620* (1990); and has edited (with Margaret F. Rosenthal) *Poems and Selected Letters by Veronica Franco* (2002).

ROSEMARY KEGL is Associate Professor of English at the University of Rochester. She is the author of *The Rhetoric of Concealment: Figuring Gender and Class in Renaissance Literature* (1994), and of essays on sixteenth- and seventeenth-century English writing. She is currently at work on a book-length project, *Inhabiting Shakespeare's "Wooden O": Theater, Intellectuals, and the Production of Knowledge.*

JENNIFER LEWIN is Assistant Professor of English at the University of Kentucky. She has published articles on eighteenth-century poetry and on the New Criticism, and she also writes on contemporary American poetry. Currently she is completing a manuscript on sleep and dreams in early modern poetry and philosophy.

JULIA REINHARD LUPTON is Associate Professor of English and Comparative Literature, University of California at Irvine. She is author of *After Oedipus: Shakespeare in Psychoanalysis* (1993), and *Afterlives of the Saints: Hagiography, Typology, and Renaissance Literature* (1996). She is currently finishing a book entitled *Citizen Saints: Shakespeare and Political Theology.*

SALLY-BETH MACLEAN is the Executive Editor and Associate Director of the Records of Early English Drama series at the University of Toronto. She has published, with Scott McMillin, *The Queen's Men and Their Plays* (1998), as well as articles on various aspects of medieval and Renaissance theater history. She is currently at work on a new electronic publication with Alan Somerset, the REED "Patrons and Performances" research and educational web site.

LAWRENCE MANLEY, Professor of English at Yale University, is the author of *Literature and Culture in Early Modern London* and is working on a study of Lord Strange's Men and their plays.

THOMAS MOISAN is Professor of English at Saint Louis University. Among his latest publications is a critical survey and assessment of recent criticism and productions of *Romeo and Juliet* for the newly reissued edition of the play by Cambridge University Press. At present he is at work on a cultural study of seventeenth-century England focusing on the poet Robert Herrick, the engraver Wenceslaus Hollar, and the gardeners and collectors, John Tradescant and son.

PATRICIA PARKER is Professor of English and Comparative Literature at Stanford University. She has published most recently

Shakespeare from the Margins (1996), and is currently at work on a new Arden edition of *A Midsummer Night's Dream.*

TANYA POLLARD is Assistant Professor of English at Montclair State University. She has published essays on early modern theater, cosmetics, sleeping potions, and poisons. She is editor of a volume of early modern antitheatrical and protheatrical writings (forthcoming, 2003), and author of a book on preoccupations with drugs and poisons in early modern drama (forthcoming).

RICHARD PYM is a Lecturer in the Department of Hispanic Studies, Royal Holloway, University of London. He has published on Calderón, Velázquez, and St. Teresa of Avila. He is currently working on questions of identity and representations of otherness in the writing of Spain's Golden Age.

MAUREEN QUILLIGAN is R. Florence Brinkley Professor of English at Duke University and Department chair. She has written on allegory, Renaissance epic, and early modern women's writing. She is currently finishing a book, *Incest and Agency: Female Authority in Elizabeth's England.*

PHYLLIS RACKIN is Professor of English Emerita at the University of Pennsylvania and a past president of the Shakespeare Association of America. Her books include *Stages of History: Shakespeare's English Chronicles* and, with Jean E. Howard, *Engendering a Nation: A Feminist Account of Shakespeare's English Histories.* She is currently completing a book on Shakespeare and women.

DAVID HARRIS SACKS is Professor of History and Humanities at Reed College. Among his works on the history and culture of early modern Britain and the Atlantic world, *The Historical Imagination in Early Modern Britain: History, Rhetoric, and Fiction, 1500–1800* (1997), a collection of essays coedited with Donald R. Kelley, appeared in paperback in fall 2002. He is presently at work on two books: *The Sweet Name of Liberty: The Culture of Freedom in Early Modern England,* and *Restoring the Distracted Globe: Richard Hakluyt and His World.*

MICHAEL SCHOENFELDT is Professor of English and Director of the Program in Medieval and Early Modern Studies at the University of Michigan. He is the author of *Prayer and Power: George Herbert and Renaissance Courtship* (1991), and *Bodies and Selves in Early Modern England: Physiology and Inwardness in Spenser, Shakespeare, Herbert, and Milton* (1999). He is currently at work on the ethics of emotion in early modern culture.

GRANT SHEN is Assistant Professor of Theatre Studies at the National University of Singapore. He has directed English versions of *zaju* opera (1995), kabuki (1998), and Sanskrit theatre (2002), all in their classical styles. He has published in *TDR, ATJ,* and *Theatre Journal.* His drama reviews appear regularly in arts magazines.

JYOTSNA G. SINGH is Associate Professor of English at Michigan State University. Her publications include *Colonial Narratives/Cultural Dialogues: "Discovery" of India in the Language of Colonialism,* and the edition, *Travel Knowledge: Narratives of "Discovery" in Early Modern Europe.*

SARA JAYNE STEEN is Professor of English at Montana State University and an American Council on Education Fellow in residence at the University of Delaware. She has published numerous books and articles related to early modern English writers and is currently working on a book about seventeenth-century women writers.

GUSTAV UNGERER, Professor of English at the University of Berne, retired, has published essays on Mary Frith and on prostitution in late Elizabethan London. He is currently working on the presence of black Africans in early modern England and on the first English slave holders and traders residing in fifteenth-/sixteenth-century Andalusia.

VALERIE WAYNE is Professor of English at the University of Hawai'i. She has edited Edmund Tilney's *The Flower of Friendship: A Renaissance Dialogue Contesting Marriage*; and Thomas Middleton's *A Trick to Catch the Old One* for the forthcoming *Collected Works of Thomas Middleton.* She is currently editing *Cymbeline* for the Arden Shakespeare, third series.

SHAKESPEARE
STUDIES

EARLY MODERN DRAMA AROUND THE WORLD

AROUND THE WORLD

The State of Study

Preface

The Editor

Under this rubric *Shakespeare Studies* presents the first in an annual series of essays on drama as practiced in various regions of the world between ca. 1500 and 1700. These pieces have been commissioned to speak to the scholarly interests of readers who may be unfamiliar with the work being done in dramatic activity outside of Renaissance England. Accordingly the editor has asked the authors of these short essays to familiarize us with the state of research, perceived problems, and the shape of future emphases in each field.

Mere synchronicity, of course, cannot in itself dictate either the shapes of problems or their solutions in ways likely to be relevant to the study of early modern English theater; the world in 1500 was vast. But in the last few years we have been continually surprised by the depth and number of instances of cultural interpenetration, and, in the end, surely we are not the worse off for knowing more about the status of dramatic practices outside of Renaissance England. The analogies that present themselves in ways that enrich our understanding of our own research projects may well be the least of the benefits accrued through the intellectual generosity of our invited authors.

This volume offers such studies of 1) the drama of the Spanish Golden Age and 2) the drama of China contemporary with England from 1500 to 1700. Spanish drama and its problems are discussed by Richard Pym, author, most recently, of "Telling Histories: Trends in Historical Criticism and Some Notes on *El alcalde de Zalamea*" in *Journal of the Institute of Romance Studies*, while Ming drama is discussed by Grant Shen, whose most recent work in this field is "Acting in the Private Theatre of the Ming Dynasty," *Asian Theatre Journal* 19 (2002): 64–86.

A Survey of Scholarship
on Late Ming Drama

GRANT SHEN

THIS PAPER COVERS the state of scholarship on late Ming drama, a period that coincided roughly with the Elizabethan (1558–1603), Jacobean (1603–25), and Caroline (1625–42) theater of Renaissance England.[1] Scholarly writings on Ming drama (1368–1644) are fewer than those on the *zaju* opera of the Yuan dynasty (1234–1368), or those on the regional genres of the Qing dynasty (1644–1911). The first work (1901) to attempt a history of Chinese literature includes one chapter on drama.[2] The author outlines the plots of three *zaju* operas of the Yuan, gives an eyewitness account of Qing theater in performance, but omits any reference to Ming drama. Similarly, a book on oriental drama published sixty years later does not include a single Ming work although it discusses some thirty translated plays of the Yuan and Qing dynasties.[3]

Ming drama was first introduced to the English-speaking world in 1936, when Yao Hsin-nung wrote about the development of the national theater of the late Ming.[4] His views are still valid today, although much has been added to that brief survey by subsequent scholarship. Yao's article evidently benefited from the then recently published *History of Early Modern Chinese Drama* by the Japanese Sinologist Aoki Masaru.[5]

Aoki's book had also benefited from the scholarly studies of his colleagues (Aoki 734–35), and especially Wang Guowei's multivolume study that initiated academic investigation of traditional Chinese theater.[6] Aoki's survey is still one of the most complete and respected works to date, despite its neglect of the performative aspects of Ming drama, a shortcoming that has yet to be fully rehabilitated even in scholarly studies today.

Another quarter-century elapsed before the surge of interest in the 1960s in the West in things Asian brought in its wake three books on the history of Chinese literature, each with a section on Ming drama. In *Chinese Literature: A Historical Introduction*, Ch'en Shou-yi discussed one music composer, no fewer than eight playwrights, dozens of plays, and introduced the structural features of the drama as well.[7] Lai Ming's *A History of Chinese Literature* covered a single playwright and one play, mistaking its heroine of sixteen years for twenty.[8] Liu Wu-chi's *An Introduction to Chinese Literature* focused on the librettos and intentions of the literati playwrights.[9] More detailed was Josephine Huang Hung's pocket-size *Ming Drama*, covering major playwrights and their representative works.[10] Both Liu and Hung also introduced the schools of dramatists of the late Ming.

In the sixties, scholarship was largely limited to the literary study of masterpieces about which scholars tended to disagree with each other. In fact, Ch'en and Liu provided two sharply contrasting views of Ming drama. While Ch'en portrayed Ming theater as contemporary, realistic, and entertaining,[11] Liu saw it as historical, poetic, and elitist.[12] If one uses *Ming Feng Ji* (*The Phoenix Singing*), a play about contemporary politics, as example and holds innovations in theater as intended to please the theatergoing public, one may agree with Ch'en. But if one reads the allusive and symbolic librettos that are a staple feature of the masterpieces of Ming drama, and regards their verses as incomprehensible to the mostly illiterate common folk, one may concur with Liu's interpretation.[13] Nevertheless, the fact remains that scholarship in the 1960s explored only a small number of plays and adopted narrow investigative angles.

In the 1970s, scholarship gradually saw a more equitable balance between attention to literature and to performance. C. T. Hsia focused on the philosophical ideas encompassed by the four dream plays of Tang Xianzu.[14] Colin Mackerras viewed Ming drama from the performative angle, and traced its historical development to the level of individual genres.[15] Combining the learning of the East and the West, Mackerras examined a large number of primary materials of the Ming era, such as the writings of Wang Jide and Zhang Dai, as well as many scholarly reports in Chinese, including the works of Zhou Yibai and Wang Gulu. Almost two hundred references are drawn from non-English sources in his paper.

In an extensive textual study using a wider range of data, Cyril Birch was able to conclude that *Ming Feng Ji* was "a rare instance, of its time, of a drama built around contemporary events" (220), and provided four more plays of the same nature (231).[16] However, the performative aspects were not addressed. On the other hand, William Dolby treated Ming theater not only as dramatic literature, but also as performing arts in *A History of Chinese Drama*.[17] He systematically tried to introduce staging elements, namely singing and music, costume and props, singing styles and role types. Performative features of Ming drama, albeit still incomplete and inaccurate, started to be addressed.

The 1980s saw the publication of the seven hundred page *The Chinese Conception of the Theatre*, in which the innovation of the Kunqu music was briefly delineated.[18] But John Hu's introductory chapter "Ming Dynasty Drama" proves insightful. It is characterized by a sensitive treatment of the available data and an objective presentation of the drama scene.[19]

In the 1990s, two alternative approaches to the performance space of Ming private theater emerged. In the introduction to his translation of selected scenes of Ming drama, Cyril Birch led his reader to a fictional garden performance, thus imagining the performance space.[20] Chen Shizheng, the director of *The Peony Pavilion* that opened the 1999 Lincoln Center Festival in New York City, strove for what "Tang Xianzu himself would have known," thus rebuilding the performance space. The centerpiece of Chen's set was a Ming style open-sided pavilion consisting of sixty hand-joined pieces—not a single nail was used. But his most unambiguous mirroring of the performance space is seen in the eighteen thousand gallon working pond next to the pavilion, complete with live ducks, fish, water-lilies and songbirds. Chen explains:

> The ducks floated on the water; the water reflected the lights; the birds chirped—these elements did not necessarily relate to the plot. But they certainly contributed to the environment in which the audience would come into contact with what the Ming literati must have experienced.[21]

Chen's authentic production in fact served an academic purpose: the Ming gardens were famous for their water features, and the Ming literati were known to stage plays at waterside pavilions.

Grant Shen's "Acting in the Private Theatre of the Ming Dynasty" describes the singing, dancing, and role playing of private actors and the functions of literati troupe owners.[22] Based on original records rather than scholarly reports, his study views its subject from the perspective of ancient theatergoers. The primary materials cited in the article are mostly new to modern scholarship. Shen also experimented with Ming methods in his reproduction of the classical style.[23]

To date, research on Ming theater has extended from dramatic literature to include performing arts, a development particularly important to the subject. Historically, the performing arts as well as the visual spectacles of theater have not developed simultaneously or proportionally with the dramatic literature. The presentation of golden age drama has been marked by immaturity and reductive simplicity. For instance, ancient Greek performance caught up with its text only during the Hellenistic age (336–146 B.C.), when Greek tragedy had long passed its golden age. The technical wonders that helped create illusionary stage images—proscenium arches, wing-and-shutter settings, painted-perspective designs, and the groove system—only became standard practice for the English Restoration theater (1660–88), when the glories of Renaissance drama had already faded.[24]

The traditional theater of China followed a pattern similar to that of the West. Whereas China's classical drama peaked during the Yuan dynasty, its performing arts matured during the Ming era. The Yuan style of presentation was relatively simple, with many vestiges of storytelling and other narrative entertainment. For instance, a Yuan *zaju* opera permitted only one singer in a play, a practice apparently inherited from that of *zhugongdiao* ballads of the Jin era (1115–1234). When a *zaju* opera called for two characters to sing, the singer would double his/her roles, just as Greek actors did when a tragedy needed more than three characters.[25] The Ming stage, on the other hand, featured sophisticated performing arts characterized by a variety of styles. The growing prominence of singing, dancing, role playing, and visual spectacles of Ming opera gradually equaled or eclipsed the importance of play scripts by the end of the dynasty.

The study of Ming drama, whether of its literary scripts or its performative aspects, has yet to match the numbers of scholarly publications on the earlier or later periods. This situation is partially due to the elitist nature of Ming drama and its sophisticated styles of performance. Even those with some experience of working on Yuan opera may encounter difficulties in evaluating a Ming text. For instance, a Ming *chuanqi* libretto was deemed "much inferior" after it was compared with a Yuan *zaju* libretto.[26] Yet the only criteria suggested for the judgment, "economy and freshness," are more suitable for *sanqu* poetry than for opera librettos (223). Not surprisingly, the fact that the Yuan lyric expressed merely a general feeling, while the Ming lyric depicted a specific dramatic circumstance is ignored.[27] Even the sentimental and stylistic similarities between the two librettos are overlooked. What's more, a *sanqu* poem, "Qiusi" ("Autumn Thought"), is used as a benchmark for the criticism. The superiority of the Yuan libretto is based on a comparison with "Autumn Thought" (223), against which it is claimed for the former that "it hardly seems inferior." No actual comparison is made between these two Yuan verses, except finding that they come from the same author. However, my research proves that only *Yaoshantang waiji*, a sixteenth-century source, ascribes the "Autumn Thought" to the celebrated Yuan author, while all three sources of the thirteenth to fourteenth centuries, *Liyuan yuefu*, *Zhongyuan yinyue*, and *Shuzhai lao xue congtan*, identify the *sanqu* poem to a folk or unknown origin.[28]

Another difficulty the researcher confronts is that Ming drama often features allusive and ambiguous language to be decoded during its performance. An investigation of the acting technique thus becomes vital in interpreting the text.[29] Even the comprehension of a colloquial passage may require some knowledge of its staging. The following text was cited to prove the playwright's debt and close affinity to the Ming novelists, because "in its easy loquacity and love of detail it smacks of *Chin P'ing Mei* brand of fiction rather than of the dialogue of the stage":

> Ah, daughter, today you talk of finding a husband, tomorrow you'll talk of finding a husband—what's so great about finding a husband? Marry some man and before you've got past his gate his first wife will be letting you know who she is. She'll soon have your coiled hair scratched down, and you'll have to kneel or kowtow any time she says kneel or kowtow. . . . Now go hurry and do your makeup and entertain your visitors, or I've got a whip here and I'll beat you to a pulp with no mercy if you go on like this.[30]

These lines were in fact meant for a farcical presentation of the *chou* (clown) role type, instead of the naturalistic persuasion of a courtesan by her mother-procuress, which may resemble the novel mode as assumed by the author.

While textual research is difficult and dependent on performance study, the latter too has its own problems. First, the primary sources are usually scattered in contemporary books, notes, letters, diaries, poems, and memoirs and are thus are hard to collect. Second, the Ming literati, from whose writings we gather much of our information, tended to write in the symbolic or allusive style, making them not readily accessible or comprehensible. For instance, Zhang Dai (1597–1679), one of the literati and private theater owners, reported how the Hades scenes as depicted by the Tang painter Wu Daizi were staged in a Ming public performance.[31] His eyewitness account vividly described the scenarios when the condemned sinners were tortured by Yaksha, Rakshasa, or Ox-headed and Horse-faced demons. However, the three-dimensional set pieces, including saws and grinding stones, freezing ice and boiling cauldron, sword-hill and blood-ditch, are compared to two-dimensional paintings; and the thousand taels of cash spent on the lavish set converted to paper hell-money in a modern interpretation:

> In a most extravagant production, the scenes of the supernatural were represented as vividly, we are told, as the Tang master Wu Daozi's painting "Various scenes from Hell". Thousands of pieces of paper sacrificial money were burnt—presumably by the audience in dread and fear of the hell which suddenly seemed so real and near to them?[32]

Zhi-za, the term in Zhang Dai's original version which stands for set, was probably first misunderstood as "paper-bundle" that was then determined as "paper sacrificial money." To read this passage correctly, one has to know that *zhi-za* means paper-made funeral objects, that the ancient Chinese considered theater as a platform for the dead, and that those appearing on it were figures of the past. The set made for their use, whether in paper or otherwise, thus comprises objects for the other world, thus named *zhi-za*.

The misreading of primary data is a common occurrence. Two more errors are located in the above mentioned paragraph:

1. *"Yu yunshu"* should not be read as "a certain Yu Yunshu," but "my uncle Yun." The show was organized and financed by Zhang Dai's uncle.
2. *"Nü-tai"* does not mean "*loges* for women," but a "smaller platform" that serves the function of a box or *loge*. The character *"nü"* does not always mean "female" in classical Chinese. For instance, *"nü-qiang"* does not mean a city wall defended

by Amazons, but that top portion of a city wall that is smaller in size.

While there is much room for improvement in existing scholarship, there is even more opportunity for discovery. The three theater worlds of the Ming—the court, the private, and the public—each generally separated from each other, and presenting different performances, demand individual critical attention. For example, Grant Shen's study covers only acting in the private theater, which differs from that in the court or public troupes with their respective styles and strengths. For another example, many have mentioned the schools of dramatists of the late Ming, yet none has shown a genuine appreciation of the technical issues that most concerned them. Academia's general support for Tang Xianzu's librettos in *The Peony Pavilion* would be more meaningful if the performance-related criticism of Tang's contemporaries were also understood.

Notes

A grant (R-103–000–007–112) is provided by the National University of Singapore to conduct thorough library research in the preparation of this article.

1. Scholarship often addresses the three hundred years of Ming drama as a whole. However, only references to the last one hundred years of the dynasty will be reviewed in this article.
2. See Herbert Giles, *A History of Chinese Literature* (London: William Heinemann, 1901), 256–75.
3. See Henry Wells, *The Classical Drama of the Orient* (Bombay: Asia Publishing House, 1965), 3–153.
4. See Yao Hsin-nung, "Rise and Fall of the K'un Ch'ü," *T'ien Hsia Monthly* 2, no.1 (1936): 63–84.
5. See Aoki Masaru's 1930 preface. The Chinese translation was published in 1936. See *Zhongguo jinshi xiqu shi*, trans. Wang Gulu (Shanghai: Commerce, 1936).
6. See Wang Guowei, *Qu lu*, vols. 3–5 (np: Fanyu Shenshi, 1909) and *Song Yuan xiqu shi* (Shanghai: Commerce, 1912).
7. Ch'en Shou-yi, "Ming Drama," in *Chinese Literature: A Historical Introduction* (New York: Ronald Press, 1961), 519–35.
8. See Lai Ming, "Libretti of the Yuan and Ming Dynasties: The Life of Tang Hsien-tsu and His Works," in *A History of Chinese Literature* (London: Cassell, 1964), 245–51.
9. Liu Wu-chi, "Dramas of the Literati and the People," in *An Introduction to Chinese Literature* (Bloomington: Indiana University Press, 1966), 247–61.
10. See Josephine Huang Hung, *Ming Drama* (Taipei: Heritage Press, 1966).

11. Ch'en concluded his study with the following:

> In the selection of plots . . . Ming drama looked persistently if not exclusively to contemporary events for inspiration. Thus, in a sense, as far as the plots go, Ming drama was on the whole much more realistic, reminding us of the rise of middle-class comedy in eighteenth-century England as well as continental Europe. Ming drama . . . has a tendency to utilize the vehicle for mere entertainment with no philosophical message. (535)

12. As if to call attention to his disagreement with Ch'en, Liu began his study of Ming drama with the following:

> [D]uring the Ming and Ch'ing periods, drama lost its intimate contact with the audience, particularly the common people, and tended to become a type of studio play for a few connoisseurs of *ch'ü* poetry rather than a stage presentation for popular entertainment. . . . Little attempt was made to invent new plots or to deal with contemporary events and stories of social import. (247)

13. Liu sees the "declining into mere feats of poetic skill" and the "loss of contact with the people" as the weakness of the dominant genre of Ming drama (260).

14. See C. T. Hsia, "Time and the Human Condition in the Plays of T'ang Hsien-tsu," in *Self and Society in Ming Thought*, ed. Theodore de Bary (New York: Columbia University Press, 1970), 249–90.

15. See Colin Mackerras, "The Growth of the Chinese Regional Drama in the Ming and Ch'ing," *Journal of Oriental Studies* 9 (1971): 58–91.

16. See Cyril Birch, "Some Concerns and Methods of Ming *Ch'uan-ch'i* Drama," in *Studies in Chinese Literary Genres*, ed. Cyril Birch (Los Angeles: University of California Press, 1974), 220–58.

17. See William Dolby, " 'Nanxi' Drama, 'Chuanqi' Drama, and the Beginnings of Kunqu Drama," and "The Theatre World during the Ming Dynasty," in *A History of Chinese Drama* (London: Elek Books, 1976), 71–113.

18. See Hsü Tao-Ching, "Changes in the Chinese Theatre since the Advent of the Drama: The Innovation of the K'un Tunes," in *The Chinese Conception of the Theatre* (Seattle: University of Washington Press, 1985), 272–76. The next chapter, although titled "The Decline of K'un Dramas and the Future of Chinese Theatre," turns to the rise of Beijing opera, the author's favorite topic, again.

19. See John Hu, "Ming Dynasty Drama," in *Chinese Theatre: From Its Origins to the Present Day*, ed. Colin Mackerras (Honolulu: University of Hawaii Press, 1983), 60–91.

20. See Cyril Birch, "Introduction: To the Readers as Fellow Mandarin," in *Scenes for Mandarins: The Elite Theatre of the Ming* (New York: Columbia University Press, 1995), 1–20.

21. Interview with the author on 5 February 2002 at the Esplanade, Singapore, which is published in *The Arts Magazine* (January/February 2003): 18–21.

22. See Grant Shen, "Acting in the Private Theatre of the Ming dynasty," *Asian Theatre Journal* 15 (1998):64–86.

23. See Grant Shen, "*Zaju* and Kabuki in English: Directing in the Classical Styles," *TDR The Drama Review* 171 (2001): 134–48.

24. By the 1630s, only the Jacobean (1603–25) and Caroline (1625–42) court entertainment employed Italian staging techniques, introduced by Inigo Jones.

25. Acting in Greek tragedy was not a profession and began as a mere append-

age to playwriting. Both Thespis and Aeschylus, for instance, acted in the tragedies they penned. As a rule, the chorus outnumbered the actors. Sophocles called
for no more than three actors in tragedy, and his judgment actually prevailed.

26. See Birch, "Some Concerns and Methods," 223–24.

27. Birch's translation of the Yuan lyric reads:

> Setting sun, wide sky, darkling river's meander,
> Hills of Ch'u, folds of green, rest on the clear air.
> Ice-jar cosmos, sky to earth,
> Trees tall and short are cloud-brocaded.
> Will someone ask Wang Wei
> For a landscape to transcribe this sorrow?

His translation of the Ming lyric reads:

> Singing strings, metal pick, body of sandalwood
> Have made a knell for oh, so many who were young.
> Startle the roosting bird from his still forest
> Make dance the dragon in his dim ravine—
> But no strum, no twang
> Can all express of this sad song of pining.

28. See *Quan Yuan Sanqu* [*Complete collection of sanqu poetry of the Yuan dynasty*], compiled by Sui Shusen (Beijing: Zhonghua shuju, 1964), 242, 1732–33.

29. See Shen, "Acting in the Private Theatre," 74–76.

30. See Birch, "Some Concerns and Methods," 225–26.

31. See Zhang Dai, *Taoan mengyi* [*Taoan' Remembrance of Dreams*], vol. 6 (Shanghai: Shanghai guji, [early 1700s] 1982), 52–53.

32. See Dolby, *A History of Chinese Drama*, 111.

Drama in Golden-Age Spain:
The State of the Art

Richard Pym

THE ESTABLISHMENT in the 1580s of two permanent public theaters or *corrales de comedias* in Madrid signalled the rapidly growing popularity in Spain of a new, if somewhat synthetic dramatic genre, the *comedia nueva*. Their appearance marked the effective beginning of the great age of Spanish drama that was to last for approximately the next hundred years. That it did so, despite the occasional, if not always universally respected, closure of the theaters in periods of national mourning, pestilence, or as a result of the objections of moralists, is a testament to its remarkable vigor. The objectors, usually churchmen, were concerned throughout the period about the potentially deleterious effects of this new, secular drama. The *comedia*, as they saw it, was too prone to court a dangerously uncontrolled populism at the expense of the proper pieties of moral instruction. The presence of women on the stage, for example, provoked much shaking of heads, while lewdly suggestive dances such as the *zarabanda*, which frequently accompanied the performances, were a favorite, soft target of criticism. Even more alarming to the worriers, however, was the thought that this new, commercial theater might encourage the imagination in ways that could easily lead to a failure to distinguish between the represented and the real, a concern reflecting that wider preoccupation with appearance and reality, art and life, which so exercised cultivated minds throughout the period. The end of the age, or at least the beginning of the end, finally announced itself with the death in 1681 of Calderón, regarded by many as the greatest of all of Spain's seventeenth-century dramatists. Over the intervening years, Spanish playwrights may have produced as many as ten thousand plays. The tally, approximate though it is, bears eloquent witness to just

how extraordinary a cultural phenomenon the explosion of drama
in early modern Spain was. It is perhaps worth noting, to take just
one example, that Calderón's production alone amounted to about
five times that of Shakespeare. And the overall figure suggested
above does not include minor forms such as the *loas* (preludes), *entremeses* (interludes), and *bailes* (dances with dialogue), which
must themselves run into the thousands. The sheer scale of the task
with which critics and literary historians are confronted in consequence will not go unremarked by the reader. Thankfully, recent
years have seen a significant, if geographically somewhat patchy,
widening of interest in Golden-Age Spanish drama. Especially notable has been the growth of interest in Spain itself, where the *comedia* was for so long the poor relation of Golden-Age studies at the
undergraduate, if not necessarily the research level. As things are,
the historically crucial and continuing contribution of scholars in
Britain, Germany, France, and the United States remains of fundamental importance to Golden-Age drama research.[1] But one could
easily argue that the center of gravity, at least in terms of volume of
activity, may now have begun to shift to Spain, where, after all, it
surely belongs.

   The early years of the *comedia nueva* were dominated, and in a
real sense shaped, by another of the period's great figures, the be-
wilderingly prolific Lope de Vega (1562–1635), a man whose tal-
ents are thought by some, especially in Spain, to surpass even those
of Calderón.[2] Driven in part by demand and economic necessity, he
may have authored over eight hundred plays. It was Lope who,
with the necessarily practical approach of the professional writer,
wrote the ground rules for this new drama on which others would
build. His *Arte nuevo de escribir comedias en este tiempo*, which
he read before an audience of Madrid's literati in 1609, represented
a spirited defence of his practice as a playwright and offered a blue-
print for others to follow. He began by insisting that, while he was
fully aware of the classical precepts, he would nonetheless lock
these away "with six keys" before beginning to write, banishing
Terence and Plautus from his study "to prevent them from calling
out to me." The *comedia nueva* should consist of three acts, or *jor-
nadas*; it should allow of a mixture of the comic and the tragic; it
should be polymetric, different meters being recommended to suit
particular dramatic circumstances. Plays should not be so long as
to excite "the wrath of the seated Spaniard," as he put it, a wrath
unlikely to be assuaged unless the former was offered "Genesis to

the Last Judgement" in the space of two hours (in fact, most *come-dias* run to three to four thousand lines). He noted the need, given such a restive audience, to maintain suspense until the final scene, the popularity of actresses appearing in male clothing, of ambiguous speech which ordinary members of the audience "think they alone understand," the emotive power of plots touching on questions of honor, the popular hatred of traitors (which was likely to pursue the unfortunate actor who performed such a role even after he had left the stage), and so on.

And yet, hugely popular as it was, the thematically eclectic *comedia* as performed on the relatively bare boards of the public *corrales*, and with which Lope was particularly concerned in the *Arte nuevo*, was by no means the only form of theater to be encountered in the Spain of the period. The *corrales* were similar in many ways to the Shakespearean playhouses. But other theatrical spaces, and other forms of drama, were equally important in their different ways. There were, for example, the performances of *comedias* at court, lavish affairs which tended to become increasingly spectacular and elaborate in their use of stage machinery and effects as the seventeenth century wore on. One thinks particularly in this connection of Madrid's Buen Retiro palace, which was built in the 1630s and which, with its picture stage, provided the splendid venue for performances attended by the aesthete King Philip IV. And then there were the *autos sacramentales*, one-act religious plays written to celebrate the feast of Corpus Christi and performed in the streets on complicated, purpose-built floats which could be pulled along by oxen. These were the three principal theatrical genres of the period. All three were dominated for much of the seventeenth century by the figure of Calderón.

And it has been Calderón, unsurprisingly, whose quatercentenary was celebrated in 2000, who has tended to dominate recent scholarship. The past few years have seen something of a flood of publications, many of them, predictably enough, treating familiar, easily obtainable, and widely taught texts such as *La vida es sueño, El médico de su honra* or *La dama duende*. But there have also been others that have offered readings of lesser-known plays like *La niña de Gómez Arias* or *Darlo todo y no dar nada*, works which have not hitherto received much critical attention. The playwright's mythological drama has also attracted scholarly interest, the seminal work in this area, published some years ago now, being Margaret Rich Greer's *The Play of Power: Mythological Court Dramas of Cal-*

derón de la Barca.[3] But perhaps the most welcome development
in Calderónian studies in recent years has been the focus on the
playwright's *autos sacramentales*. Calderón himself, rather underestimating his own production, claimed in 1680 in a letter to the
duke of Veragua to have written seventy. Certainly he monopolized
the form, at least in Madrid, from 1648 until his death. Critical editions of all of Calderón's *autos* are currently being published by the
GRISO group (Grupo de Investigación del Siglo de Oro) based at
the University of Navarre. This is an impressive international effort
under the directorship of Ignacio Arellano and draws on the exper-
tise of scholars from Spain, Britain, France, Italy, Argentina, and
the United States. Some forty volumes have appeared to date. It is
earnestly to be hoped that sufficient funding and support will in
the future be found to carry out a similar exercise in respect of Calderón's secular works. Daunting though such a project may be, it is
most certainly overdue in the case of a playwright whom Shelley,
flushed with enthusiasm, once saw fit to compare favorably with
Shakespeare himself.[4]

Work on other dramatists and a range of related topics also continues apace. The University of Barcelona's "Prolope" project,
founded by Alberto Blecua and Guillermo Serés, aims eventually
to publish all of Lope's plays grouped by the *partes* or sets of plays
published in the playwright's own day and accompanied by a brief
history of textual transmission in each case. GRISO's Instituto de
Estudios Tirsianos has set itself the task of publishing the complete
works of Tirso de Molina (1583–1648), who completes the trio of
great dramatists produced by Spain during the period. The Universities of Castilla-La Mancha, Burgos, Seville, Valencia, and Madrid's Complutense all also have Golden-Age drama projects of
various kinds under way. Research at the University of Seville continues, for example, to unearth discoveries relating to the *corrales
de comedias* both in that city and in Córdoba, and to explore the
fortunes of theater in other smaller towns like Écija and Carmona,
also in Spain's deep south. The now well established claims of cultural studies have meanwhile tended to problematize the traditional canon to a degree, at least in academic circles, and to sharpen
interest in a number of less well-known dramatists. The University
of Granada is, for example, currently engaged in publishing the
complete works of Mira de Amescua, author of *El esclavo del
demonio* and royal chaplain to Granada Cathedral in the early
1700s. Meanwhile, project work is also going on elsewhere on play-

wrights such as Francisco de Rojas Zorrilla (1607–48), Álvaro Cubillo de Aragón (1596–1661), and Francisco de Bances Candamo (1662–1704), to name just a few.

There has, too, been a marked increase over the last decade in research into Golden-Age staging, conditions of production, and, more recently still, acting. Evangelina Rodríguez Cuadros's monumental study *La técnica del actor español en el Barroco: hipótesis y documentos* has, to take one notable example of work in an area long overdue for investigation, provided scholars with fascinating information about actors and acting techniques during the period.[5] Meanwhile, the already incalculable debt owed by hispanists everywhere to the late John Varey's exemplary scholarship continued to accumulate with the publication of *El teatro palaciego en Madrid 1589–1707*.[6] This volume, which he co-authored with Margaret Rich Greer, forms part of the invaluable series *Fuentes para la historia del teatro en España [Sources for the History of Theatre in Spain]* published by Tamesis. In it, the authors explore archival material relating to actors' salaries, rents, costume, stage machines, and other sundry matters connected with the practical business of staging *comedias* at court. The resulting vignettes are fascinating, as, for example, when we read of the dispute between the Marquess of Heliche and another courtier over which man enjoyed precedence in respect of the right to arrange the disposition of spectators for a performance at the court of Philip IV. The courtier in question, whose name is celebrated now in a rather different connection, is named as one Diego Velázquez.

But there is also another important point to be made about the whole question of performance. The study and teaching of Shakespeare are, of course, much enriched by the great and continuing performance tradition associated with his work. Regular performances of Shakespeare plays in the theater are supplemented by the ready availability on video or film of numerous other excellent productions. Sadly, the same cannot be said of Spain's Golden-Age drama. It is true that professional and often excellent productions continue to be mounted in Spain, and a handful of *comedias* are occasionally staged in translation elsewhere. But the frequency and range of such productions cannot be compared with what we have quite properly come to expect in the case of Shakespeare; and, perhaps partly for that very reason, there is often an understandable reluctance to venture too far from the well-tried, traditional canon. But there are exceptions. For example, the Compañía Nacional de

Teatro Clásico's splendidly energetic production last year of a com-
pilation of five of Cervantes's *entremeses*, short, comic interludes
which were inserted between the acts of the main play being
staged, represented an encouraging recent departure in this respect.
And one production in particular, albeit not in the theater, deserves
special mention. Pilar Miró's excellent, award-winning 1996 film
of Lope de Vega's satirical comedy *El perro del hortelano* came as a
most welcome development, and of course especially so to those of
us engaged in teaching the *comedia*. However, her untimely death
in 1997 put paid to plans to film a second, very different Golden-
Age play, Calderón's dark and disturbing *El médico de su honra*.
Her version of *El perro del hortelano* stands as a poignant monument to what we have missed.

On a more general note, the growing academic interest in staging,
alluded to earlier, may well reflect a certain dissatisfaction with
hermeneutic criticism's tendency over recent decades to privilege
the productive role of the solitary reader at the expense of a properly rigorous historical contextualization of the seventeenth-century text. This tendency, that is to say, has sometimes risked
blurring the fact that these texts were written to be performed, and
to be performed, more to the point, with a particular historical audience in mind. It is therefore to be welcomed that so many
Golden-Age drama scholars should continue to recognize the fundamental importance of history, of those interwoven contextual
pressures which mediate the complex relationship between the
text, its transmission, and its articulation and reception as performance. Indeed, the importance of this recognition has been borne out
by discoveries made as a direct result of the markedly increased
interest in textual criticism over recent years. Important, too, have
been new theoretical insights into questions of textuality offered by
scholars such as Jerome McGann in the United States and the narra-
tologist Gerard Genette in France. As notions of the historicity of
the text (traditionally predicated on a search for an original purity)
have been subjected to scrutiny, there has developed a growing recognition that the in some cases quite radical instability of the texts
that have come down to us is itself the first and most obvious manifestation of their true historicity. Nor is such instability always
merely a result of faulty transmission, whether through technical
errors in the early printing process, simple tricks of memory, or
subsequent editorial "corrections." As the Calderón *autos* project
has demonstrated, the dramatists themselves were perfectly capa-

blc of rewriting their own work when the spirit, or indeed any one of a range of more pragmatic considerations, moved them to do so.[7]

Other modern theoretical approaches to Golden-Age drama seem, generally speaking, to have fared rather less well in recent years, except perhaps in the United States, where the challenges and opportunities presented by such approaches continue to occupy many scholars. And yet, despite Paul Julian Smith's undeniably powerful appeals for "an end to the resistance to theory in Hispanism" well over a decade ago now,[8] Golden-Age scholars in Europe have, for the most part, tended to be cautious in their reactions to new theories of writing. Instead, many have preferred, perhaps wisely, to nurse their suspicions in relative silence rather than engage publicly with the often more or less overtly agenda-driven debates which have characterized some other areas of literary studies. Where such approaches have been embraced, there has been a distinct tendency for large tracts of the articles or chapters in question to be devoted almost wholly to explication of the theory espoused (often, in the way of many a modern marriage, temporarily), relegating the play itself to the status of an afterthought. In the context of a discipline which has been slow to adopt such approaches, this may in one way be understandable, even necessary; but one is still quite often left with an uncomfortable suspicion that, rather than indicating the proselytizing zeal of the true convert, the tendency to otiose explication represents not so much a desire to elucidate theory for the reader as an attempt to see it pinned down safely in the author's own mind. The danger, as suggested, is that the promised critical analysis of the text can too easily turn out to be little more than a mirage, eventually evanescing into thin air in an indeterminate region somewhere between theoretical discourse and the literary archaeology of the textual scholars. In Spain itself, one should add, post-structuralist approaches have never really taken firm root.[9] One suspects that even the widespread passion for semiotics, which has characterized a good deal of criticism there for years now and which, as elsewhere, has too often seen the text shrink-wrapped in the search for determinate meaning, has now at last begun to cool.[10]

But a failure to embrace theory does not perforce imply a failure to progress. In fact, it is now clear that the essentially ahistorical formalism and moralism of past approaches to Golden-Age drama studies, most obviously represented in the highly influential work of A. A. Parker from the 1940s on through the sixties and beyond, has now definitively given way to a determination to read these plays historically. But this is not just a question of history writ large, the kind of history that investigates the drama's role in relation to great affairs of state, to the role of the monarch, to Spanish history itself, and so on. It has also, importantly, involved an increasing focus on different aspects of that country's social history. The representation of women in the *comedia*, for example, continues to excite a good deal of academic interest, as might be expected of a corpus of drama shot through with the heady contradictions of Spanish male prejudice toward the female sex. Then again, the fact that women's roles in the *comedia*, uniquely in early modern theater, were actually represented *by* women has also proved of great interest to feminist critics. But there are also areas of Spain's social history which have been rather neglected in the past, such as the complex legacy of the tripartite culture represented by Spain's Christian, Jewish, and Moorish populations in the middle ages. The suppression from the late fifteenth century on of the Jewish and Moorish traditions via expulsions, conquest, forced conversions, and the operations of the Argus-eyed Inquisition is well enough established, though some recent research suggests that the traditional, totalizing account of these events has very probably not yet told the whole story. Certainly one can detect a growing interest over recent years in the representation in Golden-Age drama of "voiceless" minorities or marginal groups such as the *moriscos* (Muslims "officially" converted to Christianity), slaves, or, indeed, the indigenous peoples of the New World. This increasingly interdisciplinary exploration of the shapes and boundaries of seventeenth-century constructions of otherness, whether constituted in terms of race, gender, status, or culture, looks set to continue. It is a trend which must, I think, be most heartily welcomed and encouraged.

But there is something else that needs to be said about the historical turn in Golden-Age drama studies, that is, that it does not generally involve the view of history theorized by adherents of the New Historicisms, which seem on the whole to have failed to convince most hispanists. It may well be that a detectable increase in the use of the historical anecdote has to some extent been stimulated by the practice of the New Historicists. But the latter's failure to convince seems due not so much to objections to their conception of history as representation, or of the historian's (or literary critic's) inescapably context-bound inability to lay claim to ideological innocence either as writer or teacher. Many or most scholars will nowadays readily sympathize with such notions. It seems rather to be due to the fact that their essentially Foucauldian preoccupation with the darkly ubiquitous workings of power seems altogether too reminiscent of the conception of Golden-Age drama advanced over two decades ago by Spanish scholars José Antonio Maravall and, somewhat later and rather less influentially, José María Díez Borque.[11] They offered a vision of seventeenth-century Spanish drama as one expression of an essentially propagandistic culture, unrelentingly univocal in its support for the power structures of the state and unwavering in its attempts to naturalize the power of Spain's social elites. But this monolithic view of the theater of the period has now been seriously challenged. Two years ago, Melveena McKendrick published her magisterial study *Playing the King: Lope de Vega and the Limits of Conformity*. In it she argues with great cogency that the stiflingly reductive Maravallian orthodoxy has simply misrepresented the complex, turbulent, and sometimes contradictory realities of the period and its art.[12] This book, which, as the author acknowledges, was "a long time in the making," certainly constitutes one of the most important pieces of *comedia* scholarship in recent years. It remains now for others to take up its challenges and carry them forward to help forge a new, more sophisticated understanding of other dramatists and their works, and of course ultimately, of Spain's Golden Age itself.

There is, of course, always more that could be said about the valuable contributions made by scholars whose names have not found their way into this brief survey, or about the status of Golden-Age literature in the universities, or about the way technological developments, not least the internet, are beginning to contribute to Golden-Age drama studies. The list could go on. But one inevitably has to draw a line and, in the process, resign oneself to being more or less unhappy about it. Perhaps the most important conclusion to draw, though, is that there now seem to be grounds for real optimism about the future of Golden-Age drama scholarship, something that has not always been the case. It was Paul Julian Smith who, in 1998, wrote of Spain's perceived cultural marginalism as the " 'woman' of European culture," excluded from serious consideration as a player in Europe's central intellectual tradition. He went on nevertheless to observe that this unenviable status might for that very reason perhaps be turned to advantage "at a time when the Utopian projects of the Enlightenment and the objective authority of empirical science are increasingly called into question."[13] Perhaps Apollo has indeed ceded some ground to Dionysus. Certainly, Spanish culture seems to have moved a little closer to the limelight. What one can say with certainty about Spain's now thoroughly "embodied" Golden-Age theater is that there is a distinct sense of a freshening of the critical air, an encouraging sense that this theater remains in many ways a world still to be discovered, still exciting, still rewarding, still as strange as it is familiar, still to be explored.

Notes

1. Among fundamentally important contributions by non-Spaniards, Melveena McKendrick's excellent *Theatre in Spain, 1490–1700* (Cambridge: Cambridge University Press, 1989) remains indispensable background reading for specialist and non-specialist alike. For Spanish speakers, Ignacio Arellano's more recent *Historia del teatro español del siglo XVII* (Madrid: Cátedra, 1995) is also highly recommended.

2. Calderón's reputation was rescued in the twentieth century by scholars in England and also in Germany, where his work had been much appreciated and performed since the Romantic era. But he did not enjoy the same critical fortune in Spain. In 1880, the young critic Marcelino Menéndez y Pelayo, writing out of a literary culture focused on the European trend toward social realism, attacked Calderón for what he saw as his artificiality, unevenness, unrestrained hyperbole, symbolism, and disregard for historical accuracy. It was to be an influential assessment which can only now be said truly to have dissipated, and this despite the fact that Menéndez y Pelayo himself eventually described the offending comments as an egregious youthful folly. The philosopher José Ortega y Gasset took more general aim at Calderón years later. He accused him of playing coldly calculating word games, like a sort of conjuror, presumably to satisfy what Ortega saw as the "mania for verse," which he claimed had flooded the Spain of Calderón's day. Citing some lines from act 2 of *La niña de Gómez Arias*, he went on liverishly to observe that the Calderónian technique of inserting successive exclamatory asides in the second half of the line gives the impression of a kind of pathological tic, producing an effect akin to belching.

3. Princeton: Princeton University Press, 1991.

4. In a letter to Thomas Peacock in 1819.

5. Madrid: Castalia, 1998.

6. Madrid: Támesis, 1997.

7. I am most grateful to Professor Alan Paterson for drawing my attention in a recent conversation to this most interesting aspect of Calderón's practice as a playwright.

8. In *Writing in the Margin: Spanish Literature in the Golden Age* (Oxford: Clarendon Press, 1988), 204.

9. Ignacio Arellano provides an example of one of those critics who have openly expressed their deep reservations about modern theoretical approaches.

10. I cannot resist adding that the number of summative diagrams, which have tended for some years now to accompany much published criticism in Spain, seems also, thankfully, to be in decline.

11. The works in question are Maravall's *Teatro y literatura en la sociedad barroca* (Madrid: Benzal, 1972) and Díez Borque's *Sociología de la comedia española del siglo XVII* (Madrid: Cátedra, 1976).

12. London: Tamesis, 2000.

13. *Writing in the Margin*, 204 and 205.

REVIEW ARTICLES

Is the Renaissance
an Aesthetic Category?

RAPHAEL FALCO

The Waning of the Renaissance, 1550–1640
By William J. Bouwsma
New Haven and London: Yale University Press, 2000

Cosmopoiesis: The Renaissance Experiment
By Giuseppe Mazzotta
Toronto: University of Toronto Press, 2001

Reviewer: Raphael Falco

I

Intellectual history flourishes in the gap between continuity and discontinuity, between the unity of thought and its disjuncture. Whether talking about turning points or paradigm shifts, the intellectual historian is obliged to highlight the moment of change. Without such marking, the theory behind the history languishes. Yet the moment of change is rarely perfectible, and its identification

makes manifest the manufactured quality of the discourse—its my-
thos. "Establishing discontinuities," as Foucault remarks in *Les
Mots et les choses*, "is not an easy task even for history in general.
And," he goes on,

> it is certainly even less so for the history of thought. We may wish to
> draw a dividing-line; but any limit we set may perhaps be no more than
> an arbitrary division made in a constantly mobile whole. We may wish
> to mark off a period; but have we the right to establish symmetrical
> breaks at two points in time in order to give an appearance of continuity
> and unity to the system we place between them?[1]

It cannot be emphasized too strongly: the marking off of periods
invariably creates an appearance of continuity and unity. The paradox of cultural history is that the continuity between periods
emerges from the establishment of a break. "Discontinuity," Foucault goes on, "the fact that within the space of a few years a culture
sometimes ceases to think as it had been thinking up till then and
begins to think other things in a new way—probably begins with
an erosion from outside, from that space which is, for thought, on
the other side, but in which it has never ceased to think from the
very beginning."[2] If I understand Foucault correctly, then the possibility he suggests is that discontinuities are manufactured by historical thought to establish those "symmetrical breaks" that allow
us to see an overarching unity of thought. The discontinuities
prove that the unity and their manufacture must be seen as a necessary part of the myth of intellectual-historical continuity.

Awareness of the manufactured quality of the discontinuities of
thought, whether ours or those of earlier periods, remains foundational to the writing of cultural history. William J. Bouwsma and
Giuseppe Mazzotta take strikingly different approaches to this form
of awareness. Mazzotta, whose *Cosmopoiesis: The Renaissance Experiment* concentrates on focused comparisons of a few texts, successfully builds a cultural-historical argument around the notion of
invented worlds. His consciousness of the presence of a Renaissance mythos in its many incarnations determines the character of
his interpretations. Although he makes large claims regarding turning points in thought, he is ultimately less concerned with the cultural historiography of the moment than with the clash of
particular texts. In contrast, Bouwsma's *The Waning of the Renaissance, 1550–1640* is a deliberate effort to retheorize cultural his-

tory. As his title indicates, he addresses himself directly to a climacteric, a turning point moment of discontinuity that occurred sometime between the late sixteenth and mid seventeenth centuries in Europe. This is a vast undertaking, and Bouwsma forcefully confronts the challenges of writing cultural history. But the results are mixed. While, to a degree, the author has solid support for the discontinuity he wishes to establish—the rejection of ancient, Aristotelian science for empirical science, the replacement of Platonic occultism with modern mathematics, the acceptance of Copernican theories—it is difficult to determine whether *The Waning of the Renaissance* ever becomes conscious of the manufactured quality of the more rhetorically driven discontinuities it seeks to reveal. Although much of Bouwsma's argument is indisputable—*something*, call it The Renaissance, waned between 1550 and 1640—the study's attention to cause and effect tends to be oversimplified, as is evident in its neglect on one hand of economic factors throughout the book, and, on the other, of the influence of discursive mythification in the transformation of culture.

Bacon and others of his generation may have turned away from the ancients, recognizing the limits of their (scientific) knowledge, yet it is mistaken to cast admiration, even idolization, of the ancients as an early Renaissance idea. Literary genealogies constructed well into the seventeenth century led back to Orpheus and Amphion. Many thinkers of the later Renaissance believed that poetic—if not scientific—knowledge led back to antiquity, and that it had an equal place beside the newer discoveries. In the eighteenth century Vico constructed an epistemological cosmos—to use Mazzotta's term—based on poetic knowledge. Samuel Butler, author of the satirical *Hudibras*, might have mocked the notion of poetic genealogical authority, but his contemporary John Milton strove to see himself in the line leading from Homer and Virgil to Ariosto and Tasso. Similarly, cultural genealogy—the notion that a later culture descends from an earlier, alien culture, as Britain was said to descend from Troy—while brought to its widest dissemination by the humanists, long outlasted the Renaissance itself, as did such innovations as the humanists' school curriculum and even the alphabet we now use. Therefore, identifying the limits of the Renaissance becomes the first step. But satisfying "dividing-lines" are hard to come by, except, maybe, in the hindsight of "symmetrical breaks."

The problem of limits is not new. "Depending on one's views,"

P. O. Kristeller once observed, "the Renaissance would seem to have lasted as much as four hundred years, or only 27 years, not counting the view of those scholars who think that the Renaissance did not exist at all."[3] Kristeller himself considered the Renaissance to be more in the three hundred year range, but tended to limit it to the achievements and influence of the Italian humanists. And he notably refused to single out one batch of ideas by which to identify humanist writings: "At the present state of my knowledge," he said with unnecessary modesty, "I should still maintain that the contribution of the Italian humanists does not lie in any particular opinions which all of them would have defended, or in any particularly strong arguments they might have offered for such opinions."[4] Such an endorsement of the diversity of views among humanist and humanist influenced authors by one of the twentieth century's most important scholars of the period should probably have a restraining effect on theories of encompassing Renaissance philosophies or of a stable structure of Renaissance ideas. But the temptation to find a unifying thread is strong. Scholars continue to want to speak of the Renaissance as a whole.

This is, and is not, true of *The Waning of the Renaissance*. Written in a clear, accessible style, the book ranges over a copious number of texts published over a lengthy period in different European countries. The title of the book refers openly to Johan Huizinga's *The Waning of the Middle Ages*, which the author called a "cultural history" long before the term became popular. Bouwsma's aim, as he puts it in his preface, is to identify a major turning point in European (high) culture brought about by a reaction to cultural liberation: "In the later Renaissance," he observes, "the impulses toward liberation seem to have become unendurable, and thus to have set in motion a reaction in the opposite direction" (x). I am wary of such a generalization, recalling Kristeller's sense of the humanists' diversity and wondering how fixed the poles of Bouwsma's opposing reactions are. But it must be said that, at least in principle, Bouwsma himself is aware of this problem. He claims to respect the complexities and ambiguities of the thinkers and writers he marshals to make his argument, and he notes in his conclusion that the "three major tendencies" he treats successively often occurred simultaneously, "playing off each other" (259). This is a significant admission in an argument about historical change, and Bouwsma misses an opportunity in not emphasizing it more throughout the text. Instead, perhaps because of the ambitiousness of the argument itself, he heaps together as evidence of the same point of view writers in vastly differently genres and cultures, with different motives, audiences, and languages, sometimes writing a hundred years apart. This happens repeatedly throughout the book. For example, in one brief paragraph on the relativity of customs, Bouwsma cites Francois Hotman's *Anti-Tribonian*, Étienne Pasquier's *Recherches de la France*, Jean Bodin's *Colloquium*, Paolo Sarpi's *History of the Council of Trent*, Burton's *Melancholy*, Hooker, *Hamlet*, Lope de Vega, and Hobbes. The sheer volume of citation has an aspect of sleight of hand, as if the author were trying to suggest that these texts all supported each other, which would be impossible to demonstrate on close reading. To take just one comparison, Shakespeare's politics, not to mention his religious views, are frustratingly difficult to pin down, while neither Hooker nor Hobbes presents the same kind of problem.

Bouwsma's profound knowledge of the period is not in doubt. His learning and his close familiarity with a stunning range of texts impel the book's aggregative style, and it is a genuine pleasure to be swept along by his confident prose. Evidently in an effort to make the text more readable, Bouwsma eschews footnotes almost entirely, citing scores of passages often without even indicating titles. There is a five page bibliographical note at the end, listing a basic set of secondary sources on Renaissance history. It is impossible not to wonder what audience Bouwsma and the series editors (of which he is one) had in mind. On one hand, it is a relief to read a book free of the burden of expository notes. On the other hand, the book, for all its learned quotations, lacks the engagement with historical scholarship that we might expect to find in a landmark study of early modern intellectual culture. Too often we have to take Bouwsma at his word when we know there are other opinions, not to mention contradictory evidence, to be considered. The citation of secondary sources in the body of the text can be counted on a few fingers—Vaclav Havel makes more appearances than any scholars. The myriad disagreements over the very authors Bouwsma unproblematically uses as evidence of his argument might never have existed. At this level, *The Waning of the Renaissance* resembles nothing so much as a general historical study for non-scholarly readers, or a Whig history in the Trevelyan mode (with quotations added), the very sort of narrative Bouwsma says he wanted to avoid (vii).

There is, however, another level, and the final product is a puzzling hybrid. Bouwsma aims to advance a new scholarly thesis, a complement and rival to such influential works as Huizinga's or Jacob Burckhardt's *The Civilization of the Renaissance in Italy*. And his thesis demands our attention—not least because it represents the long-gathered conclusions of a distinguished Renaissance scholar. We can glance back at Bouwsma's earlier work for guidance in reading the present book. For a collection of his essays in 1990, *The Usable Past*, Bouwsma supplied headnotes reflecting on his intentions in the essays, sometimes adding comments on the reactions of readers. Prefatory to an essay on Philippe de Commynes, for example, he notes that ever since graduate school it had been his "constant concern to place the results of a particular investigation in the largest possible context of significance."[5] Even more germane to *The Waning of the Renaissance* is the headnote to Bouwsma's well known and controversial article "The Two Faces of Humanism":

> Like a number of other essays in this volume, this piece was distilled from an otherwise unsuccessful—because excessively ambitious— effort to write a general book about the place of the Renaissance and Reformation in the context of the whole of Western culture. I regard this essay, however, as my most successful description of what seem to me that culture's perennial dichotomies. The essay also reflects my reliance on ideal types, although this strategy was not always recognized by reviewers.[6]

One would like to speculate that *The Waning of the Renaissance* is that "general book" placing the Renaissance and Reformation in the context of all of Western culture, and that it took decades to pare down the effort from "excessively ambitious" to a manageable, yet still ambitious, thesis. Bouwsma's reliance on ideal types in the earlier essay, moreover, might be a key to reading this later book.

The concept of ideal types is generally credited to Max Weber, who saw the use of such abstractions as "indispensable for heuristic and expository purposes." He explains the problems and the value of the ideal-typical narrative in cultural analysis. I quote at some length from Weber's famous essay "'Objectivity' in the Social Sciences":

> Whoever accepts the proposition that the knowledge of historical reality can or should be a "presuppositionless" copy of "objective" facts,

will deny the value of the ideal-type. Even those who recognize that there is no "presuppositionlessness" in the logical sense and that even the simplest excerpt from a statute or from a documentary source can have scientific meaning only with reference to "significance" and ultimately to evaluative ideas, will more or less regard the construction of any such historical "utopias" as an expository device which endangers the autonomy of historical research and which is, in any case, a vain sport. And, in fact, *whether* we are dealing simply with a conceptual game or with a scientifically fruitful method of conceptualization and *theory*-construction can never be decided a *priori*. Here, too, there is only one criterion, namely, that of success in revealing concrete cultural phenomena in their interdependence, their causal conditions and their *significance*. The construction of abstract ideal-types recommends itself not as an end but as a means.[7]

Weber's remarks on conceptualization and theory construction have considerable value for reading *The Waning of the Renaissance*. Bouwsma's search for a theory that would explain the waning of certain ideas must depend for coherence on a series of abstractions from particular texts, a series of identifiable ideal types from which he can draw a conclusion. Therefore, we should not measure his success by a facile matching up of thesis and evidence. Rather, we should look for the value of Bouwsma's book in the power of his theory construction.

The theory he constructs is far-ranging, at once innovative and explanatory of the facts we have. It can be sketched in the following way: a period of the liberation of the self, tied to humanism and certain religious upheavals, was followed by a kind of panic which led to skepticism regarding the tenets of the liberating ideas; this skepticism was in turn followed by a re-ordering of the self, accompanied by a repression of those early Renaissance ideas. Bouwsma turns often to Montaigne and Bacon as exemplars whose skepticism outstripped the Renaissance and adumbrated the re-ordering of the self emblematic of the seventeenth century. Underlying the idea that skepticism led to intellectual changes is the pivotal concept of "individuality," the self that is in flux:

Petrarch had been concerned with the individuality of his own style; and Montaigne now carried to an extreme this tendency to individuation. For Montaigne, the goal of writing was self-understanding and self-acceptance. . . . Calvinist spirituality regularly began with a review of the self, and Foxe's martyrs made their own desperate and individual

choices. Sarpi emphasized personal responsibility in religious matters.
. . . For Descartes, intellectual activity, though leading to universal
truths, had in the first instance to be private and individual. (32–33)

Again in one paragraph Bouwsma assembles a curious group of authors, forcing us to accept that a definition of individuality was in
fact shared by them all. Otherwise the ideal type "individuality"
has little meaning in the passage. And the heart of understanding
The Waning of the Renaissance lies in this distinction. The persua-
siveness of Bouwsma's argument depends, not on proving the existence of abstract categories, which are in any case "pure" forms
that do not have a reality, but on showing how those categories
have a viable connection to the period and indicate genuine historical and cultural change. The difficulty of this methodological approach—a difficulty encountered as well by Weber—is that in
seeking the general drift of particular texts in order to fit them into
an ideal-typical narrative, literary, historiographical, and linguistic
details can be missed. If the value of the general thesis is compromised by what is missed, then the use of ideal types has failed "in
revealing concrete cultural phenomena in their interdependence,
their causal conditions and their *significance*" (to quote Weber).

In these terms, *The Waning of the Renaissance* remains a conun-
drum. While Bouwsma's general thesis clearly has validity—
certain aspects of Renaissance thought began to wane in the
seventeenth century—his methodology often conceals more than it
reveals about concrete cultural phenomena. A typical instance of
this methodological problem occurs in the chapter on the theater,
"Renaissance Theater and the Crisis of the Self." The title of course
begs the question of so much recent criticism on the transformations of individuality in the period, taking for granted a "self" that
can be in crisis. But even this simple observation on my part seems
unfair in the context of the chapter because it refers to a trend in
current scholarly debates, while Bouwsma characteristically
avoids such debates. Indeed, from a scholar's perspective, the
chapter is a rather cursory analysis of the development of the theater, ample and interesting to an uninformed readership but unsat-
isfying as a serious inquiry into the subject. One might object that
in relying on ideal types, Bouwsma must forgo a detailed account
that would satisfy scholars in the field. But I think the chapter errs
too much on the side of heuristic categories, suppressing literary
detail, valuable scholarship, and historiographical and economic

evidence. Bouwsma begins by tracing the origins and transmission of the theater companies from Italy to England, from which fol lowed the theater's commercial success and its appeal to a cross-section of classes ("in early Stuart England the Queen herself attended"). He touches briefly on plays as play, and on play in general, Huizinga's subject in a later book, *Homo ludens*, and a subject much more provocatively tied to the Renaissance in Giuseppe Mazzotta's *Cosmopoiesis*.[8]

With some justification, Bouwsma ties the success of the theater in the period to the increase in theatricality and role playing in the culture in general. Acknowledging the antiquity of the idea of the world as a theater, he notes the extraordinary frequency of the metaphor of world-as-theater in the Renaissance, and the many authors (and composers) who used it, from Machiavelli to Erasmus to Monteverdi and Shakespeare. He contends that "[p]eople in this period commonly thought of themselves and of their lives as dramas" (132), and goes on to emphasize role playing in politics, the theatricality of rulers (particularly Elizabeth and James), St. Peter's at Rome, the pope, and the assembled multitudes. Here as elsewhere Bouwsma craftily elides the court, or the curia, and the other classes. Was role playing really part of the lives of everyone in the period? Were common people actually more aware of their lives as dramas when watching an Elizabethan progress than when, say, watching their fellow townspeople perform a mystery cycle in the fifteenth century? It is certainly true that there was a proliferation of books on manners and courtly conduct, Castiglione and Stefano Guazzo and Annibale Romei being only the most prominent. Poetry, private letters, and dramatic representations all record the influence of these books (on stage their influence is often mocked). But these books had a small refined audience—recall, for instance, that *The Book of the Courtier* went through more editions in Latin than in English in the sixteenth century. This is not to disagree with Bouwsma's observations regarding the theatricality of politics and its high-culture commentators, only to delimit his generalization: most people were probably not striving to achieve *sprezzatura* in their daily lives.

Still, there *does* seem to have been an increased interest in theatricality in the sixteenth century among intellectuals; there *is* evidence that role playing became a popular topic in handbooks and on stage. But it seems inadequate for Bouwsma to imply a restrictively causative relationship between the supposed increase in role

playing in society and the development of the theater in the sixteenth century. He undoubtedly realizes that many factors contributed to the theatrical phenomenon, yet he narrows his argument
unconscionably, failing to support the Weberian ideal type with a
sufficiently thick description. (In his preface, he mentions Clifford
Geertz and Mary Douglas as inspirations, so it is not presumptuous
to expect thicker descriptions.) Here again one senses that the book
is aimed at a non-scholarly readership, and as if in proof of this,
Bouwsma sums up two decades' scholarship without even a passing reference:

> because of its ability to order collective experience through plot and
> closure, theater also supplied a sense at least of the possibility of a
> moral order governing the chaos of ordinary experience. This, I suggest,
> was a major element in the emergence of theater in the age of the Re-
> naissance and helps to explain the concern of those responsible for the
> maintenance of order to control it. (134)

This is not really Bouwsma's idea, of course, despite his "I suggest."
New Historicism, Cultural Materialism, and all their offshoots have
haggled over chaos and containment since *Renaissance Self-
Fashioning*. Yet, although Stephen Greenblatt's name is one of the
few mentioned elsewhere in the book, no reference appears here. Is
this just a matter of practicality? Is Bouwsma simply trying to cover
a vast area without getting bogged down in local debates? Probably
so, but his summary method works better in some places than in
others. Toward the end of the chapter on theater Bouwsma focuses
on the subversiveness of the theater. Again he suppresses references, but here his survey of the terrain, by confining itself to a narrow area, is considerably more successful while still useful for a
general readership. It is well-trodden ground for English scholars—
Jonson, the anti-theatrical prejudice, Stubbes, Heywood, Gosson—
but the addition of continental reactions to plays and actors makes
Bouwsma's *tour d'horizon* seem more than perfunctory.

II

Half a century ago Hans Baron began his monumentally influential *Crisis of the Early Italian Renaissance* with the observation that
"[t]he method of interpreting great turning-points in the history of

thought against their social or political background has not yet rendered its full service to the study of the Italian Renaissance."[9] Baron draws many controversial conclusions, digging into a wide range of humanist writers and speculating on the spurs to their brilliance. Yet for all its range and polemical intensity, *The Crisis of the Early Italian Renaissance* starts with a simple question:

> Although the time had passed when large parts of Italy were crowded with free cities, and although Tyranny was marching toward the period when monarchical absolutism would reign supreme, yet, at the turn from the fourteenth to the fifteenth century, some of the surviving city-states and local powers led by the Florentine Republic were waging a protracted fight which succeeded in limiting the triumphant progress of Tyranny in Renaissance Italy. . . .
>
> Was awareness of the historic significance of this struggle a source of stimulation for the thought and culture of the Renaissance when Humanism and the arts, in the first great flowering, had their focus in Florence? This present book is meant to give an answer to this crucial question.[10]

I quote this as an example of how one might begin a turning point interpretation. It is not a prescription by any means, as there are many other ways of writing cultural history. The passage anticipates Foucault's doubts about establishing "symmetrical breaks," though Baron eventually overcame his reluctance and allowed himself to see both continuity and unity in the systems of thought he described. Foucault was never really so sanguine. But, in any case, the focus, and therefore the flexibility, of Baron's approach is enviable. He succeeds in establishing an opposition between socio-historical conditions and the efflorescence of humanism and the arts, without losing sight of his polemic.

Unfortunately, *The Waning of the Renaissance* provides no such focus. There is a kind of confusion in Bouwsma's argument, fostered in large part by his consecutive treatment of simultaneously occurring changes "in quite different and even contrary directions" (259)—a stylistic choice he acknowledges in the conclusion. Moreover, from an organizational standpoint, in the preface Bouwsma speaks of his book's "two-fold" structure while in the conclusion he describes the tripartite organization of chapters. Ultimately these two characterizations are compatible, but together they add little clarification. Another difficulty, and an obvious difference from Baron, is that Bouwsma undertakes to chart the turning point not in one Renaissance at one juncture, but in various European Renaissances over a long period of time. Italy, Spain, England, the Netherlands, Germany—all experienced some form of what we now term the Renaissance, but all at different times and intensities. Renaissance courts, as much as they shared ideas (even ideals), often demonstrated sharper differences than similarities. Generalities can be gleaned, and ideal types established, but eventually, as the historiographical, literary, and economic differences begin to obscure the similarities, the harvest becomes very thin.

Gianni Vattimo, in speaking of the aestheticization of the history of science, has recently noted "the emergence in contemporary epistemology of an aesthetic model of historicity opposed to the notion of a process of cumulative development."[11] He contrasts "cumulative" historicity to "the historicity produced by genius," and describes a descent from the Kantian notion of epoch making or exemplary works of genius to Thomas Kuhn's notion of the paradigmatic shifts in the history of science. Vattimo sees paradigm shift history as aestheticized history, which he links to the centrality of aesthetics in modern life. This centrality begins, he says, with the "superiority and dignity" of the Renaissance artist, continues through Vico and the Romantics, who "consider the origin of civilization and culture to be 'aesthetic,'" finally ending with the contemporary notion of aesthetic models of behavior (celebrities, for example). The upshot, and Vattimo's concern (following Nietzsche), is that the aesthetic has left the domain of philosophy and become the very model for "thinking about historicity in general."[12]

Much the same concern plagues the reader of *The Waning of the Renaissance*. Bouwsma is not naïve about historicity, nor about the evolution of ideas. He respects the complex interdependence of thinkers from period to period, and would never, so far as I can tell, fall prey to the kind of naïve evolutionism against which Huizinga himself cautions.[13] Nevertheless, his model of Renaissance intellectual culture seems to aestheticize historical change. If his study is not traditional linear Whiggish history (Bouwsma's bane), then it is an undertheorized equivalent. The wealth of examples, the sheer breadth of learning, requires a too-conscious shaping. To some extent, this problem reflects praise on Bouwsma's remarkable ability to multiply textual witnesses. But, in the final analysis, the ideal-typical narrative, the theory construction, cannot quite reconcile itself with the messy, never-really-ended assimilation of ideas. Too often conflicting voices are forced into the Procrustean bed of the polemic.

For instance, in the chapter titled "The Reordered Self," Bouwsma notes a sudden attention to the restraint of the passions in the late sixteenth and seventeenth centuries, citing some of his favorite authors: Montaigne, Sarpi, Burton, Hooker, Pasquier, Bodin, and so forth. He turns quickly from the control of the passions to the restraint of the imagination, and by extension to the multiple attacks on poets and the danger of poetic thinking. This is an important subject, and its manifest appearance at the end of the sixteenth century deserves attention. But it is hardly accurate, even in ideal-typical terms, to see a shift in attitudes that would warrant an argument for a clear reaction to past conceptions, as, in fact, Bouwsma's own text makes clear. He quotes Lodovico Castelvetro on Aristotle (1570) as evidence that intellectuals had become alarmed about poetic thought: "We cannot create a king who never existed by our imagination, nor can we attribute actions to such a king; indeed we cannot even attribute to a really historic king actions he never performed; history would give us the lie" (169). Putting aside the strong possibility that Castelvetro himself might not have believed this dictum, there is the more significant problem that other authors writing at the same time said almost exactly the opposite. In fact, earlier in the book, to support the "liberation of the self" part of the argument, Bouwsma quotes Philip Sidney from the *Defence of Poetry* (1580): "Only the Poet, disdayning to be tied to any such subjection [to nature], lifted up with the vigor of his owne inuention, dooth growe in effect another nature, in making things either better than Nature bringeth forth, or, quite a newe, formes such as neuer were in Nature . . . so he goeth hand in hand with Nature, not inclosed within the narrow warrant of her guifts, but freely ranging onely within the Zodiack of his owne wit" (30). Since Sidney is writing after Castelvetro, and indeed might have read the earlier author, it makes little sense to suggest a fear of imagination *evolving* as the century progressed. Sidney obviously admires and celebrates the "zodiac" of the poet's wit, with no evidence of anxiety about runaway imagination in this crucial passage, nor, in Castelvetro's terms, about giving the lie to history (it will be remembered that Sidney reckoned the poet superior to the historian because the poet is not tied to "the particular truth of things").[14]

This overlapping of attitudes gives me pause about the entire project of cultural history. It is so difficult to find a turning point, so rare that the reaction-formation will withstand scrutiny, that it sometimes seems the effort should be abandoned for something less ambitious. Vattimo suggests that "the emergence of a paradigm requires much more than its imposition by force from the outside. It occurs through a complex system of persuasion, active participation, interpretations and answers which are never exclusively not principally the effects of force and violence, but involve a kind of aesthetic, hermeneutic, or rhetorical assimilation."[15] This statement reminds us that Foucault says that what seems to be outside has been part of thought from the beginning, pointing in a subtler way to the manufactured quality of reaction-formation discontinuities. This is not to say that *The Waning of the Renaissance*, in tracing the emergence of a paradigmatic shift, evades that "complex system of persuasion, active participation, [and] interpretations" that Vattimo advocates. To the contrary, Bouwsma often brilliantly multiplies voices, layering the complexities drawn from his commanding store of learning. Occasionally, it is true, one gets more sense of ideological "force and violence" than rhetorical assimilation from the description of the reaction to "unendurable" impulses. The difficulty may simply be one of stylistic reticence, although it never becomes clear to me whether Bouwsma recognizes that the reactions he records are themselves products of an aesthetic approach to history, a kind of mythos *in statu nascendi*.

III

In *Cosmopoiesis*, the published version of Giuseppe Mazzotta's Goggio lectures at the University of Toronto, there is less chance that the signs of aestheticization might slip by. Originally titled "Inventing Worlds," *Cosmopoiesis*—which means "world-making"—exudes a sensitivity to authors' manipulation of language in the forming of a culture. Mazzotta brings to his readings a frank delight in figuration. His chapters on Poliziano's *Orfeo*, Ariosto and Machiavelli, utopian fictions, and *Don Quixote* sparkle with critical wit, leading us again and again toward unexpected comparisons. Mazzotta's method remains firmly grounded in close reading, the ambitions of seeing a cosmopoiesis notwithstanding. The developments Mazzotta wishes to identify with the Renaissance have less to do with historical turning points than with the recognition that different forms of representation emerged when the creation of the cosmos became a human, rather than a divine, achievement. Mazzotta promises to explore the making of philosophical, religious, and scientific cosmologies in a future volume, while in the present book he confines himself to "the invention of the world and the notion of making through utopias, magic, science, art, and the theatre" (xiii). He claims that these are the "imaginative elements that char acterize the paradigm shift from the Middle Ages to the modern age ushered in by the Renaissance" (xiii). Paradigm shifts suggest aestheticization, and Mazzotta might here stand accused of an indebtedness to a master narrative of historical imaginative evolution. But I think Mazzotta's approach will answer the accusation. Not long ago, Lee Patterson challenged "the crude binarism that locates modernity ('us') on one side and premodernity ('them') on the other, thus condemning the Middle Ages to the role of all-purpose alternative." He observed:

> That [the] claims to original forms of thought are themselves central to Renaissance self-definition—that they arose within the Renaissance and served it as part of its own cultural *prise de conscience*—should encourage literary historians to view them with skepticism. The fact is, however, that they have been accepted by both medieval and Renaissance scholars with something approaching unanimity.[16]

This last assertion, though unfortunately more true than not, has notable exceptions. Herbert Weisinger in fact wrote articles on this very subject—"The Renaissance Theory of the Reaction against the Middle Ages as a Cause of the Renaissance" and "The Self-Awareness of the Renaissance as a Criterion of the Renaissance."[17] There has also been a good deal of scholarship on Petrarch's self-serving notion of the "Dark Ages" and its influence on humanist writers.[18] But too often, as Patterson contends, literary scholars have ignored the manufactured quality of the intellectual paradigm shift, accepting as genuine a discontinuity which in reality is an imaginative element of Renaissance representation.

Mazzotta's project in the lectures therefore has potentially great value. He does not really have space to problematize the concept of the paradigm shift from the Middle Ages, but his sense of cosmopoiesis captures the self-consciousness with which certain writers invented their worlds through their texts. And let it be said that Mazzotta proceeds deliberately in his concentration on the texts as privileged forms of representation. He issues a kind of call to arms:

Only by focusing on the complexities of literary texts can one grasp
their power to challenge the truth-value of the various discourses—
politics, ethics, science, and so on. No doubt, by investing literature
with such a privilege, one runs the risk nowadays of appearing as if one
belatedly revives residual romantic aesthetic conceptions, as if one
were speaking from the standpoint of nostalgia for dead forms of discourse. Not for nothing, in fact, have literary critics all but abandoned
the practice of reading as if it were a fossil. Their extra-literary concerns, however, shed little, if any, light on the texts and are not essential
to the questions put forth by literary texts, especially those of the Renaissance. (xv)

This is a strong position, perhaps overstated but in the final analysis reasonable counsel. If the Renaissance cosmos is to a large extent the product of the authorial imagination, if economic and
political changes appear in already biased form in Renaissance
texts, as they do in any culture, then our best means of reading the
Renaissance is by focusing on the literary texts, as Mazzotta recommends.

He begins with Poliziano's *La fabula di Orfeo*, a tragedy about
the death of the mythic poet. His discussion traces the meanings of
fabula, fable, back through Horace's use of the word to its etymo-
logical origins, and finally compares it to the Aristotelian mythos.
Mazzotta demonstrates from the beginning of his lectures a welcome familiarity with myth and its uses in the construction of Renaissance ideals—philosophical, political, literary—a familiarity
conspicuously absent from Bouwsma's account of the Renaissance.
The chapter on *La fabula di Orfeo* argues that for Poliziano Orpheus's death signaled "the death of a certain way of doing art. It is
the death of an aesthetic attitude and of a specific philosophy of
harmonious order that provided the theoretical underpinning of
the political myths of Lorenzo's Florence" (7). Mazzotta is referring
to Florentine Neoplatonism and Marsilio Ficino in particular when
he speaks of philosophy and harmonious order, and he recalls that
Ficino's disciples were involved in the Pazzi conspiracy. He argues
that Ficino should be seen in contrast to Poliziano as a proponent
of an anthropocentric cosmos and controllable human passions, or
furores, a purveyor of optimistic rationalism, while Poliziano's *furores* are wild and destructive and uncontainable. So Poliziano's
play constitutes a critique of Ficino, and by extension of the Florentine court politics for which, according to Mazzotta, he was the the-

orist. This is a tricky area since Ficino wrote no political treatise and since his political influence on the Medicis is difficult to gauge. But the contrast between Ficino's rationalism and Poliziano's uncontainable furies emphasizes Mazzotta's theory regarding the Renaissance experiment: certain writers began to shift toward inventing the world in their texts, keen on representing all the chaos they saw (and, in some cases, remedies for it). In Poliziano's *La fabula*, "the frenzy of the Bacchants textually recalls Poliziano's own account of the Pazzi conspiracy" (21), and the play, while not denying the empirical world, "marks the emergence of the world as fable, the world as a language construction" (23).

Other readings are equally thought provoking. In an impressive chapter comparing Machiavelli and Ariosto, Mazzotta not only sounds the depths of his theme, but also offers detailed interpretations that persuasively defend his theory of the Renaissance transition from the notion of a pre-existing world to that of an invented world, a world "made by human art and will" (xiii). Briefly, Mazzotta casts Ariosto's critique of power against Machiavelli's *The Prince*. He begins with the familiar observation that *The Prince* "demythologizes the belief in the magic or sacred origins of power," bringing power "within the bounds of the imaginative grasp of man" (28). He adds that Machiavelli's power-centered vision tended to be represented as tragic on the Elizabethan stage and makes the acute remark that Machiavelli himself understood *The Prince* as a tragic text. Mazzotta is most interesting, however, once he begins to examine Ariosto's critique of power, which he discusses in relation to madness and to play. Mazzotta draws attention to the shift in the *Orlando Furioso* from the outward madness of war's ravages to the inward ravages of the love-mad Orlando. The "internalized passion that moves Orlando" reveals the hero to be a Petrarchan lover confronted with the maddening erotic frustration of his jealousy—this occurs in the famous grotto scene, where he reads the message about Medoro and Angelica carved on the tree (Canto XXIII). Mazzotta distinguishes Ariosto's representation of madness from that of Seneca in the *Hercules furens* and from Erasmus in the *Encomium moriae*, acknowledging, however, that the *Orlando Furioso* comes close to Folly's playful satire. But Ariosto's madness "is not merely an intellectual game that turns around all meanings" (44); it is instead a function of grief, which "marks the tragic disfiguration of the hero, his degradation into the sufferings of unaccommodated existence" (44).

Mazzotta argues that Ariosto's alternative to those sufferings, his antidote to madness, is play—specifically, the play of the poetic imagination. "The poetic imagination is sovereign," he concludes, "and this sovereignty cannot be reduced to a mere strategy of rhetorical simulations. The poetic imagination is akin to madness, yet paradoxically it retrenches from madness: It is a Platonic 'divine frenzy,' which possesses the poet and allows him to play with the world as madness" (45). This last statement links Ariosto to Mazzotta's larger theme, the Renaissance experiment itself. The poetic imagination embodies—or juggles—the cacophonous voices of war, power, politics, passion, and madness, and, through what Mazzotta terms an ethics of play, restores the sanity of the hero.

Aptly titled "The Ludic Perspective," the final chapter elaborates on the theme of play in the context of the prose of *Don Quixote*, specifically Sancho Panza's visionary flight on the back of a wooden horse. Following a less satisfying third chapter on utopian writing, this last chapter undertakes an analysis of Cervantes's use of the poetic imagination as it came down to him from the Italian Renaissance. Mazzotta identifies the *serio ludere* style as indicative of a perspectival view of knowledge and proceeds from there to trace the influence of theories of perspective throughout the period, ending with Leo Spitzer's observation that perspectivism is the dominant mode of Cervantes's writing. This observation leads Mazzotta to excellent analyses of Sancho's dream vision, of the humanists' ideal of chivalry, and finally of the remythologization of knowledge by Cervantes's knight. My own hasty account does not do justice to Mazzotta's individual readings, but should give some idea of the intricacy with which he weaves his argument about the poetic imagination. Again and again he returns to proofs of how Renaissance writers invented new worlds by challenging the accepted structures of their predecessors. And, throughout this brief but intriguing book, he reiterates the claim he makes for Cervantes, namely, "that in order to speak of politics one has to speak of literature first, that fiction is the crucial ingredient of political discourse" (92).

Notes

I wish to express my gratitude to Christoph Irmscher for his invaluable editorial comments on various drafts of this essay.

1. Michel Foucault, *The Order of Things: An Archaeology of the Human Sciences* (A translation of *Les Mots et les choses* [no translator listed by the publisher]) (New York: Vintage Books, 1973), 50.

2. Foucault, *The Order of Things*, 50.

3. Paul Oskar Kristeller, *Renaissance Thought and the Arts* (Princeton: Princeton University Press, 1980), 2.

4. Kristeller, *Renaissance Thought and the Arts*, 16.

5. William J. Bouwsma, *The Usable Past: Essays in European Cultural History* (Berkeley: University of California Press, 1990), 190.

6. Bouwsma, *The Usable Past*, 19. The article appeared in a *Festschrift* for Kristeller, which is why it received reviews.

7. Max Weber, "'Objectivity' in the Social Sciences," in *The Methodology of the Social Sciences*, trans. and ed. Edward A. Shills and Henry A. Finch (New York: Free Press of Glencoe, 1949), 90, 92. The essay first appeared in *Archiv für Sozialwissenschaft und Sozialpolitik* in 1904.

8. Bouwsma never mentions Huizinga on play, nor does *Homo ludens* appear in the bibliographical note.

9. Hans Baron, *The Crisis of the Early Italian Renaissance: Civic Humanism and Republican Liberty in an Age of Classicism and Tyranny* (Princeton: Princeton University Press, 1966), xxv.

10. Baron, *The Crisis of the Early Italian Renaissance*, xxvi.

11. Gianni Vattimo, *The End of Modernity: Nihilism and Hermeneutics in Postmodern Culture*, trans. Jon R. Snyder (Baltimore: Johns Hopkins University Press, 1991), 95.

12. Vattimo, *The End of Modernity*, 95.

13. See Johan Huizinga, *Men and Ideas: History, the Middle Ages, the Renaissance*, trans. James S. Holmes and Hans van Marle (New York: Meridian Books, Inc., 1959), esp. 29–39.

14. Philip Sidney, *A Defence of Poetry*, ed. J. A. Van Dorsten (Oxford: Oxford University Press, 1966), 32.

15. Vattimo, *The End of Modernity*, 92.

16. Lee Patterson, "On the Margin: Postmodernism, Ironic History, and Medieval Studies," *Speculum* 65 (1990): 93.

17. *Speculum* 20 (1945): 461–67; and *Papers of the Michigan Academy of Science, Arts, and Letters* 29 (1943): 561–67.

18. See, e.g., Theodor Mommsen, "Petrarch's Concept of the Dark Ages," *Speculum* 17 (1942): 226–42; Erwin Panofsky, *Renaissance and Renascences in Western Art* (New York: Harper and Row, 1972); Thomas Greene, *The Light in Troy: Imitation and Discovery in Renaissance Poetry* (New Haven: Yale University Press, 1982); Walter Ullmann, "The Medieval Origins of the Renaissance," in *The Renaissance: Essays in Interpretation*, ed. André Chastel (London and New York: Methuen, 1982), 33–82; William Kerrigan and Gordon Braden, *The Idea of the Renaissance* (Baltimore: Johns Hopkins University Press, 1989).

Imagination in History

DAVID HARRIS SACKS

Practicing New Historicism
By Catherine Gallagher and Stephen Greenblatt
Chicago and London:
The University of Chicago Press, 2000

Hamlet in Purgatory
By Stephen Greenblatt
Princeton and Oxford:
Princeton University Press, 2001

"History," the word, is Greek in origin; it derives from *historia*, a term whose primary meaning is "inquiry." At its root, it names an intellectual process, not its subject matter or its final result. But it can also mean the knowledge obtained through investigation or study, an account of one's inquiries, or a narrative of events, past or present. Arguably the title of Herodotus's famous book, *The Histories*, conveys all these meanings. In Latin, *historia* refers more narrowly to narratives of events or to fictional tales and stories; the same goes for *histoire* in medieval French. In modern English, however, the word "history" names two related but distinct concepts: it can be a narrative or study of the past, or it can be the past that is narrated or studied. We "*do* history" when we research and write about previous times and places; we *"make* history" when we cause events or participate in process which later may become a subject of historical investigation or story telling.

Nevertheless in the history of the English language, "history" understood as a written narrative represents the earlier usage. In a manner of speaking, therefore, history as written precedes history as lived. Whether the same holds in logical, ontological, or causal terms—i.e., whether *a priori* models of time and of human interactions within it define, construct, direct, or shape our experience or knowledge of historical events and processes—has been one of the central issues among humanists and historians for the last two decades. Perhaps no group of scholars has done more than the practitioners of New Historicism to make apparent the important role played by literary and institutional convention and by intellectual and ideological presupposition in conditioning our understandings of the past, our reactions to the present, and our aspirations for the future.

New Historicism came into prominence as an interdisciplinary movement in literary studies, history, and related subjects around the year 1980. The term itself was first introduced in 1982 to distinguish its form of text-based historicism not only from traditional literary history, but also from American New Criticism.[1] Assuredly it has already proven itself as a movement, not just in offering insights into a host of specific topics from the self-fashioning of artists and courtiers to the making of the modern body,[2] but also in conveying the utility of construing "cultures as texts" and of thinking of literature and the other creative arts as a "key to particular historically embedded social and psychological formations" (Gallagher and Greenblatt, 7, 9). There is also no doubt that the diverse ways of working of the founding generation of New Historicists have been widely emulated or adapted by colleagues and students in a variety of different fields and disciplines. Almost from the outset, there have been numerous attempts to summarize its accomplishment and criticize its methods; I won't endeavor to cite the huge corpus of commentaries and critiques that have appeared, let alone list all the works of scholars who identify themselves in one way or another as New Historicists.[3] I propose instead to look closely at the two books before us to see where the movement now stands.

I
Practice

According to Catherine Gallagher and Stephen Greenblatt, two of New Historicism's earliest and most important proponents, their movement is not a theory or even a school, but an evolving set of practices applied to particular problems and performed by a loose and changing coalition of practitioners with different purposes and projects. *Practicing New Historicism* is their attempt to explain the character of this interdisciplinary movement, to offer an account of its intellectual affiliations and major concerns, and to reveal by their practical example some of its paradigmatic methods and moves.

What then is a "practice"? It does not seem to be the sort of activity contemplated in the old joke: A stranger to New York City stops a man on the street who is carrying a violin case and asks "How do I get to Carnegie Hall?" Fritz Kreisler answers: "Practice! Practice!" For Kreisler—for the exemplar of violin virtuosity that he represents—it is possible not just to repeat the same sequence of actions over and over but in doing so to get closer and closer to perfection. There is an external standard of excellence, applicable by neutral observers, and practice makes perfect! New Historicism, as explained by Gallagher and Greenblatt, eschews any such idea. One can do it well or badly, but not asymptotically approach the thing in itself. Nor is New Historicism's notion of a practice the precise equivalent of what Aristotle meant by *praxis*. For Aristotelians there is an external standard toward which action is directed—namely *eudaimonia*, human flourishing. Accordingly, *praxis* involves the exercise of practical wisdom, or *phronesis*, by an individual who, guided by the moral disposition to act rightly, applies theory to circumstances. Karl Marx, perhaps the greatest of modern Aristotelians, also had a teleological conception of *praxis*. In his case, it entails the translation of theory into revolutionary action aimed to overthrow bourgeois capitalism and establish communism.

While New Historicism's idea of a practice borrows heavily from this Marxist philosophical tradition of critical-practical activity— nowhere more so than in seeking to undermine established structures of thought and power—New Historicists in general, and Gallagher and Greenblatt in particular, lack the confidence of traditional Marxists that they know the driving force of history or its final end. They are not engaged in actions intended to promote a specific social movement or political cause. In this they would perhaps agree with Marc Bloch: "No one today," he ventured, "would dare to say, with the orthodox positivists, that the value of a line of research is to be measured by its ability to promote action." But like Bloch, they no doubt would also allow that "mere amusement . . . is no longer permitted us in our day, even . . . when it is the amusement of the intelligence." Writing in 1941, after the fall of France, Bloch said, that

> in this poor world of ours which . . . has created so little happiness for itself, the tedious minutiae of historical erudition, easily capable of consuming a whole lifetime, would deserve condemnation as an absurd waste of energy, bordering on the criminal, were they to end merely by coating one of our diversions with a thin veneer of truth. Either all minds capable of better employment must be disuaded from the practice of history, or must prove its legitimacy as a form of knowledge.[4]

For Bloch what the study of history offers is understanding and explanation of historical events and developments, not merely the enumeration of factual knowledge. Nevertheless, living in Vichy France and under the menace of Nazism, he concluded that "[a] science will always seem to us somehow incomplete if it cannot, sooner or later, in one way or another, aid us to live better."[5]

The New Historicist program conforms in large measure to this paradigm, as Gallagher and Greenblatt implicitly acknowledge. To use Bloch's formulation, they aim to escape "from mere narrative," to reject the "modern poisons of routine learning and empiricism parading as common sense," and "to penetrate beneath the mere surface of actions."[6] However, in thus seeking "understanding," New Historicists have been more concerned than Bloch and others in the founding generation of the Annales school, to reveal, and sometimes to unmask, the structures of power they see being served by the particular narratives and ideological constructions they examine. They use their work to challenge the master narratives in whose thrall we sometimes have been and can still remain entrapped. In this respect, their writing has a distinct ethical dimension even more explicit than the one Bloch discussed. Nevetheless, they are too aware of the role of accident in human history, too knowledgeable of ways in which cultural forms and habits resist reduction to any one formula, and too devoted to the unpredictable play of the imagination in human activity to be able to offer their own grand narrative to replace those that have fallen under the weight of critique.

So, despite New Historicism's well-known resistance to disciplinary canons and its aspiration to bring about cultural reform, the movement's conception of itself seems to share most with the definition of a "practice" as the exercise of a profession. On the whole, its members see themselves as participating in discussions and debates about the past, the present, and the future that engage the wider world of culture and politics. But their base is in university departments and scholarly journals, most notably *Representations*, and their influence, while very broad for an academic movement, has largely been confined within the world of professional scholarship. While there is no fixed theory to which everyone adheres or a body of incontrovertible findings that all accept, the practitioners of New Historicism share a language, as it were, as well as assumptions and questions that condition their discourse and relations with others.

One feature of New Historicist practice has been reliance on anecdotes, and two chapters of *Practicing New Historicism* are devoted to describing, explaining, and defending this preoccupation. The first explores the movement's debts to Clifford Geertz's method of "thick description" and to Eric Auerbach's form of literary historicism, especially his attention to "*mimesis*." Gallagher and Greenblatt argue that New Historicism built a bridge between these two seemingly disparate approaches. Geertz's style of interpretation sought to recover the imaginative world of social groupings or communities in which individual acts could be understood as signs in a common code, while Auerbach's historicism, in effect, conjured out of a particular moment in a literary work "a complex, dynamic, historically specific spirit of interpretation" characteristic of a particular time and place (Gallagher and Greenblatt 37). In the hands of the New Historicists, the result of this union is a disposition to treat cultures themselves as texts and texts as embodiments of whole culture. While Gallagher and Greenblatt seem right in suggesting that this treatment of cultures and texts is traceable ultimately to Herder and German romanticism, whether Auerbach's historicism and Geertz's cultural anthropology belong on the same branch of this evolutionary tree is more open to doubt. But my focus here is on what lessons New Historicists learned from

Geertz and Auerbach, not on whether the apparent affinities they discovered can survive close historical or critical scrutiny, and on the former Gallagher and Greenblatt are our native informants, as it were.

The use of the anecdote focuses on the way short, self-contained narratives drawn most often from outside the realm of imaginative literature or from small fragments of larger literary works can be used to "put literature and literary criticism in touch with . . . the lived life" outside of literary texts. Anecdotes, Gallagher and Greenblatt suggest, "select or . . . fashion, out of the confused continuum of social existence, units of social action small enough to hold within the fairly narrow boundaries of full analytical attention." They convey a "touch of the real," but they also participate in and draw upon the imaginary. Whether anecdotes refer to actual events no matter how carefully recorded, they are "alike fictions in the root sense of things *made, composed, fashioned*." Just like literary works, therefore, they "are shaped by the imagination and by the available resources of narration and description" in their context (Gallagher and Greenblatt 26, 28, 31). Those facts make it possible to read anecdotes as texts, and to see in them, as Auerbach did so brilliantly in the opening chapters of his *Mimesis*, the complex, multi-layered, life-world that produced them in the first instance. As is revealed by the four chapters on art, literature, and history with which this volume concludes, the debt to Auerbach's historicism is large.

"The anecdote," Gallagher and Greenblatt say, "satisfied the desire for something outside the literary, something indeed that would challenge the boundaries of the literary. It offered access to the everyday, the place where things actually are done, the sphere of practice that even in its most awkward and inept articulations makes a claim on the truth that is denied to the most eloquent of literary texts." But it also did something more, they argue. By introducing a "touch of the real," it provided a way to "interrupt" what they call "the Big Stories," i.e., the master historical narratives treating the growth of capitalism, the course of modernization, or the triumph of communism as not only the main subject matter of historical study but the inevitable end product of a unitary history process. Anecdotes, then, became the basis for formulating what they call "counterhistories," which could be "counterpoised against more ambitiously comprehensive historical narratives" (Gallagher and Greenblatt, 31, 49, 51, 52, 54).

Here Gallagher and Greenblatt associate New Historicism not only with the interest in anecdotes evinced by "humanist or 'culturalist' British left-wing" historians, such as E. P. Thompson and Raymond Williams, but also with Michel Foucault's use of "the anecdotal rupture" in his grand counterhistorical project (Gallagher and Greenblatt 67). Again perhaps it matters little whether Thompson and Williams would have felt comfortable in Foucault's intellectual company, or he in theirs. For the purposes of *Practicing New Historicism*, it arguably is enough to know that New Historicists derived one of their most characteristic ways of working by yoking together the divergent aims and approaches that they had learned from these figures. The result is less a method, or even a set of skills, than a disposition to treat the world as composed of a kaleidoscope of fragments, something remote from the historical intuitions of Thompson and Williams, if not always of Foucault.

"Counterhistory," Gallagher and Greenblatt say, "opposes itself not only to dominant narrative, but also to prevailing modes of historical thought and methods of research" (Gallagher and Greenblatt, 52). Seen in this light, the concept of "counterhistory" shares something with Karl Popper's principle of "falsifiability" in scientific inquiry. According to Popper's formulation, all scientifically meaningful propositions must be open to disproof by contrary cases. In consequence, the truth of positive claims to knowledge is only provisional and in any given instance the demonstration of a contrary case results in the "falsification," i.e. the rejection, of the claim. Counterhistory understood in this manner also draws on the idea of "counterfactual analysis," which represents a standard way of isolating and testing causal explanations. While most historians would resist the implication of Popper's analysis that their only incontrovertibly true empirical statements are in the negative, much of modern historical scholarship proceeds by the invocation of counterfactuals in the course of making counterhistorical arguments. Historians often criticize causal arguments in the form "if X was present, Y follows" by falsifying the counterfactual into which it can readily be translated: "if X is absent, Y does not follow."

But a grand narrative, no matter the end point it identifies as its own, commonly offers no unitary causal explanation for what happened. Instead, it weaves a continuous storyline out of a series of little stories—of anecdotes, if you will—that are seen to build on one another cumulatively to produce the final result. Grand narratives do not offer their explanations in a form testable by counterfactuals, and so cannot be undermined by a single contrary case, no matter how richly resonant that case might be. The best the latter can do is challenge the larger structure and make it problematical. A counterhistory, in the terms offered by Amos Funkenstein, from whom the concept is borrowed, is something else again.[7] It not only seeks to destabilize the larger narrative framework it challenges, but to displace it. Nevertheless, it too offers its explanations in forms not readily amenable to counterfactual refutation. Grand narratives and counterhistories, then, are best understood not as a means for presenting proofs, but as devices for organizing our historical imaginations and understandings. As such they often coexist for long periods in dialogue or conflict before a new paradigm comes along to shift the debate from settled ground.

Despite this limitation, Gallagher and Greenblatt want something more from counterhistory—more perhaps than the latter can provide. "Counterhistories," they say, "have tried to revive" what they call the "alterity within" systems of thought. "The force field of the anecdote," they argue, "pulled even the most canonical works off the border of history and into the company of nearly forgotten and unfamiliar existences. There literature's own dormant counterhistorical life might be reanimated: possibilities cut short, imaginings left unrealized, projects half formulated, might be detected there," and stirred back to life "at 'the touch of the real,'" as they hoped (Gallagher and Greenblatt, 74). The remaining four chapters of the book explore the porous boundaries between the "real" and the "imaginary," alternating in pairs between early modern and modern subjects.

Two chapters focus on the Real Presence in the Catholic Eucharist. Chapter 3 considers belief in the presence of Christ's body and blood in the bread and wine of Holy Communion as a paradigmatic example of representation and its conundrums. Through a thoroughly engaging comparison of Joos van Gent's late fifteenth-century Urbino altarpiece *Communion of the Apostles* with its predella entitled *Profanation of the Host* by Paolo Uccello, the chapter explores the relations and tensions between faith and doubt, between Christians and Jews, between membership in a community and exclusion, and finally "between beliefs and representations" (Gallagher and Greenblatt, 107). Chapter 5 returns to the same territory to examine some of the controversies generated in the Reformation era by the doctrine of the Real Presence and to show how Shakespeare's *Hamlet* can be understood to have been "written in the shadow of these controversies" (Gallagher and Greenblatt, 151). Although few Reformation historians will find anything new here, and some might want a more thoroughgoing familiarity with recent revisionist and post-revisionist scholarship in Reformation studies, the play's links to Reformation themes revealed in this chapter illuminate a number of its dark corners. These two chapters resonate deeply with the renewed interest in the place of religion in shaping modernity that is apparent among scholars of early modern history and culture regardless of discipline.

Two further chapters take us into the world of Victorian England. Chapter 4, devoted to an exploration of "body history" and what Gallagher and Greenblatt call "the materialist imagination" (110), offers commentary on early nineteenth-century debates among political economists and social reformers about the value of the potato in the emerging industrial economy of the age and in the diet of the poor in England and Ireland. The object is to contrast the representational reality of Christ's presence discussed in the previous chapter with the apparent materiality of the potato and the human body and its appetites in order to show that they are themselves products of imaginative representation and provide no stable history or culture-free ground for explanation. For some commentators at the time, the potato seemed capable of breaking the cycle of famine and distress and to be the salvation of the poor, since it grew plentifully, seemingly without exceptional efforts at cultivation, and unlike grain, required no long series of productive processes to transform it into something edible. For others, however, it seemed to be the food of impoverishment, since it appeared to require no skill to grow; it turned peasants, as it were, into beings born directly from the soil, the human equivalent of the potato itself. And for many of the era's political economists, devotees of Ricardo's "iron law of wages," the fact that potatoes could be readily raised on small plots by those who ate them meant that their use would keep wages low, partly by promoting the growth of population beyond the capacity of the economy to support them.

E. P. Thompson makes another appearance in this chapter, this time in a somewhat puzzling discussion of his well-known essay "The Moral Economy and the English Crowd in the Eighteenth Century," which Gallagher and Greenblatt honor but fail fully to grasp.[8] Thompson's powerful focus on the interrelationship among political rights, social justice, and the formation of class identity manifested in the activities of English food rioters gives a rather different weight to the concept of "moral economy" than does the culturalist reading provided here. It is true, as Gallagher and Greenblatt say, that Thompson does not mention the place of the potato in the eighteenth- and nineteenth-century economy and in economic thought. He concentrates instead on grain and bread, since these not only were the subjects of the traditional regime of market regulation, but also were the targets of the collective violence of the food rioters. For him, the rioters step in to enforce the ethical and legal principles that underpinned the old system of market control when the officials responsible for assuring fair prices for grain and bread failed in their duties. The rioters focused on rights to bread, not on bread itself; and it was hunger for justice, more than for food that prompted their collective action. There is good reason, therefore, for Thompson's neglect of the potato and of the debates it engendered; and while we have learned much from the history of the body to which Gallagher and Greenblatt refer, it is doubtful that Thompson himself, or we as his readers, would have found consideration of its finding a means to "strengthen the 'culturalism' of his account" (Gallagher and Greenblatt, 126). Thompson's interest was in the mutually constitutive relations between the cultural and the social, not in cultural analysis of symbolic systems undertaken on its own. There is something still to be said for this focus on human sociability and on the ways which peoples make and remake their collective lives in their social interactions, although not always according to their own choosing.[9]

The sixth and final chapter is the longest and also the most loosely jointed. It takes up the novel in relation to modern skepticism. But unlike Odysseus's scar and the world in Pantagruel's mouth, which Auerbach had used to lay bare the essential features of Homer's epic narrative and Montaigne's Pyrrhonistic doubt, neither the novel as a genre nor skepticism as a philosophical disposition can be treated as representing any one system of signs or as being uniquely expressive of the characteristics of a particular time and place. The novel chosen for close examination is Charles Dickens's *Great Expectations* and the discussion ranges over a complex array of subjects: relations between modern skeptical doubt and the modern novel; relations between the living and the dead in the creation of ideology; and relations between fathers and sons, or the lack of them, in the shaping of imagination, the formation of personal identity, and development of a concept of society. The moves made are connected by association more than inner logic or a tight sequence of causes and effects, and in consequence the form of the chapter itself replicates several of the features of the modern skeptical outlook discussed within it.

The chapter ends by reminding readers of the place that Shakespeare's *Hamlet* has in Dickens's novel and of the cultural, intellectual, and literary "distance" between the two (Gallagher and Greenblatt, 204). But apart from invoking the role of modern skepticism in undermining structures of belief in the era of Enlightenment and beyond, no historical explanation is offered to account for the differences. The rise of the modern novel and the development of modern skepticism undoubtedly are implicated in each other's histories, but the novel and skepticism are too varied in their forms and instantiations to lend explanation of their separate and collective histories very well to historicism, old or new.

Practicing New Historicism is a subtly rich and rewarding book. It gives readers a good sense of New Historicism's intellectual and methodological debts as well as of its aims and the approaches that it uses. The discussions of individual works, whether visual or literary, always provide insights, some quite profound, even if at several points their larger arguments may seem a bit muddled or fail fully to persuade. It also gives a very fine sense of New Historicism's contributions to literary criticism. But it is not intended to be a contribution to historical study and is somewhat limited in the sense of historical process it conveys. In keeping with the modes of thought presented in this volume, there is no overarching conclusion. Its final chapter completes the cycle of argument by predicting, and simultaneously demonstrating and lamenting, the continued survival of "disbelief" free "from all ontologies, including materialism" as a mode of addressing the world (Gallagher and Greenblatt, 210).

II
Imagination

I turn now to Greenblatt's *Hamlet in Purgatory*, a work preoccupied with things imagined and with poetic and historical imagination.[10] History as written is inescapably the work of the imagination—it requires bringing into presence events or developments that are necessarily absent and communicating their presence vividly, or at least intelligibly, to readers who have neither experienced them at firsthand nor examined their traces in the surviving historical record. In some ways, therefore, doing history and reading history share something with the encounters with ghosts with which Greenblatt is engaged in his impressive, insightful, and very substantial discussion of the history of spirit and ghost lore and of the so-called "third place" of Purgatory in *Hamlet in Purgatory*. We depend for many of our present-day assumptions and presuppositions on conventions, ideas, and images drawn from the past. Sometimes they haunt us, and we must exorcise them from our souls and move on. Sometimes, however, they enter into the very core of our beings and shape or motivate our actions, as did the ghost of Hamlet's father whose presence in Hamlet provides the focus for Greenblatt's subtle and well-crafted reconstruction of the history of purgatorial conceptions before, during, and after the Reformation era.

But as Thomas Babington Macaulay noted long ago, history is also inescapably in the realm of our reasoning powers—i.e., of our skills in discovering and assessing historical records and documents, our abilities in transforming our discoveries into findings, and our capacities in organizing our findings into logical, coherent arguments. "History," Macaulay says, "at least in its state of ideal perfection, is a compound of poetry and philosophy. It impresses general truths on the mind by a vivid representation of particular characters and incidents."[11] "A perfect historian," he argues elsewhere, "must possess an imagination sufficiently powerful to make his narrative affecting and picturesque. Yet he must content himself with the materials he finds, and to refrain from supplying deficiencies by additions of his own. He must be a profound and ingenious reasoner. Yet he must possess sufficient self-command to abstain from casting his facts in the mould of his hypothesis."[12]

Macaulay professed himself to be acquainted with no work of history that was equally obedient to "its two rulers, the Reason and the Imagination," none which "approach[ed] what a history ought to be . . . no history which [did] not widely depart, either on the right hand or the left, from the exact line." Given the "insuperable difficulties" in producing such a perfectly balanced history, no one would "think it strange," he said, "that every writer should have failed, either in the narrative or in the speculative department of history." These are somewhat harsh words, but even now it is hard to argue against the conclusion that only the rare historical writer has been able to walk along "the exact line" Macaulay envisioned.

Where does Greenblatt's *Hamlet in Purgatory* fit on Macaulay's sliding scale? In certain ways, it is much more a history, in the sense that Macaulay meant the word, than Greenblatt's other works, including *Practicing New Historicism*. In asking us to remember the age in which *Hamlet* was written, it leans more to the side of the imagination, not just in its subject matter but also in the vividness of its interpretations. But in building up a picture of that distant world from the evidence of the texts studied, it also participates in an act of historical recovery that would have been familiar in its basic elements to Macaulay himself. With the possible exception of Greenblatt's study of the career of Sir Walter Ralegh,[13] none of his books offers so sustained an examination of a single, if complex, historical problem, or tells a single story in so focused a fashion. It is not the perfect history of Macaulay's aspiration, but it lies more toward the middle of the spectrum than what we might call the "pole of imagination" *tout court*.

Taken as a work of historical analysis, which it is only in part of course, the book presents a remarkably imaginative structure. "I believe that nothing comes of nothing," Greenblatt says, "even in Shakespeare. I wanted to know where he got the matter he was working with and what he did with that matter" (Greenblatt, 4). The first chapter begins with Simon Fish's *A Supplication of the Beggars* of 1529, reviews the place in English religious life of some of the institutions associated with Purgatory at the time, and examines the extensive early reformation critique of the place as a poet's fiction. The latter claim condemns Purgatory as a fraud, damning it to Hell as it were; but in the second chapter Greenblatt undertakes to evaluate in a religiously neutral way what it means to treat Purgatory as "a vast piece of poetry," i.e., as an imagined reality (Greenblatt, 47). This chapter ranges broadly over medieval literature and art and considers in depth several literary representations of *Saint Patrick's Purgatory*, a treatise originally dating from the late twelfth century. But Greenblatt applies this broader approach only to his treatment of medieval materials, not to the Renaissance or early modern ones taken up elsewhere in the book, and one may wonder whether a similarly broad, comparative perspective would have further illuminated issues arising later in the book. '

The following chapter, the third, takes up the purgatorial claims of the dead to prayer and remembrance and closely examines the medieval narrative known in its fourteenth-century Middle English version as *The Gast of Gy*. Greenblatt treats these claims as "rights of memory," to quote the chapter's title. The chapter then ends with a detailed reading of Thomas More's *A Supplication of Souls*, first published in 1529. In *The Supplication*, More, lord chancellor at the time, mounted his vigorous defense of the intercessory institutions of the Church against Fish and other critics. It is only in the fourth chapter that ghosts finally appear in full Renaissance theatrical garb. Ghosts "do not altogether vanish in the later sixteenth century," Greenblatt argues, although they are "labeled" by Protestants "as fictions of the mind. . . . Instead they turn up onstage" (Greenblatt, 151). In this fourth chapter we find a wide-ranging overview of the representation of ghosts and spirits in English Renaissance drama, including the corpus of Shakespeare's plays. This discussion then leads in the fifth and final substantive chapter to a brilliant exploration of the way *Hamlet* draws on and builds upon the materials that Greenblatt has so effectively interpreted in the previous chapters.

As the above account might suggest, Greenblatt's treatment in the early chapters necessarily gives greater weight to the views of those who believed in Purgatory and conformed to the institutions and practices associated with it than to those who opposed the intercessory regime with which it was intimately connected. Scant attention is given to the arguments of John Wycliffe, who believed in Purgatory but not in the worldly institutions of intercession to which it gave rise, and equally little is said about the views and activities of the Lollards. Although Fish and other Protestants who attacked Purgatory, such as William Tyndale and John Foxe, receive very thorough treatments, they appear effectively as outsiders bringing in new ideas with which to overturn the old. It is assumed, correctly of course, that the Protestantism of these figures accounts for their rejection of the purgatorial regime, but whether they received their Protestantism exclusively as an import or derived it in part from native roots does not engage Greenblatt's discussion. Nor does any attempt to account historically for the great paradigm shift demonstrated by the book. In consequence, the Reformation is treated as a given historical fact and only the responses to it are examined as parts of an ongoing historical development. A more satisfactory approach might have been to treat the Reformation itself as a process in which religious identities were formed, and sometimes performed, in and by the clash of rival positions.

Viewed in this manner, the debate about Purgatory would be seen as constitutive of the Reformation's history.

The presence of the Ghost in Shakespeare's *Hamlet*—the presence, that is, of that spectral figure putatively of the prince of Denmark's father, who appears on stage near the beginning of the play asking his son to "Remember me"—gives this probing and stimulating book its intellectual and critical impetus. As Greenblatt convincingly demonstrates, the Ghost's call upon Hamlet to remember repeats language traditionally associated with the regime of intercessory prayer in Catholic practice. How, then, should we understand this and other echoes of Purgatory in Shakespeare's play and, more generally, in the beliefs of his contemporaries? The story Greenblatt tells is meant to answer this deep, if simple-sounding question. Its nexus is located in the early moments of the English Reformation, when Fish's attack on the power and greed of the clergy in *A Supplication of the Beggars* was answered by More's own defense of traditional intercessory institutions and practices in *A Supplication of Souls*. Fish's *Supplication* was written in the voices of the wandering poor, the very same downtrodden beggars and vagabonds to whose plight Thomas More had drawn attention in *Utopia*. More, in response, presented his *Supplication* in the voices of dead souls pleading for prayers from kin and neighbors. For Greenblatt, the text of *Hamlet*, with its pervasive skepticism about things seen and unseen, its probing of the boundary between the imagined and the real, and its frequent references to memory and remembrance, contains within it something of the same contested territory marked out by this important early Reformation debate.

Much of what Shakespeare says in the play reveals his thoroughgoing familiarity with the forms and attractions of the Old Religion. This knowledge is not surprising, perhaps, given that the playwright came from a recusant family and early in his career may well have had personal links with Lancashire Catholics. Greenblatt, however, sensibly does not attempt to settle whether "Shakespeare himself was a secret Catholic sympathizer." Although he explores some important religious issues in considerable depth, his goal is "not to understand the theology behind the ghost, still less to determine whether it was 'Catholic' or 'Protestant'" (Greenblatt, 4, 254). Nor does he enter into current debates among English historians about the pace of the Reformation or the relative strength of Catholicism and Protestantism in the early modern era. He cites some of so-called "revisionists," such as Eamon Duffy, Christopher Haigh, and J. J. Scarisbrick, but does not offer a close treatment of their works or discuss Reformation historians who disagree with them.

Greenblatt finds no systematic defense of Catholicism in Shakespeare's play. Nor does he find in it a defense of Protestantism, although elements of a Protestant sensibility and of Protestant usage also abound in the play. Too much in its language and plot, most notably the Ghost's bloody demand for revenge, speaks against the play advancing any established religious movement or advocating a single religious stance. Instead, Greenblatt says, it mixes elements derived from the medieval literature of "wonder" and tales of miracles, in which spirits regularly manifest their presence, with those of Senecan revenge tragedy, where we also find ghosts as standard fixtures of the genre. Purgatory, which provides the foundation for the medieval forms, focuses on the cure of souls in the other world of the dead, where the justice of God is tempered with His mercy. It draws attention to what the living might do for the well being of those who have passed from this world, not to how they might avenge in this world wrongs experienced by the departed while still alive. In revenge tragedy, souls cry out for bloody retribution not spiritual redemption. "[W]hile compatible with a Christian (and, specifically, a Catholic) call for remembrance," Greenblatt argues, Purgatory "is utterly incompatible with a Senecan call for vengeance." Nevertheless in Shakespeare's hands, the tension—the seeming contradiction—between remembrance and revenge, which might otherwise have led "to derision," works, Greenblatt suggests, to "intensify the play's uncanny power." It achieves this effect, "by participating in a violent ideological struggle"—not between confessions, but between sensibilities—"that turned negotiations with the dead from an institutional process governed by the church to a poetic process governed by guilt, projection, and imagination" (Greenblatt, 237, 252).

Although Greenblatt does not emphasize the fact, 1529, the year that Fish and More published their rival *Supplications*, represents a critical moment in England's political and religious history—the point where, as it were, the needs of the state and the requirements of the conscience converged. By then Henry VIII was firmly committed to ending his marriage with Catherine of Aragon, but had not yet decided on the break from Rome. As More clearly recognized, the future course of events lay in the balance, and the power of words to persuade and condemn was concomitantly great. It was a time when the existence of Purgatory was not only of importance to the soul's welfare, but also to the church's and the state's; it was worth a fight. Whatever else Purgatory did, its putative existence emphasized the central (although, as Greenblatt correctly reminds us, not the exclusive) place of the church as an institution in interceding with God through the saints on behalf of sinful individuals living and dead. If the place was a sham—"a poet's fable" as Tyndale put it, or an idle fantasy just like *Utopia*, as Foxe would later insist—many other claims made by the church and its priests to the possession of spiritual power and to a share of the worldly wealth of its communicants were as well. The highly contested character of this moment therefore comes as no surprise.

The picture was rather different at the time of the first performance of *Hamlet* in 1601. By then not only had the official doctrine and liturgy of the Church of England erased the name of Purgatory, but the traditional institutions of intercession—the saints' cults, monasteries and chantries, and anniversary masses—also had been dismantled. While some Catholics continued to conspire against Protestant rule in England, and representatives of the rival confessions contested for converts and persisted in their vituperative debates, Greenblatt eschews any treatment of these matters. His interest is in the text, and in what Shakespeare, the author, did to make it what it was. *Hamlet*, in Greenblatt's view, took no sides in the great religious quarrels of the era, but instead incorporated elements from competing outlooks and used them for its literary purposes, inviting the members of its audience to confront if not resolve the deepest contradictions residing within the conventional concepts and practices by which they lived. Many no doubt took the play in this way, but one may well wonder whether a number might have seen more immediate religious conflicts or controversies at stake with some Protestants perhaps hoping that James VI in Scotland (Elizabeth's likely successor), would follow a more aggressive anti-Catholic stance once installed in England, and some Catholics possibly hoping he would be more tolerant toward them.

Although it is possible to differ over the interpretation of Shakespeare's aims in *Hamlet*—the play is far too rich to reduce to any single view—Greenblatt surely is correct in concluding that the playwright was not himself seeking to intervene directly in the great confessional disputes of his day. But to a surprising degree in so carefully a contextualized study, little is said about the play's first audiences or early readers and what they might have brought with them to their interpretations. The assumption seems to be that they built their views out of the same materials as Shakespeare. It is perhaps worth keeping in mind, however, that for many of them religious controversy remained fully alive at the time the play was first performed, although in retrospect we might agree, as Greenblatt seemingly does, that the institutional and cultural changes wrought by the Reformation had by then given Protestantism a nearly insurmountable dominion over the scene. Even if most contemporaries had faith in the probable victory of Protestantism, it remained uncertain what sort of Protestantism it would be. Moreover, for English men and women living ca. 1601, whether Protestant or Catholic or those yet to be firmly converted to either camp, the course of Providential history still held out the prospect of a last great battle between the forces of light and of darkness. In 1601, England was still at war with Spain; it had been threatened with the possible return of the Armada as recently as 1599. Whether England or Spain would triumph in the end was not yet certain.

No matter how deep one's faith, treating historical events as reflecting the will of God meant weighing their providential significance case by case and acting according to what one judged God demanded. The evidence was never anything but ambiguous. Was victory a sign of one's rectitude or a temptation to pride? Was defeat a test of one's faith or a warning of one's error? In consequence, among seriously committed Protestants and Catholics there was the belief that the religious convictions of the English remained in play. Indeed, as Peter Lake and Michael Questier recently have been arguing, many philosophically deep and politically important issues had been revivified in the 1590s in the course of clashes between the so-called Puritans and the Church of England's hierarchy and their conformist supporters in which the importance of ceremonies and the doctrine of predestination were once again in hotly contested debate. In these circumstances, room was opened anew for Catholic apologists to intervene on behalf of their own views. Protestants feared Catholic resurgence and felt the need to battle against anything that smacked of popery, while Catholics, or some of them, remained ever hopeful of winning back the faithful.[14] Hence, some in *Hamlet*'s first audience might well have seen the play engaged with these living political and ecclesiological issues of the day and not only with the spiritual and psychological ones to which Greenblatt so effectively draws our attention.

Although nothing that Greenblatt says contradicts the above account, it is not his purpose to explore this kind of historical territory. His interests reside elsewhere, namely "in the tragedy's
magical intensity" (Greenblatt, 4), i.e., its imaginative capacity to
call the spirits of its characters vividly into presence. For him, the
text in effect engages in an internal dialogue about the boundary
between the living and the dead. Is the apparition that Hamlet saw,
or thought he saw, truly the living spirit of his dead father or actually the work of the devil tempting the prince of Denmark to sin? Is
the boundary between this life and the next open or closed? How
can one decide? In Greenblatt's treatment, these questions also concern the boundary between material and imagined reality, and
therefore between experience and art or culture. Is the boundary
impervious or porous? Should it be one or the other? These deep
questions, which connect to but transcend the great debates of the
Reformation, were not yet settled, and it is one of the many suc-
cesses of this important book that it treats them as living problems
for the English as they confronted and accommodated to the rever-
berating consequences of the religious revolution through which
their kingdom was passing.

For Greenblatt "Purgatory exists in the imaginary universe of
Hamlet only as what the suffering prince, in a different context,
calls 'a dream of passion.'" It gave "its viewers," he says, "many of
the deep imaginative experiences, the tangled longing, guilt, pity,
and rage evoked by More." But did this "unforgettably vivid
dream," also participate "in a secularization process . . . in which
the theater offers a disenchanted version of what the cult of Purgatory once offered?" Without rejecting the possibility outright,
Greenblatt concludes that "the palpable effect is something like the
reverse: *Hamlet* immeasurably intensifies a sense of the weirdness
of the theater, its proximity to certain experiences that had been organized and exploited by religious institutions and rituals" (Greenblatt, 252, 253). A similar point is made in the book's short but apt
"Epilogue," which takes us to Shakespeare's *The Tempest*. There
the playwright famously probed the relationship between dreams
and reality, spirits and actors, prayers and applause, the theater and
"the great globe itself." Shakespeare seems to be more than playful
when he has Prospero say: "As you from crimes would pardoned
be, / Let your indulgence set me free." In the face of the desacraliza-
tion of religious institutions that accompanied the Reformation,
Greenblatt seems to be suggesting a migration of the holy to other
sites, temporal in character with the theater high among them.

Hamlet in Purgatory addresses the history it considers primarily through the close examination of texts, each seen in relation to a fabric of other texts with which it shares subject matter, concepts, and rhetoric, if not genre or form. The readings offered are as illuminating as they are subtle, and it is one of the great pleasures of the book to follow along as its author makes the connections among seemingly diverse literary motifs and images and draws out their implications. The book asks hard questions, and it presses to answer them. It is also a deeply humane book. In asking us to consider "the afterlife of Purgatory, the echoes of its dead name" (3), it is calling upon us to weigh our own encounters with the spirits of the dead in the traditions or conventions that shape our self-understanding and our actions.

III
History

Although many of the methods employed by historians in the present day might be unrecognizable to the founders of the discipline, history still retains its ancient, Herodotean roots, as a form of inquiry. As with Herodotus and Thucydides, however, the results of historical research most commonly are presented as stories, small, medium, and large. And, as in Macaulay's conception, its ideal form arguably is still a vividly told narrative, or series of interconnected narratives, grounded in the careful discovery, evaluation, and presentation of evidence. Stories, as distinct from descriptions, normally involve change of some kind.

However, in much of the work of New Historicists, such as Greenblatt's *Renaissance Self-Fashioning* or his often reprinted essay "Invisible Bullets," emphasis was given to the persistent power of political and cultural institutions or structures to contain the forces of change.[15] Change, when it was discussed at all, was understood to proceed by abrupt breaks or ruptures from settled frameworks of practice and power. Between these breaks, the movement of events disappeared entirely or became compressed and flattened. In *Shakespearean Negotiations* Greenblatt modified this position somewhat. There the emphasis was on the "circulation" of vivid representations in a reciprocal dialogue, rather than on their containment. Nevertheless, little attention was paid to the processes by which cultural forms or ideological structures changed over time.[16] A similar idea is to be found in his *Marvelous Possessions*, a book especially focused on what Greenblatt calls "the assimilation of the other." There, explicitly adapting Marx, he speaks of "the reproduction and circulation of mimetic capital," a formulation that stresses the accumulation of a stockpile of vivid images that have recognized value under existing "social relations of production" and that can be mixed and matched to make further representations.[17] In many ways the models of historical development embedded in *Practicing New Historicism* replicate these understandings.

Hamlet in Purgatory, in contrast, is simultaneously an analysis and an account of a long-term, interlocking process of change in some of England's main cultural institutions. On the one hand, it examines the development of Purgatory as an imagined place and its continued presence in Renaissance literature and culture. Although Greenblatt says that his book is about the post-Reformation life of Purgatory, there is at least as much about its long history during the middle ages as about what happened to it during and after the Reformation. On the other hand, the book seeks to explore the emergence of the theater as a major cultural institution in Renaissance England.

In making his case, Greenblatt sees the medieval and Reformation materials from which Shakespeare constructed the Ghost in *Hamlet* as the same materials from which the theater as a social form established its niche in modern culture and from which the drama and its performances derive their ideological or cultural power. The process is one in which elements from the past, often wrenched from the frameworks in which they were first established, persistently enter into the present, even though typically in different, sometimes quite new, surroundings. Although something of the idea of circulation still remains, conventions and practices from within Western Christendom's own past are transformed by the fires of the Reformation, and not simply transmitted, circulated, and reassimilated.

Viewed in its broadest terms, therefore, *Hamlet in Purgatory* is a book about how past history lives on in memory and inherited practices and continues to shape present culture. While the book does not represent the rejection of its author's previous views or abandonment of his past positions, it offers—to this reader at least—a significant move away from some of their most problematic features. While the concept of "containment" might help to explain the absence of significant historical change over long periods, it makes its occurrence something of a mystery. Similarly, while the idea of "negotiation" can go some way to account for the circulation of social energies within and between texts, it does so by downplaying the potential for change in social and cultural life. What is transmitted is the characteristic force of the person or thing within the circulating medium, not the transformative effects they might have.

In *Hamlet in Purgatory*, the focus is on how individuals and communities come to live with, participate in, and accommodate the fact of historical change. We do so, Greenblatt now seems to be saying, by adaptation and reinterpretation, rather than by destruction or replacement. In effect, the ghost of Hamlet's father becomes a figure for the continuing hold the spirit of the past has on the present. Just as for Shakespeare, so for us, "nothing comes from nothing" (Greenblatt, 4). While many historians would not endorse this view in its entirety, there is no doubt that it captures a large measure of the truth about historical processes.

Notes

1. Stephen Greenblatt, "Introduction," in *Genre* Special Topic 7: *The Power of Forms in the English Renaissance*, ed. Stephen Greenblatt, *Genre* 15, nos. 1–2 (Spring–Summer 1982), 5. This volume was reprinted as *The Power of Forms in the English Renaissance*, ed. Stephen Greenblatt (Norman, OK: Pilgrim Books, 1982). The term "new historicism" was not an entirely new coinage in 1982; see Wesley Morris, *Toward a New Historicism* (Princeton: Princeton University Press, 1972).

2. Stephen Greenblatt, *Renaissance Self-Fashioning: From More to Shakespeare* (Chicago: University of Chicago Press, 1980); *The Making of the Modern Body: Sexuality and Society in the Nineteenth Century*, ed. Catherine Gallagher and Thomas Laqueur (Berkeley and Los Angeles: University of California Press, 1987).

3. I associate myself with both sides. I made my first attempts to comment critically on certain features of this movement in two review articles published in the later 1980s: "History in Literature: The Renaissance," *Journal of British Studies* 26, no. 1 (January 1987): 107–23; "Searching for 'Culture' in the English Renaissance," *Shakespeare Quarterly* 39, no. 4 (Winter 1988): 465–88. My book *The Widening Gate: Bristol and the Atlantic Economy, 1450–1700* (Berkeley and Los Angeles: University of California Press, 1991) is number 15 in the University of California Press's New Historicism series, edited by Stephen Greenblatt.

4. Marc Bloch, *The Historian's Craft*, intro. Joseph R. Strayer, trans. Peter Putnam (New York: Alfred A. Knopf, Inc., 1953), 9.

5. Ibid., 10.

6. Ibid., 13. For Gallagher and Greenblatt's comments on New Historicism's associations with aspects of the Annales school's program, see *Practicing New Historicism*, 53, 59. It is worth noting as well that New Historicism at its founding was especially concerned to reject what it saw as the moral obtuseness of "the mainstream literary history practiced in the first half" of the twentieth century. See Greenblatt's early comments on "The Political Background of Shakespeare's *Richard II* and *Henry IV*," delivered in 1939 by Dover Wilson before the German Shakespeare Society at Weimar; Greenblatt, "Introduction," *Power of Forms*, 5–6.

7. See Amos Funkenstein, "History, Counterhistory, and Narrative," in *Probing the Limits of Representation: Nazism and the "Final Solution,"* ed. Saul Friedlander (Cambridge: Harvard University Press, 1992), 66–81; Amos Funkenstein, *Theology and the Scientific Imagination from the Middle Ages to the Seventeenth Century* (Princeton: Princeton University Press, 1986), 202–89, esp. 273–89. Gallagher and Greenblatt discuss Funkenstein's idea on p. 52.

8. Gallagher and Greenblatt cite this 1971 *Past and Present* article from E. P. Thompson, *Customs in Common: Studies in Traditional and Popular Culture* (New York: New Press, 1991), 185–258.

9. For a recent critique of cultural analysis as practiced by anthropologists such as Geertz, see Adam Kuper, *Culture: The Anthropologists' Account* (Cambridge: Harvard University Press, 1999). For a somewhat similar critique from the perspective of literary study, see Terry Eagleton's "Blackwell Manifesto": *The Idea of Culture* (Oxford: Blackwell, 2000).

10. I have also discussed Greenblatt's *Hamlet in Purgatory* in similar terms in "Exercising the Imagination," an H-ALBION review on H-NET, which also comments on Carlo Ginzburg, *No Island Is an Island: Four Glances at English Literature in a World Perspective* (New York: Columbia University Press, 2000); Davis Harris Sacks, "Exercising the Imagination," H-Album Review, for H-NET, August 2002, http://www.h-net.msu.edu/reviews/showrev.cgi?path=204381032241906.

11. Thomas Babington Macaulay, "Hallam," in *The Works of Lord Macaulay Complete*, ed. Hannah More Macaulay, Lady Trevelyan, 8 vols. (London: Longmans, Green and Co., 1873), 5: 162; a review of Henry Hallam, *The Constitutional History of England, from the Accession of Henry VII. to the death of George II*, 2 vols. (1827), first published in the *Edinburgh Review* in September 1828.

12. Macaulay, "History," in *Works*, 5: 122–23; a review of Henry Neele, *The Romance of History. England* (London, 1828), first published in the *Edinburgh Review* in May 1828.

13. Stephen Greenblatt, *Sir Walter Ralegh: The Renaissance Man and His Roles* (New Haven: Yale University Press, 1973).

14. See Peter Lake and Michael Questier, *The Antichrist's Lewd Hat: Protestants, Papists, and Players in Post-Reformation England* (New Haven: Yale University Press, 2002).

15. Greenblatt, *Renaissance Self-Fashioning*. For the earliest version of "Invisible Bullets," see Stephen Greenblatt, "Invisible Bullets: Renaissance Authority and Its Subversion," in *Glyph: Textual Studies #8*, ed. Walter Benn Michaels (1981) 40–61.

16. Stephen Greenblatt, *Shakespearean Negotiations: The Circulation of Social Energy in Renaissance England* (Oxford: Clarendon Press, 1988).

17. Stephen Greenblatt, *Marvelous Possessions: The Wonder of the New World* (Chicago: University of Chicago Press, 1991), 3, 6.

ARTICLES

Portia and the Prince of Morocco

GUSTAV UNGERER

IT IS NOT UNUSUAL for critics to view Shakespeare's Prince of Morocco in *The Merchant of Venice* merely as an exotic figure, creating, in the words of Eldred Jones, a "from-the-ends-of-the-earth atmosphere." He may indeed even enrich Portia's wooing pageant as a kind of Marlovian leftover, penetrating deep into the green world of her countryside retreat.[1] But the sequence of Morocco's ill-fated courtship can also lead us into significant vistas of the cultural world which created this complex play, one such vista comprising the intense diplomatic, commercial, and cultural interactions of the time, interactions that were taking their shape from the traffic between the court of the Moroccan sultan Ahmad al-Mansur and that of Queen Elizabeth of England. Such interactions may well command attention because, in 1589, a shaky political entente between the two courts had already made much headway. A league offensive and defensive, officially propagated as a league of amity between a Christian and a Muslim ruler, had almost been consummated, the Moroccan ambassador Marzuq Rais and the English government having been in close consultation.[2] This warmth between the kingdoms was still present in 1595 when ambassador Ahmad ben Adel with a retinue of some thirty-two persons was rumored to be on his way to London to resume these negotiations.[3]

One should also keep in mind in this connection that at the time of her death Queen Elizabeth, for the sake of assuring a political partner with whom to wage war against their mutual counterpart Philip II, had conducted a correspondence with Morocco's king, Ahmad al-Mansur, over a period of some twenty-five years (1578–1603), an exchange in which she continually praised "la buena amistad y confederación que ay entre nuestras coronas."[4] Indeed, the queen's last missive to him emphasized this close epistolary relationship as she signed herself "Vuestra hermana y pariente según ley de corona y ceptro."[5]

This particular correspondence aside, it is important to note that

Morocco under the rule of the Saadian dynasty seems to have created quite a large field of multicultural encounters that especially involved England, a matter not yet widely discussed. Especially relevant is the fact that Englishmen themselves, factors and ambassadors resident in Morocco, were adjusting to a Muslim society whose export/import trade lay entirely in the hands of the Jewish merchant class and the Jewish top echelons of the Moroccan civil service which had emigrated to Morocco under the pressure of enforced conversion in 1492. Segments of Shakespeare's society were thus in the very business of dealing with a permeable bi-continental space which had been fashioned by the Iberian Peninsula and the Maghreb for centuries, an area productive of concerns to be found in *Merchant*. A multiethnic bond situation involving the Moroccan sultan himself (Abd al-Malik: the victor in *The Battle of Alcazar*), a Jewish sugar magnate and elite official (Isaac Cabeça), and the leading partnership of the Barbary merchants, cannot help but relate to the bond story of the play with, however, surprisingly different implications. At the same time, William Shakespeare's own acquaintance with a family who not only owned property in Agadir and Marrakesh, but were involved in the real-life bond situation alluded to above, is a part of the early modern English cultural ambiance interestingly relevant to *The Merchant of Venice*.

All these concerns are the subject of this essay, which attempts a cross-cultural investigation which must begin in Andalusia because another matter, raised by Shylock at his trial, is slavery—and this is also a topic of cultural relevance to early modern English audiences. This relevance becomes clear in the earliest records of the English slave trade to which English and American historiographers seem to have turned a blind eye. For these records show that the first English slave holders and traders of black and Moorish domestic servants were the English merchants resident in Andalusia in the last decades of the fifteenth and early decades of the sixteenth centuries, and further, that the English were the pioneers of the English slave trade with Morocco.

The Historical and Cultural Setting

Early Anglo-Muslim Encounters in Spain and Morocco

Nabil Matar, in his study of *Turks, Moors, and Englishmen in the Age of Discovery*, warns us against conflating the North African

Muslims, the Moors, Berbers, and Arabs with the sub-Saharan black Africans, as did the Elizabethans, because English relations with the inhabitants of black Africa, as he cogently agues, were relations of power, dominion, and slavery, whereas relations with the Muslims of North Africa, with the sharifs of Morocco, as well as with the Ottomans, were relations based on anxious equality.[6] Matar's warning is fully justified, but I disagree with his view that the encounter between Britons and Muslims in Morocco and the Iberian Peninsula engendered no colonial dispute. On the contrary, there is ample evidence that the northwestern African Muslims, the Moors and Mooresses of Morocco, constituted colonial targets not only for the Portuguese and the Spaniards but also for the English. One of the dire consequences of the Portuguese and Spanish conquest of the Atlantic and Mediterranean littoral of Morocco in the fifteenth and sixteenth centuries was the establishment of a large-scale slave trade.

The English, lagging behind for about half a century, cashed in on the slave trade as early as the 1480s. Various records kept in several Spanish archives disprove the received view that the English as a slaving nation were late coming in the 1550s.[7] Hence it is no longer opportune to argue that the Moors and Mooresses of Morocco constituted colonial targets only for the Portuguese and the Spaniards, they were also victims of the English who bought the captured slaves at the slave markets of Andalusia. The trade with enslaved Moroccans led to a serious depopulation of the coastal regions of Morocco.[8]

The first Englishmen to settle along the Christian/Muslim or Hispano/African border were the merchants stationed in Seville, Sanlúcar de Barrameda, Huelva, Cádiz, and Valencia. Their early encounters with the Moors in Andalusia and across the Straits of Gibraltar were the result of a concerted campaign launched by their company's expansionist commercial policy. A shroud of silence has been cast over the history of early English slaveholding in Spain by Gordon Connell-Smith's study of the English Andalusia Company.[9] It is time to recognize as a historical fact that the majority of the English merchants resident in Andalusia—I mention only some of the prominent figures such as Robert and Nicholas Thorne, the geographer Roger Barlow, and Thomas Malliard—were slave owners. Alfonso Franco Silva, the medievalist of the University of Cádiz, has provided ample evidence that some of them were also slave dealers.[10] Malliard's inventory, drawn up after his death on 29

August 1522 by his English business partners and executors Robert Thorne, Thomas Bridges, and Roger Barlow, lists sixteen slaves, among them three Moroccan Moors, five Mooresses, four mulattoes ("loros"), and five negroes.[11] The Malliards must be ranked among the leading slave owners in the Iberian Peninsula considering that the average number of slaves owned by the landed nobility was fifteen.[12]

English trade with Morocco was a natural extension of the existing trade established by the Andalusia company in Spain and in the Levant. Individual voyages can be traced as far back as the 1520s or 1530s when Roger Barlow visited Agadir, which then was still in the hands of the Portuguese. Regular trade, however, began after the Portuguese had withdrawn from Agadir and Safi in 1541, and it increased after 1549 when Charles V forbade Spanish merchants to trade with North Africa, Morocco included, which by then had emerged as an independent sovereign state under the Saadian sharifs. The following years until 1603 were a period of experimentation when the merchants sought the ideal form into which the trade should be cast. Trade was maintained by the Barbary merchants for more than a generation without control or regulation. Then in 1585, under the pressure of the earl of Leicester, it was subjected to the control of a regulated company. Leicester saw in the Barbary Company a vehicle for selling strategic goods, munitions, iron, lead, tin, timber, and oars for the professional army and navy of Ahmad al-Mansur. The monopoly of the Barbary Company came to an end in 1597 when the trade reverted to its former freedom, giving way to uncontrollable deregulation, damaging rivalry, and fraudulent practices; its demise caused heavy losses among the English merchants.[13]

The Anglo-Moroccan merchants made the painful discovery that they were interacting with Moroccan Muslims not from an overwhelming position of strength, but from a position of near-impotence and vulnerability. The centralized rule of the Saadian sharifs had infused a sense of nationhood into the Moroccan tribes, and its mercantile policy, relying on exports to European countries, was conducted on Morocco's own terms. Thus the English merchants were often at the mercy of the Moroccan sultans and their marabouts. The sultans dictated the fiscal terms of the trade and the marabouts banned the export of saltpetre and the famous Barbary horses. It is true that the trade had unilaterally been pioneered, in chronological order, by the Genoese, Portuguese, French, and English merchant adventurers who had the advantage of the superior sailing technology of ocean-going vessels, but once the trade had been established, the sultans, on the whole, gained the upper hand. It was quite a humiliating experience for English merchants in Morocco and their authorities at home to realize that their commodities were not always under their own disposition and that their policy to cut out the Jewish middlemen proved a dismal failure. This must be taken as a reminder that trade as a key to imperial success ultimately proved a failure for the English in the Mediterranean.[14]

Early Anglo-Jewish Encounters in Morocco

The nature of Anglo-Moroccan trade and its cross-cultural aspect, moreover, cast some doubt on the alleged Elizabethan horror of the Jews. Charles Edelman has recently argued that the horror was probably a myth.[15] The evidence at my disposal supports Edelman's view. Morocco offers a hitherto unexplored long-term scenario of Anglo-Jewish face-to-face encounters which have gone unnoticed in Shylock criticism. The entire Moroccan import/export trade had been monopolized by the Jews. Trade was simply not possible without their help and good offices. Their services were indispensable at the ports, the royal customs house in Marrakesh, the running of the sugar farms, and the hiring of camels for the transport of goods. The fact that the Jews had monopolized the export trade was brought home to the Elizabethans by the anonymous English chronicler of the Battle of the Three Kings (1578).[16]

The records of the English Barbary merchants also disclose that English encounters with Jews mainly took place in Morocco and not in England. The Jews who had settled in England, for instance the musicians under Henry VIII, such as the Bassanos and Lupos, had been assimilated within a generation or two; and the Iberian conversos, among them the anglicized elite physicians Dr. Ruy López and Dr. Hector Nuñes, were in a position that was not unlike the status of the Elizabethan recusants. The best modus vivendi for a secret Judaist in Elizabethan London was a pragmatic compromise between inward conviction and outward conformity. The same observation applies to the English recusants, Shakespeare's father included. [17]

The business pioneered by the English Barbary merchants was prone to be harassed by commercial conflicts and cultural frictions.

Their factors trading with Morocco under the Saadian sharifs found themselves transplanted in a country which was a part of the permeable bi-continental space as it had been fashioned by the Iberian Peninsula and the Maghreb. They had to learn how to adjust to a multicultural society which carried on the tradition of religious cohabitation, confessional pluralism, freedom of worship, and racial tolerance as it had evolved in medieval Spain and in North Africa and had abruptly been cut short in 1492 by the national policy of the Catholic Kings in their attempt to put an end to intercontinental hybridity and to subject reconquered Spain to rigid cultural conformity. About twenty thousand Sephardic expellees, among them historians, physicians, scientists, merchants, goldsmiths, artisans, a printer, highly qualified military experts, and gun casters took refuge in Morocco. Within a decade or two, the best qualified among them had worked their way up to the upper echelons of the civil service, had set up a nationwide network of business connections, and had modernized the trade under the auspices of the sharifs. For the English merchants in Morocco there was no way of avoiding the ubiquitous Jews. The political and social circumstances brought them together as neighbors and partners who under the tutelage of the Saadian rulers came to understand and respect each other's humanity.[18]

Thus the English merchants and soldiers dispatched to Morocco by the Elizabethan government as ambassadors or agents were obliged to honor the Saadian court protocol and, like all the other foreign diplomats, to reside in the mellah (the judería) of Marrakesh. One might have expected the Saadian authorities to have accommodated the Englishmen with diplomatic status in the Alfandica, the Christian borough, where some English merchants, among them the Gores, owned houses . The reasons that induced the Saadian government to adopt a different policy must have been manifold. In the first place, the mellahs in Morocco were far less discriminatory and exclusionary than the ghettoes in European countries. Morocco was a young nation still in the making, and the Saadian sharifs were acutely aware that the unifying process generated by their military, economic, and religious struggle (jihad) against the domination of the Portuguese invaders would be jeopardized without the experience and collaboration of the Jews. Their integration into the nascent Moroccan state was, it seems to me, a necessity to achieve political independence and a sense of national identity. The Sephardic Jews, living within the permeable borders of the Moroccan mellahs, were considered the neighbors of the Muslims. David Corcos has argued that the spiritual leaders of the Moroccan Jews, unlike their European naguids and rabbis, did not encourage the Moroccan communities to live separate lives.[19]

Furthermore, it must be taken into account that the mellah in Marrakesh was a showpiece of urban development which the Saadian rulers took pride in showing off to the European visitors. Their object was quite obviously the projection of a positive image of their country in western Europe. The houses of the Jewish intelligentsia and the Jewish top officials of the Saadian court were stately mansions, standing in large plots of parkland that had been denied to the Christian inhabitants of Marrakesh. The mellahs, moreover, functioned as cultural buffer zones, as linguistic oases, as it were, which helped to mitigate the cultural differences between the foreign envoys and the Muslim authorities. Hebrew, of course, was the language that prevailed among the Jewish elite, but as the majority of the mellah residents were Spanish and Portuguese expellees, and most western diplomats were proficient in Spanish or Portuguese, the Jewish hosts had no difficulties in welcoming, accommodating, and getting to know their Christian guests. All the English envoys had a sound command of Spanish, one of them being of Spanish and a second of mixed English/Portuguese descent. Some of the Jewish hosts must have also served as court interpreters who were indispensable for establishing an understanding between England and Morocco.

Edmund Hogan, a London mercer, was the first English ambassador to submit his credentials to Abd al-Malik. From May 1577 until the end of July he resided "not farre from the Court"—the mellah was close to the court—in a house that was "faire after the fashion of the Countrey, being daily well furnished with all kind of victuall at the Kings charge."[20] Henry Roberts, a soldier and privateer, was appointed governor of the Barbary Company and ambassador of Queen Elizabeth to the Saadian court, a double function which was to cause some friction and litigation. He resided in one of the best houses of the mellah from August 1585 until August 1588.[21] Roberts confirmed the outstanding quality of his accommodation in a short report published by Richard Hakluyt. In it he defined the "Juderia" for the English readers of *The Principal Navigations* as "the place where the Jewes have their abode, and is the fairest place and quietest lodging in all the citie." His wording and use of the superlative was undoubtedly a piece of self-aggrandizement.[22]

The next two English ambassadors experienced Morocco in a negative way. John de Cardenas, commissioned in September 1589, lived at an undisclosed address in Marrakesh,[23] but the address of Edward Prynne, commissioned in April 1590, is known. The son of a cross-cultural marriage between an Englishman stationed in the Azores and a native Mooress, Prynne had entered the service of Dom Antonio as interpreter. He complained about being detained in Marrakesh against his will until March 1592, unimpressed by the fact that the sharif had granted him a personal "alowance of sixe ounces a daye" and had ordered shaykh Jacob Rute to bid him "wellcome" and to "lodge" him in the mellah in a house befitting his status as accredited representative of Queen Elizabeth.[24] Jacob Rute, like his father Jacob (I), had made his way up to the highest echelons of the Saadian government, rendering indispensable services to Ahmad al-Mansur as interpreter, intelligencer, and minister of foreign affairs. His is the example of an influential Jew in Moroccan politics who was accustomed to crossing cultural boundaries, to moving in both the upper circles of the Muslim and Jewish society of Marrakesh. In his double capacity as a prominent figure of the Saadian court and leading member of the Jewish community he was the best choice for providing suitable accommodation and generous hospitality for Prynne in the mellah and for preparing the royal audiences.[25]

The cross-cultural interactions that took place between the Christians and the Jews in the mellahs of Fez and Marrakesh were consciously ignored by the contemporary Christian chroniclers of Saadian history, particularly by the annalists of The Battle of the Three Kings (1578), who focused their attention on the military dimension and political implications of the defeat suffered by the Christian army under King Sebastian. Some of them did not hesitate to distort the truth, inventing fictional incidents in order to vilify the Jews and denounce their cruelty to the Christians. Fortunately, one Christian annalist abstained from joining his colleagues in the malevolent defamation of the Jews. Jerónimo de Mendonça, in his *Jornada de Africa* (Lisbon, 1607), records how much the Jews respected their prisoners' dignity as human beings. Thus, the eighty Portuguese noblemen accommodated in the judería of Fez were looked after by their Jewish hosts, among them Abraham Rute, the brother of Jacob (II) Rute, in a spirit of tolerance, commiseration, and, most surprisingly, commensality. The acceptance of each other's humanity transcended religious barriers and cultural differences. Prisoners and hosts felt free to engage in religious disputations under the supervision of the naguid, the head rabbi, and the Dominican Friar Vicente da Fonseca. The disputations took place in the house which had been prepared for Francisco Portugal, son of the count of Vimioso, as his residence in the mellah. There were conversions generated under the impact of the disputations.[26]

Surprisingly, the mellah in Marrakesh was converted into a political arena in which the war between Protestant England and Catholic Spain was fought out between the English merchants residing in the Alfandica and the Spanish envoy residing in the mellah. When the news of the English victory over the Armada reached the Saadian court about the beginning of September 1588—Queen Elizabeth's letter breaking the news to Ahmad al-Mansur is dated 5 August[27]—the English merchants immediately set out to mount the victory celebrations in the Alfandica. They treated the European community of Marrakesh, about three hundred Christian merchants, to fireworks, public dances, and street banquets. The following day a cavalcade consisting of over forty English merchants and factors, among them presumably the factors of the Gores , and some Dutch and French residents, paraded through the various boroughs of the city. The vanguard of the procession, according to one source, flew a standard displaying the triumphant queen of England with the king of Spain lying prostrate at her feet, and according to another source, the riders carried effigies of the king of Spain and Pope Sixtus V which they set on fire.[28]

The cavalcade then entered the mellah and proceeded along the main road, the Derbe, as far as the residence of Matias Becudo, ambassador of Dom Antonio and claimant to the Portuguese throne who had taken refuge in England. There the spectacle came to an unexpected halt. It was attacked by Diego Marín, one of King Philip's representatives in Marrakesh. He was seconded by two comrades-in-arms whose identity was known to António de Saldanha.[29] One was Joao Gomes de Silva, a Portuguese gentleman, who was a captive of the Moroccan government charged to serve Diego Marín. The other assailant was Juan de Heredia, a native of Córdoba, who had been taken prisoner at The Battle of the Three Kings, had been ransomed, and had been staying on in the Spanish embassy. The three hotspurs, brandishing their swords, unsaddled three unarmed English merchants and slew them. According to another source, they put to death seven Englishmen and wounded many others, one of them being Arnold Tomson (it was probably Tomson who reported the lethal incident to George Wilkins, who is believed to have co-authored *Pericles*). [30] Diego Marín was imprisoned and not released until twenty years later, in 1608.

The dire spectacle of Christians killing each other under the very eyes of the Jews in the mellah of Marrakesh caught the Muslim ruler Ahmad al-Mansur completely unaware. He had masterminded the bringing together of Jewish and Christian merchants in the sugar business as peaceful partners and competitors. All the sugar mills in Morocco were the sharif's royal property, and he farmed out the so-called "ingenios" to the leading Jewish businessmen who in turn leased them to English merchants. These merchants were, in effect, the first English industrial producers of sugar cane, decades before their followers were operating sugar plantations and sugar refineries in the West Indies. They can also claim the privilege of having been the sugar purveyors of the royal household, the queen insisting on the consumption of Moroccan sugar. The development and success of the sugar industry depended as much on the interplay between the English merchants, the Christian and Jewish specialists in sugar processing, and the large salaried native labor force of Berbers and Arabs (up to two thousand workers for each farm and refinery), as it did between the lessees (the Jews) and the royal monopolists. Power relations, however, were unevenly distributed. [31]

The economic importance of the sugar industry as the major source of the sultans' wealth, along with gold, was brought home to the English consumers by one Robert C. [32] Yet despite their enormous revenues and the heavy taxes levied on their subjects, Ahmad al-Mansur and his two brothers before him kept increasing the terms of the sugar leases because they were lavishly spending money on building up the most advanced professional army among the Mediterranean countries. In 1578, its technology and combat experience proved superior to the European invasion army under the chivalrous but inexperienced Portuguese King Sebastian. [33] As a result of the sultans' steady increase of the sugar leases, the Jews suffered three bankruptcies, one in 1568, the next in 1583, and the worst in 1589. [34]

Isaac Cabeça's Insolvency

One of the Jewish sugar barons doing business with the English was Isaac Cabeça. Isaac and his brother Abraham Cabeça were members of a Sephardic family that had taken refuge in the Canary Islands and had found a permanent abode in Marrakesh before the 1530s. They enjoyed the generous protection of Muhammad ash-Shaykh, who advanced their public careers from accredited interpreters and translators to intelligencers, merchants, and bankers controlling the flourishing trade in ransoming captured Christians, mainly Portuguese and Spaniards. Abraham was even entrusted with political negotiations with the Portuguese government. Under the threat of persecution in Spain, the Cabeça family had been forced to convert, but under the liberal regime of Muhammad ash-Shaykh, Isaac and Abraham reverted to Judaism. Thus on his diplomatic mission to Mazagan, Abraham enjoyed the status of a Jewish representative of a Muslim country. In 1568, Isaac Cabeça, who had been a successful banker and businessman, went bankrupt. He was imprisoned by the new sultan Abdullah al-Ghalib for a debt of fifty thousand ounces of silver, that is 6,250 pounds, which the sultan claimed as the annual rent for three sugar farms.[35]

Isaac Cabeça's imprisonment, in 1568, was a matter of serious concern to a partnership of English Barbary merchants. Sir Willam Garrard, Edward Jackman, Francis Bowyer, Arthur Dawbeney, and the brothers Gerard and Thomas Gore had been selling English cloth to Isaac Cabeça, who owed them about one thousand pounds. His imprisonment, however, made it difficult for the English partnership to recover his debts, for the sultan Abdullah al-Ghalib forbade the sale of Cabeça's sugar production as long as the Jewish sugar magnate was in prison for failing to pay his debt of 6,250 pounds. The efforts made in Morocco by the factors of the partnership, by Edward Grey, John Richardson, Philip Westcott, and Henry Colthurst, to recover Cabeça's debts reveal a paradigm of labyrinthine interdependences, a tight system of interlocking sureties and personal bonds which beset the sugar trade in Morocco. The historic value of the existence of an elaborate transnational network of legal sureties lies in the fact that the various parties involved were Christians, Muslims, and a Jew. In view of these commercial, legal and cultural complexities binding partners of different nationalities and ethnicities it seems quite logical to argue that the bond story involving Isaac Cabeça, Abdullah al-Ghalib, and the partnership of English Barbary merchants affords a real-life parallel to the bond story of Shylock and Antonio in *The Merchant of Venice*.

The hearings concerning Isaac Cabeça's insolvency took place in the High Court of Admiralty, in London, in the absence of Cabeça and Abdullah al-Ghalib. The deponents heard and examined were some of the factors of the English partnership, and their depositions touched mainly upon the English response to Cabeça's insolvency. Thus it emerges from the testimony of John Whaley, the twenty-two year old apprentice to Philip Westcott, that in July 1568 the four English factors stationed in Morocco had come together to have talks with Isaac Cebeça "to this ende that yf he woulde promys vnto them to dischardge the old debt" of one thousand pounds and would "graunte vnto them . . . a bargaine of certen his ingenios of sugers" for the crop of 1569, "they woulde be earnest suters to the kinge for his libertie." Cabeça agreed to honor these terms and apparently bound himself to supply the English partnership with sugar to the value of sixteen thousand pounds in 1569.[36]

The next step undertaken by the English factors to recover the debt was to win over a high court official, "a certen More beinge cheffe aboute," Abdullah al-Ghalib. Thus they asked the Moor Tangarffe to intercede with the sultan "for the saide Jewes enlargement & deliveraunce." Tangarffe agreed provided Edward Grey and Philip Westcott "woulde first promys to become bounde to him for his indempnitie" and "to save him harmeles therein." Thereupon Tangarrfe "moved" the sultan and "obteyned of him the said Jewes releace and settinge at libertie" provided he "woulde be bounde" to Abdullah al-Ghalib "to pay him all suche debt as he asked of the sayde Jewes handes. . . . And so" Tangarffe "entred bande to" his sultan "in that behalf accordinglie." Finally the other factors, John Richardson and Henry Colthurst, were also "bounde over againe" to Grey and Westcott "for their dischardge." In consequence of these interlocking bonds, none of the factors, "whose masters be the saide Jewes creditors, . . . coulde be suffered" to leave Morocco. But it was agreed that only Grey and Westcott "shoulde be principallie bounde" to the sultan and remain behind as sureties in Morocco, whereas John Richardson, Sir William Garrad's factor, was allowed to "repaire home . . . for the better provision of wares necessarie for the complyenge of the said bargaine" with which to bail out Cabeça and restore his sufficiency. [37]

John Richardson, accordingly, went back to England to pursue the matter. In his hearing he testified that he had seen "the saide bandes writen . . . and concluded at Morocus, a Cittie in Barbary in Julye" 1568, in the presence of Grey, Westcott, Colthurst, and himself and of "moores sundrie."[38] The agreement moreover, ruled that Sir William Garrard was to pay one-fifth of the debt Isaac Cabeça owed the sultan, Edward Jackman and Francis Bowyer two-fifths, and Gerard and Thomas Gore the remaining two-fifths.[39]

It is noteworthy that the multiracial reality of the Christian/Jewish/Muslim bonding in 1568/69 did not give rise to outbursts of racial discrimination. Commercial interests and the lure of fat profit obviously prevailed over religious reservations. The English Barbary merchants and Isaac Cabeça helped one another in the face of a commercial and financial setback brought about by the sultan's increase of the sugar leases. The English merchants were clearly looking forward to resuming their sugar trade with Isaac Cabeça, the Jew, who in one of the hearings in the High Court of Admiralty was straightforwardly acknowledged as being "a famous and jolie merchant." This statement reads like a compliment paid in an English court to one of the most prominent Jews in the service of the Saadian sharifs. It sounds refreshingly honest and appears to be uncontaminated by the fear and cultural anxiety that Jews are said to have instilled in English society.[40]

Shakespeare and the Cabeça Incident

The capitalist world of elaborate credit relations and moneylending (usury) had been brought home to Shakespeare by his father John.[41] There are good reasons for believing that it was the experience of the Gores as Barbary merchants and their involvement in the bankruptcy of Isaac Cabeça that awakened Shakespeare's interest in how Christians and Jews came to be interlocked in business relations and moneylending, the Gores themselves or their cousins the Davenants serving as likely sources of information. The Gores were what Willan has termed the first Anglo-Moroccan family. The brothers Gerard (1516–1602) and Thomas Gore (1526–1597) invested heavily in the Moroccan trade. They owned a house in the Alfandica of Marrakesh, and Gerard, with his sons Richard and Gerard junior, another house in the Playe, that is, the Playa of Agadir.[42] Four of Gerard eight sons, Richard, Gerard junior, John, and Williams were trading with Morocco in the 1590s, Gerard and Williams as their father's factors assisted by John Swinnerton and John Tedcastle.[43] The Gores were highly cultivated members of the Merchant Taylors Company. In 1561, the brothers Gerard and Thomas, the two of them liberal advocates of learning, had supported the foundation of the Merchant Taylors School, one of London's elite academies, where Gerard's sons spent their formative years under the supervision of Richard Mulcaster, the famous headmaster known for his promotion of school theatricals. [44]

Gerard Gore was also instrumental in shaping the careers of James and John Davenant (c. 1540–1606). The two brothers were apprenticed to Gerard Gore, who was their brother-in-law by virtue of his marriage to Ellen Davenant. Gerard presented his two brothers-in-law for freedom of the Merchant Taylors Company, James in October 1559 and John in October 1562. The second generation of the Gores doing business with Morocco were first cousins of John Davenant (1565–1622). He, too, became free of the Merchant Taylor's Company on 22 June 1590 by virtue of the freedom enjoyed by his father John. It is very plausible that Shakespeare knew John Davenant, who was a theater enthusiast, before John moved to Oxford in 1601, where he fathered William Davenant, Shakespeare's godson, in 1606. One of John's cousins, whom Shakespeare is likely to have sought out, was Thomas, the son of Gerard and Ellen Davenant. He married the widowed mother of Nicholas Tooley in 1584 and died the following year. Tooley was to be apprenticed to Richard Burbage and became one of the principal actors and shareholders of the King's Company.[45]

The likelihood that Shakespeare was acquainted with the Gores undermines the current view that the first real-life aristocratic Moor whom Shakespeare had the opportunity to watch was the Moroccan ambassador Abd al-Ouahed ben Messouad, who, on 17 November 1600, attended the Accession Day Tilt. In point of fact, the first Moroccan ambassador ever to set foot in Elizabethan London was Marzuq Rais (Mushac Reyz). He made his entry "by torchlight," riding in the coach of Henry Roberts, on Sunday night, 12 January 1589, and escorted by "the chiefest marchants of the Barbary Company well mounted all on horsebacke, to the number of 40 or 50 horse."[46] We can take it for granted that among the forty or fifty charter members of the Barbary Company on horseback there were the sons of Gerard Gore; Gerard himself, then seventy-three years old, and his brother Thomas, sixty-three, were hardly on horseback, but were among those responsible for footing the bill for the torchlight cavalcade. The Muslim ambassador stayed on until mid-summer 1589, attending the Portugal expedition in Dom Antonio's flagship disguised as a Christian nobleman from Portugal.[47]

The nocturnal influx of Moorish diplomats crossing London Bridge by torchlight must have given Londoners the feeling of being witnesses to history. It set the stage for the spectacular arrival of the North African ambassador and his retinue, who were empowered by Ahmad al-Mansur to negotiate an alliance of amity. The Admiral's Company of players immediately responded to the latest political situation by performing George Peele's *The Battle of Alcazar*, a historical play featuring Ahmad al-Mansur (Muly Mahamet Seth) as one of its three protagonists.[48]

The Prince of Morocco's Pilgrimage to Portia's Shrine

The Dramatization of Cultural Exchange: Mercantile Miscegenation

One of the aims of the present overview of the political, commercial, and cultural encounters between England and Morocco has been to discredit the commonly held opinion that in Shakespeare's day the attitude to the Moor and the Jew can hardly have been based on direct intercourse with these people. On the contrary, direct intercourse with the unmythologized Jew and Muslim in Morocco, as has been demonstrated, was a historical reality. Taking this fact into account, it is, I think, legitimate to suggest that the Gores' response to the mercantile and cross-cultural experience they had made in trading with Morocco was known to Shakespeare when he was creating the characters of Shylock and the Prince of Morocco. Moreover, Shakespeare may have recognized an opportunity to attract and regale Londoners with the Prince of Morocco's pilgrimage to Belmont (a displacement of an English country seat and estate) as an allegory of the political and cultural rapprochement between Saadian Morocco and Elizabethan England. The Londoners had witnessed the presence of the Moroccan embassy welcomed by the Barbary Company and had flocked to the theater to see Peele's Moroccan play in 1589. Shakespeare's "Venetian" play was staged at the very moment the embassy of Ahmad ben Adel was rumored to be on its way to England to sign a league of amity between the two countries.[49]

Shakespeare did not choose to stage the conclusion of a political bond of amity; instead, he dramatized the preliminary ceremonies of a potential match between a Muslim prince and a Christian gentlewoman, which is doomed to failure because of cultural and sexual incompatibility. The Prince's prominence is foregrounded by the fact that none of Portia's other international suitors, all of them

Christians, is given an opportunity for self-representation except for the Prince of Arragon. Arragon, however, is accorded just one reception, whereas Morocco is given the privilege of two: one in which to articulate his otherness, fashion his self-image, define his identity, and make a bid for racial equality in proposing a blood test among Portia's suitors; and a second in which to undergo the casket trial. Morocco's foregrounding, as compared to the demotion of the other foreign suitors to backstage figures bereft of a chance to defend themselves against the barbs of Portia's mocking criticism and sexual innuendoes, serves to confront the Elizabethan theatergoers with the issue of cultural difference.

The Prince of Morocco, a Moor clad in the white regalia of the ceremonious fashion of the royal court of Morocco, does not conform to the Elizabethan stage stereotype of the villainous black Moor.[50] Though of noble origin, he has no chance of concluding a cross-cultural alliance with a Christian lady, just as the real-life Moroccan ambassadors, in the end, stood no chance of persuading Queen Elizabeth to sign a League of Amity with Ahmad al-Mansur. At the last moment the queen shrank from signing a treaty that would have obliged her to provide the logistics, the manpower, and the material to modernize the Moroccan navy. The strategic targets of al-Mansur were an invasion of the Spanish mainland, in emulation of the English sack of Cádiz of 1596, as well as the conquest of the West Indies in a joint English/Moroccan enterprise against Philip II. But there was, understandably, no reason to trust a Muslim ally who, in 1589, had left Elizabeth in the lurch when she launched the disastrous Portugal expedition to reinstate Dom Antonio, the prior of Crato, as king of Portugal. The Moroccan ambassador Marzuq Rais had, as we have seen, boarded the English flagship, dressed up as a Portuguese observer; but al-Mansur had not honored his word to provide financial support to Elizabeth for compelling reasons of his own. At the time, he feared that Philip II would openly support the claims to the Moroccan throne of a Saadian prince who had taken refuge in Spain.[51]

Various levels of ironies permeate the Prince of Morocco's quest for Portia's portrait, which he is sure he will find represented in the figure of "an angel in a golden bed" (2.7.58), lying enshrined in the golden casket.[52] For the Prince, the "golden bed" as a symbol of procreation is heavily invested with political expectations; for Portia, it is an "unproper" bed fraught with cultural, sexual, and gender anxieties. As a rule, the Muslim elite were much more open to transcultural interrelations than the Christian upper classes. Thus, Ahmad al-Mansur and his brother Abd al-Malik had adopted some western habits. They did not sleep on mattresses spread on the floor but in beds which they imported from western countries. Cervantes, who had been incarcerated in the prisons of Algiers, the notorious "baños de Argel," from 1575 to 1580, knew that "Muley Maluco," as he called Abd al-Malik, "duerme en alto, come en mesa/sentado a la cristianesca."[53] One of Ahmad al-Mansur's royal beds and coaches happened to be made in London.[54] The ordering, making, licensing for export, shipping, transporting, and delivering of the royal goods involved a sequence of negotiations which has been called "mercantile miscegenation." In a perceptive essay, Daryl W. Palmer uses the concept to refer "to all the ways that people and things 'pass into traffique', mingle and form attachments."[55] Acquiring things English from beds to cannons and musical instruments had become a cross-cultural norm for the Saadian royals, as had enticing qualified craftsmen from their jobs in England.[56] These skilled workers were granted the status of privileged foreign residents with a work permit and do not seem to have apostasized. Other Englishmen, however, did cross the religious divide. For example, the commander of the garrison of Safi and a cryptographer employed by the Saadian intelligence service seem to have been renegades.[57]

The irony inscribed in the play's text is aimed at conveying to the original audience that, while several prominent London craftsmen, woodcarvers, joiners, cabinet-makers, gold foilers, and embroiderers of valances met with the approval of the Elizabethan authorities for making a miscegenetic artefact destined, as it were, to secure the survival of the Saadian dynasty, the "golden bed" which the Prince of Morocco yearns for lies beyond his powers of procreation. What for him is a symbol of miscegenetic generation is for Portia a symbol of pollution; what for him is the only possible choice in the context of his cultural background and his country, which venerated Ahmad al-Mansur as the Golden Ruler, the "adh-Dhahabi," turns out to be the wrong choice in a prenuptial test devised by Portia's Christian father.

Numismatic Miscegenation

There is unanimous agreement that one of the major themes pervading the play is the equating of sexual with monetary generation.

An ironical variation of this theme occurs in the story of the golden casket. The Prince of Morocco has found out that "They have in England / A coin that bears the figure of an angel / Stamped in gold" (2.7.55–57). Understandably, he sees in it a good omen favoring his interracial union with Portia. The irony inherent in Morocco's invocation to the English angel can be grasped only if one bears in mind that the Saadian kings were among England's main purveyors of gold. Jewish middlemen supplied the Barbary gold either in the form of sand, as mined in the African kingdom of Songhay, or in the form of sequins, as coined in the royal mint in Marrakesh, with Christian renegades supervising the minting process of 1400 hammers pressing the coins. Richard Gore, one of the sons of Gerard Gore, was selling Barbary gold as late as 1601,[58] and the eminent mathematician Edward Wright was advised, in 1600, to design "some instruments in brasse or silver" and sell his "magnetical instrument of declination" to the Moroccan ambassador in London, for it "would be commodious" for navigating the annual "voyage . . . over a sandy sea" across the Sahara to Gago to fetch gold and salt.[59] As the Moroccan sequins were of superior quality, the royal mint in the Tower of London seized the opportunity to remelt them, debasing them with an English copper alloy. The official debasement of the coinage, begun in the 1540s, was called in numismatic parlance "la mutacion du poids" and "la mutacion de la matière." In consequence of this mutation, the English angel, which, as the Prince says, bears (on the obverse) the impress of the archangel St. Michael, an emblem of Christian faith and English ethnocentrism, was, numismatically, a coin of bastard quality, a cross-breed "à titre inférieur," of less value than the Moroccan sequin. For the Christian government in England the inflationary process of multiplying the angels was, to borrow a term from Shylock, a way to thrive. The mutation effectively bred more angels, and thereby the English government shrewdly contrived to bring its own quest for the golden fleece to a seemingly happy end. Considering the play's strategy to reconcile love with money, the Prince's unexpected reference to the English angel can be read as his personal attempt to intimate that the interracial marriage between a Christian lady and a Muslim prince was bound to work and thrive as did the crossing of English with Moroccan gold.

Portia's Anxieties about Rape and Miscegenation

Resistance to miscegenation, as Nabil Matar has demonstrated, was strongest in the English upper classes and weakest in the lower ones. When King James acceded to the English throne, miscegenation, however, was no longer a cultural aporia for the upper classes; and among the merchant class, the religious and cultural divide between Christians and Muslims was disintegrating. Thus in 1614, the East India Company entered into negotiations for the marriage of the daughter of a "gentleman of honorable parentage" with the sultan of Aceh, the city-state in Sumatra. The merchants were of the opinion that the cross-cultural union would no doubt be "beneficial to the Company." Accordingly, they marshalled some Anglican theologians to prove "the lawfulness of the enterprise . . . by scripture." The marriage never took place, but what is culturally of crucial importance is the readiness of the Company's directors to encourage the union between a Christian woman and a Muslim ruler, known for his harem exotics, with a view to legitimating the marriage.[60]

Spanish, Portuguese, and even English chronicles bear witness to the fact that the imagination of western Europeans had been captured by their idea of the sexuality of the Saadian sharifs. Thus both Ro(bert) C., a competent insider, and George Wilkins, a hack when it came to writing a chronicle on Morocco, made significant contributions to the incipient cultural debate on polygamy. Ro. C. offered his readers factual and sensible information on how polygamy actually worked, observing that "Though the liberty of poligamie be granted, yet not one amongst a hundred hath foure" wives, the reason being that "the wives friends will never suffer any to marry their kinswoman without first they have a bill of dowry sufficient for the maintenance of her. Therefore the great and rich men have three and foure wives, but the poore most but one, few two." Unlike his contemporary, George Wilkins fed his readers inaccurate episodic information on Ahmad al-Mansur's polygamy, which he fashioned as an induction to the calamities and what he chose to call the *Three Miseries of Barbary:* the plague, famine, and civil war that befell Morocco at the turn of the century.[61]

Thus, instead of explaining to his readers the fateful law of succession, which led to the downfall of the Saadian dynasty and to the civil wars between Ahmad al-Mansur's sons, Wilkins dished up the platitude that Ahmad al-Mansur had "more Wiues then any of his fore-fathers: his Concubins were fairer and more in number."[62] He then launched into a seemingly intimate account of the female members of the royal family, unfolding the hot news that "Of all the Wiues and Concubins that this Emperor had, three onely,

108 GUSTAV UNGERER

(aboue the rest) had a soueraignty ouer his amorous affections."
The favorite wife was Lalla Aisha, "Lilia Isa," as Wilkins calls her,
the mother of the first-born son Mulay Zaydan. She "was the fairest" of the three, obviously a fair-skinned Mooress, and "empresse
ouer the rest," having "the supreame commaund of the kinges
house," the magnificent and sumptuous Badi (the Marvel), which
Ahmad al-Mansur had built in emulation of the Alhambra. The
wife who had "a second place in his heart" was Lalla Al-Djauher
(the Pearl), also called Al-Kheizuran (the Liana) and by Wilkinson
"Lilia Ageda." She was a cultivated mulatta, the mother of the
princes Ash-Shaykh al-Mamum ("Muly-Sheck") and Abd Allah
Abu Faris ("Muly-Beferris"), and, on António de Saldanha's authority, a patroness of the Christian captives working in the Badi.
The third wife mentioned by Wilkins was Lalla Meriem ("Lilia My-
riem"), "a black woman," who gave birth to Abu al-Hassan.[63] Wilkins does not mention that among the many concubines in the
seraglio of the Badi there were fifteen virgins, the daughters of the
king of Gago, whom Ahmad al-Mansur had exacted as part of his
booty of the Sudan expedition.[64]

To reassure English readers, Ro. C. provided a corrective to Wilkins's inaccuracies. He told his contemporaries that Ahmad al-
Mansur's overblown seraglio was much more a showplace of his
wealth and greatness, a self-representation of his royal power than
a beacon of his unbridled sexuality or eastern voluptuousness.[65] It
was precisely the sexual problem raised by legal concubinage that
appealed to Wilkins's sense of chronicling history in episodic form.
It induced him to spice up his rudimentary historical narrative
with a boudoir anecdote about the rivalry between Lalla Al-Djauher
and Lalla Aisha. Wishing to "draw this Barbary-picture, with as
much life and delightfull colours as" he "could," Wilkins found it
not "amisse . . . to set downe a pretty combat betweene" the two
wives, "playd before the Emperour himselfe" (sigs. B3v–B4r).

The common knowledge that the Saadian princes were seasoned
polygamists was certainly less alarming to the Elizabethans than
the reports that they were also rapists of a kind, at least from a western European perspective, endowed with the impressive gift of celebrating their conquests in lyrical encomia of female beauty.
Ahmad al-Mansur was a man of learning and taste with interests
ranging from grammar, poetry, theology, and jurisprudence to ar-
chitecture, astronomy, astrology, military science, and mathematics. He was said to have studied Euclid's *Elements* on his own; for

he was a man whom God, as the Moroccan historian Abdallah
Eloufrani notes, "had bestowed with a nonpareil piercing intelligence."[66] An enlightened despot, he wielded uncontested power in
his kingdom and in his seraglio. Men and women who put up resistance were eliminated. Thus António de Saldanha relates the tragic
case of the Andalusian convert Ahmad Monfadal and his daughter
which he qualifies as unique in the memory of mankind.[67] The trib-
ulation the young Christian woman must have undergone in the
Badi as a forced concubine can be guessed from the example set by
Ahmad al-Mansur's father in breaking down the resistance of the
Portuguese governor's daughter of Agadir in the early 1540s.

The celebrated story of Muhammad ash-Shaykh al-Mahdi and
Dona Mencía (also Mecía) de Monroy caused quite a stir in western
Europe. A Christian, on reading or hearing it, was bound to be
struck by the basic ingredients of a tale of horror charged with the
emotional issues raised by racial difference: attempted rape, enforced conversion, psychological terror, submission, miscegenation, and death. No wonder that the disconcerting news of a noble
Moor marrrying an upper-class white gentlewoman alarmed the
Portuguese queen Catherine of Austria and dominated the head-
lines of the contemporary Iberian commentators. But what today
strikes us about this union of a Muslim potentate and a Christian
lady is not only the alleged brutality initially unleashed by the
cross-cultural encounter, but also the nascent understanding of the
male partner for the need to transcend his racialized notions of the
female other and recognize his wife and father-in-law as individuals irrespective of creed, race, blood or color.[68]

Shakespeare scholars might be prompted to see in their story a
mirror inversion of the Othello/Desdemona relationship: Muhammad ash-Shaykh, a North African sultan in his fifties, triumphs
over his alleged initial cruelty, transforming into ardent affection
his consuming desire for the body of a Christian gentlewoman in
her early twenties. He grounds the social bond of his marriage on
passionate love and espouses a humanist philosophy of life, propa-
gating tolerance as a guiding principle beyond the reach of dogma.
In some lines he composed, Muhammad ash-Shaykh did voice his
belief that all human beings share common attributes, the differences that exist between them being brought about not by ideological views but by the different degrees in which each individual
strives to improve his/her inner self. The sultan's sense of human-

ity, honor and nobility, as the anonymous chronicler avows, was respected by his Portuguese adversaries.[69]

Muhammad ash-Shaykh is remembered as the Saadian sharif who lay the foundations for the centralization of political authority and successfully initiated the jihad, the reconquest of occupied Moroccan territory. As sharif reigning over a united kingdom (1544–57), he generated a technological innovation and social change which, as Vincent J. Cornell has observed, was unparalleled elsewhere at that time in the Arab countries bordering on the Mediterranean.[70] He was a despotic ruler imposing heavy taxes on his subjects, but he was also a man of letters who passed on his exceptional literary endowments to his sons Abd al-Malik and Ahmad al-Mansur. Posing as a redoubtable warrior, he prided himself on his superior knowledge of warcraft. In 1541, his capture of Agadir broke the backbone of the Portuguese colonial establishment set up in Morocco since 1415. His subsequent victories against internal rivals earned him recognition as a potential contestant in the political power game played between the Spanish and Ottoman empires in the Mediterranean. Diego de Torres has brought to life his impressive appearance in a close-up portrait; it shows the stocky figure of a middle-sized man, strong-limbed, round-faced, fair-skinned, the eyes great and lively, two upper incisors (or canines) oversized, a full gray beard cut round, reddish hair dyed with henna, a nobleman on horseback.[71]

The course of Dona Mencía's ordeal can be reconstructed as follows. From March 1541 (the fall of Agadir) until June 1544 (the deposition of Ahmad al-Araj as ruler of the kingdom of Morocco) the indomitable Dona Mencía was detained as a Christian captive in Muhammad ash-Shaykh's royal residence in Tarudant, where she was, no doubt, sexually subjugated. She converted to Islam on Muhammad ash-Shaykh's assumption of power as sultan of Morocco. At this time,the sultan acknowledged her publicly as his third wife and, to believe Diego de Torres, he fell madly in love with her, neglecting his other wives.[72] In 1545, Dona Mencía gave birth to a daughter, who died within eight days; eight days after the death of her infant, she, too, was dead.[73] The theory of a palace intrigue against her remains unproven. There were rumors that she had been poisoned or had fallen victim to the witchcraft of the other wives, but Torres is of the opinion that she died of a miscarriage.[74]

Despite her cultural and spiritual adjustment at the Saadian court, Dona Mencía's presence established an alien flavor. At the request of the enamored sultan, she maintained the garb of a Spanish or Portuguese gentlewoman, took her meals in Christian manner, sitting at a table (not on a cushion) with sword and dagger as Christian insignia of royalty by her side and displaying her handkerchief in her girdle.[75] Her cultural otherness seemed to intrigue the tolerant sultan and his sons Abd al-Malik and Ahmad al-Mansur, who both adopted, as we have seen, some of her western idiosyncracies, which were resented by the Muslim traditionalists.

Notwithstanding his initial disregard for Dona Mencía's desperate plight, Muhammad ash-Shaykh seemed determined to set an example of moral strength in overriding the entrenched categories of cultural and ethnic difference. Thus he claimed consanguinity with both Dona Mencía and her father Gutierre de Monroy. His claim of consanguinity with his wife derived from the belief that sexual activity engendered an exchange of blood, that with his father-in-law was the personal expression of his understanding that all human beings share common qualities. His statement that there was no such thing as Muslim or Christian blood, that there was only human blood, would seem to transcend racial barriers.[76] In the presence of many caids, Muhammad ash-Shaykh invited his Christian father-in-law to stay on in Marrakesh as a brother and counsellor advising him on how to rule his kingdoms and seigniories. If Gutierre de Monroy accepted the offer, his son-in-law was ready to give him *plein pouvoir*, half of his revenues, and the licence to build a Christian church in Marrakesh. These were no courtly compliments but serious propositions. However, Dom Gutierre de Monroy, who was in his mid-sixties, declined the invitation on the grounds that he was old and preferred instead to return to Portugal and proclaim in Christendom the greatness of Muhammad ash-Shaykh's power and the noble-mindedness of his way of thinking.[77]

Gutierre de Monroy's intention to propagate the example of toleration set by Muhammad ash-Shaykh was doomed to failure. Cultural assumptions about polygamy as sanctioned by Islam and as practiced by the Saadian rulers, and about the violent nature of their sexuality prevailed over the rare accounts of their cultural achievements and exercise of tolerance. Thus George Wilkins, as mentioned, peddled sensational anecdotes about the sexuality of Ahmad al-Mansur. Those Englishmen who turned to Diego de Torres's *Relacion* for information, such as Sir Walter Ralegh, would have also known of Muhammad ash-Shaykh's passion for Dona Mencía de Monroy.[78] But for others, in addition to the alarming examples of cross-cultural marriages of real-life figures in Muslim countries, there were fearsome fictional instances of interracial marriages between a Muslim ruler and a Christian wife, such as the novella (the forty-first) in William Painter's *Palace of Pleasure* (1567) about the love of Muhammad II, the Ottoman conqueror of Constantinople (1453), for Hyerenee (Irene), a sixteen-year-old Greek beauty.[79]

The body of comment by Christian authors on the aggressive sexuality and cruelty of Muslim rulers left its imprint on the stage portrait of the Prince of Morocco. The Prince conforms, in the first instance, to the paradigm of the transgressive Moor who strives for a miscegenational union which is doomed to pollute his European partner. He has come from Morocco, a liminal country situated on the edge of the western world, on one of "the four corners of the earth" (2.7.39), in order to kiss the "shrine" of his "mortal breathing saint" in Belmont (2.7.40).[80] On his voyage he has braved the "watery kingdom" of the Atlantic Ocean and Mediterranean Sea, negotiating the storms and dangers as if crossing "o'er a brook to see fair Portia" (2.7.44–47). However, his greatest flaw as a suitor, as I see it, is neither his bravado as a warrior under the Ottoman Sultan Suleyman the Magnificent, nor his tawny complexion, nor his cultural otherness; it is the self-indicting pose he assumes as the imperial rapist. Thus he boastfully addresses Portia (2.1.8–11):

> I tell thee, lady, this aspect of mine
> Hath feared the valiant; by my love I swear
> The best-regarded virgins of our clime
> Have loved it too.
>
> (2.1.8–11)

The "renowned prince" (2.1.20) has no second thoughts about advertising to his bride-to-be the sexual reputation he enjoys in Morocco, suggesting to her that he is a past master at the art of deflowering the virgins of the Moroccan nobility and thereby intimating that the Moroccan virgins of the ruling class take pride in dwelling in his sumptuous seraglio, where they contribute to his status as a Muslim potentate. In Elizabethan eyes, this violent sexuality doubtlessly appeared quite in tune with the rapes reportedly perpetrated by the Moroccan sultans Ahmad al-Mansur and Muhammad ash-Shaykh.[81] It therefore does not come as a surprise that the Prince of Morocco finds himself to be among the "losers"

(2.7.77). His unwitting self-description as a violator of women is tantamount to the admission that he aspires to the lordship of Belmont for reasons of self-aggrandizement. He desires to "gain what many men desire" (2.7.37) not out of love but primarily out of self-love.[82]

The Prince's mischoice relieves Portia from what she sees as the unpleasant, if not repellent, prospect of maintaining the bloodline of a Moroccan prince. Her seemingly insensitive comment "Let all of his complexion choose me so" (2.7.79) savors of racial discrimination, casting a slur on all Africans. Portia's education as a Christian gentlewoman would have left her unprepared for an unexpected cross-cultural transfer of her person, body, and the property of Belmont to a Muslim husband. However, she has no objections to Lorenzo's cross-cultural bond with Jessica, the convert, and she and Bassanio will have to put up with Launcelot's impregnation of a Mooress and the black offsping of their miscegenetic union in Belmont. Launcelot's pairing up with a Mooress reads like a subcultural ploy to offset Portia's denigration of the Prince of Morocco and opens up an alternative perspective on cross-cultural encounters.

As a loser the Prince faces the penalty that Portia has taken the trouble to explain explicitly only to him: "Never to speak to lady afterward / In way of marriage" (2.1.40–42). The forfeiture of lawful propagation helps obviate the cultural anxieties engendered by the Prince's sexuality, but the possibility of unlawful propagation through rape and enforced marriage nonetheless remains an alternative to the Prince, particularly in a Muslim country.[83]

In addition to the negative undertones of miscegenation, however, Morocco's courtship of Portia evokes the ennobling dimensions of Muhammad ash-Shaykh's love of Dona Mencía. Morocco's attempt to take the rules of the casket test into his own hands and to propose a blood test among Portia's international suitors has, to my mind, less to do with a Moorish nobleman vying for martial valor with his Christian competitors than with the struggle for recognition of his human identity and his claim to racial equality. His bold request,

> Bring me the fairest creature northward born,
> Where Phoebus' fire scarce thaws the icicles,
> And let us make incision for your love
> To prove whose blood is reddest, his or mine.
>
> (2.1.4–7)

is orchestrated to shift Portia's attention away from his tawny complexion to blood, that is, from outer surface to inner substance.[84] The clever move functions as a thematic parallel to Shylock pleading for his humanity as a Jew (3.1.46 ff.), its ideological message being that all human blood is red, be it a Jew's, a Christian's, or a Muslim's. This view of human consanguinity had been publicly voiced by the sultan Muhammad ash-Shaykh, the son-in-law of the Portuguese nobleman Dom Gutierre de Monroy, when he made the memorable attempt to transcend the racial barriers on the occasion of his marriage to Dona Mencía de Monroy.

I have argued that the Prince of Morocco's ethnically oriented casket trial situates itself within the political, cultural, and racial discourse of the age, and that his mischoice and subsequent elimination expose England's cultural and racial incompatibility with Morocco. The rapprochement that had been achieved between the two countries was not strong enough to warrant a political alliance. Rather than reinforcing a mutuality of interests, their encounters foundered on the duplicity of western merchant capitalists, who conducted business with the Moroccans while at the same time disdaining their Muslim partners as inferior beings.

Concerned mainly with exploitable resources, the Elizabethans developed an unbalanced perspective on Saadian Morocco. Both the merchant class and the political establishment continued to harbor contradictory views about Moroccans despite the continuous interrelations over half a century. While men like Roger Bodenham and Edmund Hogan came to look upon Morocco as a neighboring country, lying "as neer as Spayne," the majority of the Elizabethans were still patronizing it as a liminal place situated on the edge of the world. John Chamberlain, the unparalleled letter writer, epitomizes the profound ambivalence of the Elizabethan elite's response to Morocco. Surprisingly, he was brought up in the house of Thomas Gore, the prominent member of the Barbary Company, who owned property in Morocco. Nonetheless, Chamberlain dismissed the members of the Moroccan embassy, who in 1600/ 1601 came to London to resume negotiations for a political alliance, as "Barbarians" representing a cultural wasteland. His comment that "yt is no small honor to us that nations so far remote, and every way different, shold meet here to admire the glory and magnificence of our Quene of Saba" reveals the myopic outlook of this geography of difference.[85]

Notes

1. See Eldred Jones, *Othello's Countrymen: The African in English Renaissance Drama* (London: Oxford University Press, 1965), 68–71; Nicholas Brooke, "Marlowe as Provocative Agent in Shakespeare's Early Plays," *Shakespeare Survey* 14 (1961), 34–44.

2. A study of the Anglo-Moroccan political interactions of the sixteenth century remains a desideratum. The best historical survey available in English is Dahiru Yahya's *Morocco in the 16th Century: Problems and Patterns in African Foreign Policy,* Ibadan History Series (Harlow: Longman, 1981). Jack D'Amico provides a useful introduction to the historical setting in *The Moor in English Renaissance Drama* (Tampa: South Florida University Press, 1991). I have not been able to consult T. H. Weir, *The Shaykhs of Morocco in the 16th Century* (Edinburgh, 1904). Carmen Martín de la Escalera's "Marruecos en la política peninsular de Inglaterra," *Cuadernos de Estudios Africanos* 2 (1946), 147–53, focuses on the events of 1588. Manuel Fernández Alvarez, *Felipe II, Isabel de Inglaterra y Marruecos* (Madrid: Instituto de Estudios Africanos, 1951) covers the ground in a nutshell. For a solid handbook on Morocco containing a comprehensive bibliography, see Thomas K. Park, *Historical Dictionary of Morocco,* new edition (Lanham and London: The Scarecrow Press, 1996).

3. On the rumors of the embassy, see Henry de Castries, *Les sources inédites de l'histoire du Maroc. Série 1: Dynastie Saadienne, III, Archives et bibliothèques d'Angleterre,* 3 vols. (Paris, 1918–35), vol. 2 (1925), 89–90; henceforward quoted as *SIHM.* This is the most exhaustive collection of original records on Morocco kept in European archives and libraries. The only important class of material missed out by Henry de Castries are the records of the High Court of Admiralty in the Public Record Office, Kew. The 1595 embassy did not materialize, but the 1600 embassy did. It was headed by Abd al-Ouahed ben Messouad ben Muhammad Anun. See Bernard Harris, "A Portrait of a Moor," *Shakespeare Survey* 11 (1958), 89–97; reprinted in *Shakespeare and Race,* ed. Catherine M. S. Alexander and Stanley Wells (Cambridge: Cambridge University Press, 2000), chap. 2. The portrait hangs in The Shakespeare Institute, Stratford.

4. Queen Elizabeth praised "the good amity and confederation existing between our crowns" in her letter dated 10 April 1600. See Castries, *SIHM, Angleterre,* 2:154. Both sovereigns had a sound command of Spanish and had arranged for their originals in English and Arabic respectively to be rendered into Spanish by one of their secretaries.

5. The letter, dated 3 April 1603, is signed "Your sister and kin according to the law of the crown and sceptre." See Castries, *SIHM, Angleterre,* 2:220–21. The originals of the royal correspondence are preserved in the Public Record Office, State Papers Foreign, Barbary.

6. Nabil Matar, *Turks, Moors, and Englishmen in the Age of Discovery* (New York: Columbia University Press, 1999), 7–8.

7. This view has been advocated by Winthrop D. Jordan, *White Over Black: American Attitudes Towards the Negro, 1550–1812* (Chapel Hill: University of North Carolina Press, 1968; rpt., New York, 1977), 6; James Walvin, *Black and White: The Negro and English Society, 1555–1945* (London: Allen Lane, 1973),

chap. 1; Peter Fryer, *Staying Power: The History of Black People in England* (London: Pluto Press 1984; rpt., 1992), chaps. 1 and 7.

8. Moors and Mooresses were the main commodities of the trade between Andalusia and the Portuguese strongholds in Morocco. It reached a dismal peak in 1521/22 with the famine that ravaged both Morocco and Spain. See Robert Ricard, "Les places portugaises et le commerce d'Andalousie," *Annales de l'Institut d'Etudes Orientales* 4 (1938), 128–53. For the consequences of the military and slaving raids, the so-called "cavalcadas," undertaken by the Portuguese nobles in Morocco in order to improve their financial situation and maintain their military prowess at home and abroad as valiant Christian champions, see Malyn Newitt, "Prince Henry and the Origins of European Expansion," in *Historiography of Europeans in Africa and Asia, 1450–1800*, ed. Anthony Disney (Brookfield: Variorum, 1995), 85–111; Andrzej Dziubinski, "L'armée et la flotte de guerre marocaines à l'époque des sultans de la dynastie saadienne," *Hespéris Tamuda* 13 (1972), 61–94. For the Spanish slave raids on the Maghreb and Morocco, mounted as commercial enterprises, see Aurelia Martín Casares's pioneering work on slavery, *La esclavitud en la Granada del siglo XVI. Género, raza y religión* (Granada: Universidad de Granada, 2000), 162–64, 326.

9. Gordon Connell-Smith, *Forerunners of Drake: A Study of English Trade With Spain in the Early Tudor Period* (London: Longmans, Green & Co., 1954). His study despite its total disregard for slaveholding still commands admiration.

10. Alfonso Franco Silva's latest study, *La esclavitud en Andalucía, 1450–1550* (Universidad de Granada, 1992), is the result of a lifelong commitment to research in Andalusian archives, the Archivo General de Indias, the Archivo de Protocolos de Sevilla, notarial records, and parish registers. In our private correspondence, he has confirmed my query about the involvement of English merchants in the slave trade: "se dedicaban también al mercado de esclavos" [they dedicated themselves to trading in slaves]. The researches of Consuelo Varela also leave no doubt that the English merchants were slavers. Thus William Holburn (Guillermo Lebrón), who settled in Huelva about 1486, kept eight "esclavos y esclavas" in his house and transported slaves on his vessels which were plying to Lisbon. See Consuelo Varela, *Ingleses en España y Portugal, 1480–1515, Aristócratas, Mercaderes e Impostores* (Lisbon: Ediciones Colibri, 1998), 71, 73, 166. Whether Holburn's vessels bound for Bristol contained human cargoes remains, I think, an open question.

11. Archivo General de Simancas, Consejo Real, 12/6/32v. The will and inventory cover folios 22–43. In his will, dated from Seville on Saturday, 23 August 1522, Malliard left his wife Beatriz Fernández three female slaves and one male slave (fol. 27). For more information on Malliard's properties in Andalucía, see Blanca Krauel, "Events Surrounding Thomas Malliard's Will," *Proceedings of the II Conference of the Spanish Society for English Renaissance Studies*, ed. S. G. Fernández-Corugedo (Oviedo: Universidad de Oviedo, 1992), 157–65.

12. The total number of slaves owned by the Malliards was much higher. Thus I owe to Alfonso Franco Silva's generous disposition the information that Malliard in 1520 had the slave Catalina baptized in the church of Santa Ana de Triana in Seville (Libro de Bautismos, fol. 96) and the slaves Guillermo, Beatriz, and Catalina in the church of Sagrario. For the social prestige of holding slaves measured in numbers see A. C. de C. M. Saunders, *A Social History of Black Slaves and*

Freedmen in Portugal, 1441–1555 (Cambridge: Cambridge University Press, 1982), 66, 101.

13. The uncontested authority on the commercial relations between England and Morocco is T. S. Willan, *Studies in Elizabethan Foreign Trade* (Manchester: Manchester University Press, 1959; rpt., 1968), chap. 4, 92–312. A reliable overview is given by Jacques Caillé in "Le commerce anglais avec le Maroc pendant la seconde moitié du XVIe siècle," *Revue Africaine* 84 (1940), 186–219.

14. C. Funk-Brentano, in his entry on Ahmad al-Mansur, notes that the Christians who had settled in Morocco were "Quasi-prisoners of the Sharif and his people" and "always liable to extortion." See vol. 5 of *E. J. Brill's First Encyclopaedia of Islam*, ed. M. Th. Houtsma et al. (Leiden: Brille, 1927; rpt., 1987), 250–54. The British subjects captured by the Maghreb states in the sixteenth and seventeenth centuries experienced a painful reversal of Western superiority. See Linda Colley, "Britain and Islam, 1600–1800: Different Perspectives on Difference," *The Yale Review* 88 (2000), 1–20.

15. Charles Edelman, "Which is the Jew that Shakespeare Knew? Shylock on the Elizabethan Stage," *Shakespeare Survey* 52 (1999), 99–106.

16. In the introduction to *A dolorous discourse of a most terrible and bloudy battel fought in Barbarie* (London, 1578), the anonymous chronicler informs his readers that "In this countrye are manie Jewes enhabiting, in whose handes consisteth the most parte of the trafique of the country, being the onely marchantes of sugers, mallasses, and other ritche marchandize which the same yeldeth: for the which they paye great sums of money to the King." Quoted from H. de Castries, *SIHM*, Angleterre, 1:331. The Moroccan setting disproves Appiah's view that Elizabethan attitudes to the Moor and the Jew "do not seem to have been based on experience of these people." See Kwame Anthony Appiah, "Race," in *Critical Terms for Literary Study*, ed. Frank Lentricchia and Thomas McLaughlin (Chicago: University of Chicago Press, 1990), chap. 20, p. 277.

17. For the Bassanos and Lupos, see Eleanor Selfridge-Field, "Venetian Instrumentalists in England: A Bassano Chronicle (1538–1660)," *Studi Musicali* 8 (1979), 173–221; Roger Prior, "Jewish Musicians at the Tudor Court," *The Musical Quarterly* 69 (1983), 253–65; David Lasocki, "The Anglo-Venetian Bassano Family as Instrument Makers and Repairers," *Galpin Society Journal* 38 (1985), 112–32. As Jewish studies are steadily increasing, I restrict myself to listing those I have found most helpful: Lucien Wolf, "Jews in Elizabethan England," *Transcations of the Jewish Historical Society of England* 11 (1926), 1–91; Cecil Roth, *A History of the Jews in England*, 3d ed. (Oxford: Clarendon Press, 1964); C. S. Sisson, "A Colony of Jews in Shakespeare's London," *Essays and Studies* 23 (1938), 38–51; Roger Prior, "A Second Jewish Community in Tudor London," *Transactions of the Jewish Historical Society of England* 31 (1988/89), 137–52; James Shapiro, *Shakespeare and the Jews* (New York: Columbia University Press, 1996).

18. For the expulsion of the Sephardi from the Iberian Peninsula and their emigration to Morocco, which assumed the epic proportion of a demographic, ethnic, and cultural challenge to the Muslim population, I have drawn on Haym Zeew Hirschberg, *A History of the Jews in North Africa*, 2d rev. ed., vol. 1 (Leiden: Brille, 1974), and 2 (1981); Jonathan Israel, "The Jews of Spanish North Africa, 1600–1669," *Transactions of the Jewish Historical Society of England* 26 (1979), 71–86; Jane S. Gerber, *Jewish Society in Fez, 1450–1700: Studies in Communal and Eco-*

nomic Life (Leiden: Brille, 1980); Henry Kamen, "The Mediterranean and the Expulsion of Spanish Jews in 1492," *Past and Present* 119 (1988), 30–55; Michel Abitbol, "Juifs d'Afrique du Nord et expulsés d'Espagne après 1492," *Revue d'Histoire des Religions* 210 (1993), 49–90; Jane S. Gerber, *The Jews of Spain: A History of the Sephardic Experience* (New York: Free Press 1994); Haim Zafrani, *Juifs d'Andalousie et du Maghreb* (Paris: Maisonneuve et Larose, 1996); and José Alberto Rodrigues da Silva Tavim, *Os Judeus na expansão portuguesa em Morrocos durante o século XVI: origens e actividades duma comunidade* (Braga: Edições APPACDM Distrital de Braga, 1997). Tavim's study is a superbly researched repository of information, but the absence of an index is most regrettable.

19. David Corcos, "Les Juifs au Maroc et leurs mellahs" (1972), in *Studies in the History of the Jews in Morocco*, by David Corcos (Jerusalem: R. Mass, 1976), 64–130.

20. Hogan was very much taken in by the favors showered upon him by Abd al-Malik. The account of his embassy was edited by Richard Hakluyt in *The Principal Navigations* (London, 1598–1600), 2:64–67, and reprinted by H. de Castries, *SIHM*, Angleterre, 1:239–49. For his political agenda and his illegal trade, see Willan, 118–19, 147–51; and Yahya, 76–79.

21. H. de Castries, *SIHM*, Angleterre, 3:597–98.

22. R. Hakluyt, 2:117; H. de Castries, *SIHM*, Angleterre, 1:511–12. For Henry Roberts's difficult mission see Willan, 225–33, 261–62; and Yahya, 133–35.

23. In his incisive report addressed to Walsingham from Agadir, on 18 October 1589, he draws a negative picture of the state of Morocco and assumes a hostile view of Ahmad al-Mansur, whom he keeps dismissing throughout his report as the "Moor." For his embassy, see Willan, 234–35, 267–68, 272–74, 276–77; Yahya, 171–74, 186. On his Spanish descent and career in England, see Gustav Ungerer, *A Spaniard in Elizabethan England: The Correspondence of Antonio Pérez's Exile*, 2 vols (London: Tamesis, 1975 and 1976), 2:250, 273 n., 276, 322.

24. Quoted from Edward Prynne's report to Sir Francis Walsingham dated from Marrakesh on 30 May 1590. See H. de Castries, *SIHM*, Angleterre, 2:10–14. The original document is in the PRO, State Papers Foreign, Barbary States.

25. There is much information available on the extraordinary career of Jacob (I) Rute, but virtually none on his son Jacob. For the success story of the Sephardic Rutes in Morocco, see David Corcos's entry in the vol. 14 of *Encyclopaedia Judaica* (Jerusalem), 323, under "Rote". For Jacob (I) see Abitbol, 77 ff.; Gerber, 89–91. Tavim's researches have brought to light the broad spectrum of the career of a man who cut a figure in Portugal, Spain, Morocco, and the Vatican, and felt at home with Christian and Muslim rulers. see Tavim.

26. See Edward Glaser, "Le chroniqueur portugais Jerónimo de Mendonça et son esprit de tolérance," *Bulletin Hispanique* 56 (1954), 38–48; Robert Ricard, "Le Maroc à la fin du 16e siècle d'après la *Jornada de Africa* de Jerónimo de Mendonça," *Hespéris* 44 (1957), 179–204. Fray Bernardo da Cruz in his *Chronica de ElRei D. Sebastião*, ed. Alexandre Herculano (Lisbon, 1837), 371–72, confirms that the captives lived a life of luxury in the houses of their wealthy Jewish hosts. Abraham Rute, who, about 1610 was to be appointed naguid of Fez, was the host of the duke of Barcelos. See Tavim, 104–7, 341.

27. The letter has been published by H. de Castries, *SIHM*, France, 2:151.

28. Gaston Duverdun, 1:445–46; António de Saldanha, chaps. 53 and 54.

29. António de Saldanha, *Crónica de Almançor, Sultâo de Marrocos (1578–1603)*, ed. António Dias Farinha with a French translation by Léon Bourdon (Lisbon: Instituto de Investigaçâo Científica Tropical, 1997). The editor has identified Saldanha as the author of the anonymous chronicle. Saldanha was the son of the Portuguese governor of Tangier. In 1592, he was taken prisoner by the Sharifian army and held hostage until 1606, when he was ransomed by Sir Anthony Shirley who was then staying in the mellah of Marrakesh. Saldanha became an insider and shrewd observer of Moroccan politics and society. He kept an open house for Christian captives and Christian renegades.

30. For George Wilkins the Armada victory parade in Marrakesh was newsworthy. He has published a potted, fictionalized version in his rudimentary chronicle *Three Miseries of Barbary: Plague. Famine. Ciuill Warre. With a relation of the death of Mahamet the late Emperour* (London: W. Jaggard, for Henry Gosson, [1607]). Thus he misinformed his readers that the English ambassador, obviously Henry Roberts, was present in Marrakesh. But he had taken leave on 28 August 1588. See facsimile edition, The English Experience, 178 (Amsterdam: Da Capo Press, 1969), sigs. B1v–B2r. Arnold Thompson (or Tomson) was obviously a member of a family that had great interests in the Moroccan trade. The most prominent member of the family business was Richard Thompson who was criticized for being an interloper. In 1596, one year after the charter of the Barbary Company had expired, he supplied Ahmad al-Mansur with a shipload of weapons and was accordingly rewarded with privileges which the Company had never obtained. His factors in Morocco were George and Jasper Thompson. He seems to have served as a seaman in the battle against the Armada. See Willan, 276, 282–84, 302–3. There is an entry in the *DNB* under Richard Tomson.

31. The most comprehensive study of the Saadian sugar farms is Paul Berthier, *Les anciennes sucreries du Maroc et leurs réseaux hydrauliques*, 2 vols. (Rabat, 1966). Andrzej Dziubinski addresses the sugar production from the perspective of a social historian in "La fabrication et le commerce du sucre au Maroc aux XVIe et XVIIe siècles," in *Acta Poloniae Historiae* 54 (1986), 5–37. For the sugar consumption of the royal household see Willan, 269, 325–26. António de Saldanha in his *Crónica*, chap. 31, mentions eighteen sugar farms in the Sus, each of which employed at least two thousand workers from wood cutters and carters to technicians operating the sugar presses. For the importance of the paid native labor force, see Vincent J. Cornell, "Socioeconomic Dimensions of Reconquista and Jihad in Morocco: Portuguese Dukkala and the Sa'did Sus, 1450–1557," *International Journal of Middle East Studies* 22 (1990), 379–418, resp. 403, 409.

32. Ro[bert] C. reports in *A True Historicall Discourse of Muley Hamets rising to the three Kingdomes of Moruecos, Fes, and Sus* (London, 1609) that "by husbanding his *Maseraws*, or, *Ingenewes*, where his Sugar Canes did growe," as "is sufficiently knowne, all of them about *Morruecos*," that is Marrakesh, "*Taradant*, and *Mogador* , were yearely worth to him, sixe hundred thousand ounces at the least" (sig. B1v), that is sixty thousand pounds. The chronicle has been reprinted by H. de Castries, *SIHM*, Angleterre, 2:318–408. Its authorship has remained elusive. The following candidates have been put forward as author: Captain Robert Coverte, Robert Chambers, Sir Robert Cecil. Henry de Castries has ascribed it to Shakespeare's colleague, George Wilkins. The attribution to Cecil and Wilkins can be ruled out. The *OED* definition of "ingenios" as sugar-works in the West Indies

is historically and geographically inaccurate, and its first entry (1600) can be antedated as far back as 1564. There is no *OED* entry for the synonym "Maseraw" from Arabic "masserat." Further antedatings of Ro. C. with references to the reprint in *SIHM*: "Morruecans," inhabitants of Marrakesh, pp. 372, 377, *OED* 1860; "Brebers," Berbers, pp. 324, 398, *OED* 1842; "Larbies," pp. 328, 329, that is, Arabs, *OED* 1634.

33. The authority on the rearmament of the Saadian army is Westin Franklin Cook, *The Hundred Years War for Morocco: Gunpowder and the Military Revolution in the Early Modern Muslim World* (Boulder: Westview Press, 1994). See also Andrej Dziubinski, "L'armée et la flotte de guerre saadienne à l'époque des sultans de la dynastie saadienne," *Hésperis Tamuda* 13 (1972), 61–94.

34. From a request made by the English merchants in 1583 it appears that the bankruptcy of the Jews cost the English merchants forty thousand pounds. See H. de Castries, *SIHM*, Angleterre, 1:418–21. For more information on the bakruptcies of the Jews and losses sustained by the English Barbary merchants, see Henry Roberts's clash with the Barbary Company, which erupted on his return from Morocco in January 1589. H. de Castries, *SIHM*, 1:543–52.

35. For further information on the Cabeças, see vol. 5 of *Encyclopaedia Judaica*; and Tavim, 158–61, 383, 436–37. The case heard in the High Court of Admiralty (HCA) put the figure of the debt at 6,250 pounds; an interrelated case heard twenty years later in the Court of Chancery put the figure of the same debt at sixteen thousand pounds. See Willan, 129 n. 3.

36. PRO, HCA 13/16/384v–387v. The hearing is dated 17 January 1569. For more information on John Whaley, see Willan, 134.

37. HCA 13/16/386.

38. HCA 13/16/365–366v. The examination is dated 7 December 1568. For the various English partnerships involved in Isaac Cabeça's insolvency, see Willan, 126–33.

39. See Willan, 129–30.

40. See Willan, 127. Willan, unfortunately, does not specify in which of the hearings he has come across the compliment, and I have failed to trace the relevant passage in those photographed documents I ordered from the PRO.

41. E. A. J Honigman, " 'There is a World Elsewhere': William Shakespeare Businessman," in *Images of Shakespeare: Proceedings of the Third Congress of the Internal Shakespeare Association, 1986*, ed. W. Habicht et al. (Newark: University of Delaware Press, 1988), 40–46.

42. The relevant passage in Gerard Gore's will, dated 19 December 1602, reveals that Moroccan law secured his property rights. Its wording is as follows: "And where, as I am Owner of a Howse with th'appurtenaunces scituate and beinge in the *Alfandica in Morocus in Barbarie* formerlie belonginge to my self and my brother Thomas Goare deceassed and nowe properlie belonginge to my self and my heires & assigned forever accordinge to the lawes of the saide Countrie. And am alsoe Owner ioyntlie with my sayde twoe sonnes Richard and Gerrard Goare of one other Howse with th'appurtenaunces scituate and beinge in the Playe in Barbarie aforesaid which was buylte at the charges of my self & my sayde twoe sonnes Richard and Gerrard" (P.R.O., Prob. 11/111/54–56). Other merchants who owned property in Morocco were Arthur Dawbeney, the doyen of the Barbary merchants, freeman of the Merchant Taylors Company, who introduced his

brother-in-law Gerard Gore to Morocco as a marketplace. Thomas Starkey, alderman and sheriff of London, bought part of a house in Agadir from Dawboney in the 1570s (Willan, 217, 289).

43. On the Gores as the first Anglo-Moroccan family, see Willan, 202–5.

44. For the foundation of the famous Merchant Taylors School and Richard Mulcaster's curriculum, see Richard L. DeMolen, *Richard Mulcaster (c.1531–1611) and Educational Reform in the Renaissance* (Nieuwkoop: De Graaf, 1991).

45. On the Davenants and Tooley, see Mary Edmond, *Rare Sir William Davenant: Poet Laureate, Playwright, Civil War General, Restoration Theatre Manager* (Manchester: Manchester University P, 1987), chaps. 1 and 2; Park Honan, *Shakespeare: A Life* (Oxford: Oxford University Press, 1998), chap. 16.

46. H. de Castries, *SIHM*, Angleterre, 1:510–12; reprinted from Hakluyt, *The Principal Navigations*, vol. 2, pt. 2 (1598–1600) 117.

47. On the Moroccan embassy, see Yahya, *Morocco in the 16th Century*, 135–36; Willan, 233–34; Richard Bruce Wernham, ed., *The Expedition of Sir John Norris and Sir Francis Drake to Spain and Portugal, 1589;* Navy Records Society Publications 127 (Aldershot: Temple Smith, 1988). Richard Gore subscribed twenty-five pounds to the Portugal expedition. See Wernham, 26.

48. The play was printed in 1594. Its title page mentions that it had been acted sundry times by the Admiral's Company before 1594. John Yoklavich, in his introduction to the play in *The Dramatic Works of George Peele* (New Haven: Yale University Press, 1961), 221–26, argues that the play was written before the Portugal expedition weighed anchor on 18 April 1589.

49. The strategy of anchoring *The Merchant of Venice* in the context of Elizabethan politics pervades the whole play. Thus the text takes up the issue of the rights of the foreign merchants and retailers to do business in England, which Parliament had been debating in 1594/95. Some of the members supported the rights, invoking the example of the Republic of Venice as the commercial and political model to follow. See Sir Simonds D'Ewes, *The Journals of all the Parliaments during the Reign of Queen Elizabeth* (London, 1682), 505–11.

50. When Ahmad al-Mansur granted the first royal audience to the Spanish ambassador Don Pedro Venegas de Córdoba, on 30 July 1579, he was dressed all in white, wearing a turban. See H. de Castries, *SIHM*, France, 2:33–54, resp. 49–51. The emblem of his military power was the great royal standard called "Ellinâ al-Mansur." See Abdallah Eloufrani (al-Ufrani), *Nozhet-Elhâdi: Histoire de la dynastie saadiene au Maroc, 1511–1670*, trans. Octave Houdas (Paris: E. Leroux, 1889), 199. For the symbolic and social value of honorific garments, see Patricia L. Baker, "Islamic Honorific Garments," *Costume: The Journal of the Costume Society* 25 (1991), 25–35.

51. Dahiru Yahya, "The Role of Pretenders and Fugitives in Moroccan External Relations in the 16th Century," *The Maghreb Review* 14 (1989), 97–107.

52. Quotations of *The Merchant of Venice* are taken from The New Cambridge Shakespeare, ed. M. M. Mahood (Cambridge: Cambridge University Press, 1987).

53. "He sleeps lying high, takes his meals at the table sitting in Christian manner." See Miguel de Cervantes, *Los Baños de Argel*, ed. Florencio Sevilla Arroyo and Antonio Rey Hazas, in *Teatro Completo* (Barcelona: Planeta, 1987), 269, lines 2603–4.

54. After the death of Ahmad al-Mansur (25 August 1603), the London mer-

chant Thomas Pate submitted a petition to King James and the Privy Council from which it appears that John Wakeman had been acting as a factor of Ahmad al-Mansur, "supplying" the sultan, among other things, with "necessaries and furnitures for his owne use" through the agency of Thomas Pate, who was also responsible for the transportation of the goods. This well-established traffic was known to the Lords of the Privy Council, "to whome" Pate had been "lately suitor for transportation of a coach and bedd for the same late King." Ahmad al-Mansur's death left John Wakeman with "a great stock" and with the sugar farms he had rented. He lost his store of goods and the sugar farms in the ensuing turmoils of the civil war and was therefore unable to pay his debts to Pate. See H. de Castries, *SIHM*, Angleterre, 2:236–37; Willan, 301–2.

55. Daryl W. Palmer, "Merchants and Miscenegation: *The Three Ladies of London, The Jew of Malta, and The Merchant of Venice,*" in *Race, Ethnicity, and Power in the Renaissance*, ed. Joyce Green Macdonald (Madison, NJ: Fairleigh Dickinson University Press, 1997), 36–66.

56. John Smith confirms in *The True Travels and Adventures and Observations . . . in Europe, Asia, Affricke and America* (London, 1630) that there were "so few good artificers" available in Morocco that Ahmad al-Mansur "entertained from England goldsmiths, plummers, carvers, and polishers of stone, and watchmakers, so much hee delighted in the reformation of workmanship; hee allowed each of them ten shillings a day standing fee, linnen wollen, silkes and what they would for diet and apparell, and custome-free to transport or import what they would: for there were scarce any of those qualities in his kingdomes." Some of them went back to England at the outbreak of the civil wars (1603) and were still living in London in 1630. Smith mentions the watchmaker Henry Archer and his servant John Bull. His book of travels was partly reprinted by H. de Castries, *SIHM*, Angleterre, 2:266–73.

57. The native muskateers of the Safi garrison were under the command of an Englishman when the Spanish ambassador Don Pedro Venegas de Córdoba arrived in August 1579 on a mission to congratulate Ahmad al-Mansur on his succession to the Saadian throne. See H. de Castries, *SIHM*, France, 2:35. He may have been one of the soldiers of Thomas Stukeley's contingent who survived The Battle of the Three Kings (1578) and obviously converted to Islam to be released from captivity. The English cryptographer decoded the correspondence of the Portuguese ambassador Francisco da Costa with Philip II after the annexion of Portugal (1580). See Saldanha, *Crónica*, chap. 44.

58. Willan, 299.

59. For this daring plan to offer English craftsmanship and scientific knowledge in order to boost Ahmad al-Mansur's colonial policy in Africa, see the enthusiastic letter of Thomas Bernhere, Wright's brother-in-law, written from Marrakesh ("Morocco") on 24 June 1600, published in Samuel Purchas, *Hakluytus Pothumus* (London, 1625), 2:852, and reprinted by H. de Castries, *SIHM*, Angleterre, 2:168–70.

60. N. Matar, 40. For more information on the Sultan's request lodged with the Company for two English maidens see John Keay, *The Honourable Company. A History of the East India Company* (London: Harper Collins, 1991), 19. In like manner, the Virginia Company promoted miscegenation as a colonial practice in Virginia between 1605 and 1622, a practice that was actually propagated by Angli-

can ministers. The Virginia Company's official discourse effaced cultural taboos against ethnic intermarriages between English settlers and female Algonquins. See David Stymeist, "'Strange Wives': Pocahontas in Early Modern Colonial Advertisement, *Mosaic* 35 (2002): 109–25.

61. Ro(bert) C., *A True Historicall Discourse* (1609), chap. 20. Chapter 20 is one of the parts reprinted by H. de Castries, *SIHM*, Angleterre, 2:318–408.

62. George Wilkins, *Three Miseries of Barbarie* (1607), sig. B1r.

63. George Wilkins, sig. B3r. For more information on Ahmad al-Mansur's wives, see H. de Castries, *SIHM*, France, vol. 1 plate 5; Roger Le Tourneau, "Histoire de la dynastie Sa'dite," *Revue de l'Occident Musulman et de la Méditerranée* 23 (1977), 7–109. António de Saldanha, *Crónica*, calls Lalla Al-Djauher "moura negra" who was "mui bem entendida" (chap. 88). In chap. 20, Saldanha observes that the Badi in Marrakesh was the most beautiful palace he had ever seen. The apartments were designed to hold a thousand women. A great number of the female servants he had seen were Christian captives.

64. Zakari Dramani-Issifou, *L'Afrique noire dans les relations internationales au 16e siècle. Analyse de la crise entre le Maroc et le Sonhai* (Paris: Editions Khartala, 1982) is a perceptive study of the Moroccan expedition to the Sudan and the kingdom of Gago, of the salt, gold, and slave trade launched by Ahmad al-Mansur's expansionist policy. The fifteen daughters of the king of Gago taken on a memorable camel ride across the Sahara are also referred to in E. W. Bovill, *The Golden Trade of the Moors*, 2d ed. revised and with additional material by Robin Hallett (London: Oxford University P, 1968), 190.

65. As Ro. C. put it, Ahmad al-Mansur's "sumptuous prouisions for the Seraile, and maintenance of his women" did not mean that he was "so much delighting in the sinne, as his predecessors had done before, as to shew his glorie, because the fashion of the Countrye is such, to shewe their riches and greatnesse" (sig. B1v). The objective account made by Ottaviano Bon, the Venetian ambassador to the Ottoman court (1604–07), is quite in line with Ro.C's. See the translation made by Robert Withers from Bon's text and published by Samuel Purchas in *Hakluytus Posthumus or Purchas his Pilgrimes* (1625, part II). There is an annotated edition by Godfrey Goodwin, *The Sultan's Seraglio. An Intimate Portrait of Life at the Ottoman Court* (London: Saqi Books, 1996), chap. 4. The royal seraglio as a feature of self-representation was made fun of by the Inns-of-Court students and their professional readers during the Christmas revels. The mock seraglio, run by the Prince of Love (impersonated by the lawyer Richard Martin) on the occasion of the Middle Temple Revels of 1597/98, was a landmark of the Prince's holiday kingdom. The *dames de joie* were expected to "humble, and submit themselves to his Highness pleasure." See Benjamin Rudyerd (ed.), *Le Prince d'Amour or The Prince of Love* (London for William Leake, 1660), 30.

66. Under the rule of Ahmad al-Mansur, Marakkesh reached the peak of its cultural efflorescence. Virtually all functionaries were notable scholars from all over Islamic Africa. For the king's brilliant cultivation of the arts and sciences, his precious library of rare books, most of them annotated with his marginalia, his outstanding command of rhetoric, his amatory letter riddles, and samples of distichs saturated with erotic intoxication and of sensual poems addressed to his concubines Amina and Nasîm, see Abdallah Eloufrani (al-Ufrani), *Nozhet-Elhâdi*, 216, 217, 225–33. His library was inherited by his son Zaydan who kept the Irish Dom-

124   GUSTAV UNGERER

inican Antoine de Sainte-Marie as a captive for eight years. The Dominican's task
was to translate the Latin books into Spanish. In 1612 the library was seized by
Spanish vessels and deposited in the holdings of the Escorial, sixty-three big bun-
dles of books in Arabic. See G. Duverdun, 1:435.

67. "Tragedia por ventura nova na memória dos homens." Saldanha, *Crónica*,
chap. 90.

68. Their story is much better documented than the abduction and prospective
rape of Monfadal's daughter whose only written source remains the private chronicle of António de Saldanha published in 1997. There are the Christian testimo-
nies of Luis del Mármol Carvajal's, *Primera parte de la descripcion general de
Affrica* (Granada, 1573), the *Segunda parte y libro septimo de la descripcion general de Africa* (Málaga, 1599), and Diego de Torres's *Relacion del origen y sucesso
de los xarifes, y del estado de los reinos de Marruecos, Fez, Tarudante* (Sevilla,
1586). A modern edition of Mármol Carvajal's chronicle was published by the Instituto de Estudios Africanos (Madrid, 1953), and Mercedes García-Arenal presented a modern edition of Diego de Torres's *Relacion*. The two memoirists
garnished their chronicles with lurid details. The partisan editorial policy Diego
de Torres pursued to catch the eye of the Christian reader becomes manifest in the
wording of the title of chapter 107: "El Xarife reinó treinta y siete años y fue ca-
sado quatro vezes" [The Sharif ruled thirty-seven years and was married four
times] denounces Muhammad ash-Shaykh as a polygamist. By far the best and
most reliable historian is the anonymous memoirist of the chronicle of Agadir, an
officer of the Portuguese garrison of Agadir, who was an eyewitness of the fall of
the "presidio" and the subsequent events. He was ransomed and released from
captivity in 1546, that is after the death of Dona Mencía, and wrote his account of
the events in Portugal in the 1560s for private circulation. His original Portuguse
text and a French translation have been edited by Pierre de Cenival, *Chronique de
Santa -Cruz du Cap de Gué* (Paris: Paul Geuthner, 1934).

69. For comment on the lines composed by Muhammad ash-Shaykh, see Yahya,
Morocco in the 16th Century, 26. His epitaph in the mausoleum of the Saadian
rulers in Marrakesh puts his birth to the year 896, that is, 1490/91. See Gabriel
Rousseau and Edmond Doutté, *Le mausolée des princes sa'diens à Marrakech:
Texte arabe et traduction par Félix Arin* (Paris: Paul Geuthner, 1925).

70. For a perceptive assessment of Muhammad ash-Shaykhs's reign, see Vincent J. Cornell, "Socioeconomic Dimensions of Reconquista," 379–418, resp.
399–407.

71. "Fue ombre de mediana estatura, doblado, rezio de miembros, el rostro redondo, los ojos grandes y alegres, era blanco, tenía dos dientes de parte de arriba
mui grandes, la barva larga y cana, hecha en redondo, los cavellos traía alheñados.
A cavallo era gentil ombre." Diego de Torres, *Relación*, chap. 107, p. 283. The
same style of beard was worn by the Moorish ambassador to Queen Elizebeth in
1600/1601. See plate in Harris and in E. A. J. Honigman's *Othello*, The Arden
Shakespeare (Walton-on-Thames: Thomas Nelson & Sons, 1997). Note that Muhammad ash-Shaykh's reddish hair does not correspond to the stereotyped head
of hair of the Elizabethan and Jacobean stage Moor.

72. Torres, chap. 36. For an account of his other wives, see chap. 107 and R. Le
Tourneau, 27 n. 80.

73. Anonymous chronicler; see Cenival, 139–41. The earliest possible date of

the birth and death is, I think, March 1545. Mármol Carvajal records that Dona Mencía gave birth to a son. See Cenival, 140, n. 1.

74. Torres, chap. 36.

75. Torres, chap. 36; Mármol Carvajal as quoted in Cenival, 138 n. 2.

76. The anonymous Portuguese officer and chronicler of the fall of Agadir is the only writer to comment on the relations between the Muslim sultan and his Christian father-in-law. The chronicle used to resort to direct speech whenever he wished to drive home a point. In the present case, Muhammad ash-Shaykh addressed the following words to Gutierre de Monroy, who, strange to say, until this memorable encounter, had remained captive in a prison in Marrakesh: "o meu sange he o teu ey a todo hum" [my blood is yours and I consider our blood to be one and the same]. See Cenival, 152–53.

77. Dom Gutierre's answer in the Portuguese chronicle reads: "Já sou muito velho e fraquo como vês e cansado; antes quero ir ser apregoeiro pela Cristandade de quem és e quam gram senhor e poderoso." See Cenival, 152. Gutierre de Monroy, governor of Agadir (1533–34, 1538–41) was born about 1480, the son of the Spanish gentleman don Alonso de Monroy of the Order of Alcántara, who settled in Portugal at the close of the fifteenth century. See Mercedes García-Arenal, ed., *Relación*, by Torres, 112 n. 229.

78. Sir Walter Ralegh's copy of Diego de Torres's *Relacion* (1586), which contains his marginal annotations, is now in the British Library, shelfmark 583.c.4. Ralegh owned a good many Spanish books, some of which I helped Walter Oakeshott identify for his reconstruction of "Sir Walter Ralegh's Library," *The Library*, Fifth Series, 23 (1968), 285–327. Besides the "Relation del Diego de Torris" (no. 88) Ralegh acquired the "Descriptio of Afrik Spanish" (no. 225), which I am now sure was a copy of Luis del Mármol Carvajal's *Primera parte de la descripcion general de Affrica* (Granada, 1573) and the *Segunda parte* (Málaga, 1599).

79. Salih Mahdi Hameed has drawn attention to Painter's novella in "The Prince of Morocco in *The Merchant of Venice*," *Journal of Education and Science* 7 (1989), 5–24.

80. On the Shakespearean pattern of the Moor as an erring barbarian and promiscuous voyager, see John Gillies, *Shakespeare and the Geography of Difference* (Cambridge: Cambridge University Press, 1994), 32.

81. Arthur L. Little Jr. is the only critic I know to have spotted the Prince's aggressive sexuality. See his magisterial study *Shakespeare Jungle Fever: National-Imperial Re-Visions of Race, Rape, and Sacrifice* (Cambridge: Cambridge University Press, 2000), 63, 71.

82. The point that the Prince of Morocco and also the Prince of Arragon conceive of marriage as a matter of selfish pursuit is convincingly argued by David Lucking, "Standing for Sacrifice: The Casket and Trial Scenes in *The Merchant of Venice*," *University of Toronto Quarterly* 58 (1989), 355–75.

83. Joan Ozark Holmer has addressed the issue of penalty in her outstanding study *The Merchant of Venice: Choice, Hazard and Consequence* (London: Macmillan, 1995), 56, 87–88, 97; and Kim F. Hall has noted that the cultural threat has been obviated by the Prince's mischoice in "Guess Who's Coming to Dinner? Colonization and Miscegenation in *The Merchant of Venice*," ed. Mary Beth Rose, *Renaissance Drama*, n.s., 23 (1992), 87–111.

84. See Alan Rosen, "The Rhetoric of Exclusion: Jew, Moor, and the Boundaries

of Discourse in *The Merchant of Venice*," in *Race, Ethnicity and Power in the Renaissance*, ed. Joyce Green Macdonald (Madison: Fairleigh Dickinson University Press, 1997), 67–77.

    85. A shortened version of Chamberlain's letter, dated 15 October 1600, has been edited by H. de Castries, *SIHM*, Angleterre 2:192.

Black *Hamlet:* Battening on the Moor

Patricia Parker

> Could you on this faire mountaine leaue to feede,
> And batten on this Moore . . . ?

In the closet scene of *Hamlet*, the prince of Denmark forces his mother to look upon the portraits of her husbands in lines that draw the familiar contrast between the two, the second declining or falling from the "grace" of the "faire" first:

> Looke heere vpon this Picture, and on this,
> The counterfeit presentment of two brothers,
> See what a grace was seated on this browe,
> *Hiperions* curles, the front of Ioue himselfe,
> An eye like *Mars*, to threaten and command,
> A station like the herald *Mercury*,
> New lighted on a heaue, a kissing hill, [F: heauen-kissing hill]
> A combination, and a forme indeede,
> Where euery God did seeme to set his seale
> To giue the world assurance of a man,
> This was your husband, looke you now what followes,
> Heere is your husband like a mildewed eare,
> Blasting his wholsome brother, haue you eyes,
> Could you on this faire mountaine leaue to feede,
> And batten on this Moore . . . ?[1] (Q2)

The passage foregrounds one of the many polarities constructed in this play, between an idealized old Hamlet and his usurping brother, who appears here as a "Moore" in the double sense commonplace in early modern England—familiar, for example, from the seal of Thomas More (or "Moore"), which juxtaposes the head of a black Moor with the moorfowl of wastelands, fens or "moors."[2]

Dover Wilson's suggestion in the first New Cambridge edition of the play (that "batten on this Moore" simultaneously evokes the figure of a black "Moor") is noted in the fine print of some modern editions.[3] But it has not yet penetrated the consciousness of most critics, readers, and audiences of this most canonical of plays— from a corpus in which Moors are assumed to belong only to *Titus Andronicus*, *Antony and Cleopatra*, *The Merchant of Venice*, or *Othello*. The appearance of a "Moore" in Hamlet's contrast of a "faire" dead father to his mother's present husband is underscored, however, as Harold Jenkins notes, by the corresponding lines of the First Quarto's version of this scene:

> Looke you now, here is your husband,
> With a face like *Vulcan*.
> A looke fit for a murder and a rape,
> A dull dead hanging looke, and a hell-bred eie,
> To affright children and amaze the world:
> And this same haue you left to change with this.
> What Diuell thus hath cosoned you at hob-man blinde?
>
> (*TTH*, 166, 168)

"Face like Vulcan" (with "hell-bred eie") explicitly invokes an infernal blackness for this second husband, in lines whose "dull dead hanging look" summons the combination of dullness, death, and Moors reflected in the "dull Moor" of *Othello*.[4] The identification of Vulcan with the "blackness" of devil and Moor was routinely applied to the blacksmith hurled from heaven, like Lucifer himself, transformed from angel of "light" to prince of darkness. "Black as Vulcan" is the comparison used for the blackened face of Antonio in *Twelfth Night*, "besmeared / As black as Vulcan in the smoke of war" (5.1.46–47), in a play that makes the traditional association of the sooty or "foul collier" with "Satan" (3.4.117).[5]

"Face like *Vulcan*," however, simultaneously evokes the darkening of a white actor's face with soot, cosmetic counterpart to the racialized figure of blackness as sullied, "besmear'd" or "smirch't."[6] The Clown chosen to play Vulcan in Dekker's *Welsh Embassador* complains that he has to "smutt" his "face," as well as "hire a hammer" and "buy a polt [or lame] foote" (5.3.227–29).[7] The "soot" or coal associated with blackface, colliers, and Vulcan produces the "coal-black" hue of Aaron the Moor in *Titus Andronicus*, joined by the "sooty bosom," "begrim'd" face, and "collied" judgment of Othello.[8] In his discussion of abjection in *Othello*, Michael Bristol argues that blackface simultaneously evoked carnival, an argument strengthened by the fact that Emilia's moronic or "dull Moor" appears in a scene that assigns to him the "coxcomb" of the "fool" (5.2.233).[9] Smearing, sullying, or blackening the face with soot to produce a "face like Vulcan" or a "Moore" was familiar from the mumming, morris dancing, and carnival that the early texts of *Hamlet* repeatedly invoke, associating the present king of Denmark with the black face not only of the collier but of carnival misrule—the "King of shreds and patches" (Q2 and F) that criticism has long linked to a carnival reversal or *mundus inversus*.

The sooty Vulcan and the black face associated with a carnival "Moore" is thus part of all three early texts of the Closet Scene. As in the case of the Lucifer who was once an angel of light, Hamlet's polarized contrast of "faire" and "Moore" posits an original white or light as the point of departure for his mother's decline, echoing the Ghost's "what a falling off was there" (Q2/F).[10] What I want to argue here is that this summoning of a "Moore" enables us to reconsider these early texts of *Hamlet*, rereading their preoccupation with blackness, soiling, sullying, and dulling, in relation both to contemporary discourses of blackness and to the "tropical" reversibility or indistinguishability of white and black, angel and devil.

*

such blacke and grained spots,
As will not leave their Tinct.

—Folio

such blacke and greeued spots
As will leave there their tin'ct.

—Second Quarto

Blackness is evoked repeatedly in these early *Hamlet* texts—in the "night" watch of the opening scene; in Hamlet's "sable sute" and "inky cloak"; in "Thoughts blacke," "raven," and "mixture ranke, of Midnight Weeds collected"; in the "cursed hebenon" associated by some editors with ebony; in "let the Divel weare blacke, for Ile have a suite of Sables"; and in the "dread and blacke complexion" of "hellish *Pyrrhus*," whose "sable arms" ("Blacke as his purpose") evoke the bodily as well as heraldic sense of "arms" exploited in the graveyard scene. Even the "Nero" of Hamlet's " 'Tis now the very witching time of night, / When Churchyards yawne, and hell it selfe breakes out / Contagion to this world" may resonate not just with the name of this famous matricide but with the Italian sense of "nero" as "black, darke, sable."[11] Hamlet's "inky cloak" adds (to the blackness that surrounds him) the "ink" that like "soot" provided another form of cosmetic blackening, associated with sexual and other blots or stains in the inky "blots" of *Much Ado*, the play with which it shares the "nothing" that lies between maids' legs. Both blackface and sexual "blackening" are evoked by the allusion in the play scene to the morris or "morisko" already connected with Moors, in the "Hobby-horse" that was a familiar term for a prostitute or "blackened" woman.[12]

In the closet scene itself, Hamlet's "Moore" or black-faced "Vulcan" for the present king is joined by the black "spots" of the queen whom Hamlet attempts to purify in this scene, counterpart in the Folio and Second Quarto to Q1's "I'le make your eyes looke downe into your heart, / And see how horride there and blacke it shews" (166). Maculation or spottedness is contrasted to the immaculate or pure as early in Shakespeare as the "maculate" Jacquenetta (*LLL*, 1.2.92). In Q2, Hamlet later speaks of himself as having not only "a father kild" but "a mother staind" (190). In the variant texts of the closet scene, the queen's "blacke and grained spots, / As will not leave their Tinct" (F)—a "leave" that suggests both a stain and its removal—appear in Q2 as "such blacke and greeued spots / As will leave there their tin'ct." "Greeued spots" suggests simultaneously the blackness of grieving and the graphic or engraved, as in the later figure of the blackened Desdemona as a "fair paper" inscribed or written on by a Moor. The fact that the Folio's "blacke and grained spots" appear in the Second Quarto as "blacke and greeued spots" suggests a logic of variants connecting both "greeued" and "grained" to the contemporary lexicon of blackening, soiling, or staining. Soiling and grieving are combined, for example, in ways we might not expect, as the "soile of griefe" in Marston's *Antonio's Revenge*.[13]

The contrast of black and "faire" in Hamlet's portraits of two brothers is thus joined by the adulterous declining of the queen—described in F and Q2 as an "act" that sets a "blister" or blemish on the "faire" forehead of an "innocent loue" (166–67). Q1's "Forbear the adulterous bed to night" (172) makes even clearer the attempt by her son to remove her from the adulterate mingling or mixture of coupling with this second husband. In the language of

decline and Fall that is so much a part of this rhetoric, the blackness associated with Denmark's "spotted" queen simultaneously
recalls the familiar black bride of the Song of Songs, introduced
early in Shakespeare in the "grained" or engrained as well as
"swart" bride of *The Comedy of Errors* (3.2.101–18), the Ethiope to
be made "white" by baptism. The adulterate coupling of this queen
raises the pollution danger associated by Douglas, Kristeva, and
others with Leviticus, recalled in these early *Hamlet* texts by the
unclean beasts of weasel, mole, and mouse.[14] Hamlet's mother—
whose "spots" simultaneously recall the spotted leopard and
"Moor" of Jeremiah 13:23, the biblical counterpart to the proverbial
blanching of the Ethiope—is distinguished from the spotless or immaculate Virgin Mother evoked (as Janet Adelman observes) in the
opening night watch, which summons the tradition of waiting for
an apocalyptic dawning, the final separation of day and night that
in this tragedy never comes.[15]

*

> Why say thy sinnes were blacker than is ieat,
> Yet may contrition make them as white as snowe
>
> —Q1

   The "Moore" of the closet scene is there opposed to Hyperion or
the God of Day, recalling Hamlet's earlier figure of his mother's decline from Hyperion to a satyr (Q2/F). The polarities join the Manichean contrast of "night" to the "God of Day" in all three texts of
the opening scene, which itself sounds—in "dead wast and middle
of the night"—one of the contemporary senses of wasteland or
"moor." Even before the closet scene, these polarities are sounded
in Hamlet's determination, at the sight of the praying king, to find
a more appropriate time to "trip him," that his "Soule may be as
damn'd and blacke / As Hell, whereto it goes."[16] The king and second husband soon to be compared to a black Vulcan or a "Moore"
invokes for his own sin the proverbial impossibility of washing the
Ethiope white, a connection made even clearer in these early texts.
The Folio's "Oh bosome, blacke as death! / O limed soul," and "Is
there not Raine enough in the sweet Heavens / To wash it white as
Snow"—lines closely paralleled in Q2—evoke not only the blackness of death but the "lime" of the "whitelime" that masks a blackness beneath, familiar from the "white-limed walls" of *Titus*

Andronicus (4.2.98–100) or the "birdlime" attached to the white devil of *Othello* (2.1.126). Blanching an Ethiope (with baptismal washing) is even more explicit in the First Quarto here, where the king, for his "adulterous fault," prays "O that this wet that falles vpon my face / Would wash the crime cleere from my conscience!" and observes of his "vnpardonable" crimes: "say thy sinnes were blacker than is ieat [jet], / Yet may contrition make them as white as snowe."[17]

In relation to the language of washing an Ethiope, in this context of maimed rites and adulterate mixtures, the most telling index may be the choice of the name "Baptista" for the wife of the play within the play. It is an unusual name choice here, as editors note, since it is almost never used for a woman, with the striking exception of Baptista Sforza, whose name juxtaposed a reminder of baptism with the black or *schwarz*. "Baptista"—which appears in all three early texts of the Mousetrap play, where names otherwise differ radically—evokes both baptism and John the Baptist (herald of another "God of Day"), part of the lexicon of blanching the black or stained to "white as snowe." It thus connects the maculate wife of the "Mousetrap" (and her ironic name) with the "spotted" queen.

The familiar biblical text on the "Moore," which corresponds to blanching the Ethiope ("Can the black Moor change his skin? or the leopard his spots?," Jeremiah 13:23), is related not only to the "spots" of this maculate queen but to the "curse placed on the adulterate offspring of Ham."[18] The king who invokes this blanching for his "black" or "adulterous" sin alludes in this same scene to the curse on Cain—the "primall eldest curse" (F/Q2) of a brother's murder, a "trespasse" for which the "earth doth still crie out" (Q1, 160). The "curse" on Cain was conflated by long tradition with the curse of blackness on Canaan or Ham, whose punishment for his own "adulterous" sin figured the origin of "black Moors" as well as the maculation of racial mixing.[19] Chus, son of Ham, identified with southern or "tropic climes," had mingled offspring both white and black.[20] Through his descendant Tubalcain (recalled in *The Merchant of Venice*), said to have founded Spain, Spenser's "most mingled" of nations, Cain was also associated with Vulcan.[21] The "primall eldest curse" (F/Q2) on fratricide thus recalls the curse that identified Cain with the "curse" on blackness itself.

*

I am too much i' th' Sun.

—Folio

Blackness likewise surrounds the prince of Denmark, as if he were a kind of *memento mori*, reminder of the Death or *Mors* already traditionally conflated with Moors. When the opening darkness of the night watch yields to the public court, the blackness of "night" becomes the color of Hamlet's grief, the "nighted colour" (Q2; Folio "*nightly* colour"), "Inky Cloake" (F), and "suites of solemne Blacke" (F) that the First Quarto (with its "sable sute") associates with the prince's "sad and melancholy moodes" (Q1) and Hamlet himself (in the Folio) with "shewes of Griefe."

Returning to these lines from the closet scene's "Moore" or the prayer scene's black bosom, we might even revisit Hamlet's "I am too much i' th' Sun," lines that align his theatrically striking blackness with the putative origin of blackness, reflected in the "complexion" of Morocco in *The Merchant of Venice* ("shadowed livery of the burnish'd sun") and in *Antony and Cleopatra*'s Egyptian queen ("Think on me, / That am with Phoebus' amorous pinches black").[22] Though obscured by a critical tradition that has concentrated instead on Hamlet's sonship and the multiple fathers of this play, being too much in the "Sun" or "Sonne" (its Q2 and variant early modern spelling) is explicitly aligned with blackening in the later scene where the "excellent white" Ophelia is warned against being too much in the sun ("Let her not walke i' th' Sunne: Conception is a blessing, but not as your daughter may conceiue").[23] Hamlet's punning "too much i' th' Sun" (or "Sonne") is thus strengthened in its overtones of blackening by its repetition in a context in which the danger to the purity of "white" Ophelia anticipates the blackening of Desdemona's sexual "wit" or "white" (2.1.129–49). Ophelia is described as "white" in both Q2 and F, in the letter from Hamlet read by Polonius before the king and queen: "*To the Celestiall and my soules Idoll, the most beautified Ophelia, . . . thus in her excellent white bosome, these & c.*"[24] The corresponding First Quarto text does not include the "excellent white bosome" of this letter's elaborate address; but it does feature the loosing that is so much a part of the language of such exposure.

Tainting, adulterating, or sullying is simultaneously part of the postlapsarian decline from "honesty," figured as the purity of an immaculate or unspotted "white," a decline evoked by the post-Edenic "vnweeded" garden of Q2 and F and distance from a definitive final Doom. The combination is underscored in the exchange on the "strumpet" Fortune (Q2) who reigns in that ambiguous interim: "What newes? / *Ros.* None my Lord, but the worlds growne

honest / *Ham.* Then is Doomes day neer" (Q2).[25] Hamlet's "there is
a kinde [Q2 'kind of'] confession in your lookes; which your mod-
esties haue not craft enough to color" (F) joins the contrast between
the "modesty" and whiteness of Ophelia and the maculate, "adulterate," or cosmetic. The cosmetic colorings of dissimulation and
rhetoric are recalled in the king's "The Harlots Cheeke beautied
with plaist'ring Art / Is not more vgly to the thing that helpes it, /
Then is my deed, to my most painted word" (F, 123). In the lines
of the Folio and Second Quarto where Polonius warns his daughter
to be less "free and bounteous" (Q1 not "too prodigall") of her presence, Q2's "Not of that die which their inuestments showe" adds
the "dye," tincture or taint later associated with the "tinct" or spots
of the maculate queen, in a speech whose "plaine tearmes" (in Q2
and F) invoke once again the "plain" as opposed to the rhetorically
colored, from the tradition of both kinds of cosmetic paintings.[26]

The metaphorics of staining "fairness" as well as "honesty" pervades Hamlet's challenge to Ophelia in the nunnery scene, where
the "faire" of "honest and faire" registers in both of its contemporary senses, of "beautie" and of purity or whiteness (88, 124–25).
The sullying of purity by an adulterating sexual "commerce" is iterated in a passage which has a counterpart in all three texts, including the First Quarto's "pure as snowe," sounded much earlier,
before the Players' entrance:

> *Ham.* If thou doest Marry, Ile giue thee this Plague for thy Dowrie. Be
> thou as chast as Ice, as pure as Snow, thou shalt not escape Calumny.
> Get thee to a Nunnery. Go, Farewell. . . . (Folio, 127)

"As pure as Snow" here anticipates the king's hope in the prayer
scene that his "bosome blacke as death" may be washed as "white
as snowe," while the figure of plague or disease joins the lines of
the closet scene that contrast the queen's "faire" first husband to a
"Moore" described as "a Mildew'd eare / Blasting his wholsome
breath" (F, Q2, "brother"). "Batten on this Moore" is usually
glossed as grazing or feeding upon wastelands or moors.[27] But "Mil-
dewed ear" simultaneously associates this "Moore" with the "murrian," pestilence, or plague identified in other contemporary texts
with Moors (Heywood, for example, conflates a "Murrian" infection with the "black face" of a "Moorian" kissing the lips of his
"fair" maid).[28] The connection between tainting a "white" and a
"wholsome" that can be infected (staple of contemporary accounts

of blackness itself as an infection) is suggested in the text in which Guildenstern demands of Hamlet "a wholsome aunswere," and the latter replies that he cannot because his "wits diseasd"—a "wit" collapsed with its homophone "white" in *Othello* (2.1.131–33). "Nunnery" itself is tainted with its apparent opposite, its inferred purity sullied by the sexual inverse this word simultaneously conveyed.

Coloring, tincturing, or sullying purity, honesty, and a "plain style" already aligned with whiteness are all part of the network of terms ranging from sallets and sallied to sullying and soiling in these early texts. In Hamlet's contrast of a play "set down with as much modestie, as cunning," with no "Sallets in the lines to make the matter savoury," the "honest" of this "honest method" (F, 109) resonates with the "honesty" Ophelia is warned not to permit to have "Commerce" with her "beauty," in the speech that invokes the sexual honesty whose sullying would taint her "white." The variants of "sallied" and "solid" in Hamlet's opening soliloquy produce the homophonic ghost effect of "sullied" that has since become the frequently remembered text, though it nowhere appears. The Q1 version of Hamlet's soliloquy, which has "grieu'd and sallied," may reflect the same combinatory logic as Marston's "soile of griefe." The glossing of "sallied flesh" as "sullied flesh" is famously enabled by the later lines in which Polonius instructs the spy on his son ("laying these slight sallies on my sonne / As t'were a thing a little soyld with working," Q2; "laying these slight sulleyes on my Sonne, / As 'twere a thing a little soil'd i' th' working," F), lines whose "sallies" (Q2) or "sulleyes" (F) are linked with the "soiled" (Q2, "soyld"; F, "soil'd"), in a passage that has to do (in both Q2 and F) with "taints." "Soiling" as "besmerching" appears in Laertes's reference to the "chaste vnsmirched brow" of his "true Mother" and his warning to his sister not to open her "chast Treasure" to the prince of Denmark ("Perhaps he loues you now, / And now no soyle nor cautell doth besmerch the vertue of his feare").[29]

The early texts of *Hamlet* are filled with this emphasis on staining, sullying, or soiling, joining the iterated references to "ground," "earth," or "soil," including the "old Mole" described as a "pioner" working in the "earth" or "ground," the exploitation of "ground" itself as both soil and cause, and the description of the Courtier known in the Folio as "young Osricke" as "spacious" in the "possession of dirt" (Q2/F). The latter says in the Second Quarto, "me thinkes it is very sully and hot, or my complection"

rather than the Folio's more familiar "soultry and hot," in lines
whose "sully" may be influenced by "dirt" or the tropical sense of
"hot" as well as by "complexion." In Laertes's advice to Ophelia,
the association of the opening of her "chaste treasure" with soiling,
fouling, or besmerching comes in a speech whose "weigh what
losse your Honour may sustaine" (in Q2 and F) echoes the "stain"
that is part of this pervasive network. The present king of Denmark
is associated (in Q2) with a reputation that doth "Soyle our addition" and a "vicious mole of nature," a "mole" linked elsewhere in
Shakespeare with bodily and other kinds of stains.[30]

The affinity between "sallies," "sullies," and "soiled" in the
speech of Polonius used to justify hearing "sullied flesh" in Hamlet's opening soliloquy is followed (in Q2 and F) by allusion to "a
house of sale, / Videlizet, a brothell," a term for the commerce of
flesh that resonates with "sale" in the sense of dirtied or sullied.[31]
Immediately following this exchange, there is another reminder (in
Q2 and F) of the soiled or "foul'd," in Ophelia's description of
Hamlet's appearance in her "closset" (Q2, 72), "his stockings
foul'd, / Vngartred, and downe giued to his Anckle" (F). What the
king in Q2 and F calls "*Hamlets* transformation" is termed in Q1
the "cause and ground of his distemperancie" (Q1, 76), the causal
sense of "ground" that joins its meanings elsewhere of earth or
soil, combined in the Gravedigger's equivocating "Vpon what
ground?"[32]

The earthy or abject bodily sense of sullying as muddying is
sounded both in Ophelia's "muddy" death (4.7.182) and in the
variants of the soliloquy known as "O what a rogue and peasant
slave am I," where Hamlet's "dull and muddy-mettled rascal" recalls the Ghost's "duller shouldst thou be" than the "fat weede"
that "rootes [F: 'rots'] it selfe in ease on *Lethe* wharffe" (Q1, 2).
Hamlet's reference to himself as a "dull and muddy-mettled rascal"
(in Q2 and F) comes in a soliloquy whose Q1 counterpart begins
"Why what a dunghill idiote slaue am I," suggesting in "dunghill"
the excrement associated with muddiness or fouling in the lines
from the Henriad on the "melancholy of Moorditch," which combine London's excremental waste with the "waste" and "black
bile" associated with "Moores."[33] "Muddy"—synonymous in the
period with muddled or confused—was used for the darkening (or
collying) of the mind or spirit (as in the "collied" judgment or
"puddled" spirit of Othello) as well as for a sexual or moral sullying.[34] "Reward not hospitality / With such black payment. . . . /

Mud not the fountain that gave drink to thee," ontreats the still-unviolated Lucrece (*Lucrece*, 577), invoking the muddying as well as the blackening of her purity by Tarquin's rape. The opposition of "pure" to "muddy" (as both sexualized and racialized terms) joins the parallel opposition of "white" and "black." "Christall is muddy," declares Demetrius in *A Midsummer Night's Dreum* (3.2.139), searching for a contrast to the purity of Helena's eyes, in scenes that racialize the opposition of "Ethiope" and "tawny Tartar" to a contrasting "fair" (3.2.246–63).

Sander Gilman, Kim F. Hall, and others have examined the racialized metaphorics of blackness itself as a sullying, dirtying, or muddying. Othello's reference to Desdemona's "name" as "begrim'd, and black / As mine own face" (3.3.386–88) joins the description there of the "filthy bargain" of her marriage, to a Moor described by Emilia as "ignorant as dirt" (5.2.158, 164). In the case of *Hamlet*, evocation of a "Moore" (or blackened "Vulcan") within the scene that goes on to accuse the queen of coupling in a bed "stewed in corruption" (Q2/F) and "making loue" over the "nasty Stye" (F/Q2) connects a racialized blackness to the rhetoric elsewhere in these texts of soiling, muddying, and disease. Though it has all but lost this sense in modern usage, "nasty" had as its contemporary synonyms "filthie," "beastlie," "sluttish," "sullied," "soyled," and "uncleane."[35]

*

stained with the obscure and dark spots
of melancholy.
　　　　　　　　　　　—Timothy Bright, *Treatise of Melancholie*

moody, muddy, Moorditch melancholy.
　　　　　　　　　　　—John Taylor, *The Penniless Pilgrimage*

black-faced tragedy.
　　　　　　　　　　　—George Chapman, *Bussy d'Ambois*

bosome, blacke as death!
　　　　　　　　　　　—Folio

Multiple forms of blackness might be expected in these early texts not just because of their preoccupation with sullying, soiling, or fouling but because of the explicit identification of melancholy,

mourning, tragedy, and death with racialized figures of blackness
in the period. Melancholy—identified with the "black" humor of
atra bilis or "black bile"—was aligned with "waste" and "Moors,"
not only in contemporary discourses but in the "sable-colored melancholy" of *Loves Labours Lost* and the Henriad's reference to "the
melancholy of Moorditch," the phrase that conflates both kinds of
"Moor" with the black bile of melancholy, muddying, and excrement.[36]The melancholic was frequently described as "black" or
"swart"—from the predominance of black bile thought to impart to
"the skin a 'swarthy' appearance."[37] An influential physiognomy
text translated into English in 1571—which identifies the "black
colour" of the "Melancholick" with "them which dwel farre South,
like as the Indian," "Egyptians," and "Moores"—claims that a
"swartishe" (or black) color "doth declare the dominion of the
black choller," the root of blackness in "melancholia" that it shares
with the pigment of blackness, or melanin.[38] Continental texts variously associate southerners with an excess of black bile, an identification of melancholia with blackness that persists whether that
association is positively or negatively framed.[39] Timothy Bright's
Treatise of Melancholie (1586)—which draws, among other
sources, on Levinus Lemnius's *Touchstone of Complexions*
(1576)—remarks of melancholics: "Of colour they be black, according to the humour whereof they are nourished, and the skinne al-
wayes receauing the blacke vapors, which insensibly do passe from
the inward parts, taketh die and staine thereof."[40] Bright describes
the process whereby even the "white" body of a melancholic ultimately "altereth" its "colour," turned by the "dye" and "staine" of
this "earthie and darke humour" into the "blacke colour" that is
"the nature of the humour." A "morphew" that "staineth melancholicke bodies, and bespeckleth their skinne" is combined with
that humour's "blacke staines," "obscur[ing] the former beautie"
and leaving the melancholic maculate or spotted ("stained with the
obscure and dark spots of melancholy").[41]

As the humor connected with earth or soil—as well as with
"black" bile—melancholy thus had the power not only to turn
white skin black but to "staine," "dye," or "spot." In Bright's description, its counter is "the expiatorie sacrifice of the vnspotted
lambe" (194), capable of washing the Ethiope. The blackness associated by Bright and others with the blackness of the devil and melancholy's *atra bilis* has been identified with the epilepsy or
"falling" sickness of the "Moore" in *Othello*.[42] The association of

"dullness" with Moors in Emilia's "dull Moor" and the "dull dead hanging looke" (Q1) of the closet scene is part of the lexicon of what Shakespeare and others called "dull melancholy" (*CE*, 5.1.79).[43] Malvolio protests that he is "Not black in my mind, though yellow in my legs," a "black" glossed as the "melancholy (thought to be caused by black bile)." In *Much Ado*, Don John ("born under Saturn") is "saturnine or morose," a *morosus* that was already a familiar homophone of *Morus* or Moor (opposed to the *candidus*, "candid" or "white" foregrounded in *Titus Andronicus*). The Spanish Armado of *Loves Labours Lost* describes how "beseiged with sable-colored melancholy, I did commend the black oppressing humor to the most wholesome physic of thy health-giving air" (1.1.231–44), in a passage whose "ebon-coloured ink" summons not only "ebony" but the black "ink" identified with melancholy. The connection with the excremental here is observed by the play's latest Arden editor, who glosses its "black oppressing humor" through the "jakes" of "the melancholy Jaques."[44]

The blackness of "Melancholie, or blacke choler caused by adustion [or burning] of the blood" was itself associated with "soot."[45] Timothy Bright's *Treatise on Melancholy* (1586) describes the soul as "smothered with this soote of melancholie" (21.123), making "natural actions . . . weaker" (21.123). Melancholy "adust" was at the same time part of a developing lexicon of racial terms. Bright treats of the "soote of melancholie" in relation to the "complexion" of the melancholic, together with the "sootie and smokie excrementes, whereby the spirites become impure."[46] "Adust" connected the discourses of melancholia and racial darkness, signalling not only the tanning or scorching by the sun that turned the Ethiope black but a melancholic adustion or burning. The soot associated with Vulcan, blackness, and blackface as its cosmetic counterfeit, as well as with sin, was thus at the same time part of the humoral discourse of melancholia, already associated with blackness and Moors.

The emphasis on blackness in the early texts of *Hamlet* might also be expected from the association of a personified blackness or of Moors with tragedy, mourning, revenge, and death. The tragic stage was traditionally hung with black (the "sable garment" of Tourneur's *The Atheist's Tragedy*), assimiliating it to the blackness of night described in Marston's *The Insatiate Countess* ("The stage of heaven, is hung with solemn black, / A time best fitting to act tragedies"). "The stage is hung with black; and I perceive / The auditors prepared for tragedy," intones the Induction to Heywood's *A Warning for Fair Women*. Drayton's *Peirs Gaveston* invokes the "cole-black darknes" of "eternall night," and "black spirits" with "sable pens of direfull ebonie / To pen the process of my tragedie" (1–30).[47] Black was the color of tragedy and of revenge tragedy in particular. "Vengeance" is colored "black" in *Othello* ("Arise black vengeance, from thy hollow cell," a text that appears in the Folio as "hollow hell"). Racializing or personifying such figures of blackness was commonplace in the period. "Night" is personified as a "black-eyed Negro" in Daborne's *A Christian Turn'd Turk* (10:13–22) and as a "black Negro in an ebone Chair" in Mason's *The Turk* (2.2). Tragedy itself is given a Moorish or black face, in the "black-faced tragedy" of *Bussy D'Ambois* (4.1) and "black-visaged shows" of Marston's *Antonio's Revenge*, personified counterpart of "black tragedy" (5.3.177–78) and its "sullen tragic scene" (prologue, lines 7, 20).

Death—apostrophized in the Folio's "Oh proud death, / What feast is toward in thine eternall Cell. / That thou so many Princes, at a shoote, / So bloodily hast strooke" (267), by the Fortinbras (or Fortenbrasse) who looks upon the final "tragicke spectacle" (Q1, 266)—is similarly figured in the period as black or Moor. John Gillies has observed that on early modern maps "Africans seem to be interchangeable with skulls," an identification reflected in the "carrion Death" of the casket chosen by Morocco in *The Merchant of Venice* (2.7.63). In one of the many contemporary portraits that uses blackness as a contrasting foil for whiteness, a black attendant bears a *memento mori*, a *mori* whose Latin case ending simultaneously denotes "death" and "Moor." "Black" is the color of "Death" in *Tamburlaine* (1 *Tamb.*, 4.1.59–61), while in *Romeo and Juliet*, the conflation of Moors with Death or *Mors* is reflected in its description of "death" itself as a "black word" (3.3.27). In *Hamlet*, the king calls his "bosome" as "blacke as death."[48]

In these early texts, where Hamlet's own blackness suggests a *memento mori*, death is further embodied (and given a black name) in Q2's description of the mysterious "Lamord," in lines whose "Vpon my life Lamord" juxtapose "life" and death as the tragedy approaches its end. Described (in Q2 and F) as "incorps't" (in the combined senses of corpse, corporeal, and the Pauline "body of death" recalled elsewhere in Hamlet's "quintessence of dust"), this figure reminiscent of the horsemen of the Apocalypse or Doom bears in the Second Quarto a "French" name ("Lamord") that simultaneously evokes the homophones More/Moor and death or "Mort." The blackness associated with tragedy and revenge sounds within this mysterious Q2 name, enabling the compound resonances of "mordre," "murdre," and *remords* or remorse, embodying or incorpsing the multiple forms of blackness in this tragedy as it moves to the corpses of its final scene. Even the Folio text here (which prints "Lamound" instead of "Lamord") suggests the earth or "mound" heaped up as a sign of burial in the Gravediggers' scene, with the French "monde" or "globe" that provided a familiar *memento mori*.[49]

The Death that was traditionally "Antic" or fool as well as black—ruler of the black carnival of *danse macabre* and *memento mori*—recalls the carnival misrule associated elsewhere in these early *Hamlet* texts with the king of Denmark described by his nephew as both a "Moore" and a King of Misrule. It may also influence what all three texts call Hamlet's "Anticke disposition." "Anticke measures" are likened to "cole black moores" in Mason's *The Turke* (2.1), where the Moor Muleasses is termed a "hellish Anticke" (3.4). "If black, why Nature, drawing of an antic, / Made a foul blot," in *Much Ado* (3.1.63–64), connects that play's blotting and fouling with this "antic" figure. The "antic" identified with grotesque masks in *Romeo and Juliet* (1.5.55–57) and "antic" entertainment in *Loves Labours Lost* (5.1.112, 147) suggest the blackface familiar from mumming, morris dancing and other theatricals, as well as the "antic" masks of carnival inversion.[50]

*

if he doe not bleach, and change at that,
It is a damned ghost that we have seene.

—Q1

the Lady shall say her minde freely:
or the black verse shall hault for't.

—Q2

The lexicon of "black" and "white" (or their counterparts, *negro* and *blanco*) may even affect—at a micro level—some of the curious variants of these early *Hamlet* texts. In the soliloquy following the Player's speech, Hamlet determines (in a line that is close in Q2 and F): "Ile tent him to the quicke; If he but blench / I know my course."[51] The First Quarto has nothing corresponding at this point, but has Hamlet utter a similar intention just before the play scene itself, in lines that have the king not "blench" but "bleach":

> Marke thou the King, doe but obserue his lookes,
> For I mine eies will riuet to his face:
> And if he doe not bleach, and change at that,
> It is a damned ghost that we haue seene.
>
> (Q1, 136)

Harold Jenkins comments in the Arden *Hamlet* on the "blench" used in most modern texts: "*blench*] flinch. The word is related to *blink* but not to *blanch*, with which it is sometimes *confused*."[52] In the early modern environment of homophones and exchangeable spellings, "not" is a firmly boundary-setting term. But—given that "blench" itself was scarcely fixed in the single meaning of "swerve, flinch, or turn aside" but could substitute for blanching or bleaching, or that a "blancher" was one who flinched or turned aside as well as one who bleached or whitened—we need to find an approach different from the traditional assumption of simple error or mistake.

Even in Shakespeare, "blench" can suggest blanching or turning white. David Bevington's Arden 3 edition of *Troilus and Cressida* glosses "lesser blench at sufferance than I do" (1.1.28) not only as "flinch" or "quail" but as potentially "turn pale."[53] In *Macbeth* ("keep the natural ruby of your cheeks, / When mine is blanch'd with fear," 3.4.116), "blanch'd" suggests "whitened" or made pale but simultaneously gestures in the direction of "blench" as "shrink, start back, give way." The boundaries between "blench" and "blanch," in other words, were easily elided. The early textual variants here (F's "If he but blench," Q2's "if a doe blench," and Q1's "If he doe not bleach and change at that") may therefore call not so much for a commentary that assumes fixed borders between blench, blanch, and bleach as for an awareness of the ways in which such terms—like the "sullied flesh" that appears nowhere in any early text—function as homophonic ghost effects, in this case part of the language of whitening important to all three.

Bleaching, blenching, and blanching were part of the sexual as well as cosmetic and racialized discourses of whitening in the period. The reference in *Loves Labours Lost* to "maidens" who "bleach their summer smocks" (5.2.916)—in a play that already contrasts the "maculate" to the "immaculate" (1.2.90–92)—

invokes a washing of linens whose sexual inference is shared by Leontes's anxiety about what might "spot" or "sully" the "purity and whiteness" of his "sheets" (1.2.320 ff.), recalled by the "white sheet bleaching on the hedge" (4.3.5) in the song of Autolycus, whose "traffic" is in "sheets." Bleaching appears in suggestive relation to the blanching of sexual stains in Massinger's *City Madam* ("some chandler's daughters, / Bleaching linen in Moorfields," 4.4), in lines that summon the proverbially unblanchable blackness of Moors as well as the "moors." "Blanch" was employed for whitening in its multiple senses, including the counterpart in alchemy to "albification" (or "albation," from the *alba* or "white" that provides the name of Albion) and the familiar term for washing the Ethiope white, used for the English king's alleged power to "blanch an Ethiop" in Jonson's *Masque of Blackness*.[54]

"Bleaching" and "blanching" were simultaneously part of the contemporary cosmetic discourse of whitening, producing a "fair" complexion by disguising or covering over stains—one of the reasons, perhaps, for the choice of "Bianca" for the courtesan of *Othello*. Philemon Holland's translation of Pliny describes the white paint that "serveth to make an excellent blanch for women that desire a white complexion" and the "blanch of cerusse" (or white lead) used to create the heightened cosmetic effect of whiteness.[55] Lucretia calls for "blanching water" to whiten her face before applying the cosmetic "tincture" or "tinct" provided by her lover—in a play where the name of "Motticilla" suggests the covering of maculate "spots."[56] "Blanching" a harlot's cheek connects dyeing, laundering, and bleaching—including the stain to "honesty" reflected in *Merry Wives* (4.2.126) on "clothes" sent forth to "bleaching"—with cosmetic whitening. "Bleaching" house was a contemporary synonym for "brothel," not only because of the identification with stains but because "dying and bleaching houses were situated along the Thames at Bankside, amongst the brothels,"[57] making bleaching, blanching, and blenching part of the antithetical rhetoric conveyed by "nunnery" in relation to this purifying. In *King John*—another Shakespearean play preoccupied with the stain of the adulterate—the name "Blanche" is iterated so frequently, in lines that underscore the link with "fair" and "pure," that it suggests the importance of being "Blanche" (or "white") in all senses.[58] The variants "If he but blench" and "If he doe not bleach" may therefore be part of this extended network of significations, within and beyond these early *Hamlet* texts.

Like "blanch," English "blank" was also part of the racialized lexicon of color, in which Spanish *blanco* or white (counterpart of Italian *bianco* or *bianca* and French *blanc*) figured the opposite of *negro* or black. Florio's *Worlde of Wordes* defines *bianca* in one of its senses as "a blanke," *bianche* as "blanks," *bianco* as "white, pale, blanke, wan" as well as "a blanke." Cotgrave translates French *blanc* as "A blanke, white, whitenesse, or white thing; the white, or marke of a paire of buts; a blanke of paper; a blanke in a lotterie; also, whitelime, or whiting for walls," the double-meaning "lime" evoked for the "birdlime" of Iago, the white devil of *Othello*, the "white-limed walls" of *Titus Andronicus*, and the "limed soul" of the king of Denmark later called a "Moore."[59]

We might, then, revisit the lines of *Hamlet* in which "blank verse" appears instead as "black verse." Greeting the newly-arrived players, Hamlet delivers the line familiar from the Folio: "the Lady shall say her minde freely; or the blanke Verse shall halt for't." In the Second Quarto, however, this "verse" is not "blank" but "black": "the Lady shall say her minde freely: or the *black* verse shall hault for't" (my emphasis). The difference in Q2 may be explained by the mistaking of "n" for "c" in secretary hand or as a manuscript ~ ("blǎck" for "blanck") ignored by a compositor.[60] "Blank," however, elsewhere in these early texts of *Hamlet*, is used explicitly in the sense of blanching or whitening. Both the Folio and the Second Quarto contain, for example, the speech of the Player Queen (in the Folio speech prefix "Baptista") in which she protests "Each opposite that blanks the face of ioy" (Q2, 146), a "blanks" that here "blanches" or "makes pale" a personified "face."[61] As an explanation for "black verse," a compositorial or other error is certainly possible, but there may also be other possibilities that are worth considering, rather than foreclosing the matter from the outset by declaring Q2's "black" to be a simple mistake.

"Blank" in early modern English had its own connections with cosmetic whitening. But even in the more familiar modern sense of empty or void, "blank" could denote a sexualized or racialized whiteness—as in the description of Desdemona as a fair "paper" to be written upon or the letters Falstaff writes to the wives of *Merry Wives*, described as "writ with blancke-space for different names," in preparation for an adulterous writing.[62] In the one other place in the early texts of *Hamlet* where *blank* appears—the king's "As leuell as the Cannon to his blanck, / Transports his poysened shot"

(Q2)—"blank" suggests (as in *Othello*) the "white" of a target that can be "blackened" or "hit."[63]

"Blank" is hence another of the early modern English terms suggesting pallor or whiteness. If we return, then, to the Folio's "the Lady shall say her minde freely; or the blanke Verse shall halt for't" and the Second Quarto's "The Lady shall say her minde freely: or the black verse shall hault for it" (a "hault" that is routinely glossed as "limp"), the alternation of "black" verse for "blank" verse might be approached as itself caught within the network and (reversible) polarity of "black" and "white" that pervades these early texts. Coming from the variants of the closet scene, which evoke a blackened "Vulcan" as well as "Moore," I find myself unable to read the Second Quarto's "The black verse shall hault for't"—with its personification of a halting or limping as well as a "black" body—without thinking once again of the blackened and limping Vulcan.

The situation becomes even more complex when we consider that early modern English "black" and "blank" were not only polarities—like "white" and "black"—but synonyms, capable of turning "tropically" into one another, in a linguistic environment that includes the early Quarto text of Shakespeare's Sonnet 77, whose "waste blacks" editors routinely emend to "waste blanks." In the Quarto of Sonnet 77, "waste" is combined with "blacks" (and with the *memento mori* of "how thy present minutes waste")—as in the "wast [instead of 'vast'] . . . middle of the night" (in the opening scene of *Hamlet*), or the waste or wasteland evoked by "batten on this Moore." Here again, we may have "moors" of different kinds—a "waste" that can be simultaneously empty or "blank" and "black," conflated with "waste" in this and other senses.[64] The tendency of such terms to turn into their apparent opposites might be demonstrated by "blankless," a contemporary term that could mean without "spot" or "blot," as if "blank" (or "white" in one of its senses) could simultaneously (through its meaning of target, perhaps) designate what blotted it.[65] Even "bleach" could be used in the sense of "blacken" as well as blanch or make "white," serving as a synonym for the "bleakness" of moors.[66]

*

as a beautifull body is never more louely then when she is
placed neer a Black-More, . . .
the Gem receives luster from the foile.

—Alexander Ross, *Alcoran* (1649)

I need no foile, nor shall I think me white only between two
Moores.
                                   —Jasper Mayne, *The City Match* (1639)

The King shall drinke to *Hamlets* better breath,
And in the cup an Onixe shall he throwe.
                                   —Second Quarto of *Hamlet*

From these multiple contexts for blackness and whiteness, we
might now return to the contrasting portraits of "faire" and
"Moore" with which we began. Kim F. Hall has described the ways
in which such portraits contributed to the articulation of racial and
class distinctions, in a period in which whiteness itself was defined
through the differentiating blackness of the Moor. Roy Strong, Patricia Fumerton, and others have related the vogue for such representations to the increased supply of ivory, ebony, and other
materials that enabled striking visual contrasts or foils.[67] The distinguishing "foil" (from *foglio* or *feuille*) is directly evoked within
these early texts of *Hamlet*, in ways that connect the material creation of racial and other contrasts to the figure of opposition made
explicit in the final duelling scene. Hamlet's "I'll be your foil
Laertes; in mine ignorance / Your skill shall like a star i' th' darkest
night / Stick fiery off indeed" (5.2.255–257), when he asks for the
"foils" that are to distinguish between them in another sense,
comes directly from this contemporary material discourse, as *Richard II* makes clear in "A foil wherein thou art to set / The precious
jewell of thy home return" (1.3.266). Within the early texts of *Hamlet*, "foil" joins the description of Ophelia as "metal more attractive" or of Lamord as "the brooch indeed / And gem of all the
nation."[68]
     The epigraphs to this section employ this term central both to the
early texts of *Hamlet* and to the contemporary visual representation
of differentiation or distinction.[69] "Miniature jewels and portraits"
(like "pendants and brooches") circulated, as Hall observes, "as ra-
cially coded signifiers of aristocratic identity in the late sixteenth
century." The 1576 inventory of English goldsmith John Mabbe includes "a brouche of gold like a Mores-head, the ground being
Mother of pearl . . . a broache with a very fair Agott like a Blacka-
more enamelled all white about the said agott . . . a jewell with an
Agott having a woman cut on it like a More." The famous Gresley
jewel features the cameo of a female Moor, whose black skin contrasts with the miniature portraits of the English aristocrats it en-

closes.[70] The cameo given by Elizabeth to Sir Francis Drake superimposes the profile of a black Moor on that of a white woman, in ways that not only provide a contrasting "foil" but evoke, as Hall suggests, the specter of racial mixture, adulteration, or mingling. The "vnion" or pearl of the Folio's duelling scene—the kind of white "pearl" frequently pictured, as a visual contrast, in the ear of a female Moor in the period—is itself (as Jenkins and other editors point out) an explicit recall of a famous story about Antony and Cleopatra, a union that foregrounded an adulterate (as well as adulterous) mixture, of Roman Antony with his Egyptian queen.[71]

The vogue for black cameos in European courts was enabled by the "increased supply of black onyx" described by Strong and Fumerton.[72] In this regard—given the opposed "faire" and "Moore" of Hamlet's contrasting pictures—the other all but effaced variant we might revisit is the mysterious onyx that appears in the Second Quarto, where the other two texts have "vnion" or pearl. Following "Ile be your foile," the Q2 text has "The King shall drinke to *Hamlets* better breath, / And in the cup an Onixe shall he throwe," an onyx that reappears in Hamlet's "Drinke of this potion, is the Onixe heere?" instead of the familiar Folio "Drink off this Potion: Is thy Vnion heere?"[73] This "Onixe" is virtually effaced from conflated editions, as well as from *Hamlet* criticism. But as the material whose layering or mixture of white and black provided a contemporary basis for racialized contrasts or "foils," its appearance in the Second Quarto may warrant more serious attention than it has received.

Hamlet's "counterfeit presentment of two brothers" has frequently been assumed to involve miniature portraits, part of the vogue for "limning" already suggestive of the intimate private space or "Closet" of a queen.[74] That Hamlet's contrasting portraits may be such miniatures is suggested by his remark elsewhere that "my uncle is King of Denmark, and those that would make mows at him while my father lived, give twenty, forty, fifty, a hundred ducats a-piece for his picture in little" (2.2.363–66).[75] Miniature portraits were frequently used to contrast white and black, fair and Moor. Miniaturists kept "a stock of cards ready grounded for fair or dark complexions," while the vogue for "limning" reflected the new variety of pigments from "Inde or Afrike."[76]

In *The Merchant of Venice*, the Death's head associated with Africa and Moors, in the casket chosen by the Prince of Morocco, provides both a disappointing contrast and a foil for "fair" Portia's picture. Even more strikingly, such contrasts are directly evoked in the play that most clearly recalls Hamlet's portraits of two husbands—*Two Noble Kinsmen*, where Emilia enters (in the Quarto stage direction) "with 2. Pictures" usually assumed to be "miniatures, such as were often exchanged by lovers," comparing the portraits of Arcite and Palamon, the lovers between whom she must choose.[77] In lines that closely resemble Hamlet's opposition, Emilia contrasts the picture of Arcite (whose "Pelops" shoulder recalls the "ivory" or "white" of that Ovidian story) with Palamon's "swart" or dark "complexion" ("Palamon / Is but his foil; to him, a mere dull shadow; / He's swart and meagre, of an eye as heavy / As if he had lost his mother," 4.2.25–28). In lines whose praise of the ivory-white Arcite ("What a brow, / Of what a spacious majesty," 4.2.18–19) echo Hamlet's "See what a grace was seated on this brow," Emilia confesses a Gertrude-like weakness for the darker of the two. But the scene simultaneously suggests (as Lois Potter comments) that "the two men are meant to be indistinguishable."[78] Arcite is elsewhere called a "gypsy" (4.2.44), the "black-haired man" he is characterized as earlier in the play (3.3.31). Emilia ends her own comparison of these two pictures with "What a mere child is Fancy, / That, having two fair gauds of equal sweetness, / Cannot distinguish, but must cry for both" (4.2.52–54).

*

So you mistake your husbands.

(Q2)

Marry how? Tropically.

(F)

I quote this strikingly parallel passage on "2 Pictures," not only because it underscores the contrast of "faire" and "Moore" in the closet scene by its recall but because it presents the contrast itself as a *rhetoric* of distinction, the construction of polarity and difference where none may exist. The passage closest to Hamlet's "counterfeit presentment of two brothers" thus invokes the "foil" used to set off "fair" from "swart" and simultaneously draws attention to their indistinguishability. In the closet scene itself, Hamlet's contrast of "faire" and "Moore" is immediately followed in Q2 and F by "Haue you eyes?," a question posed to a mother who has mistaken husbands, in all of the senses these texts exploit. The Second Quarto adds lines that call even further attention to what might "serue in such a difference" (168). "How should I your true love know from another one?" (Q2 and F: "How should I your true loue know / From another man?," Q1)—the opening of the mad scene of Ophelia in all three texts—adds the problem of telling counterfeit from true, in texts filled with counterfeit presentments of all kinds.[79]

The early texts of *Hamlet* repeatedly construct such oppositions—of white and black, heaven and hell, angel and devil—and simultaneously undo these polarities. The "night" made "joint laborer" with the "day" (in all three texts) and the emphasis on poisoned unions or oxy-morons complicate or confound the Manichean rhetoric of "night" and "Day," blending even mighty opposites into one another.[80] "Black" Hamlet and the king called a "Moore" converge in the murderer Lucianus and the "Black" Pyrrhus of the Player's speech (*TTH*, 108–11). The "Cyclops hammers" of this "hellish *Pyrrhus*" anticipate not only Hamlet's presentation of his uncle as a hellish "Vulcan" but Hamlet's own "imaginations," described as "foule / As *Vulcans* stithy" (Q2, 136). "Old Mole," applied to the Ghost (in the lines that assimilate him, as Jenkins observes, to the "foul collier" associated with the devil), recalls in Q2 the "vicious mole of nature" from the description of the present king, connecting the fathers and husbands Hamlet seeks to distinguish, even as they are joined within the closet scene itself, in the "King of shreds and patches" capable of reference to both at once.[81] Even Hamlet's "Anticke disposition" participates in this inversion of polarities, suggesting the carnival reversal shared by the king he calls a "Moore" and a king of Misrule.

The Ghost (with characteristic modesty) compares himself to a "radiant Angell" (Q2, "radiant Angle"), casting the "adulterate Beast" who won the "will" of his most virtuous-seeming queen as a contrasting devil. But angel and devil in these texts are not only reversible but indistinguishable. The lines themselves invoke the figure of the devil disguised as an angel of light (or "shape of heauen"), the Luciferic counterfeit or double recalled in Hamlet's soliloquy on the devil's power to "assume a pleasing shape" (Q2/F).[82] Hamlet's "counterfeit" representations (in the double sense of constructed or made and forged) summon the racialized counterpart of what has been called the "passion for differences," in the midst of the collapse of distinction itself.[83] The polarized rhetoric that Abdul JanMohamed has identified with the Manichean contrasts of a later imperial history is here confounded, in a crisis of undifferentiation in which opposites turn into one another, in the very mixture, mingling, or "union" Hamlet seeks to prevent.

Hamlet's contrasting portraits of "faire" and "Moore" are part of a scene that goes out of its way to call attention to empires and imperial histories. Jenkins notes an echo of Mercury's descent to Roman Aeneas in African Carthage, in the "herald Mercury" of the lines that introduce these portraits, evoking in the closet of the maculate or "spotted" Danish queen the figure of Dido, called in an influential contemporary translation "A Moore among the Moores."[84] The echo joins the unmistakable allusion to Cleopatra and Antony in the poisoned "union" of the final scene, routinely cited by editors but not yet an integral part of our apprehension of this play, though such allusions are familiar from other Shakespeare plays in which Moors or imperial conflicts prominently appear.

The continuing influence of Romantic or psychologizing conceptions of *Hamlet* may still obscure the importance of empire within it—though it is repeatedly and variously underscored in these early texts, not just in "Imperiall Ioyntresse" or "Cutpurse of the Empire and the Rule," in the names of Horatio and Marcellus, or the invocation of Alexander, Brutus, Caesar, and Nero, whose relation with his mother and stepfather Claudius is recalled at the threshold of the closet scene, but in their allusions to more contemporary struggles: Norway, Denmark, England, and the Poland reflected in the "Polonius" of Q2 and F; reminders of the "Turke" not just in the lines that survive into modern editions ("if the rest of my Fortunes turne Turke") but in usually effaced lines from Q1 (on "Christian, Pagan, / Nor Turke"); evocations of contemporary piracy (a notorious part of imperial rivalry) in Q2 and F; and of the Diet of Worms (Q2/F, 182–85), which was preoccupied not just with the Lutheran schism routinely cited for these lines but with the threat from the Ottoman Turk, or Moor.[85]

One of the original contexts for the present study was a conference devoted to "Dislocating Shakespeare."[86] *Hamlet* itself has been dislocated in recent years—by its transportation to a South African setting in the debate over Wulf Sachs's *Black Hamlet* (1937) and by work on its first recorded performance in 1607–8, aboard an East India Company ship off the coast of Sierra Leone.[87] Readers who turn from the familiar conflated *Hamlet* to its earliest texts may find that experience dislocating in another sense, estranging a play we thought we knew. What awaits are not only the variants foregrounded in the last decade of "unediting" (radically changing even "To be or not to be") but other striking differences, including not only the "Moore" or blackened "Vulcan" of the closet scene but *"guyana"* rather than Vienna as the location of the Mousetrap murder in Q1, the quarto published in the same year as the trial of Raleigh, whose "Discoverie" of "Guiana" had already been invoked in *Merry Wives*.[88]

Hamlet's opposition of "faire" and "Moore" iterates the polarizations of its culture, foregrounding its material "foils," in a context in which empire itself is ironized, its triumphant *Veni, Vidi, Vici* replayed in the cadences of the Gravediggers' scene: *"Alexander* died: *Alexander* was buried: *Alexander* returneth into dust," stopping a "Beere-barrell" as "Imperious" or "Imperiall *Caesar*" is "turn'd to clay."[89] Returning to these early texts enables us to reexamine what has been lost in the conflation. It may also enable us to read them against the rhetoric of their time.

Notes

1. The Second Quarto (Q2) here is cited from *The Three-Text Hamlet: Parallel Texts of the First and Second Quartos and First Folio*, ed. Paul Bertram and Bernice W. Kliman (New York: AMS Press, 1991), 166, 168 (hereafter *TTH*), the source of page references to Q1, Q2, and F in notes and text . Unless otherwise noted, all other Shakespeare citations are to *The Riverside Shakespeare*, ed. G. Blakemore Evans (Boston: Houghton Mifflin, 1974). This essay had its origins in talks delivered at a Folger Shakespeare Institute session on "Shakespeare and the Designs of Empire" directed by Michael Neill in 1993 and at the University of Pennsylvania in 1994. I am grateful to readers and audiences who responded to subsequent versions delivered at the 1998 School of Criticism and Theory, and in 1999–2000 at the London Renaissance Seminar, the University of Alabama, Oxford, and other universities in Britain, Australia, New Zealand, Canada, and Spain, and the "Dislocating Shakespeare" conference organized by Michael Neill and others at Auckland. I am also indebted to Bruce Boehrer, Michael Bristol, Karen Cunningham, Peter Donaldson, Catherine Gallagher, Jonathan Gil Harris, Sujata Iyengar, Evelyn Fox Keller, Bernice W. Kliman, François Laroque, Ania Loomba, Randall McLeod, Gail Kern Paster, Lois Potter, Shankar Raman, Virginia Mason Vaughan, Daniel Vitkus, Paul Yachnin, and others who provided insightful comments on its earlier versions.

2. For "moors" of both kinds in the iconography of Thomas More or "Moore" (whose Latin name *Morus* meant "black" as well as "fool"), see J. B. Trapp's expo-

sition in *Ephialte* 2 (1990): 45–49, with Germain Marc'hadour, "A Name for All Seasons," *Essential Articles for the Study of Thomas More,* ed. R. S. Sylvester and G. P. Marc'hadour (Hamden, CT: Archon Books, 1977).

3. John Dover Wilson, ed., *Hamlet* (1934; 2d ed. 1936; rpt., Cambridge: Cambridge University Press, 1961), 85, 213. Subsequent editions vary as to whether they note the double-meaning "moor." Harold Jenkins's Arden 2 edition (London: Methuen, 1982), 322, notes that "a play on blackamoor" (suggested by the contrast with a "fair" mountain) "may be what prompts Q1 'With a face like Vulcan.'" Philip Edwards's New Cambridge edition (Cambridge University Press, 1985), 177, notes the suggested "undertone of 'blackamoor' in 'moor'"; Everyman *Hamlet,* ed. John F. Andrews (London: Dent, 1989), notes "moor" as both barren "wasteland" and "wet marshland" and the "pun on Blackamoor"; *The Norton Shakespeare* (New York: W. W. Norton & Co., 1997), 1721, glosses "batten on this moor" as "glut yourself on this poor pastureland (possibly punning on 'blackamoor')." G. R. Hibbard's edition (Oxford: Oxford University Press, 1987), David Bevington's *Complete Works of Shakespeare* (London: Scott, Foresman and Company, 1980), Stanley Wells and Gary Taylor's *William Shakespeare: A Textual Companion* (Oxford: Clarendon Press, 1987), the Riverside edition, and the new Pelican *Tragical History of Hamlet Prince of Denmark,* ed. A. R. Braunmuller (New York: Penguin Books, 2001) do not note the double-meaning "Moore."

4. On "dull Moor," see Michael Neill, *Issues of Death: Mortality and Identity in English Renaissance Tragedy* (Oxford: The Clarendon Press, 1997), 148; Marc'-hadour, "Name," 544–54, on "Moor" and "moron" in Latin *morus* and oxy-moron as "sharp dull."

5. See Ulipian Fulwell's *Like Will to Like, quote the Devil to the Collier* (1568), cited in the Arden 2 edition of *Twelfth Night,* ed. J. M. Lothian and T. W. Craik (London: Methuen, 1975), 99–100; and "smirched complexion" of the "Prince of Fiends" in *Henry V* (3.3.15–18).

6. On this racializing, see the important comments in Kim F. Hall, *Things of Darkness: Economies of Race and Gender in Early Modern England* (Ithaca: Cornell University Press, 1995), 259–60, with Sander L. Gilman, *Difference and Pathology* (Ithaca: Cornell University Press, 1985), 30–31; and Winthrop D. Jordan, *White Over Black* (Chapel Hill: University of North Carolina Press, 1968), 15, 17, 248–49, 518–21.

7. See Thomas Dekker, *The Welsh Embassador,* 4:386. On soot, coal and other forms of face darkening, see Eldred Jones, *Othello's Countrymen* (Oxford: Oxford University Press, 1965), esp. 66–68, 122; Antony Gerard Barthelemy, *Black Face, Maligned Race* (Baton Rouge: Louisiana State University Press, 1987); Hall, *Darkness,* 87–89, 116–17, 130–31, 179; Jack D'Amico, *The Moor in English Renaissance Drama* (Tampa: University of South Florida Press, 1991), esp. 53–58; Annette Drew-Bear, *Painted Faces on the Renaissance Stage* (Lewisburg: Bucknell University Press, 1994), esp. 32–34; William Carleton on the "Troop of lean-cheek'd Moors" in Jonson's *The Masque of Blackness,* cited in *Ben Jonson: The Complete Masques, 1572–1637,* ed. Stephen Orgel (New Haven: Yale University Press, 1969), 4; François Laroque, *Shakespeare's Festive World,* trans. Janet Lloyd (Cambridge: Cambridge University Press, 1991), esp. 289–302.

8. See Janet Adelman, "Iago's Alter Ego: Race as Projection in *Othello,*" *Shakespeare Quarterly* 48, no. 2 (summer 1997), 125–44, 143, on *Othello*'s "col-

lied"; *MND*, 1.1.145 ("collied night"); *Loves Labours Lost*, 4.3.263 ("colliers counted bright"); *Romeo and Juliet*, 1.1.2; *Twelfth Night*, 3.4.117; and *Othello*, 3.3.387.

9. Michael D. Bristol, "Charivari and the Comedy of Abjection in *Othello*," *Renaissance Drama*, n.s., 21 (1990): 3–21, esp. 10.

10. *TTH*, 58–59. On the Fall in relation to *Hamlet*, see Janet Adelman, *Suffocating Mothers* (New York: Routledge, 1992), chapter 2. On its combination of decline and fall with grammatical declension (characterized elsewhere as a denigration or blackening), see my *Shakespeare from the Margins* (Chicago: Chicago University Press, 1996), 179–80.

11. See *TTH*, 28–29, 58–59, 108–111, 148–49, 156–57, 226–27; *nero* in John Florio, *A Worlde of Wordes* (1598). Jenkins's Long Note (456) on the Folio's "iuyce of cursed Hebenon" points out that "The word is the same as *ebony* (L. *ebenus* or *hebenus . . .* which the Elizabethans often spelt *(h)eben(e)* as well as *ebon*." I am very grateful to Bernice W. Kliman for sharing with me the accumulated variorum debate concerning F's "Hebenon," Q2's "iuyce of cursed Hebona" (58), Q1's "iuyce of Hebona" (58), the poisonous "juice of hebon" from *The Jew of Malta* (3.4.98), and Cotgrave's "*Hebene*: m. Heben, or Ebonie; the blacke, and hard wood of a certaine tree growing in AEthyopia, and the East Indies." Even when arguing the inappropriateness of poison to "ebony," Nicholson's 1882 edition (for example) cites the appearance of "heben" in Spenser's *Faerie Queene* (including the "Heben sad" of Mammon's garden, in a description that starts with "direfull deadly black").

12. See *TTH*, 138–39; Jenkins, 501 and Edwards, 158 on morris dance allusions in *Hamlet* and the "hobby-horse" of *Othello*, 4.1.154; Wendy Wall, "Reading for the Blot: Textual Desire in Early Modern English Literature," in *Reading and Writing in Shakespeare*, ed. David M. Bergeron (Newark: University of Delaware Press, 1996), 131–59, esp. 138–39 on inky blots and stains in *Much Ado*. The resonances of "Nothing" both in Q2 and F *Hamlet* and in *Much Ado about Nothing* (whose homophone "Noting" includes blotting or staining as well as observing) may include not only the already well-known "O" and "naught/nought" but *Nothus* as a term for bastard (or the son of an adulteress) in the period. In *Illegimate Power: Bastards in Renaissance Drama* (Manchester and New York: Manchester University Press, 1994), 20–25, Alison Findlay cites William Clerke's *Triall of Bastardie* (1594, EIv) on *spurius* as the Latin for the son of a concubine and *nothus* for the son of an adulteress. Thomas Laqueur, in *Making Sex* (Cambridge: Harvard University Press, 1990), 56, cites Isidore's argument that bastards are called *spurius* because they "spring from the mother alone" and the ancients "called the female genitalia the *spurium*." Laqueur (56) also cites Plutarch's report that "the adjective *spurius* derived from a Sabine word for the female genitalia and was applied to illegitimate children as a form of abuse." Latin "Nothus" is cited for "bastard" in John Minsheu's *Ductor in Linguas, or Guide unto the Tongues* (London, 1617) and in the "Nothus" (or "Bastard") emblem (of Hercules) in Alciati's widely-disseminated *Emblemata*. In Thomas Thomas, *Dictionarium Linguae Latinae et Anglicanae* (1587) (Menston, Eng.: The Scolar Press, 1972), "Nothus" is defined as "Base borne, or bastard, not lawful, counterfeit."

13. See respectively *TTH*, 168–69; *Othello*, 4.2.71; *Antonio's Revenge*, 1.2 (sig. Bv).

14. Weasel, mole, and mouse are cited together in Leviticus 11:29–30 as "vn-cleane" beasts (Geneva, 1560). See Mary Douglas, *Purity and Danger* (London: Routledge & Kegan Paul, 1979); Julia Kristeva, *Powers of Horror: An Essay on Abjection* trans. L. S. Roudiez (New York: Columbia University Press, 1982), 12, 105–31; "mouse" and "weasel" in Gordon Williams, *A Dictionary of Sexual Language and Imagery in Shakespearean and Stuart Literature* (London: Athlone Press, 1994), 2:916–18 and 3:1509; and *Omnia Andreae Alciati V. C. Emblemata cum commentarius . . . per Clavdium Minoem* (Antwerp, 1577), 293–94. On the combination of "swart," "in grain," "grime" and echoes of the black bride of the Song of Songs with a baptismal "Noah's flood" in *CE*, 3.2.101–18, see Parker, *Shakespeare from the Margins*, 65–68.

15. For the spotted "leopard," see *Richard II* (1.1.173–76); on Jeremiah 13:23 ("Can the black Moor change his skin? or the leopard his spots." Geneva Bible) and the proverb "To Wash an Ethiope White," see Geoffrey Whitney, *A Choice of Emblemes* (1586) ["Aethiopem Lavare"]; Karen Newman, *Fashioning Femininity and English Renaissance Drama* (Chicago: Chicago University Press, 1991), chap. 5; and Hall, *Darkness*, 107–15. On the birth of Christ (evoked in all three texts)—from an immaculate Virgin Mother—contrasted with Denmark's Eve-like Queen, on "waste/waist," and adulterous/adulterate mixtures, see Adelman, *Mothers*, chap. 2.

16. Folio; similar in Q2 (162). Q1 has "trip him" that "his heeles may kick at heauen, / And fall as lowe as hel." Hamlet's speech in the Folio text of the prayer scene (2354 in the "Through Line Numbers" established by Charlton Hinman in *The Norton Facsimile: The First Folio of Shakespeare* (W. W. Norton & Co., 1968), has "A Villaine killes my Father, and for that / I his foule Sonne, do this same Villaine send / To heauen," where Q2 has "sole sonne." On Baptista, see *A New Variorum Edition of Shakespeare: Hamlet*, ed. Horace Howard Furness (New York: Dover Publications, 1963), 1:255.

17. See Drew-Bear, *Faces*, 64, with *TTH*, 160–61; Jenkins, ed., 314–15, on bird-lime, limed soul, and echoes of Psalm 51:7 and Isaiah 1:18 in "white as snow."

18. See Neill, *Issues*, 145–46, who discusses the leopard's spots as sign of its adulterate nature, from "the adultery of a lioness with a pard." On the "adulterate" disobedience of Ham, see also Benjamin Braude, "The Sons of Noah and the Construction of Ethnic and Geographical Identities in the Medieval and Early Modern Periods," in *William and Mary Quarterly* 54 (1997): 103–42; Jordan, *White Over Black*, esp. 15, 17–20, 35–39, 41–42; Joseph R. Washington Jr., *Anti-Blackness in English Religion, 1500–1800* (New York: The Edward Mellen Press, 1984), 6–21; Newman, *Femininity*, 79–80, 161; John Gillies, *Shakespeare and the Geography of Difference* (Cambridge: Cambridge University Press, 1994), 18–19, 25, and 172–73.

19. Tubalcain is associated with the blacksmith in the biblical genealogies in which he appears. On the conflation of Cain with Canaan/Ham, see Ruth Mellinkoff, *Outcasts* (Berkeley: University of Califonia Press, 1993); and *The Mark of Cain* (Berkeley: University of California Press, 1981); John Black Friedman, *The Monstrous Races in Medieval Art and Thought* (Cambridge: Harvard University Press, 1981); and Washington Jr., *Anti-Blackness*, 465, 470.

20. On the tropical location as well as troping/trapping evoked by the Mouse-trap, see Graham Holderness and Bryan Loughrey, eds., *The Tragicall Historie of*

Hamlet Prince of Denmarke (London: Harvester, 1992), 75, 122. On Ham, see Peter Fryer, *Staying Power: The History of Black People in Britain* (London: Pluto Press, 1984), 143.

21. On Tubalcain, Tubal, and Spain, see Richard Lynche, *An Historical Treatise of the Travels of Noah into Europe: Containing the first inhabitation and peopling thereof* (London, 1601), e.g., sigs. Giv and Hiiiv. A brilliant paper by Janet Adelman on *The Merchant of Venice* (delivered in Auckland in July 2002) examines these connections.

22. Q2 (28): "I am too much in the sonne"; F (20): "I am too much i' th' Sun." See Song of Songs, 1:4–5; *Antony and Cleopatra* (1.5.27–28); *The Merchant of Venice* (2.1.1–17); Jordan, *White Over Black*, 11–15; Hall, *Darkness*, 66–69, 92–107, 110; Washington, *Anti-Blackness*, 70–101; James Walvin, *The Black Presence: A Documentary History of the Negro in England, 1555–1860* (New York: Schocken, 1972), 32–47.

23. "Let her not walke i' th' Sunne" here is cited from Folio, but virtually identical in Q2 (92–93). This later exchange relies on the contemporary sense of "tanning" as a sexual blackening, sullying, or staining, exploited in Thomas Kyd's *The Tragedye of Solyman and Perseda* (1.4.13–14), ed. John J. Murray (New York: Garland Publishing, Inc., 1991), 22, where "fair" is used in its doubled sense of "white": "Faire Ladies should be coye to showe their faces, / Least that the sun should tan them with his beames."

24. Cited from Q2 (82); virtually identical in Folio (83). Q1's Corambis says "I haue a daughter, / Haue while shee's mone; for that we thinke / Is surest, we often loose" (82). Q2 and F (86–87) also have Polonius promise to "loose" his daughter to the prince.

25. F (97) is virtually identical. The variations on the names of "Rosencrantz" and "Guildenstern" suggest (among other possibilities) the association of "colors" and "craft."

26. See Q2 and F (48–49), with Shirley Nelson Garner, " 'Let Her Paint an Inch Thick': Painted Ladies in Renaissance Drama and Society," *Renaissance Drama*, n.s., 20 (1989): 123–39; Frances E. Dolan, "Taking the Pencil Out of God's Hand: Art, Nature, and the Face-Painting Debate in Early Modern England," *PMLA* 108 (1993): 224–39.

27. Jenkins notes (322) the animal metaphors here ("directly or indirectly, from Belleforest and ultimately from Saxo"); Edwards (177) suggests animals' (difficult) feeding on barren moorlands. For "wholsom breath" (F),"wholsome brother" (Q2), see 166–67.

28. See Robert K. Turner Jr., ed. *The Fair Maid of the West Parts I and II* (Lincoln: University of Nebraska Press, 1967), 87, who glosses Heywood's "Moorian" in part I (5.2.80–81) as "a play on 'murrain',," "murrion," or "plague"; and the "monstrous murrian black-a-moore" of Anthony Munday's *John a Kent and John a Cumber* (1.1), with the note on "Murrian" and "morian, or moorish" in J. Payne Collier's edition (London: Shakespeare Society, 1851). "Murrion" (itself connected with spotting) could be used for any blight or pestilence, including with reference to the biblical texts cited by *Hamlet* editors here (Genesis 41:5–7, 22–4; 1 Kings 8:37; Amos 4:9; and Haggai 2:17). Infection is part of the complex metaphorics of tainting in other contemporary contexts. See Jonathan Gil Harris, " 'With Spanish Gold, you all infected are': Taint and Transnational Usury in *The*

Merchant of Venice," in his forthcoming *Etiologies of the Economy: Dramas of Mercantilism and Disease in Shakespeare's England.*

29. In relation to the soiling or blackening of Ophelia's whiteness by exposure to Denmark's Sun/Son, it is important to note that puns on "Sol" (Latin "sun") and "soil" are already part of the story of the origin of blackness—in Ovid's account of the Chariot of the Sun driven by the son of Hyperion or Apollo, scorching the originally white Ethiope, classical counterpart of the sunburnt bride of the Song of Songs. See Frederick Ahl, *Metaformations: Soundplay and Wordplay in Ovid and Other Classical Poets* (Ithaca: Cornell University Press, 1985), 55–56, 169–91, 180–81. For the variants above, see *TTH*, 32–33, 43–44, 70–71, 198–99.

30. See *TTH*, 42–43, 50, 66–67, 234–35, 248–49; Laertes on Ophelia's "faire and vnpolluted flesh" (Q2, 238) and "hold off the earth awhile" (Q2, 238); Jenkins, 457–58 on "Old Mole" and "foul collier," with Margreta De Grazia, "Teleology, Delay, and the 'Old Mole,'" *Shakespeare Quarterly* 50, no. 3 (fall 1999): 251–67. For "mole" as stain or blot, see *MND*, 5.1.409–11, *Cymbeline*, 2.5.135–40.

31. See *TTH*, 72–73; John Minsheu, *Ductor in Linguas* (London, 1617), under "Soile or Land . . . L. Solum, quia solidum . . . Vi. fundament. Vide etiam Ground"; John Florio, *A Worlde of Wordes* (1598), *Salare, Salato, Sale, Saletta* ; Randall Cotgrave, *A Dictionarie of the French and English Tongues* (1611; Menston, Eng.: The Scolar Press, 1968), under *Sale, Salir.*

32. *TTH*, 234–35. Exploitation of the multiple senses of "ground" include "grounds/More Relatiue than this" (F, 119; Q2, 118: "grounds / More relatiue then this").

33. See *TTH*, 114–15; *1H4*, 1.2.78; "muddied . . . smell" in *All's Well*, 5.2.4. Jenkins, 270, links "dull and muddy-mettled rascal" to the "dull" of his 1.5.32. In the Folio, the king called a "Moore" appears in this same scene as "blunt" (synonym of "dull") rather than "bloat [or 'blowt'] King" of Q2 (174–75). For conflations of mud, excrement, waste, fens, moors, and Moors, see Edward H. Sugden, *A Topographical Dictionary to the Works of Shakespeare and His Fellow Dramatists* (Manchester: Manchester University Press, 1925), under "Moorditch," "Moorfields," and "Moorgate." On Ophelia's "muddy" death, see *TTH*, 222–23, with *OED*, s.v. "muddy" ("Morally impure or 'dirty'"), below, and Parker, *Shakespeare from the Margins*, 255–56. I am grateful to Gail Kern Paster for allowing me to read her work on the "melancholy of Moor-ditch" in particular, in the course of a mutual sharing of work in progress of which the present essay has been part since it was presented in Auckland in July, 2000.

34. For muddied/muddled/puddle, see *Othello* (3.4.143: "puddled his clear spirit"); and Q2 and F, 196–97 ("the people muddied"). *OED* under "muddy" (a. and n. 2) cites Leontes's "muddy" (*WT*, 1.2.325), for 5.a., "Not clear in mind; confused, muddled"; H. CROSSE *Vertues Commw.* (1603) (1878 ed., 128), "She is a muddie queane, a filthy beast" for 7: "Morally impure or 'dirty' "; the combination of mud and dung under 1.a: "Wet and soft soil or earthy matter; mire, sludge"; the figurative sense of "what is worthless or polluting"; and for muddying a pure liquid, *Rape of Lucrece* (577). See also "mud," "morris," and "murrion" in *MND*, 2.1.97–98; "rude, raw, and muddy" morris dances in *Two Noble Kinsmen* (3.5.118–20); and chap. 4 of Sujata Iyengar, "Nutbrown Maids and 'Sunneburnt' Men: Rural Nostalgia and Racial Exchange in Early Modern England" (Ph.D. diss., Stanford University, 1998), on "mud."

35. See respectively Hall, Gilman, and Jordan in n. 6; Adelman, "Iago's Alter Ego," 143, on the projection/abjection of excremental "waste" in *Othello*; the Ghost on his queen as preying on "garbage" (*TTH*, 58–59). For "nasty," see Cotgrave *Sale* ("Foule, soyled, nastie, sluttish, uncleane, filthie, loathsome, beastlie"); *Salet* ("Sullied, slubbered soyled; somewhat nastie, sluttish, or uncleane"); *Salir* ("To foule, soyle, sullie, beray, begrime; pollute, make sluttish, defile, or fill with ordure").

36. See, for example, Robert Burton, *Anatomy of Melancholy* (Oxford, 1521; New York: Dent, 1932), 12 ("black men"); 79, 87, 94 ("bogs, fens," "waste" lands, "barren heaths" and "fens, bogs, and moors"); 145 (mixed passions "like a chequer-table, black and white men"); 152 (on "black choler" and "excrement"); 169 (on the Greek root of melancholy's "black choler"); 172 ("swarthy, black" and "complexion"); 209 (on "black spots"); and 224 ("muddy" and "unclean" waters); Marc'hadour, "Name," 553–54, on melancholy, *morosus* or "morose," and Moors; Juliana Schiesari, *The Gendering of Melancholia* (Ithaca: Cornell University Press, 1992), esp. chap. 2 ("Black Humor?") and 97 on black bile and "grief" (with Marston's "soile of griefe"); Mary Floyd-Wilson, "Temperature, Temperance, and Racial Difference in Ben Jonson's *The Masque of Blackness*," *ELR* 28 (1998): 183–209, and 1996 University of North Carolina doctoral dissertation, "'Clime, Complexion, and Degree': Racialism in Early Modern England." On humoral discourses and Hamlet, see Gail Kern Paster, "The Body and Its Passions," *Shakespeare Studies* 29 (2001), 44–50.

37. Albert Boime, *Art of Exclusion: Representing Blacks in the Nineteenth Century* (Washington, D.C.: Smithsonian Institution Press, 1990), 5.

38. See Thomas Hill, trans., *The contemplation of mankinde, contayning a singuler discourse of phisiognomie* (London, 1571), 16–18.

39. On Bodin and others, see Winfried Schleiner, *Melancholy, Genius, and Utopia in the Renaissance* (Wiesbaden: Otto Harrassowitz, 1991), 14, 177, 197, 294; Floyd-Wilson, "Racial Difference," 205. Milton's *Il Penseroso* ("divinest Melancholy," 12) and *L'Allegro* ("loathed Melancholy, / Of Cerberus and blackest midnight born," 1) attest to the continuation of both positive and negative representations of melancholy.

40. Timothy Bright, *A Treatise of Melancholie* (1586), ed. Hardin Craig (New York: Columbia University Press, 1940), 128–29, the facsimile edition cited in all references here.

41. Bright, *Treatise*, 128–29, 148, 177–78, 196, 214. The white and black morphew of Philemon Holland's 1601 translation of Pliny is argued by Macdonald P. Jackson and Michael Neill in *Notes and Queries*, n.s. 45, no. 3 (September 1998): 358–86 to have influenced Marston's *Antonio and Mellida*, and to date it as after *Hamlet*.

42. In Daniel J. Vitkus, "Turning Turk in *Othello*: The Conversion and Damnation of the Moor," *Shakespeare Quarterly* 48, no. 2 (1997): 145–76, esp. 155; see also Bright, *Treatise*, 192 (on "the disaduantage of the melancholicke complexion: whose opportunity Sathan embraceth to vrge all terror against you to the fall"); Schleiner, *Melancholy*, 67, on Wittenberg and Luther's view that "the devil has particular insight into melancholic characters and uses them as instruments."

43. See *The Faerie Queene* (1590), 1.12.38 ("dull Melancholy"); Bright, *Treatise*, chap. 22, 129 ("melancholie causeth dulnesse of conceit"); Burton, *Anatomy*,

8 (on the "black fumes" of "melancholy" that "dull our senses"); Marc'hadour, "Name," on melancholy, Moors, and *Moria* or dullness; see also Robert Tofte, *Alba: The Months Minde of a Melancholy Lover* (1598), where "tawny" and "black" are cited as the colors of melancholy and "Alba" evokes the white of both "fair" beloved and Albion or England.

44. See H. Woudhuysen, ed., *Love's Labour's Lost* (Walton-on-Thames, Eng.: Thomas Nelson and Sons, 1998), 127; the gloss on 3.4.24–25 in Roger Warren and Stanley Wells, eds., *Twelfth Night* (Oxford: Oxford University Press, 1995), 170; Wall, "Blot," 140; *Much Ado*, ed. A. R. Humphreys (London: Methuen, 1981), 1.2.10–12 and 2.1.221; *Titus Andronicus*, 1.1.185 (with its Saturn[inus]/Moor); *1 Henry IV*, 1.2.83–88; melancholy and "ink" in *The Revenger's Tragedy*, 4.2.47–50.

45. See Minsheu, *Ductor* ("Melancholie, or blacke choler caused by adustion of the blood"); homophonic "soots" and "suits" in Hamlet's "suites" (*TTH*, 28–29), above.

46. *Treatise*, 127 ("this soote of melancholie"), and 159 ("sootie and smokie excrementes, whereby the spirites become impure"). See also 32 (on adust). Iyengar examines the use of "adust" for "black-skinned Moor or Indian" in her forthcoming *Changing Color: Mythologies of Race and Skin-Color, 1549–1668*. Floyd-Wilson, *Racialism*, 80, notes the "adust" or "burning kind" of melancholy which (according to Ficino) "makes you dull and stupid" (8).

47. See *1H6* (1.1.1: "Hung be the heavens with black! yield, day, to night!"); Cyril Tourneur, *The Atheist's Tragedy* (2.4.30–33); John Marston, *The Insatiate Countess* (3.65); Thomas Heywood, *A Warning for Fair Women* (Induction, 82–83); *The Works of Michael Drayton*, ed. J. William Hebel, 4 vols. (Oxford: Basil Blackwell, 1961), 1:158; George Chapman's *Bussy D'Ambois* (4.1.110–12); Neill, *Issues*, 30–32, 210, 274, 277–79, 282, 284–85, 292; E. K. Chambers, *The Elizabethan Stage*, 4 vols. (Oxford: Clarendon Press, 1923), 3:79.

48. F, 161 (virtually identical in Q2, 160). See Gillies, *Geography*, 161; William E. Engel, *Mapping Mortality* (Amherst: University of Massachusetts Press, 1995), 14, on Moors-Mors and Death as "der schwarze Mann"; Neill, *Issues*, 89 and 147; Marc'hadour, "Name," 554–55, on *Mors*, *memento mori*, *moriens*, and "Morians" or Moors; Philip Ziegler, *The Black Death* (London: Collins, 1969), 17–18, on *atra Mors*; Hall, *Darkness*, 5, 227–29, on the portrait of Lord Willoughby d'Eresby and its *memento mori*.

49. See *TTH*, 216, 218 (Q2: "incorp'st, and demy natur'd"; "Vppon my life Lamord), 217 (F: "encorp'st and demy-Natur'd"), 219 (F1's "Vpon my life Lamound," whose emendation to "Lamode" is cited in *The New Variorum Hamlet*, ed. H. H. Furness, 1:363); Margaret W. Ferguson, "Hamlet: Letters and Spirits," in *Shakespeare and the Question of Theory* (London: Methuen, 1985), 292–309, 301–5 (who relates this "Brooch indeed,/And Iemme of all our Nation" in Q2 and F here to Hamlet as "the glass of fashion and the mould of form"); Richard Helgerson, "What Hamlet Remembers," *Shakespeare Studies* 10 (1977): 67–97, esp. 85–93; Marjorie Garber, "'Remember me': Memento Mori Figures in Shakespeare's Plays," *Renaissance Drama* 12 (1981): 3–25; John Kerrigan, "Hieronimo, Hamlet, and Remembrance," *Essays in Criticism* 31 (1981): 105–26; for the "biter bit," see Neill, *Issues*, 239, 244–46, with 4, 237.

50. On "Antic" Death and Hamlet the "antic," see Neill, *Issues*, 5, 62–88, 225, 235; Helgerson, "What Hamlet Remembers," 85–93; with Talbot on "antic Death,

which laugh'st us here to scorn" (*1H6*, 4.7.18), Death the "antic" in *Richard II* (3.2.162). For "antic" in contexts suggesting blackface or carnival, see also *Two Noble Kinsmen* (4.1.75); *Antony and Cleopatra* (2.7.132); Michael Drayton, *Ide* (1594), 424; F. Quarles, *Jonah* (1620; 1638), 41: "Your mimick mouthes, your antick faces"; Robert Greene's "Anticks garnisht in our colours" in *Shaks. Cent. Praise* (1592), 2; Bishop Joseph Hall, *Sermons*, 5.113 ("Are they Christians, or Antics in some Carnival?"); Milton, *Samson Agonistes* (line 1325): "Jugglers and dancers, antics, mummers, mimics."

51. Cited here from the Folio, 119, Q2 (118) has "Ile tent him to the quicke, if a doe blench / I know my course." Both appear in the soliloquy that begins in Q2 and F with some version of "Oh what a Rogue and Pesant slaue am I?" (F, 115); but in Q1 with "Why what a dunghill idiote slaue am I?" (114).

52. Jenkins gloss (273) here continues "(Hence Q1 bleach at III.ii.80–81)." He argues (118) for Q1's "bleach" as an intermediary between Q2 and the German *Tragoedia der Bestrafte Brudermord oder Prinz Hamlet aus Dännemark*, which has "entfärbt" ("turned pale or changed color").

53. David Bevington, ed., *Troilus and Cressida* (Walton-on-Thames, Eng.: Thomas Nelson and Sons, 1998), 133. See also Massinger and Fletcher's *Fat. Dowry* 2.1 ("soldiers? Blanch not!"), where "blanch" is used in the sense of "blench" or flinch.

54. See Dekker's "Patience has blancht thy soul as white as snow," in *Sir Thomas Wyatt* (1607), 126; the King's power to "blanch an Ethiope" in Jonson's *Masque of Blackness* (lines 223–25). As Floyd-Wilson observes in "Racial Difference," his power to "blanch" included transforming "a subject's material debt to the crown into a merely ceremonial display of allegiance," since "blanching" was the Scottish legal term for transforming "black-ward" (or "tenure by military service") into "blanch" ("rent paid in silver, instead of service, labour, or produce").

55. See Philemon Holland's 1601 translation of Pliny II.520, 529; with Garner, "Paint," 132; Drew-Bear, *Faces*, 1–52, esp. 21–22; Dympna Callaghan, " 'Othello was a white man': properties of race on Shakespeare's stage," in *Alternative Shakespeares 2*, ed. Terence Hawkes (London: Routledge, 1996), 192–215. For important studies of whiteness, see Kim F. Hall, " 'These bastard signs of fair': Literary whiteness in Shakespeare's sonnets," in *Post-Colonial Shakespeares*, ed. Ania Loomba and Martin Orkin (London: Routledge, 1998), 64–83; Peter Erickson's "Profiles in Whiteness," *Stanford Humanities Review* 3 (1993): 98–111; Erickson, "Seeing White," *Transition* (1996): 166–85; Erickson, " 'God for Harry, England, and Saint George': British National Identity and the Emergence of White Self-Fashioning," in *Early Modern Visual Culture: Representation, Race, and Empire in Renaissance England*, ed. Peter Erickson and Clark Hulse (Philadelphia: University of Pennsylvania Press, 2000); and Barbara Bowen, "Amelia Lanyer and the Invention of White Womanhood," in *Maids and Mistresses, Cousins and Queens: Women's Alliances in Early Modern England*, ed. Susan Frye and Karen Robertson (New York: Oxford University Press, 1998). For surveys of major work on race in the period, see Peter Erickson, "Representations of Blacks and Blackness in the Renaissance," *Criticism* 3 (1993): 499–528; Erickson, "The Moment of Race in Renaissance Studies," *Shakespeare Studies* 26 (1998): 27–36; Erickson, "Representations of Race in Renaissance Art," *The Upstart Crow: A Shakespeare Journal* 18 (1998): 2–9; and his reviews in *The Art Bulletin* 78 (1996): 736–38 and *Shake-*

speare Quarterly 48 (1997): 363–66; *Race, Ethnicity, and Power in the Renaissance*, ed. Joyce Green MacDonald (Madison, NJ: Fairleigh Dickinson University Press, 1997); the special issue on "Constructing Race: Differentiating Peoples in the Early Modern World," *The William and Mary Quarterly*, 3d series, 54, no. 1 (1997); and the forum on "Race and the Study of Shakespeare" in *Shakespeare Studies* 26 (1998), as well as the important individual studies by scholars such as Margo Hendricks, Ania Loomba, Emily Bartels, Jyotsna Singh, Arthur Little Jr., Ian Smith, Virginian Mason Vaughan, Shankar Raman, and others over the past decade, cited in these surveys.

56. Cited in Drew-Bear, *Faces*, 52. In Warner's *Albion's England* (1592), 7.39.193, "blanch" is also already a synonym for "deceive" or "cheat."

57. Williams, *Dictionary*, s.v. "bleaking house" (1:112), includes Middleton's *No Wit* (c. 1613), 4.2.129, and the "blanch'd harlot" of Middleton's *Mad World* (1604–7), 3.3.42. Callaghan ("Othello," 206) observes that the cosmetic whiteness of "Bianca" in Cyprus may have the racial implication "that she is 'passing' as a white Venetian beauty." As Margreta de Grazia's analysis in the same volume (79) of the blank as "unstruck metal" in relation to Blanches, Biancas, and Hamlet's "here's metal more attractive" (3.2.108) makes clear, the material discourses of coining and metallurgy were readily combined with adulteration in the cosmetic and other senses.

58. See the rhetoric of the adulterate and unclean analyzed in Joseph Candido, "Blots, Stains, and Adulteries: The Impurities of *King John*," in *King John: New Perspectives*, ed. Deborah T. Curren-Aquino (Newark: University of Delaware Press, 1996), 114–27.

59. See Florio, *A Worlde of Wordes* (1598) and *Queen Anna's World of Words* (1611) under *bianco, bianche*. See also Cotgrave under *blanchissage, blanchisseur*. On *negro* and *blanco* as aesthetic terms naturalized as racial signifiers, see Boime, *Exclusions*, 5.

60. See *TTH*, 102–3; Jenkins, 255. With other editors, Edwards glosses "halt" as "limp" (132). *Variorum*—citing "black" from Q2 and Q3—records Johnson and others on the implied "lameness" of the verse (162).

61. See *TTH*, 146–47; Jenkins (301) on "blanks" here as "blanches"; Bevington (1098), on "blanks" as "causes to blanch or grow pale"; Hibbard (260), "blanches, makes pale."

62. Cotgrave's entries for *blanc* include "whitelime" as well as other forms of whitening; *blanc de plomb* as "Ceruse, or white Lead, wherewith women paint." Early modern English "blank" retains the sense of white. *OED*, s.v. "blank" (adj.) cites French *blanc*, Pr. *blanc, blanca*, Sp. *blanco*, Pg. *branco*, Ital. *bianco*, med. L. *blancus*, as well as OHG *blanch* and the meaning of "white . . . pale, colourless" in examples from c. 1325 to 1821; "paper" that is "left white or 'fair'; not written upon, free from written or printed characters, 'empty of all marks'" (including *Merry Wives*'s letters "with blancke-space for different names"). For "blank" as verb, *OED* cites for "to make white, whiten; to make pale" 1483 Caxton G. de la Tour liv on a "baronnesse" who "blanked and popped or peynted her self." The infamous "blank" charters of Richard II suggest both empty (*carte blanche*) and "white," translating Latin *alba charta* (French *blanke chartre*). "Blank" could also designate "blench" (as flinch or turn aside).

63. See *Othello*, 2.1.131–32, with *TTH*, 180, for this Q2 text. *OED* and Jenkins

differ on this "blank." *OED* glosses the noun as the "white spot in middle of target" (as in *Othello*, 3.4.129), but Jenkins argues that "blank" here means "in the line of direct, or level, aim (i.e. point-blank)." In *Othello* itself, however, it is impossible to isolate the meanings.

64. See Katherine Duncan-Jones's Arden 3 *Shakespeare's Sonnets* (Walton-on-Thames, Eng.: Thomas Nelson and Sons, 1997), 264–65, which emends "waste blacks" to "waste blanks" reluctantly: "The conventional emendation of Q's 'blacks', based on a plausible supposition that the MS used a contraction sign for 'n', has been adopted with some reluctance. Reading (b) of l.3 permits the description of pages of *Son*, though marked with black lines (63.13), as waste, containing nothing of value until they bear the impress of the youth's reflections on his own image" (264–65 of her edition).

65. See *OED*, s.v. "blankless" ("without spot or blemish"), which cites 1589 R. ROBINSON *Gold. Mirr.* (1851) 4 "No blotte of blame Their banners blanckles, of any euill part."

66. See *OED*, s.v. "bleach" (noun 2), as "any substance used for blacking; e.g. ink, soot, lamp-black, and esp. shoemakers' or curriers' black used for leather," citing 1580 Baret's *Alvearie* (B794) on "Courriors bleach . . . *atramentum sutorium*" and Cotgrave on "Attrament, inke; or bleach for Shoomakers. Ibid., Suye, soot of a chimney; any bleach" and its application to "a company of sutors" (or sooters). See also *OED*, s.v. "bleach" (verb 2) "to blacken, make black," citing Cotgrave, "Poislé . . . smeered, bleached, begrymed with soote. Ibid., Noircir, to blacke, blacen, bleach, darken," opposite of "bleach" (verb) 1, "to free from stain" and "to blanch or make white." See also "a bleach barren place," cited from 1655 FULLER *Ch. Hist.* I.vi; with Neill, *Issues*, on the "undifferentiating blankness" of "death," figured as "pale" as well as "black." Like "black" and "blank" (in relation to "waste"), the polarities of "bleach" could turn tropically into one another. Randall McLeod has suggested to me the relevance of the common Indo-European root of "bleach," "blank," and "black" as strengthening the meeting of apparent opposites here.

67. On these and "advantageous use of the layers of an oynx," see Roy Strong, *Princely Magnificence: Court Jewels of the Renaissance, 1500–1630* (London: Debrett's Peerage, 1980), 62; Patricia Fumerton, *Cultural Aesthetics: Renaissance Literature and the Practice of Social Ornament* (Chicago: University of Chicago Press, 1991), esp. 75, 94; Hall, *Darkness*, esp. 211–26; Nicholas Hilliard, *A Treatise Concerning the Arte of Limning* bound with Edward Norgate, *A More Compendious Discourse Concerning ye Art of Limning*, ed. R. K. R. Thornton and T. G. S. Cain (Ashington, Eng.: Carcanet New Press, 1981), 43, 91; Alfred Maskell, *Ivories* (Rutland, VT: Charles E. Tuttle, 1966), 25; Jim Murrell, *The Waye Howe to Lymne: Tudor Miniatures Observed* (London: Victoria & Albert Museum, 1983), 67–70.

68. See *TTH* 258–9, 138–39; Jenkins, 409: "foil] background against which a jewel shows more brightly"; Edwards, 236: "foil material used to set off or display some richer thing, as a jewel"; Hibbard, 346: "Originally the setting of a jewel, a foil came to mean anything that sets off another thing to advantage (*OED* sb. 1 5b and 6)." Rayna Kalas provides insightful observations on the "foyle of contraries" in relation to George Gascoigne's *The Steele Glass* in "The Technology of Reflection: Renaissance Mirrors of Steel and Glass," in the *Journal of Medieval and Early Modern Studies*, 32, no. 3 (fall 2002).

69. See Jasper Mayne, *The Citye Match* (1639), 2.2. On blackness as a foil for whiteness, see Lorne Campbell, *Renaissance Portraits* (New Haven: Yale University Press, 1990), 134, with Hall, *Darkness*, 211, 213, 227–29.

70. See respectively Hall, *Darkness*, 222, with figure 12; 213, and 215, citing Joan Evans, *English Jewellery from the Fifth Century A.D. to 1800* (London: Methuen, 1921), 98. On the Drake jewel, see Roy Strong, *The English Renaissance Miniature* (London: Thames and Hudson, 1983), 85; Karen C. C. Dalton, "Art for the Sake of Dynasty: The Black Emperor in the Drake Jewel and Elizabethan Imperial Imagery," in *Early Modern Visual Culture*, ed. Peter Erickson and Clark Hulse (Philadelphia: University of Pennsylvania Press, 2000), 178–214; Hall's comment (222) that this jewel is "featured in a Gheeraerts portrait of Drake done in 1594 (figure 14)," where Drake's hand "rests on a globe that is turned to display the continent of Africa." On the Gresley jewel, see Strong, *Magnificence*, 62; Fumerton, *Aesthetics*, 74–75; Hall, 218–21.

71. Jenkins, 568; Hibbard, 347: "The business of drinking a pearl dissolved in wine goes back as far as Pliny, who tells how Cleopatra made a bet with Antony that she could spend a hundred million sesterces on a single meal. She won it by putting a priceless pearl in her wine and then drinking it off (*Natural History* ix. 120–1). Ben Jonson refers to the story in *Volpone* 3.7.191–3, where Volpone says to Celia: 'See, here a rope of pearl; and each more orient / Than the brave Egyptian queen caroused: / Dissolve and drink 'em.' "

72. See Strong, *Magnificence*, 70; Fumerton, *Aesthetics*, 74–75. *OED* defines *onyx* (from the Greek for "nail, claw, onyx-stone") as "A variety of quartz allied to agate, consisting of plane layers of different colours: much used for cameos," citing among other examples 1601 HOLLAND Pliny II.615 ("The Indian Onyx hath certaine sparkes in it. . . . As for the Arabian Onyches, there bee found of them blacke, with white circles") and biblical instances including Ezekiel 28:13 and Job 28:16, the latter of which combines reference to the "precious Onix" with "the golde of Ophir" (1611 Bible translation), the Solomonic treasure that played a major role in James's imperial vision.

73. See *TTH*, 258–59. "Onixe" also appears in Q3–4 (Q1 has for the second instance "Come drinke, here lies thy vnion here"). For one explanation, see Edwards (236): "Q2 printed first 'Vnice', which could be a misreading of 'Vnio'; the press-corrector, using his wits rather than the MS., changed this to 'Onixe'. When F again has 'Vnion', at 305, Q2 again prints 'Onixe.' " See also *New Variorum Hamlet* for Pope's printing of "onyx" and the tradition of commentary here.

74. On this vogue, see Roy C. Strong, *The English Icon: Elizabethan and Jacobean Portraiture* (London: Routledge and K. Paul, 1969), 13–15, 17–21 (with melancholy and the colors black and tawny, on 34); *The English Miniature*, ed. John Murdoch et al. (New Haven: Yale University Press, 1981); Graham Reynolds, "The Painter Plays the Spider," *Apollo* 79 (April 1964): 279–84; Fumerton, *Aesthetics*, chap. 3.

75. Q2 and F have "picture in little" (F with caps); Q1 has "picture" (*TTH*, 104–5). On the portraits as miniatures, and Burbage as limner and painter, see Reynolds, "Painter," 280, 283, with Hibbard, 280. The "faire"/"Moore" contrast does not depend on their being miniatures, since blackness was used as a foil in multiple representational forms.

76. See Fumerton, *Aesthetics*, 94, citing Hilliard's use of colors (including from "Inde or Afrike"), and the best "velvet black" in relation to African ivory.

77. For this gloss and the Quarto text, see Lois Potter's Arden 3 edition of John Fletcher and William Shakespeare, *The Two Noble Kinsmen* (Walton-on-Thames, Eng.: Thomas Nelson and Sons, 1997), 271, with Reynolds, "Spider," 280.

78. Potter (272) cites "Pelops' shoulder" as "ivory" from *Metamorphoses* (6.403–11), comparing Marlowe's *Hero and Leander* on "the white of Pelops' shoulder." See also her gloss (272) for "What a brow" as "Cf. 'See what a grace was seated on this brow' (*Ham.* 3.4.55–62)" and Emilia's "Oh, who can find the bent of women's fancy?" (4.2.33).

79. *TTH*, 192–93. See Stephen Orgel, "'Counterfeit Presentments': Shakespeare's Ekphrasis," in *England and the Continental Renaissance*, ed. Edward Chaney and Peter Mack (Rochester, NY: Boydell Press, 1990), 177–84, esp. 177; Michael Neill, "'In Everything Illegitimate': Imagining the Bastard in Renaissance Drama," *Yearbook of English Studies* 23 (1993): 271–72, on Hamlet's uncertain paternity, in relation to counterfeiting and adulteration; for the play on mis-taking (and mistaking) husbands, in lines that echo the Ceremony of Matrimony, *TTH*, 148–49. "Tropical" turning is introduced in the Mousetrap's "tropically/trapically" (*TTH*, 146–47), which includes "trope/trap" and the "Tropick" that was the geographical and solstitial point of turning.

80. On the role of this rhetoric in later discourses of racial distinction, see Abdul JanMohamed, *Manichean Aesthetics: The Politics of Literature in Colonial Africa* (Amherst: University of Massachusetts Press, 1983).

81. On "old Mole," see Jenkins, 457–58. For the texts cited here, see *TTH*, 50, 66–67, 170–71. For the variant descriptions of Pyrrhus above, see *TTH*, 108–11.

82. See respectively *TTH*, 58–59; 118–19.

83. On the "crisis of differentiation" in *Hamlet*, see Neill, *Issues*, esp. 9–14, 24–25, 234, 241, 248, quoting Richard D. Fly, "Accommodating Death: The Ending of *Hamlet*," *Studies in English Literature* 24 (1984): 257–74, on Hamlet's "passion for differences" as a counter to the "relentless force operating . . . to erode hierarchies of value and collapse systems of differentiation" (261, 263); Adelman's discussion in *Suffocating Mothers*.

84. For this citation from "Thomas Phaer's highly influential translation of the *Aeneid*" (1573), and the identification of Dido's African suitor as a contemporary Turk or Moor, see Jerry Brotton, "'This Tunis, sir, was Carthage': Contesting Colonialism in *The Tempest*," in *Post-Colonial Shakespeares*, 23–42, 41. Brotton stresses the importance of ancient imperial allusions (and the *Aeneid* in particular) in early modern contexts.

85. On this aspect of the Diet of Worms, see Dorothy M. Vaughan, *Europe and the Turk: A Pattern of Alliances, 1350–1700* (Liverpool University Press, [1954]), 108. See *TTH*, 148–49, where Q1 has "neither the gate of Christian, Pagan, / Nor Turke" (132) while Q2 has "Christian, Pagan, nor man" (132) and F has "Christian, Pagan, or Norman" (133). Jenkins (289) and Edwards (153) print "nor the gait of Christian, pagan, nor man" (289); Hibbard (248–49) Prints "Christian, pagan, nor no man." Both F and Q2 have "If the rest of my Fortunes turne Turke with me" (F 149) and "if the rest of my fortunes turne Turk with me" (Q2 148), where there is no corresponding "Turk" in Q1. For a fascinating account of early modern piracy in relation to the plays of Shakespeare and others—beginning with *Hamlet*—see Lois Potter, "Pirates and 'turning Turk' in Renaissance drama," in *Travel and Drama in Shakespeare's Time*, ed. Jean-Pierre Maquerlot and Michele Willems

(Cambridge: Cambridge University Press, 1996), 125–40. Though there is not space to do so here, it is important to trace the differences as well as the similarities among these three early texts, which draw in differing proportions on reminders of empire and the contemporary lexicon of blackness, suggested more elliptically in the parenthetical references of the present essay.

86. Title of the Sixth Biennial Conference of the Australia and New Zealand Shakespeare Association, held in Auckland in July 2000, featured on the cover and in articles published in *Shakespeare Quarterly* 52, no. 4 (2001), under Michael Neill as guest editor.

87. See Andreas Bertoldi, "Shakespeare, psychoanalysis, and the colonial encounter: The case of Wulf Sachs' *Black Hamlet*," in *Post-Colonial Shakespeares*, 235–58; *Black Hamlet*, ed. Saul Dubow and Jacqueline Rose (Baltimore: Johns Hopkins University Press, 1996); and Phillip Armstrong's *Shakespeare in Psychoanalysis* (London and New York: Routledge, 2001). On the reported 1607 shipboard performance of "Hamlet" enroute from England to India, see Ania Loomba, "Shakespearean transformations," in *Shakespeare and the National Culture*, ed. John J. Joughlin (Manchester: Manchester University Press, 1997), esp. 111–13; Michael Neill, "Post-colonial Shakespeare," in *Post-Colonial Shakespeares*, 164–85, esp. 171–72; Gary Taylor, "Hamlet in Africa 1607," in *Travel / Knowledge: European "Discoveries" in the Early Modern Period* (New York: Palgrave, 2001), including materials on 211–22. Jonathan Crewe, in "Out of the Matrix: Shakespeare and Race-Writing," *The Yale Journal of Criticism* 8, no. 2 (1995): 13–29, also cites the importance of recognizing that what he calls "race-writing" in Shakespeare is "not confined to overtly racialized characters and situations in a handful of plays" (13). For pioneering treatments of the issue of reading in texts where race does not seem to matter (or has been minimized or ignored), see Margo Hendricks, "'Obscured by dreams': Race, Empire, and Shakespeare's *A Midsummer Night's Dream*," *Shakespeare Quarterly* 47, no. 1 (Spring 1996): 37–60; and Kim F. Hall, "Reading What Isn't There: 'Black' Studies in Early Modern England," *Stanford Humanities Review* 3, no. 1 (1993): 23–33, with her more recent "Object into Object? Some Thoughts on the Presence of Black Women in Early Modern Culture," in *Early Modern Visual Culture: Representation, Race, and Empire in Renaissance England*, ed. Peter Erickson and Clark Hulse (Philadelphia: University of Pennsylvania Press, 2000).

88. On Q1's "*guyana*," which does not appear in the collations of most modern editions, see my "Murder in Guyana," *Shakespeare Studies* 28 (2000): 169–75. For death as an undiscovered country (in all three texts), see *TTH*, 123–24.

89. The three early texts here have the following (*TTH*, 236–37): Folio: "Alexander died: Alexander was buried: Alexander returneth into dust," with "stopp a Beere-barrell" and "Imperiall Caesar, dead and turn'd to clay"; Q2: "Alexander dyed, Alexander was buried, Alexander returneth to dust," with "stoppe a Bearebarrell" and "Imperious Caesar dead, and turn'd to Clay"; Q1: "Alexander died, Alexander was buried, Alexander became earth," with "stoppe the boung hole of a beere barrell? and "Imperious Casar dead and turnd to clay."

Deforming Sources: Literary Antecedents and Their Traces in *Much Ado About Nothing*

Thomas Moisan

In one of her most verbally expansive moments in *Much Ado About Nothing*, Hero directs her attendant "gentlewomen," Ursula and Margaret, on where to have Beatrice positioned to overhear the "honest slanders" and other misrepresentations through which Beatrice is to be led to believe that Benedick loves her:

> And bid her steal into the pleached bower,
> Where honeysuckles, ripened by the sun,
> Forbid the sun to enter, like favorites
> Made proud by princes, that advance their pride
> Against that power that bred it.
>
> (3.1.7–11)[1]

Leaving aside the temptation to hear in it a topicality that editors routinely admonish us to resist,[2] and disregarding the malice toward Beatrice it implies, what surprises us at first about the political commonplace[3] in Hero's comparison is simply who says it, or, as Harry Berger reminds us, that "Shakespeare oddly allows the usually quiet Hero to break into epic simile."[4] Its deeper effect, however, is to challenge us to recognize why we should feel surprised, and to discern the discursive demarcations the play asks us to accept as integral to its geography. In part, of course, these are demarcations of gender: how little we know Hero that we should take this utterance as surprising is a reminder of how little we hear her voice in "mixed" company elsewhere in the play and how much she is kept infantilized within the bounds of the "pleached bower" erected for her by the social and linguistic segregation of the sexes in the play, a segregation that Beatrice, on the other hand, at once italicizes and renders herself conspicuous by transgressing.[5]

Yet at the same time, we also hear in Hero's simile an evocation of the martial, heroic romance world of the writings most commonly taken to be the literary antecedents of *Much Ado About Nothing,* works by Bandello, Ariosto, *et alia*, works which provide the core elements of the Claudio-Hero plot in the play and which are metamorphosed into the determinedly holiday world of Messina.[6] Decontextualized and rendered conspicuous in its incongruity, Hero's simile reminds us of the way in which references to these writings populate *Much Ado About Nothing.* Surprising us in varying degrees of incongruity, evocations of its literary background cling to the play as a kind of scattered verbal residue by means of which the play summons its antecedents only, it seems, to distance itself from them, investing their recollections with the force of ironic, parodic allusions, or elements of a foreign fictive economy intruding upon the dramatic fiction that is Shakespeare's Messina. Indeed, the charge Benedick levels at the teasing Don Pedro and Claudio is applicable to the play as a whole: the "body of [its] discourse is sometime guarded with fragments, and the guards are but slightly basted on neither" (1.1.286–87).

Drawing upon the compilations and discussions of putative, probable, and possible sources so helpfully arraigned by Charles Prouty, Geoffrey Bullough, and Kenneth Muir,[6] reading *Much Ado* by reading its reading of these antecedents, I propose to look at the way in which juxtapositions of the sort introduced by Hero's simile help to shape the peculiar dramatic space the play configures and our experience thereof. In part, of course, what we encounter in *Much Ado About Nothing* merely offers a paradigm of the problematically furtive and mutually revealing relationships Shakespeare's plays regularly assume with the materials that influence them. More particularly, however, I would argue that in the degree to which *Much Ado* deflects even as it glances at the various literary productions that are its nutrients, it mirrors in this relationship a more significant furtiveness and ambivalence that mark its representation of character, of politics and power, and, indeed, of representation itself. With the multiple meanings of its title, *Much Ado About Nothing* teases us to "note" the divers ways in which it makes good on its eponymous claim to make much ado about nothing; beyond the ways that critics have already enumerated,[7] in the

degree to which it renders its sources shadows, decoupling itself
from the tropes and *topoi* to which it is heir, we find one more
sense in which the play brings much and nothing into a precarious
and comic proximity.

To be sure, discussions of Shakespeare's use of sources have not
infrequently been colored by a regard for Shakespeare's integrative
powers and a Coleridgean appreciation for his ability to assimilate,
to "weave" disparate source materials into organically and dramatically coherent fabrics.[8] In italicizing elements drawn from the idi-
oms of literary romance and decontextualizing them through
incongruous juxtapositions, *Much Ado About Nothing* veers away
from the sort of assimilation for which Shakespeare is praised and
exposes the rough edges of its own fictive world, or, rather, exposes
itself as a world of rough edges, of dissidences that give voice to
the margins of a discourse and undo, to recall Derrida's coinage, its
"unicity."[9]

Indeed, even as the play labors sociologically to form a comic
community in Messina from its disparate assortment of domestic
lords and family, "friendly" interloping overlords, hangers-on and
loyal retainers with divided loyalties, designated malcontents, and
socially insecure petty officials and commoners, so the discursive
divisions asserted by recollections of their literary antecedents expose the faultlines and fissures in that community. "Do you question me, as an honest man should do, for my simple true judgment?
or would you have me speak after my custom, as being a profess'd
tyrant to their sex?" (1.1.166–69). So Benedick quizzes Claudio
when Claudio quizzes him early in the play as to whether he has
"noted" Hero and whether Hero is "not a modest young lady"
(165); Benedick's question, in fact, the parrying of questions in the
exchange as a whole, is interesting, not only for the mutual guard-
edness it reveals between these two supposedly fast friends, and
not only for the evidence it affords of the inability of anyone in this
play to speak the truth about anything that matters,[10] but also for
the sense it conveys of two characters who communicate, if at all,
along discursive frontiers erected by the kinds of works to which
the play is heir and behind the characteriolgical masks those conventions entail. We have seen Benedick elsewhere, Benedick implies, and his insight into and ability to distance himself from his
own conventionality render him only more discursively wary of
Claudio's.[11]

Now such dissociative allusions have generic implications as well and ignite in *Much Ado* a powerful metatheatricality through which the play seems to insist upon its generic difference from the very sort of materials from which it proceeds. To be sure, as Jean Howard has maintained, one way in which *Much Ado* intensifies its theatricality is in its addition of something its antecedents are commonly taken to lack, namely the plot involving Beatrice and Benedick, a plot which in turn provides the site for Don Pedro's theatrically contrived manipulations of the pair.[12] Nor, though, is it in merely supplying what is not in the sources that *Much Ado* asserts its theatrical difference from them. Rather, as elsewhere in Shakespeare's plays, *Much Ado* recalls the textual character of or textual elements within the works that inform it only to marginalize texts and writings or italicize them as problematic or suspect, or, at least, not worth the "ado" they receive: "Thou wilt be like a lover presently, / And tire the reader with a book of words" (1.1.306–7), a bibliophobic Don Pedro chides Claudio when the latter with unwonted loquacity confesses his infatuation with Hero (296–305), the "book of words" a hendyadic gibe at both the volume of Claudio's effusions and their bookishness.[13]

Indeed, marginalization of the written begins at the very beginning of the play, as *Much Ado* opens by simultaneously alluding to and taking leave of a missive laying out the circumstances bringing Don Pedro and company to Messina (1.1.1–11), effectively recalling the literary background provided in Bandello only to foreshorten it. And when writing next appears it is as a site of empty epistolary formalities invoked by Claudio and Don Pedro in mockery of Benedick's conversational forms (1.1.281–84). How estimable can texts be, after all, the play seems to ask, if Dogberry insists upon being inscribed in one (4.2.86–87)?

Texts are problematic, of course, not simply for who wants to be written down—or up—in them, but for how they are used and for what gets written in them. As to the former, in the assorted love scribblings attributed to or adduced as so many *literas ex machina* against Beatrice and Benedick, the play mocks the amorously compromising and intercepted missives conventional in its sources,[14] reminding us, as if in a comically irreverent anticipation of Lacan, that as long as there is a destination letters will always exist to arrive there. At the same time, playful as its use of such writings is, through them the play also underscores its oxymoronic proximity to a world it ostensibly shuns, offering comic reminders of what it

could be even as it insists upon being something different, eschew-
ing only to associate itself with a literary world whose "slanders"
are not of the "honest" sort with which Hero proposes to "stain"
Beatrice (3.1.84).

And no less problematic are texts for the aphorisms and *sententiae* they often purvey and toward which *Much Ado*, again, like
other of Shakespeare's plays, articulates an ironic skepticism.[15]
"Shall quips and sentences and these paper bullets of the brain awe
a man from the career of his humour?" demands Benedick in mock-
soliloquy (2.3.240–42), and even as *Much Ado* answers this rhetorical question by permitting us to smile at Benedick's ability to ratio-
nalize his way against the very stock of quips, sentences, and paper
bullets of the brain that had been his barricades against emotional
humors, it exposes the sententious as a particularly flimsy fortifi-
cation. Thus, Leonato, whose *badinage* at the opening of the play
with the facile Messenger—soon to be rhetorically disarmed by
Beatrice[16]—voices the sort of platitudinous *sententiae* (1.1.8–9,
26–29) that lard commonplace books and conduct books, comes
after Hero's disgrace to spurn precisely this kind of textually predi-
gested, one size fits all wisdom when Antonio invokes it as a sop
for Leonato's grief. For Leonato such "counsel" comes to represent
an attempt to "[p]atch grief with proverbs" wholly inadequate to
the grief of his experience, a point he will rehearse with considerable vehemence in more than thirty lines of proverb-laden and sententious declamation against proverbs and *sententiae* (5.1.3–32,
34–38), a solipsistic speech whose emotion Barbara Everett has
called "surely something odder than passionate":[17] a speech occasioned, presumably, by the misfortunes of Hero, but in which Hero
rather disappears, a speech that sounds like an elegy, but for someone we know and Leonato knows hasn't died, a speech through
which *Much Ado* daringly collapses the distance between the
world of Messina and the paternal grief-smitten world of its literary
antecedents even in the act of parodying its—to use a word that re-
verberates significantly in the play—"fashion."

Still, in no instance does *Much Ado About Nothing* seem more to
trumpet its distinctness from at least its non-dramatic antecedents
than in the moment when, paradoxically, it seems most loudly to
recall the narrative form of those works and eschew its own theatricality, keeping unstaged what its antecedents show in perfervid detail. That moment, of course, comes in Shakespeare's curious
decision *not* to stage what would seem to be the eminently stagea-

ble impersonation, faux-infidelity, balcony scene in which the on-looking Claudio and Don Pedro are led by Don John to believe that Borachio is making love to Hero, only to have the event reported later by Borachio in his bibulous homily against the "deformed thief," "fashion" (3.3.95–172). In the works Much Ado recalls it is a moment that, as Katharine Eisaman Maus has demonstrated, met-onymizes the duped lover's emotional susceptibility and, pace Othello, his masochistic obsession with ocular proof.[18] And in a play which, starting with the homophonic joke in its title, persis-tently makes much ado about noting (1.1.162–64, 2.3.54–57, 3.2.55, 4.1.158, 5.1.260), and which seems otherwise not reluctant to ren-der its action theatrically, it is a moment conspicuous for its ab-sence. In electing to leave it unstaged and recorded, instead, in the inebriated Borachio's narrative, Shakespeare has been accused by one quizzical critic of forgoing "a transparent record of the event for a fuddled divagation."[19]

It could be argued that in leaving this event invisible, Much Ado, true to its name, is only underscoring the infidelity that hasn't oc-curred, one more instance of the eponymous nothing that the play makes much ado of. More important, in banishing the scene off-stage and representing the visual through Borachio's ragged report-age, Much Ado pays homage to the narrative nature of much of its putative source material—but pays homage to its unreliability, to what it doesn't represent.

For, indeed, whether the narrative antecedents for this scene ac-tually produce a "transparent record" or are any less "fuddled" than Borachio's "fuddled divagation" is questionable. For duped lovers in such scenes seem invariably not to see a lot, as it were, by watching, or, at least, see only what their jealous susceptibilities allow them to see.[20] Exemplary is Spenser's contribution to the genre in which the deceived Squire, Phedon, not one to allow his emotional convictions to be deterred by the absence of corrobora-tive physiognomic facts, recalls that at the critical moment at which he was led to believe that his lady Claribell, impersonated by her "handmayd," Pryene, was being unfaithful to him, "Her proper face / I not descerned in that darkesome shade, / But weend it was my love, with whom [the treacherous "friend," Philemon] playd."[21] And indeed, that jealous lovers will see and hear through representation what they are inclined to see and hear is a lesson turned into a brilliant piece of theater, we will recall, by Iago when he contrives to have Othello see and hear what his jealousy has led him to expect in Iago and Cassio's locker room banter over Bianca (4.1).

Already "blinded with the veil of jealousy," as the narrator in *La Prima Parte de le Novelle del Bandello* captiously remarks of his protagonist, Timbreo,[22] the deceived lovers in these narratives find a correlative for their blindness in the opacity of narrative itself, in its ability to filter data and conceal under the very pretext of revealing, whetting the lover's voyeurism while impairing his physical—and intellectual—sight. So it is that representations of the scene in Shakespeare's antecedents tend to be obsessively cluttered with visual detail, with descriptions of balconies, ladders, occluded sight lines, women's apparel and gems, and, in varyingly titillating degrees of breathiness representations of amatory embrace. Nowhere, perhaps, more breathily and distractingly fulsomely than in Peter Beverly's *Ariodanto and Jenevra* (1565–66?), an enlargement and reworking in 'fourteeners of an episode involving lovers of the same name from Ariosto's *Orlando Furioso*. In this account, it is the Don John surrogate, the villainous Duke, rather than an underling, who personally takes charge of making love to the woman, Dalinda, impersonating the lady, Jenevra, she serves, the lady whom the Duke seeks to defame in the very sight of her lover, Ariodanto:

> but see, with glistring light
> Of gould, Dalinda doth appeare lyke angell to the sight.
> And as the Duke had given in charge so she in bravest wyse:
> With Shining robes, w^t Diamonds set that gleme before the eyes
> Lyke burning torch in winter night is come into this place:
> Wher Polinesse like Judas doth her scorned limmes imbrace,
> And to th'end, [Ariodanto] should more perfectly behould:
> His loving toyes, her kisses eke, and how his armes do fould
> Her griped wast he doth approch as nere as window will
> Geve leave to him, to [Ariodanto's] sight that he mought vew his fill
> Therof, & how she clasps her armes about his stretched necke:
> Whose store of kisses do declare, her mynd voyd of suspect.[23]

Aglow in a "glistring light of gold" that blinds rather than illuminates, the description draws attention to the impersonated lady's "[s]hining," diamond studded dress. Ubiquitous in the erotic decor of these deception narratives, "the dress" is expressive of an amatory rhetoric in which clothes and other adornments are not simply representative but constitutive, rendering the women beneath iso-

morphic and hence interchangeable.[24] So it is that one of the imper-
sonators actually recalls feeling that in donning her mistress's
robes she felt herself "very like her,"[25] while in *Orlando Furioso*
the lover, Ariodante, is deceived, in part because he "stood so farre
aloof," but also because he "beleev'd against his owne behoofe, /
Seeing her cloth[e]s that he had seene her face."[26]

Banished offstage with the rest of the balcony panto, and excised
from Borachio's account in 3.3, "the dress" in *Much Ado* is displaced only to be analogically resurrected in 3.4 in Margaret's prenuptial conversation with the presciently apprehensive Hero on
the superiority of Hero's gown to the gown of the Duchess of Milan
"that they praise so":

> Margaret: By my troth's but a night-gown [in] re-
> spect of yours: cloth a' gold and cuts, and lac'd
> with silver, set with pearls, down sleeves, side
> sleeves, and skirts, round underborne with a bluish
> tinsel; but for a fine, quaint, graceful, and excellent
> fashion, yours is worth ten on't.
> Hero: God give me joy to wear it, for my heart is
> exceeding heavy.
>
> (3.4.16, 18–25)

At once proleptic and retrospective, it is an exchange that anticipates the "ado" we know lies just ahead, but simultaneously reminds us in Margaret's comparative discourse on Hero's and the
Duchess of Milan's gowns of what we haven't seen, echoing with a
sartorial inflection the word "fashion" (3.4.15) so central to Borachio's intoxicated harangue in the previous scene, gently reminding us in her detailed description of the Duchess of Milan's dress
that Margaret is "into" clothes and may well recently have been
"in" Hero's.

Rendering invisible the scene various of its narrative antecedents
labor hard to detail, *Much Ado* makes risibly audible the kind of
moralizing, sentimentalizing editorialization those narratives not
atypically voice. "But Fortune," Bandello's narrator exclaims—
waxing especially indignant by investing Fortune's normally impersonal operations with a malevolence of intent to match its
"unfortunate" effects—"which never ceases to work against the
wellbeing of mankind, found a novel means of stopping a marriage
so agreeable to both the parties concerned."[27] As "noted" earlier, a

hint of this editorializing voice comes in the platitudes Leonato at first purveys and then reviles. It is ventriloquized more volubly, however, in the digression by Borachio on "the fashion" that disrupts and displaces his account of the "villainy" against Hero he performed for Don John (3.3.107–38). With its obsessive reiteration on "fashion," Borachio's account brings a narrative "fashion" of the play's antecedents into comic alignment and parodic nexus with the tendency in *Much Ado* to turn human behavior, like wedding gowns, into "fashions," a "fashion" epitomized here when Borachio, trying his auditor Conrade's patience (140–43), turns Don John's malefaction into an *exemplum*, evil *à la mode*, digressively subordinating the "tale" he had promised to tell, the "what" that happened, to the "what" it represents. And parody turns to outright travesty when in one of the more enduring bits of misprision in the play, one of the Watch misconstrues Borachio's allegorical personification of the "deformed thief" that is fashion as a reference to the "vile thief" named "Deformed" (125). Here the literalism of the Watch produces at once a "deformation" not only of what Borachio has said, and of the allegorizing "fashion" Borachio at once deplores and indulges, but also an inadvertently apt reflection of Borachio's truly "deformed," genuinely preposterous narrative—where what should come first comes last (144–48, 154–63), where declamation on the tyranny of "fashion" precedes the account of the event that has occasioned that declamation (117–38), and where the account of the event "vildly"—by Borachio's own admission—inverts reportorial decorum in leaping ahead to what was seen before saying who was looking, and how or why they came to be there and whether they could see anything "afar off" (148–52): an account, that is, whose narrative imperfections show as through a glass darkly the misprision abundant in *Much Ado*'s antecedents.

On the other hand, for whatever dramatic possibilities it passes up in leaving unstaged the scene in which Hero is falsely represented, *Much Ado* more than compensates in bringing to melodramatic life the scene in which Hero is falsely accused, giving expressionistic form to the patriarchalism and misogyny of its sources through what Marta Straznicky has called the "frantic incantation" of Leonato's filicidal denunciation of Hero.[28] With a willingness to judge character by physiognomy and take blushes for guilt—"Could she here deny / The story that is printed in her blood"(4.1.121–22)—and a deference to status—"Would the two

princes lie?''—Leonato asks, rhetorically, why he ever had a daughter? why not have adopted "a beggar's issue at my gates,"

> Who smirched thus and mir'd with infamy,
> I might have said, 'No part of it is mine;
> This shame derives itself from unknown loins'?
> But mine, and mine I lov'd, and mine I prais'd,
> And mine that I was proud on, mine so much
> That I myself was to myself not mine,
> Valuing of her—why, she, O she is fall'n
> Into a pit of ink, that the wide sea
> Hath drops too few to wash her clean again,
> And salt too little which may season give
> To her foul tainted flesh!
>
> (4.1.129–43)

Here the misogyny and sexual defensiveness that shadow, for example, Leonato's humorous bantering with Benedick early in the
play about Hero's paternity (1.1.105–8) seize the foreground; and
we feel them all the more keenly here for their absence, or comparative mutedness, in the outcries of Leonato's counterpart, Lionato,
in the work that most closely anticipates this part of Shakespeare's
play in detail, *La Prima Parte de le Novelle del Bandello.* To be sure,
when Bandello's Lionato is presented by his presumptive son-in-
law Timbreo with the accusation that his daughter Fenicia has been
guilty of fornication and that the impending nuptial must be can-
celled, he hardly takes the news well and evinces a defensiveness
of his own. Yet his defensiveness is socioeconomic; unlike Shakespeare's Leonato, who takes Don Pedro and Don John's nobility as
a guarantee of their credibility and assumes the worst of Hero, Bandello's Lionato suspects the noble Timbreo of social snobbishness
and assumes the best of his daughter. "Friend," Lionato declares,
in an harangue equal in volume—and, perhaps, paranoia—to his
Shakespearean counterpart's, if different in theme,

> I always feared, from the first moment when you spoke to me of this
> marriage, that Sir Timbreo would not stand firm to his request, for I
> knew then as I do now that I am only a poor gentleman and not his
> equal. Yet surely if he repented of his promise to make her his wife it
> would have been sufficient for him to declare that he did not want her,
> and not to have laid against her this injurious accusation of whoredom.
> It is indeed true that all things are possible, but I know how my daugh-

ter has been reared and what her habits are. God . . . will one day, I believe, make known the truth.[29]

And if the kingly father figures in the more heroic antecedents to *Much Ado* are more restrained in their responses, a restraint imposed on them in part by their positions as upholders of chivalric laws, still, their authors strive to make us feel the fathers' grief, a grief left uninflected by the kinds of recriminations that punctuate Leonato's. Hence, in a sequence recalled in *Much Ado*, in which the accused woman slips into a death-like trance from the trauma of the accusation, the king in Beverly's Ariostan *Ariodanto and Jenevra*—and unlike Shakespeare's Leonato, who thinks that Hero would be better off dead and isn't much cheered when she recovers (4.1.154, 170–75)—labors hard to revive Jenevra from her swoon and is much cheered by her recovery:

> The aged King that sees this fitte, nye caught with like disease,
> With shaking hands her temple rubs and seekes eche way tappease
> These choking griefs, but all in vain he rubs and chafes his childe:
> For death hath nummed every part, and life is now exilde.
> Til panting hart with strained might receives his wonted force:
> And lets in wholsome breath againe into the senceles corse.
> Which joyful king (with hart revyved) doth see and driveth feare
> Away, and strayning his sprites, he thus the Princes doth cheare.[30]

Still, though Leonato's paternal counterparts manage to behave a bit better, the misogyny that informs the credence Leonato gives to Hero's accusers is hardly absent from the works *Much Ado* recalls. "Oh, they are full of deceit, cogging, flattery, foisting, twittle-tattle." So the duplicitous Pedante of Anthony Munday's *Fedele and Fortunio* (1585), the proverbial pot calling the kettle black, advises the disillusioned lover Fedele that woman's inconstancy is a theme, a *"genus demonstravum,"* so large that "[a]ll the tongues in the world are not able to set it out," and adds that "[w]hen they anger you, bid the Devil take them all, and make no more ado."[31]

And, indeed, what happens to Hero hints at the slight inconsistency we find throughout these antecedents: women are presumed guilty of sexual misbehavior as representatives of their sex; they are exonerated as individuals, the exceptions that leave the rule intact. In his translation of *Orlando Furioso* Harington offers a sly variation on the norm when to a misogynist imprecation in the text condemning the compromised heroine and *"all her kinde,"* Harington

gallantly adds the marginal gloss, "Not all women kind, but faithl-
esse women," thus calling attention to the canard while pretending
to qualify it.[32]

Representative of the misogyny that inflects the genre, Leonato's
speech anticipates his monody in solipsistic grief that we have considered in act 5, and like that speech his words here have the remarkable effect of making the person who occasioned them
disappear, rhetorically a greater challenge in this instance since
Hero is actually physically present throughout. But with a self-ab-
sorption aurally punctuated and intensified with the reiteration of
the word "mine," Leonato manages, not only to advertise himself
as the party to whom condolences should be addressed, but to di-
vert attention from the person who has occasioned this grief, Leonato's rhetoric putting into violent execution the violent directive
with which the speech had opened: "Do not live, Hero" (4.1.123).
And, true to his word, Leonato turns the daughter he addresses in
the outset of his tirade into a third person *topos* at its terminus.

Yet in the process, Hero is not only de-personified but conven-
tionalized. "[F]allen," dropped, rather, "[i]nto a pit of ink," defamed and immersed, Hero becomes indistinguishable from the
other defamed women whose misadventures she now shares, and,
as the scene unfolds, "little more than a pawn," as Janice Hays puts
it, "on a masculine chessboard,"[33] an object of contending theories
of moral physiology, and of a divergence of opinion among Claudio, Leonato and Friar Francis on how to read blushes: do blushes
reveal guilt? do they reveal innocence? do they reveal at all (4.1.34–
40, 121–22, 158–61)?

Thus, in the relationship of *Much Ado* to its sources, a certain
paradox emerges, for the play makes use of the sources it evokes,
not to gloss character, and characters, in the play, but to call attention to the possibility of their unknowability. The more recognizable Hero is as a convention, the greater her tangency with other
defamed, ink-pitted women, the more we question who she is and
how we shall know her.

Recalling the misogyny of its narrative antecedents in its own
representation of gender, *Much Ado* would seem simultaneously
to distance itself from the heroic romance values and tropes those
narratives embody. Yet the heroic is not absent from Shakespeare's
Messina; rather, it is summoned just enough to remind us of how
unheroic the world of Messina is, the foreignness of the heroic sub-

liminally reinforced with every reference to Hero's name, a Hero with no Leander in sight. "Kill Claudio," Beatrice commands Benedick (4.1.289), a remark which in casting Beatrice in the unfamiliar role of a lady imposing a love test, assigns to Benedick the equally unwonted, and apparently unwanted, part of champion, an assignment which in confronting Benedick with the necessity of choosing between love and friendship, renders him momentarily, and uncharacteristically, at a loss for words—"Ha, not for the wide world" (4.1.290)—and shoves the play into a parodic tangency with the chivalric ethos of Ariosto and his imitators, where the duel and trial by combat are the preferred methods of conflict resolution and the means by which libelled ladies get exonerated. Resolving to "challenge" Claudio (4.1.331), Benedick proves he is no Rinaldo, nor even an Ariodanto, and his failure is revealingly discursive: underscoring the interjection of the heroic as some alien idiom, and underscoring the degree to which it is assumed by what Harry Berger calls the Men's Club of Messina[34] that Benedick the quipster is never fully serious, Benedick has a difficult time making his departure from levity understood by Claudio and Don Pedro, and making his challenge understood by its designated target, Claudio (5.1.143–95).

Yet the aborted irruption of the heroic into the discursive space of the play is but a transitory reminder of a more obtrusive incursion into the physical and political space of Messina, that of Don Pedro of Arragon, along with Leonato, one of the two characters whom by name and position Shakespeare draws from Bandello's novella. In Bandello, Don Piero occupies the frame of the story. An imperialist interloper—indeed, for Belleforest *"ce Roy inhumain*[35]—from Spain who, taking advantage of the void in Sicily caused by the slaughter of the French in the Sicilian Vespers, "came quickly thither with his army, and made himself lord of the Island,"[36] he disappears from the romantic fable at the center of Bandello's story involving two of his knights and the daughters of Lionato, only to reimpose himself, if more benignly, at the end, investing Lionato's daughters and the knights they marry with the sorts of dowries which Lionato, it is made clear, cannot afford to provide, and to which Don Piero feels any knights of his are entitled.[37] In turning Don Piero into Don Pedro and giving him a prominent presence throughout *Much Ado*, Shakespeare elides the two aspects Don Piero bears in Bandello, muting his territorial aggression and subsuming it and his royal magnanimity within a no less

aggressive proclivity for matchmaking, as evinced in the proactive
guises he adopts, both in personally wooing Hero for Claudio, and
more vicariously, but no less manipulatively, in getting Benedick
and Beatrice to think each in love with the other, a campaign which
if successful would, Don Pedro brags, in a gush of *gloire*, displace
Cupid: "his glory shall be ours, for we are the only love-gods"
(2.1.384–87)—once an hegemonist, it seems, always an hegemonist!

And yet the elision is hardly seamless. From the opening lines of
the play, and the deixis with which Leonato, scanning the letter the
Messenger has brought, couples a reference to "this action" with
the news of Don Pedro's arrival (1.1.1–6), the play by preterition
permits us not to forget what it pretends to suppress, attaching references to Don Pedro's anterior, martial self and to his status as an
outsider, even as it would appear to labor to integrate him in the
comic community and doings of Messina. We hear, of course, a typically simultaneous evocation and displacement of things Spanish
in the verbal joke fusing "civil" with "seville oranges"—the citrus
of choice, it seems, in Messina, where "seville" oranges make civil
hands unclean (see 2.1.294, 4.1.32).[38] Apart from this playfully ca-
sual allusion, however, the play incarnates in Don Pedro—and in
the importunate residual "baggage" the play creates for him in the
figure of the sociopathic Don John—traces of some greater world, a
world of political *imperium*, intrigue, and power relations, a world
toward which Hero's simile in the "pleached bower" fecklessly
gestures. So it is that when roughly halfway through the play, and
before Claudio's marriage, Don Pedro announces that he will soon
be leaving the community in which he has recently been so active
a player. Claudio's offer to accompany him, coupled with the
Prince's demurral that he will settle for the company of the unmarried Benedick instead, serves not only to remind us of division between the sexes in the play and the tenuous grip even the pre-
disillusioned Claudio has on his relationship to Hero, but to bring
to the foreground an orb of political claims that the insulation of
male camaraderie and the merrymaking of the play repress (3.2.1–
14).

In turn, ambiguities in the nature of Don Pedro's relationship to
the community of Messina expose the hybrid nature of Messina itself, *almost* masking its status as a client city-state[39] behind the ge-
nial civil disarray that is its "normal" civil rule, a rule enforced on
the street by a constable who would have hypothetical transgres-

sions addressed by ignoring them, and who solves real crimes despite, and not through, his best efforts.[40] To be sure, in demoting Don Pedro to prince from the king he had been in Bandello and Belleforest, *Much Ado* may soften Don Pedro's authoritarian edges and make him a more approachable fellow whose offers of wedlock Beatrice can decline with a joke and seeming impunity (2.1.326–33), but it renders the nature and extent of his authority in Messina, and, for that matter, the nature of his relationship to that other figure of authority in Messina, Leonato, unclear, and surely less clear than the relations between their counterparts in Bandello. Certainly, in *Much Ado* Leonato greets Don Pedro with a rhetoric sufficiently obsequious as to suggest the posture of a political, if not social, inferior (1.1.99–102). At the same time, as Straznicky has argued, Leonato's tirade against Hero and his subsequent maneuvers to compel Claudio to bow to his pleasure in the re-nuptials as readily suggest a concern with status and power and the desire to maintain and regain them against Don Pedro and Claudio as they do the grief of a father for a daughter shamed.[41] In fact, it is a measure of the ambiguity of Don Pedro's relationship to the power structure of Messina that when Dogberry calls his crew "the Prince's watch" (3.3.6), tells them that they may "bid any man stand in the Prince's name" (3.3.26), and reminds them that they are to "meddle" only with "the Prince's subjects" (3.3.33), we could ask "Which Prince?" For though we would surmise that it is Don Pedro to whom Dogberry refers—for lack of any other prince in town—still, nothing in the play clearly articulates that Don Pedro is in charge, and the situation only grows more confusing when in the very next scene Dogberry, with an instinct, if not aptitude, for deference, assures Duke Leonato that he and his watch are "the poor Duke's officers" (3.4.20).

At the end of *Much Ado About Nothing*, and in that recuperative rush toward nuptials and festivity Howard has anatomized,[42] the curious presence Don Pedro assumes as something of a "fifth wheel"—a status his counterpart does not bear in Bandello, where he comes fully mated with a queen—is symptomatic, not only of the tensions of his own status in the play, but of the curious relationship *Much Ado* negotiates with its source materials, particularly, in this case, Bandello's story.[43] For like *Much Ado About Nothing*, Bandello's story looks beyond the bounds of its romantic fiction when at its very end its narrator begins to enumerate the noble progeny to descend from the union of Timbreo and Fenicia, only to catch himself, coyly, in the act of violating generic decorum, for "without noticing it, I have digressed from telling stories to making panegyrics!"[44] In *Much Ado* the slippage for which Bandello's narrator archly apologizes is folded into its dramatic action and discourse, making us aware of what it excludes, something rather like Don Pedro himself, something integral to our experience of the play but not fully assimilated, our sense of which gives our experience of *Much Ado About Nothing* its peculiar richness.

Notes

1. All references to *Much Ado About Nothing* and other plays by Shakespeare come from *The Riverside Shakespeare*, ed. G. Blakemore Evans, 2d ed. (Boston: Houghton Mifflin Company, 1997), and are cited parenthetically.

2. See George Lyman Kittredge, ed., *Much Ado About Nothing*, rev. Irving Ribner (Waltham, MA: Blaisdell Publishing Company, 1967), 44; A. R. Humphreys, ed., *The Arden Shakespeare Much Ado About Nothing* (London: Methuen, 1981; rpt., Walton-on-Thames, Surrey, U.K.: Thomas Nelson & Sons, 1997), 143–44; F. H. Mares, ed., *Much Ado About Nothing* (Cambridge: Cambridge University Press, 1988), 90; Sheldon Zitner, ed., *The Oxford Shakespeare Much Ado About Nothing* (Oxford: Oxford University Press, 1993), 139. Following Horace Howard Furness, *Much Ado About Nothing: A New Variorum Edition* (New York: American Scholar Publications, 1966), xvii, Mares cites Furnivall's speculation that the simile is a reference to Essex and his misadventures, albeit "a late two-line addition" to a play generally taken to have antedated the insurrection by two years (90).

3. The figure of the intractable honeysuckle offers but a negative variation on the behavior described in the contemporary prose character of "a loyal Subject [who] like [the] Marigold should open and shutt with the Sunn"; cited in W. J. Paylor, *The Overburian Characters* (Oxford: Oxford University Press, 1936), 111. Both Mares, 90, and Zitner, 139, underscore the likelihood that as part of her aristocratic upbringing Hero would not have been unlikely to have encountered such a *sententia*. But the point here is not that Hero is incapable of employing such figures, but that such figures, and a tendency to employ them, are nowhere else a part of her verbal *repertoire*.

4. Harry Berger Jr., "Against the Sink-a-Pace: Sexual and Family Politics in *Much Ado About Nothing*," in *Making Trifles of Terrors: Redistributing Complicities in Shakespeare*, ed. Peter Erickson (Stanford: Stanford University Press, 1997), 14.

5. That the women in *Much Ado* may internalize those barriers, see Carole McKewin, "Counsels of Gall and Grace: Intimate Conversations Between Women in Shakespeare's Plays," *The Woman's Part: Feminist Criticism of Shakespeare*, ed. Carolyn Ruth Swift Lenz, Gayle Greene, and Carol Thomas Neely (Urbana: University of Illinois Press, 1980), 124–26.

6. For surveys of possible sources, see Charles Prouty, *The Sources of Much*

Ado About Nothing: A Critical Study, Together with the Text of Peter Beverly's Ariodanto and Ieneura (New Haven: Yale University Press, 1950); and Geoffrey Bullough, ed., *Narrative and Dramatic Sources of Shakespeare*, vol. 2 (London: Routledge and Kegan Paul, 1958); see also Kenneth Muir, *The Sources of Shakespeare's Plays* (New Haven: Yale University Press, 1978), 113–15; Humphreys, Arden ed., 24, and Zitner, Oxford ed., 12. For speculation that the characterization of Benedick in particular may have been inspired not by literary sources, but by the courtier, poet, and translator of Ariosto, Sir John Harington, see Juliet Dusinberre, "Much Ado About Lying: Shakespeare and Sir John Harington in Dialogue with *Orlando Furioso*," in *The Italian World of English Renaissance Drama: Cultural Exchange and Intertextuality*, ed. Michele Marrapodi (Newark: University of Delaware Press, 1998), 239–57.

7. For a summary of the significations found in the title of the play, see Zitner, Oxford ed. 14–15. See also the titles of Dusinberre, cited above, n. 6, and Leo Salingar, "Borachio's Indiscretion: Some Noting about *Much Ado*," in *The Italian World of English Renaissance Drama*, 225–38.

8. Representative is A. R. Humphreys, Arden ed., 13, who treats the evocations of Bandello and Ariosto in *Much Ado* in terms reminiscent of the "secondary Imagination" and very much as a function of a controlling, assimilative artistry. "Interweaving Bandello's materials with Ariosto's," Humphreys observes, "Shakespeare shows a mind ranging over elements loosely similar but so markedly variant in tone and incidents that only the shrewdest of judgements could co-ordinate them into a theme of such tragi-comic force."

9. Jacques Derrida, *Margins of Philosophy*, trans. Alan Bass (Chicago: University of Chicago Press, 1982), xvi.

10. For Salingar, "Borachio's Indiscretion," 228, in *Much Ado* "[s]ocial transmission becomes a medium of distortion." This propensity in *Much Ado* is highlighted and counterpointed for Dusinberre, "Much Ado About Lying," 254, by the figure of Benedick, "a man who will wear his faith but as the fashion of his hat," and yet "is nevertheless an honest man."

11. To be sure, what have been seen as the oddities in Claudio's behavior, the misogyny that erupts so readily when he supposes that Don Pedro has "got" his Hero, the calculated violence of his rejection of Hero, the coolness with which he behaves when he supposes her dead, the tendency of the figure in the play most identifiable as a "lover" to act so amorously challenged, lead Prouty, in *The Sources of Much Ado About Nothing*, 39–47, to read Claudio, not as a conventionally literary lover at all, but as a product of social "realism," a figure for whom marriage is a practical, contractual affair, a *mariage de convenance*, and thus one for whom a prospective bride's virginity was central to the assessment of her "market" value.

12. Jean E. Howard, "Renaissance Antitheatricality and the Politics of Gender and Rank in *Much Ado About Nothing*," in *Shakespeare Reproduced: The Text in History and Ideology*, ed. Howard and Marion F. O'Connor (New York: Methuen, Inc., 1987), 173.

13. Recall the travesty of the literary in the ubiquitous letter writing of *The Two Gentlemen of Verona* and, most memorably, the reminder supplied the bookish Horatio by the no less bookish Hamlet that "[t]here are more things in heaven and earth, Horatio, / Than are dreamt of in your philosophy" (1.5.166–67).

14. Hence, in George Whetstone's *The Rocke of Regard* (1576), in *Illustrations of Early English Poetry*, ed. J. Payne Collier vol. 2 (London, 1866–70), 73, a forged missive imbedded by a jealous rival and a treacherous maidservant in a suggestively post-lapsarian apple poisons, at least for the next eighteen pages, the relationship between Rinaldo and Giletta, while in *Ariodanto and Ieneura, daughter to the King of Scottes, in English verse, by Peter Beuerly* (1565–66 [Prouty, 68]), *The Sources of Much Ado About Nothing*, 94, we find a letter from the eponymous heroine to the eponymous hero, the amorous contents of which are rendered so compromising in the repressive courtly society of the protagonists that it must be destroyed lest it fall into the wrong hands.

15. "Good sentences, and well pronounced" is Portia's drily dismissive response to the *sententiae* Nerissa invokes in her attempt to invalidate the feeling of world-weariness Portia expresses upon her entrance in *The Merchant of Venice* (1.2.1–10). See also the treatment of the sententious Friar Lawrence in *Romeo and Juliet*, whose moral apothegms may be "true," but are inadequate to cope with the irruption of events and "rude" human nature in the play, an irony remarked upon by G. Blakemore Evans in his introduction to *The New Cambridge Romeo and Juliet* (Cambridge: Cambridge University Press, 1984), 24–25.

16. Or, as Zitner, Oxford ed., 10, dubs him, the "caste-obsessed messenger with no concern for the merely common dead."

17. Barbara Everett, "*Much Ado About Nothing*: The Unsociable Comedy," in *English Comedy*, ed. Michael Cordner, Peter Holland, and John Kerrigan (Cambridge: Cambridge University Press, 1994), 71.

18. Citing the recurrence of such scenes, Maus argues in *Inwardness and Theater in the English Renaissance* (Chicago: University of Chicago Press, 1995), 120, that "[a]ttempts at surveillance are the way the cuckold ritually defines himself, inside and outside the playhouse."

19. Salingar, "Borachio's Indiscretion," 225–26.

20. That seeing should not always be believing is timelessly affirmed by Chico Marx in *Duck Soup*, when in response to Margaret Dumont's surprise at finding him in her bedroom when she had just seen him leave, "with my own eyes," he asks, "Well, who you gonna believe, me or your own eyes?"

21. *The Faerie Queene*, in *The Complete Poetical Works of Spenser*, ed. R. E. Neil Dodge (Cambridge: The Riverside Press, 1936), 2.4.28, 11.3–5.

22. Bullough, *Narrative and Dramatic Sources*, 2:116.

23. Prouty, *The Sources of Much Ado About Nothing*, 115–16. For the corresponding scene in Ariosto, see *Orlando Furioso*, 5.42–51, in Bullough, *Narrative and Dramatic Sources*, 2:92–94.

24. On the concern among contemporary antitheatricalist polemicists that clothes did, indeed, make the man and woman and that theatrical cross-dressing undermined the essence of gender distinctions, see Laura Levine, *Men in Women's Clothing: Anti-theatricality and Effeminization, 1579–1642* (Cambridge: Cambridge University Press, 1994), esp. 1–25.

25. Such is Dalinda's recollection in *Orlando Furioso*, 5.49.5–8, in Bullough, *Narrative and Dramatic Sources*, 2:94.

26. *Orlando Furioso*, 5.50.1–4, in Bullough, *Narrative and Dramatic Sources*, 2: 94.

27. Bullough, *Narrative and Dramatic Sources*, 2:114.

28. Marta Straznicky, "Shakespeare and The Government of Comedy: *Much Ado about Nothing*," *Shakespeare Studies* 22 (1994), p. 155.

29. Bullough, *Narrative and Dramatic Sources*, 2:118.

30. Prouty, *The Sources of Much Ado About Nothing*, 127–28.

31. Anthony Munday, *A Critical Edition of Anthony Munday's Fedele and Fortunio*, ed. Richard Hosley (New York: Garland Publishing, 1981), 152.

32. Bullough, *Narrative and Dramatic Sources*, 2:95. Consider, however, the argument that Dusinberre makes that Harington "thought of himself as a writer for women, aiming the *Orlando* at the queen's ladies to make them laugh," in "Much Ado About Lying," p. 241.

33. Janice Hays, "Those 'soft and delicate desires': *Much Ado* and the Distrust of Women," in *The Woman's Part: Feminist Criticism of Shakespeare*, 87.

34. Berger, "Against the Sink-a-Pace," 14.

35. Not surprisingly, in the *histoire* by the French writer Belleforest, the arrival of the Don Pedro figure in Sicily hot upon the massacre of the French is viewed with considerable asperity. See François de Belle-forest, *Le Troisiesme Tome Des Histoires Tragiques, Extraite des oeuvres Italiennes de Bandel* (Paris 1572), 475.

36. Bullough, *Narrative and Dramatic Sources*, 2:112.

37. Bullough, *Narrative and Dramatic Sources*, 2:133.

38. A tart reminder, perhaps, of the minatory associations of things Spanish only sharpened by the heightened sense of nationalism in post-Armada England, recalled in A. J. Hoenselaars, *Images of Englishmen and Foreigners in the Drama of Shakespeare and His Contemporaries* (Rutherford: Fairleigh Dickinson University Press, 1992), 26–27. See also the simile "civil as a civil orange" in Nashe's *Strange News*, in *The Works of Thomas Nashe*, ed. Ronald B. McKerson, 5 vols. (Oxford: Basil Blackwell, 1958), 1:329.

39. Not that *Much Ado* is any more convincingly "urban" than it is "heroic." See Gail Kern Paster in *The Idea of the City in the Age of Shakespeare* (Athens: University of Georgia Press, 1985), 178; and Salingar's symptomatically elusive reference, in "Borachio's Indiscretion," 229, to the play's "comparatively realistic urban atmosphere."

40. That Dogberry's precarious grip on power and authority may all too aptly have mirrored the lot of local constabularies, see Theodore B. Leinwand, "Negotiation and New Historicism," *PMLA* 105 (May 1990), 481–85; and Phoebe Spinrad, "Dogberry Hero: Shakespeare's Comic Constables in Their Communal Context," *Studies in Philology* 89 (1992), 163–69.

41. Straznicky, "The Government of Comedy," 155–56.

42. Howard, "Renaissance Anti-theatricality and the Politics of Gender and Rank," 179.

43. For Zitner, Oxford ed., 10, there is no tension: "Shakespeare dismantles Bandello's framework and reassembles it as irony," an irony that knocks Don Pedro from "Bandello's pedestal."

44. Bullough, *Narrative and Dramatic Sources*, 2:134.

"Your Actions Are My Dreams": Sleepy Minds in Shakespeare's Last Plays

JENNIFER LEWIN

IN MAKING HIS famous declaration "We are such stuff / As dreams are made on; and our little life / Is rounded with a sleep" (4.1.156–58),[1] Prospero has long been thought to be saying goodbye to his magical powers with an analogy between the insubstantiality of the masque for Ferdinand and Miranda that now has ended and the fragility of humanity and human endeavor itself. As he prepares to drown his book, Prospero's tone becomes more elegiac, and he seems to place less emphasis on fleeting things. The presence of sleep and dreams in his valedictory language reveals a very different tendency, however, in which the contemplation of such powerlessness creates an anxious awareness in him of mental life itself, more than it inspires awe and wonder concerning the shape of human existence.[2] Although Prospero's elegant words have an air of lofty certainty, there is no solace in such a tenuous grip on the world. What unnerves him, what he wrestles with here, is the unfixed quality of the "dreams" and "sleep" he refers to. Their ungroundedness is precisely what makes mental life and language itself both extraordinarily sensual and urgent. T. G. Bishop remarks that

> By this late stage in his career, Shakespeare's dramatic language has become an instrument subtle and searching enough to register not only the surface gestures of a character, but also the secret affections or intentions that inform those gestures. The imagination has become a layered thing, often obscure to itself, inventing its purposes moment by moment at several levels.[3]

The most salient aspect of the imagination's opacity in the last plays is its consistent investigation of the reality of mental life, its evocation of an absorbingly staged drama of the mind even as—or perhaps *because*—the plays readily attempt to achieve certainty in the midst of discrepancies between surfaces and secrets, and the affective sources of action. During their most memorable moments, these plays claim in paradoxically sensual terms that that we *are* our mental experiences, and that mental experiences have undeniably sensual effects.

Northrop Frye remarks that the romances contain an "imaginative faith" that "is something much more positive than any mere suspension of disbelief, however willing"; sleep and dreams put intense pressure on that faith by affirming the difficulty of measuring the distance between perception and truth, knowledge and belief, and memory and action.[4] They permit characters to go far in avoiding knowledge that would prove either threatening or embarrassing, and to nourish false beliefs, memories, and desires. Shakespeare's plays precede Freud and contemporary neurological research in noticing that sleep and dreams expose and create unsettling emotions far more often than they instill happiness in those who experience them.[5] Dreams show that characters know both a little more and a little less than they think they do about themselves, others, and the world.[6] Thereby dreams create a skeptical stance toward self-knowledge by alienating such figures from themselves, from a firmer familiarity with the content of their own minds. Nowhere do sleep and dreams more insistently frame these fundamental topics than in Shakespeare's last plays. Clearly they are relevant to discussions of earlier works including *Richard III*, *Midsummer Night's Dream*, and *Macbeth*, but they permeate the last plays in specific ways that are shared by those plays as a whole, and especially by the two plays this discussion will focus on, *The Winter's Tale* and *The Tempest*.

The skepticism that Stanley Cavell persuasively finds to dominate *The Winter's Tale* is immersed in the language of sleep and dreams. Cavell argues that Leontes' jealousy is rooted in a deep reluctance to recognize his own fatherhood.[7] Such a recognition would put an end to "the very intensifying of his identification with Polixenes,"[8] an identification that is aided by sleep. Sleep allows their identification to prolong itself; dream signals its extreme end in that it illustrates the play's need to face its own startling, implicit recognition that the identification already has gone too far. Sleep is as close to a perfect escape from intractable prob-

lems, great and small, as characters ever achieve. In the opening
scene of the play, Archidamus remarks that when his turn comes to
host the Sicilian king in Bohemia, he will be forced to remedy his
own country's deficiencies with "sleepy drinks" that render those
who taste them "unintelligent of our insufficience" (1.1.14–15).
The brief but highly significant mention of this drug-induced state
literalizes a forcible if somewhat desperate reconciliation between
perception and reality, as if it were the only way to maintain a
friendship built on sameness, the mutual exchange of gifts, and vis-
its of equal extravagance. Sleep permits the avoidance of discrepancies between expectations and the way things really are, between
wishful thinking and the stubborn presence of difference.

In a similar move that may not seem so at first, the Bohemian
shepherd who later discovers the infant Perdita remarks that he
"would there were no age between ten and three-and-twenty, or
that youth would sleep out the rest" (3.3.58–60). In his silly way
the shepherd reveals the sheer versatility of sleep as a compellingly
flexible solution to problems ranging from the scaring off of sleep
to the damage to reputation caused by pregnancy out of wedlock.
The shepherd and Archidamus realize the detrimental effects of the
availability of ordinary cognition, judgment, and will to people
whose minds and bodies one seeks to influence. When rhetorical
persuasion or physical violence cannot succeed, putting someone
to sleep is always a viable, albeit temporary, solution. In the play's
very next scene, the chorus, Time, asks the audience to suspend
disbelief as the play jumps ahead sixteen years, imagining that they
"had slept between" (4.1.17). Time effectively makes the play fulfill the shepherd's wish, imposing Frye's "imaginative faith" by
skipping over the years reminiscent of those in which friendships
such as Leontes and Polixenes' are solidified, and hence their identification with one another is forged. And yet the Old Shepherd
quickly forgets this wish when he says of Florizel, disguised as Dor-
icles, that if he chooses his daughter "she shall bring him that /
Which he not dreams of" (4.4.181–82).

As if in response to the concerns and ambitions of the older generation, the young prince and princess themselves address these
matters later on in the same scene. Florizel reveals his haste in
showing the Old Shepherd that the younger generation will exceed
expectation with dreams: "One being dead, / I shall have more than
you can dream of yet; / Enough then for your wonder" (4.4.382–
84). And when we see Perdita talking with Florizel, she memorably

uses the language of dreams to show him that the game of love is over: "this dream of mine / Being now awake, I'll queen it no inch farther" (4.4.452–53), lines that Coleridge found some of the most affecting in the entire play.[9] With declarations like this, Perdita brings us toward the end of the illusionary world of Bohemia and toward the reunion with the real queen in the final act. The idea that sleep is the great reconciler of significant theatrical problems reflects a solution within the play that an earlier play, *Midsummer Night's Dream*, situates at its very end in an address to the audience: "Think but this, and all is mended, / That you have but slumber'd here / While these visions did appear" (5.1.432). In *The Winter's Tale*, sleep is asked to heighten the credibility of the world onstage; by contrast, Puck suggests that sleep protects the theater against the incredulity that waking consciousness facilitates.[10]

Sleep and dream, then, are collapsed into one. They are no longer ontologically distinct because from the play's very first act the identification with Polixenes that Leontes suffers from is a form of sleep, in which dreams are common property that protect sleepers from waking into an unfamiliar and hence destabilizing world.[11] Polixenes admits as much for himself when he fondly reminisces about the "innocence" of their friendship: "we knew not / The doctrine of ill-doing, nor dream'd / That any did" (1.2.69–71). Such a dream would have constituted an intense, nightmarish crisis—it would have meant entering a far more suspicious world peopled by minds whose interiors one cannot access. Until now their friendship has protected them from the shock of that inaccessibility, but even "the best case of knowledge" is vulnerable to "the transformation of a scene of knowing for oneself into a sense that true knowledge is beyond the human self, that what we hold in our minds to be true of the world can have at best the status of opinion, educated guesswork, hypothesis, construction, belief."[12] With the consistent aid of sleep and dreams, this transformation is exactly what Leontes experiences in the course of the first three acts of the play. The former self becomes the dreaming self, the self dreaming of omniscience because it deeply fears its own shortcomings.

The instrumentality of the sleep and dreams of childhood I have described as sheltering Leontes from exposure to the disturbing epistemological discrepancies between one's perceptions and the world quickly combines, however, with Leontes' rapid descent into doubt. A prescient Cartesian, he assumes that one can never know that one is not dreaming (Perdita will later examplify someone who can). Using the language of dreams yet once more, he inflicts the consequences of this doubt about the validity of his own perceptions onto the body and activities of Hermione. With his chilling retort "your actions are my dreams" (3.2.82), a line that responds to Hermione's "My life stands at the level of your dreams," it becomes clear that he is so infected with jealousy that Hermione ceases to be a real person to him, and his own mind is at once a source of disgust and denial; it becomes all he knows. He is "an Othello who is his own Iago."[13] Her actions are his dreams because like a dreamer, he cannot control his mental life so it completely controls him and the world he sees. I read Leontes as saying not that her actions are so nightmarish that they haunt him as such, as resembling a dream that contains clues meant to challenge his belief in her faithfulness. With "your actions are my dreams," he suggests that he cannot imagine her actions or Hermione herself as literally existing anywhere else but inside his own delirious mind. Her existence turns him inward because she frighteningly embodies what is uncontrollable and unknowable about other people; that is all he can know about her. Unable to acknowledge that he is implicated in this process of making her into such a creature, that in fact his version of her existence is a construction of his own, he becomes fixated on removing himself from such a daunting association as if she is the one who is out of reach. The jealous mind is an inward looking one because all it has are its own thoughts to feed on, and yet it is this very quality that causes it to become disgusted by itself. Without thinking it cannot be so; without his own thoughts she cannot exist, and his thoughts repulse him. Until Leontes' mind is rid of this absorption the play cannot move beyond him.[14] It stays in a dream world, capitulating to the temptations of sleep.

In an early scene in *The Tempest*, Ariel initiates a series of episodes that distinguish this play as being preoccupied in other ways with sleep as an ingenious mechanism of psychosomatic control. It is seldom remembered that just after the tempest itself with which the play begins, Ariel forces the boatswain and the mariners to fall asleep until late in act 5, and Ariel performs the same trick with many of the island's visitors, including Gonzalo, in the middle of the play. Sleep is Ariel's focal point for simultaneously managing affect and plot alike. Thus Prospero prolongs his control over those he needs to manipulate, without doing any noticeable physical harm. The question of what they have done to the sleepers' newly awakened minds, however, remains tantalizingly open. Even for those who are already awake, something of a reawakening occurs. Take the moment, for example, when Antonio turns to Sebastian and speaks like a would-be seducer of wrongdoing, playing the role of Lady Macbeth to Sebastian's Macbeth:

> Ant. . . . Th'occasion speaks thee, and
> My strong imagination sees a crown
> Dropping upon thy head.
> Seb. What? art thou waking?
> Ant. Do you not hear me speak?
> Seb. I do, and surely
> It is a sleepy language, and thou speak'st
> Out of thy sleep. What is it thou didst say?
> This is a strange repose, to be asleep
> With eyes open—standing, speaking, moving—
> And yet so fast asleep.
> Ant. Noble Sebastian,
> Thou let'st thy fortune sleep—die, rather; wink'st
> Whiles thou art waking.
> (2.1.207–17)

Sebastian lets Antonio take the lead in this conspiracy plot whose rhetoric centralizes an idea of sleep that moves between the word's literal and metaphorical meanings. The "sleepy language" Sebastian hears is one he will not acknowledge being attracted to. It allows Ariel stealthily to succeed in his mission to get him to try to turn treasonous ideas into dangerous actions, to manage their expressions of desire and their urgently deceptive motives. Just before the two plotters are able to murder the sleeping Alonso and Gonzalo, Ariel rescues them by means of a song whispered to Gonzalo that vaguely informs him of the imminent threat to his life. Here Ariel brilliantly uses sleep to show off his magical ability to control both mental perception and the bodies of characters under his spell, an ability shared by Prospero and wished for in *The Winter's Tale* by characters such as Time, the Shepherd, and Archidamus in the moments we have already discussed. The process of thinking paradoxically is sleepy and a form of sensation in scenes like these, titillating the evil characters with temptation and making them aware of the degree to which mental activities like cognition, for Sebastian, are sensual: they prompt, resemble, and create

heightened awareness of bodily states, especially sleep. Whether
one is trying to seize political power or to reminisce about youthful
indiscretions, sleep can represent either the vulnerable lure of
oblivion or the eerier attractions of seizing control over one's circumstances. When it does so it also creates an obscured sense of
mental agency, as we shall see it does for Miranda in the second
scene of act 1. Here, Gonzalo is on his guard when he awakens but
does not say whether he knows who is to blame or to thank for his
new state of mind. We do not see him reasoning his way through
the meaning of the song in his ear, but merely responding to it.
What does Gonzalo know, consciously and unconsciously? Has he
heard pieces of the conversation while asleep? Alonso, for all we
know, still believes that Antonio and Sebastian have protected him
from grave harm. Sleep enables the audience to know somewhat
differently. It silently exposes unusually resonant discrepancies between what characters know and what we know, but it also shows
us that characters can have interiorities that we cannot know in
full.

The products of sleep can be tellingly diverse: they enable plots
or narratives to unfold, they alert characters to expressions of desires for power, and they show the success of magical projects
(Prospero's and, by extension, Ariel's) in subtly undermining a
sense of control over destiny even before that sense of control has
made itself felt.[15] When sleep overtakes a character onstage, it turns
waking characters into an audience of sorts and can arouse strange,
and even menacing, emotions or temptations in them. The plot
against the lives of Gonzalo and Alonzo hatched while they sleep
surely gains urgency by their vulnerable bodily presence onstage.
Likewise, because of their sleep onstage, wakened characters such
as Gonzalo unknowingly attain unusual relationships between language and self-knowledge. Sleep may have provided them with
some way of understanding the world that we have no access to,
and will never know. Their minds are filled with ideas that they
cannot quite register as their own, and yet they are unable to dismiss the same ideas as foreign or irrelevant. Nor are the ideas any
longer in the full possession of the magus. We watch the character
ruminate on or accept some truths as given without fully knowing
how they arrived at them. Whether or not we can have this knowledge, and what it would mean to, are two of the deeper questions
that sleep and dreams ultimately point us to but cannot answer.[16]
As David Bevington remarks, "As sleep becomes more theatrical,

it serves as an apt vehicle for explorations of carnival inversion, indeterminacy of meaning, uncertainty as to the will of Providence, and the ironies of human lack of self-awareness."[18]

An example of what I have been arguing is also a *sensual* uncertainty highlighted by sleep and dreams occurs in act 1 scene 2, when Prospero puts Miranda to sleep without her knowledge that he is doing so, right after she asks about his responsibility for the tempest. He says "I know thou canst not choose" (1.2.186). Sleep in this case creates an excess of interpretation whereby it is difficult to know whether or not the character's utterances about it or upon waking are expressive of his or her own thoughts or if the mind remains fettered by the outside force, in this case Prospero. Miranda's sleep raises several possible interpretations that are far from mutually exclusive: first, that Prospero believes she needs to sleep in order to understand, that is to remember, his narrative; second, that it enables her to forget the question as soon as she asks it about his role in the tempest's origins; and third, that it further illustrates Prospero's willfulness. One recent analysis Heather James puts forth is that "by lulling her into an involuntary sleep, Prospero puts an end to a line of questioning that cuts across the grain of his paternal absolutism. . . . Unable to acknowledge his plans [for the men who have arrived], he cuts short her questions and plunges her into sleep."[18] Prospero may also go one step further, and cause Miranda later on to offer the following: "The strangeness of your story put / Heaviness in me" (1.2.306–7). Whether or not Prospero inspires this sentiment is left unspecified, but the play intimates the possibility. Surely, as James implicitly suggests, the ensuing conversation between Prospero and Ariel would have alerted Miranda to her father's control over the storm. In turn, this very control (and the conversation about it that she sleeps through) again directly involves sleep: during their conversation we learn that Prospero has had Ariel put the mariners on the ship to sleep too. Ariel won't release them until act 5, when their account of their bewilderment and uncertainty about whether they sleep or wake will resemble that of Sebastian in act 2, though without implying any of his greed: "even in a dream, were we divided from them, / And were brought moping hither" (5.1.239–40). Release from sleep's bondage does not entail immediate detachment from its effects. As we have seen, sleep often suffuses characters with a deeply mournful, and sense-driven conceptualization of their own emotional lives. It leaves them in the thrall of forces that seem, and in this case in fact are, out of their control. In a parallel development it establishes a wildly vivid sense of the same characters' physicality with words like "moping."

Echoing and parodying its previous manifestations, sleep permeates another hostile, if somewhat comic, attempt to alter the power imbalance on the island that Ariel and Prospero have already proven themselves capable of using it to establish. When Caliban in act 3 proposes that he and Stephano destroy Prospero while he sleeps, he reveals his own knowledge of how sleep exposes one's vulnerability to several kinds of assault. Caliban uncannily seems to be repeating what has already happened in act 2, telling Stephano that in order to take control of the island they need to seize Prospero's books and by doing so they will have turned him into the "sot" that Caliban is. Caliban's plans call for violent collaboration ("I'll yield him thee asleep, / where thou mayst knock a nail into his head" [3.2.60–61]) and he repeats his instructions involving sleep:

> Why, as I told thee, 'tis a custom with him
> I' th' afternoon to sleep. There thou mayst brain him,
> Having first seiz'd his books . . .
>   Remember
> First to possess his books; for without them
> He's but a sot, as I am;
>
>   (3.2.87–93)

Finally, Caliban again turns to Stephano: "Within this half hour will he be asleep. / Wilt thou destroy him then?" (3.2.114–15). Sleep exposes Caliban's foolish plotting, because no one takes him up on the idea, more than it poses as a real threat to Prospero, but in doing so it reveals an intimacy between Caliban and Prospero, whose sleep patterns Caliban is well aware of.[19] Caliban's familiarity with the island extends to its inhabitants in surprising ways, though sleep takes revenge on the revenger himself in that Stephano and Trinculo fail to follow through.

So far sleep has been shown to be a condition that purports to solve a range of epistemological and moral issues both within the late plays and about them; specifically it allows characters to control or to imagine controlling one another's private actions or thoughts, political and social power, and perception. It also allows them to posit a private space of obliviousness: with its suspension of physical mobility and normal cognition, sleep also shields others from full knowledge of their conditions, as witness the boatswain's reaction to his bewildering experience on the island. None of these instances, however, quite prepares us for Caliban's account of sleep and dream in act 3. In his well-known speech, sleep registers a private access to worlds that lie outside his immediate, daily life, whether we believe the passage to be "one of the loveliest passages in the play" or "the matrix for the culminating masque-like depiction of the monster's flawed ideal,"[20] to quote from two of the diverse responses he has succeeded in generating:

> Be not afeard, the isle is full of noises,
> Sounds, and sweet airs, that give delight and hurt not.
> Sometimes a thousand twangling instruments
> Will hum about mine ears; and sometime voices,
> That if I then had wak'd after long sleep,
> Will make me sleep again, and then in dreaming,
> The clouds methought would open, and show riches
> Ready to drop upon me, that when I wak'd
> I cried to dream again.
>
> (3.2.135–43)

Caliban questions not only the ontological specialness of the real world but also the preference for it. Music leads him to sleep which leads to dream, creating such intense longing for its repetition that he prefers the dream to all else. The plenitude that dreaming offers is an escape from the impoverishment that characterizes the existence he desperately wants to transform, and it also indicates the plenitude that is what one reader recently has called Shakespeare's "compensatory powers of language."[21] It is a moment of complete concentration; nothing else matters but the recollection of a oneness with "the isle" and the "riches." Vicariously experiencing his "delight" in his intimate knowledge of the island and the sensual pleasures of listening, sleeping, and dreaming, we are watching Caliban come as close as any Shakespearean character does to creating the very circumstances he describes. Another striking feature is that the *readiness* is what predominates: Caliban recounts the infinitely enjoyable, repeated experience of a perpetual state of anticipation. The riches never do come either in the dream or elsewhere and we cannot know if Caliban is drawn to replay the scene because the riches may one day drop or because it is delightful as is; the promise itself seems nourishing enough. Caliban's dreaming mind is a retreat from everyday life so superior to that life that it becomes a blissful form of self-fulfillment. His mental life is so intense that it momentarily compensates for, and almost causes us to lose sight of, the suffering of his ordinary existence even as his crying hints at that suffering. We hold both aspects of his experience in mind and acutely experience both of them with him. Even to himself, and to us, he is a little out of reach. The fervency with which he encourages the tramps to attack Prospero gives way to an indulgence in sensuous experience that returns us to enchantments that are neither dangerous nor didactic.

The only other experience of dreaming that comes close to Caliban's in intensity is Antigonus's dream in the third act of *The Winter's Tale*. Earlier I suggested in brief that in order for the effective purgation of Leontes' skepticism to occur, a readily identifiable sacrificial moment is required that dissolves all the epistemological doubts that his jealousy has engendered. Antigonus's dream transforms him from a peripheral character into that crucial sacrifice; as such, it is an episode with which interpretations of the play have not sufficiently been concerned.[22] With it, Shakespeare realizes manifold possibilities for how dreams can reflect complex mental states, carefully demonstrating the deepest truth they do in all the last plays: *the palpable reality of mental life greatly differs from its truthfulness.* As we have seen, the less true Leontes' beliefs become, the more he separates himself from the social world of the play, and the harder it is to envision his eventual return to normalcy. The swift expulsion of falsity—and, before that can happen, the beliefs' physical and mental separation from Leontes and full embodiment in another character—are the most convincing means Shakespeare ever designs for restoring a character and an entire play to the ready acceptance of knowledge that such skepticism had prevented for three long acts.[23] Just as it looks back to and is an attempt to solve the problems raised in the play's first three acts, to think about how one would stage it also calls attention to its anticipation of Hermione's appearance in act 5. As Kenneth Gross has written about the latter scene, in which the statue's "silence speaks out of a paradoxical, resistant inwardness" at the same time that its "more gently elegiac air" is remarkable,[24] Antigonus's dream-figure betrays the frustrations and inadequacies, as well as the wondrous epistemological ambiguities, of its own task. Although the dream

authorizes the restitution of Leontes' court, its price tag is Antigonus's life; it looks ahead to another consequence, that of Leontes
and Hermione's final failure to achieve a successful reunion. Even
as (marital) life is restored, the play challenges the idea that one
ever can fully recover the lost object of desire. Antigonus investigates these matters long before act 5.

First and foremost, Antigonus's dream is dramatically useful in
that it facilitates the movement of the action of the play from the
Sicilian court to the green world of Bohemia.[25] The transition is as
psychological as it is physical, marked by the altered quality of
Antigonus's language, which is suffused with an elegance and cal-
mness that it never had before. I quote the dream in full, as well as
some of Antigonus's reflections on the dream:

> I have heard (but not believ'd) the spirits o'th' dead
> May walk again. If such thing be, thy mother
> Appear'd to me last night; for ne'er was dream
> So like a waking. To me comes a creature,
> Sometimes her head on one side, some another—
> I never saw a vessel of like sorrow,
> So fill'd, and so becoming; in pure white robes,
> Like very sanctity, she did approach
> My cabin where I lay; thrice bow'd before me,
> And (gasping to begin some speech) her eyes
> Became two spouts; the fury spent, anon
> Did this break from her: "Good Antigonus,
> Since fate (against thy better disposition)
> Hath made thy person for the thrower-out
> Of my poor babe, according to thine oath,
> Places remote enough are in Bohemia,
> There weep, and leave it crying; and for the babe
> Is counted lost forever, Perdita
> I prithee call 't. For this ungentle business,
> Put on thee by my lord, thou ne'er shalt see
> Thy wife Paulina more." And so, with shrieks,
> She melted into air. Affrighted much,
> I did in time collect myself and thought
> This was so, and no slumber. Dreams are toys,
> Yet for this once, yea, superstitiously,
> I will be squar'd by this. I do believe
> Hermione hath suffer'd death, and that
> Apollo would (this being indeed the issue

> Of King Polixenes) it should here be laid,
> Either for life or death, upon the earth
> Of its right father. Blossom, speed thee well!

$\qquad\qquad\qquad\qquad\qquad\qquad\qquad\qquad\qquad$ (3.3.16–46)

Hesitant and yet insistent, Antigonus shares his new experience with benign incredulity. He utters two of Leontes' false beliefs, namely that Hermione is adulterous and that she is dead. It is puzzling that Antigonus assumes both of these to be the case. As for the second belief, he is already on his way to deliver Perdita, according to Leontes' instructions, "to some remote and desert place" (2.3.176) when Paulina later falsely attests: "I'll say she's dead; I'll swear't" (3.2.203). In addition, when Hermione tells Antigonus that "places remote enough are in Bohemia" she uses two words Leontes had used in the speech just quoted from in act 2, when he tells Antigonus to bring Perdita away (2.3.176), resonating with Freud's observation that dreams yield "evidence of knowledge and memories which the waking subject is unaware of possessing." Hermione was in jail when Leontes spoke these words to Antigonus and presumably could not have heard them. Paulina, who may have repeated his instructions to Hermione, was also absent during the conversation between Antigonus and Leontes. Dreams are wish-fulfillments in creating better, more well-integrated responses to situations than one feels one has given in waking life; the dream lets Hermione address Leontes' charge and control the dramatic situation from what Antigonus considers to be beyond the grave. But it is at the same time a simple, pithy plot device. Antigonus thereby gets to perform an act of condensation: several duties are taken care of at once. He not only embodies Leontes' false beliefs, he responds (through Hermione) to Leontes' wishes, changing their potential consequences, in ways that he could not imagine before.

Finally, there is a delicately ekphrastic quality to the dreamed Hermione. She is a statue of sorts. Hermione's "pure white robes / Like very sanctity" clearly have religious overtones and suggest that she has sacrificed herself like Alcestis. One of the most conspicuous aspects of the visual description here is its distinctive emphasis on Hermione's ceremonious liquidity. She is "a vessel" that is "fill'd" and that releases tears through her eyes as if they were a fountain's "spouts" soon "spent." The account invites us to remember Gail Kern Paster's observation that this sort of attention to the female body was "a culturally familiar discourse" that "in-

scribes women as leaky vessels by isolating one element of the female body's material expressiveness—its production of fluids—as
excessive, hence either disturbing or shameful. It also characteristically links this liquid expressiveness to excessive verbal fluency."[26]
Here Hermione is literally a "vessel" of both bodily fluids and a
speech that has extraordinary effect, but Antigonus's perspective
on what comes from her is much more sympathetic than Paster's
tends to be. He clearly pities her and is in awe of her presence and
gestures, facing with trepidation and unease this last task of his
life as a member of Leontes' court and, in doing so, unwittingly
transforming the nature of that court. Toward the end of *The Body
Embarrassed* Paster notes how several contemporary manuals recommended that women who have just given birth not be emotion-
ally excited or made upset, which makes this scene a significant
extension, through the mind of Antigonus, of how Leontes in the
trial scene performs "a clearly unwarranted intrusion of patriarchal
power."[27]

The language of Antigonus's "spiritual visitation," according to
J. H. P. Pafford, makes him seem to exist "in one sense outside the
play."[28] Antigonus describes Hermione's appearance as achieving a
beautiful purity (in her white robes and intricate evasions of likeness she looks ahead to the late-espoused saint in Milton's sonnet).
Her distress, her turmoil, and the quality of her agony clearly echo
the trial scene and address the question of Leontes' jealousy in a
way that allows her to embody its wrongful effects. In conveying
this picture, Antigonus himself becomes a vessel of sights and
sounds that he is barely in control of, and he uses a different rhetorical technique, reminding us that he is unable to undergo the kind
of transformation Leontes will.

The dream foreshadows the attention that the statue of Hermione
receives at the end of the play. If, according to Janet Adelman,
"identified with Cleopatra in his longing for Antony, Shakespeare
in effect locates the recuperative power of his own art in the female
space of her monument, making her imaginative fecundity the
model for his own; and in his imaginative alliance with her, he is
able to recuperate theater itself, rewriting its dangerous affiliation
with the female in *Macbeth* and *Coriolanus*,"[29] then with Antigonus's dream Shakespeare distances the play from one model of
imaginative fecundity in order to make room for the final monu-
ment-turned-flesh in the final act of the play. Thereby Shakespeare
offers us two Hermiones at the end of the play: Antigonus's Hermi-

one and Paulina's Hermione, with the former making way for the latter. Comparing Paulina to another magus with whom this essay has been concerned, namely Prospero, Stephen Orgel notes: "Paulina requires much less in the way of apparatus, only a discovery curtain and a Hermione capable of standing absolutely motionless for eighty lines; but her demand for a suspension of disbelief, her invocation of wonder, and most of all, her claims for the therapeutic quality of her performance sound much more like Renaissance apologias for theatre than like any Renaissance version of religious experience."[30] Antigonus's speech likewise evokes wonder and requires no apparatus. He not only demands that the audience suspend their disbelief, he admits to having imaginative faith in the sensual reality of his own mind and acting on the impulses it urges him to accept as truth.

Antigonus thereby makes possible the shifting rhetoric of act 5 in which a single word that signifies the play's definitive movement away from sleep and dreams and therefore away from Leontes' false surmises, the word "awake," is able to accrue multiple thematic connotations as *The Winter's Tale* draws to a close. Remember that Perdita herself had used it in relation to the dream of Florizel in act 4. Just after instructing her audience that "It is requir'd / You do awake your faith" Paulina brings the statue of Hermione to life. She does so with the command "Music! awake her! strike!" (5.3.94–95; 98). Using the same imperative not only to control the collective frame of mind and response that her dramatic spectacle should elicit, but also to animate the statue of Hermione, Paulina indicates her directorial role and assumes an ability to manage belief, affect, and, indeed, the very ontological existence of those around her.[31] She replaces her husband's Hermione with the real thing, but the real thing requires a different kind of imagination. By doing so she carefully shifts Leontes' and our attention from his initial willingness to experience "what you can make her do" (5.3.91) into active mental participation. Forbidding the audience to remain "content" hearers and "lookers-on," she attempts to make them achieve the heightened state of apperception reminiscent of that with which dreams are experienced and their meanings pondered by characters like Antigonus, or Caliban when he cries to dream again. Lastly, Paulina's act of awakening strategically, if literally, banishes Leontes' false beliefs by evoking the trial scene in which Hermione invokes metaphorical versions of the same set of somatic conditions, calling Leontes' accusations "surmises (all proofs sleeping else / But what your jealousies awake)" (3.2.112–13). Here being "awake" means leaving behind that jealousy and the destruction it created. Hers is one of the final attempts of the last plays to shape the reality of characters' minds, an attempt made possible by dreams and demises.

Paulina, like Ariel, now will be done with such tricks, leaving Prospero as the single artificer continuing to bewilder characters such as the boatswain: "even in a dream, were we divided from them, / And were brought moping hither" (5.1.239–40).[32] Although Prospero has renounced his magic and prepared himself for a new life in which every third thought will be his grave ironically it is the realm of sleep, brother of death, that remains the world in which his effects, as on this still confused character, linger. *The Winter's Tale* attempts to replace dreams and sleep with an awakened faith; with the effects of Prospero's use of sleep, the residual powers of his magic succeed in haunting the end of *The Tempest*.

Notes

1. *The Riverside Shakespeare*, ed. G. Blakemore Evans (Boston: Houghton Mifflin, 1997). All quotations of the plays, unless otherwise noted, are from this edition.

2. For good recent discussions of Prospero's sense of "the pressure of mortality" see Mary Ellen Lamb, "Engendering the Narrative Act: Old Wives' Tales in *The Winter's Tale, Macbeth,* and *The Tempest*," *Criticism* 40 (1998): 552–53, and David Lindley's introduction to his edition of *The Tempest* (Cambridge: Cambridge University Press, 2002), 30.

3. Bishop, *Shakespeare and the Theatre of Wonder* (Cambridge: Cambridge University Press, 1996), 149. See also Russ McDonald's recent *Shakespeare and the Arts of Language* (Oxford: Oxford University Press, 2001). McDonald remarks on how Shakespeare's last plays show "a renewed faith in the theatrical enterprise, a devotion to the surface, a commitment to the material value of the medium, a positive assessment of such potentially dubious phenomena as illusion, ornament, and the signifier as signifier" (47–48).

4. Frye, *A Natural Perspective: The Development of Shakespearean Comedy and Romance* (New York: Harcourt Brace Jovanovich, 1965), 19. The dream in Shakespeare's romances is discussed at great length by Marjorie Garber in *Dream in Shakespeare: From Metaphor to Metamorphosis* (New Haven: Yale University Press, 1975), 139–214. My discussion is indebted to hers, and especially to her sense of the distinctive quality of dreams in the romances and that of the poetry of the plays itself.

5. J. Allan Hobson writes that "anxiety, fear, and surprise are the most common affects to undergo a marked intensification during dreaming" (*The Dreaming*

Brain: How the Brain Creates Both the Sense and the Nonsense of Dreams [New York: Basic Books, 1988], 7).

6. In a much contested passage, Freud noted, "it is a very common event for a dream to give evidence of knowledge and memories which the waking subject is unaware of possessing" (*The Interpretation of Dreams*, in the *Standard Edition of the Psychoanalytic Works of Sigmund Freud*, ed. James Strachey, 24 vols. [London: Hogarth Press, 1955], 4:14). This point will become particularly relevant when I explicate Antigonus' dream. But for a discussion of Freud's notion of "evidence" in dreams, see Jacques Lacan who treats Freud's dream of the burning son as being a suggestion of "a mystery that is the world of the beyond" (*The Four Fundamental Concepts of Psychoanalysis*, trans. Alan Sheridan and ed. Jacques-Alain Miller [New York: Norton, 1981], 34; see also pp 54–60), and also Dan Merkur, *Unconscious Wisdom: A Superego Function in Dreams, Conscience, and Inspiration* (Albany: SUNY Press, 2001). Whether or not we should even call the "evidence" about which Freud writes either "knowledge" or "memories" has long been debatable by neuroscientists and philosophers. For example, Hobson himself begins his "psychophysiological theory of dreaming" with a distinction between Freud's reliance on subjective knowledge and "obscurity" and his own focus on dreams as "transparent" and yielding discoveries about the brain that can objectively be known (Hobson, 12–14). For a rebuttal to Hobson, see Patricia Kitcher, *Freud's Dream: A Complete Interdisciplinary Science of Mind* (Cambridge: MIT Press, 1992), 113–49. Some philosophers claim, contra Freud, that dreams should not be taken seriously as experiences. In *Dreaming* (1959) Norman Malcolm claims that all we can know about the dream is the awake subject's report and that the report indeed is the dream—unlike public events, dreams are not verifiable or to be considered occurrences. In "Are Dreams Experiences?" Daniel C. Dennett makes a distinction between memories and experiences and argues that dreams cannot be the latter because they are the former, and recent ones at that: "the dream one 'recalls' on waking was composed just minutes earlier" and that the "subject is not in a privileged position to answer" questions about whether or not the dream is an experience (*Brainstorms: Philosophical Essays on Mind and Psychology* [Montgomery, VT: Bradford Books, 1978], 129–148).

For psychoanalytic readings of Shakespeare's plays variously indebted to Freud, though not always to his work on dream interpretation, see Norman N. Holland, ed., *Shakespeare's Personality* (Berkeley: University of California Press, 1989) and Julia Reinhard Lupton and Kenneth Reinhard, *After Oedipus: Shakespeare in Psychoanalysis* (Ithaca: Cornell University Press, 1993). Janet Adelman's *Suffocating Mothers: Fantasies of Maternal Origin in Shakespeare's Plays,* Hamlet *to* The Tempest (New York: Routledge, 1992), especially 198–238, Christopher Pye's *Vanishing: Shakespeare, the Subject, and Early Modern Culture* (Durham, NC: Duke University Press, 2000); Stephen Greenblatt, "Psychoanalysis and Renaissance Culture," in *Literary Theory/ Renaissance Texts*, ed. Patricia Parker and David Quint (Baltimore: Johns Hopkins University Press, 1986), 210–24 and Cynthia Marshall, "Psychoanalyzing the Prepsychoanalytic Subject" *PMLA* 117 (October 2002): 1207–16.

7. "Recounting Gains, Showing Losses: Reading *The Winter's Tale*," in *Disowning Knowledge in Six Plays of Shakespeare* (Cambridge: Cambridge University Press, 1987), 193–221. For a psychoanalytic reading of the play that argues that

Leontes' jealousy is based on his latent homosexuality, see J. I. M. Stewart, *Character and Motive in Shakespeare* (London: Routledge, 1949). Compatible with my argument is Randal Robinson's point that Leontes "is frightened by uncontrollable fantasies of disgrace when circumstances make him intensely libidinal," and that he does "make progress toward the acceptance and development of his libidinal ego" though I do not agree that Leontes "responds to [Hermione] warmly" at the play's end ("Stage Images in *Titus Andronicus* and *The Winter's Tale*," *From Page to Performance: Essays in Early English Drama*, 224). For an interpretation that holds that Leontes is equally uncomfortable with and threatened by "his own interior" for reasons having to do with his philosophical skepticism, see David Hillman, "Visceral Knowledge: Shakespeare, Skepticism, and the Interior of the Early Modern Body," in *The Body in Parts: Fantasies of Corporeality in Early Modern Europe*, ed. Carla Mazzio and David Hillman (New York: Routledge, 1997), 95–96. Other sources of Leontes' jealousy not discussed herein are the idea of maternal self-sufficiency, noted by Madelon Sprengnether in relation to dreams and fantasy in Freud, *The Spectral Mother: Freud, Feminism, and Psychoanalysis* (Ithaca: Cornell University Press, 1990), 76–77; for a related discussion, see Jessica Benjamin's article "The Primal Leap of Psychoanalysis, from Body to Speech: Freud, Feminism, and the Vicissitudes of the Transference," in *Freud 2000*, ed. Anthony Elliott (New York: Routledge, 1999), 110–38.

8. Cavell, 213.

9. Coleridge's marginalia are reprinted in the Signet edition of *The Winter's Tale*, ed. Frank Kermode (New York: Penguin, 1998), 146. For a persuasive view of the relationship between Florizel and Perdita which lends credence to the idea that they are really in love, see William Empson, "Hunt the Symbol," in *Essays on Shakespeare*, ed. David B. Pirie (Cambridge: Cambridge University Press, 1986), 232–35. For a view that takes seriously the perspective of Derek Traversi, in which the plot of the last plays is secondary to the poetry, see Russ McDonald, "Poetry and Plot in *The Winter's Tale*," *Shakespeare Quarterly* 36 (1985): 315–29. I agree with the idea that "[the verse] illuminates and comments on two central themes of *The Winter's Tale*, the complexities of perception and the importance of time in the process of perception," (328).

10. See also David Bevington's comments that "Sleeping onstage in Shakespeare often occurs at moments of otherworldly visitation, as in medieval drama, or evokes at least a powerfully ominous world of magic," ("Asleep Onstage," *From Page to Performance: Essays in Early English Drama*, ed. John A. Alford (East Lansing: Michigan State University Press, 1990), 69).

11. T. G. Bishop makes a similar point (*Shakespeare and the Theatre of Wonder*, 144). Another positive version of the work of the dream, namely its creation of a "great constancy" (in the words of Hippolyta) that affirms the imagination's power, is discussed by Kathryn L. Lynch, "Baring Bottom: Shakespeare and the Chaucerian Dream Vision," in *Reading Dreams: The Interpretation of Dreams from Chaucer to Shakespeare* (Oxford: Oxford University Press, 1999), 99–124.

12. Cavell, 7.

13. Harold Bloom, *Shakespeare: The Invention of the Human* (New York: Riverhead Books, 1998), 639.

14. Kaplan and Eggert, "'Good queen, my lord, good queen': Sexual Slander and the Trials of Female Authority in *The Winter's Tale*," *Renaissance Drama* 25 (1994): 110.

15. These comments should indicate that I agree with Janet Adelman that Leontes "in his inability to tolerate the unreliable world outside himself, had retreated to the space of his delusion," (*Suffocating Mothers*, 235). While Adelman locates the costs of Leontes' return to the world in terms of control of the female, I instead read Antigonus as the central victim. Perhaps these readings are not mutually exclusive. Although his focus differs from mine in that his seems to be on whether or not the ghost of Hermione is "real or unreal" (203), a view closer to my own would be that of Stephen Greenblatt, who writes of this speech that "to the extent that *The Winter's Tale* is centrally about horrible consequences of taking fantasies as realities—the whole cause of Leontes' viciously false accusation against his wife—then we are meant to distance ourselves from Antigonus' dream and to think of his ghost story as a psychological projection" (*Hamlet in Purgatory* [Princeton: Princeton University Press, 2001], 202).

16. For a brief argument about Shakespeare critics and their acceptance of Prospero's cruel control over others, see Empson, 238–43.

17. To a certain extent, this is also the theme of Howard Felperin's " 'Tongue-Tied Our Queen?': The Deconstruction of Presence in *The Winter's Tale*," in *Shakespeare and the Question of Theory*, eds. Patricia Parker and Geoffrey Hartman (New York: Methuen, 1985), 3–18.

18. Bevington, 53.

19. James, "Dido's Ear: Tragedy and the Politics of Response," *Shakespeare Quarterly* 52 (2001): 370.

20. As Leslie Katz and Kenneth Gross remark, "In thwarting Caliban's attempt to remove and replace oppressive hierarchies, Stephano and Trinculo pick up on the gleeful ease with which puppets refuse to take sires . . . Puppets can be seen as all revolt, all spirit of contradiction. Caliban seeks to channel precisely this species of aggressive momentum into a shared dream of usurpation" ("The Puppet's Calling," *Raritan* 15 [1995]: 22). See also Simon Palfrey, *Late Shakespeare: A New World of Words* (Oxford: Clarendon Press, 1997), 24–7.

21. See, respectively, Hallett Smith's introductory essay to *The Tempest* in the Riverside edition, 1660; and John G. Demaray's *Shakespeare and Spectacles of Strangeness:* The Tempest *and the Transformation of Renaissance Theatrical Forms* (Pittsburgh: Duquesne University Press, 1998), 121. For the eloquently argued view that Caliban shows us "the wonderful quality of the island becomes here an image of frustration for Caliban-frustration both in the dream and out of it, because even if the riches did descend, what value would they have on the island?" see Stephen Kitay Orgel, "New Uses of Adversity: Tragic Experience in *The Tempest*," in *In Defense of Dreading: A Reader's Approach to Literary Criticism*, ed. Reuben A. Brower and Richard Poirier (New York: E. P. Dutton, 1962), 124.

22. The phrase is Russ McDonald's (*Shakespeare and the Arts of Language*, 188).

23. References to the dream in recent years include that which Stephen Orgel includes in his edition of *The Winter's Tale*, where he writes of Antigonus's dream of the ghost of Hermione that "Roman Catholic thinking admitted the existence of ghosts, but Protestantism was skeptical and in the official view, ghosts were delusions produced by the devil. To the drama of the period, however, they were indispensable, and Antigonus keeps all the options open" (Oxford: Oxford University Press, 1996), 153. For an argument about Antigonus' illogical thinking, see David

Thatcher, "Antigonus' Dream in *The Winter's Tale*," *The Upstart Crow* 13 (1993): 130–42.

24. If, according to Adelman, "*The Winter's Tale* restores the mother to life and makes the father's generativity and authority contingent on her return," (*Suffocating Mothers*, 236) it can only do so after the father's delusions are gone. See also Valerie Traub, "Jewels, Statues, and Corpses: Containment of Female Erotic Power in Shakespeare's Plays," *Shakespeare Studies* 20 (1987): 215–38. While I disagree with Traub's assertions that "Hermione's 'unmanageable' sexuality must be metaphorically contained and psychically disarmed" and that "her silence toward Leontes" in act 5 "bespeaks a submissiveness most unlike her previous animation" (230), it is clear from the rest of my article that I agree with her useful point that "the anxieties that incited him to impose stasis upon her are still immanent, indeed, inherent, in their relationship" (233). Paulina attempts to assuage such anxieties in her "audience" broadly conceived, as does the play itself with the death of Antigonus, but we have no reason to believe that they do not linger in the mind. Marjorie Garber's observation that in Antigonus's dream Hermione's "death" symbolizes Antigonus' "failure of belief, another instance of unawakened faith" (171) is relevant here.

25. Gross, *The Dream of the Moving Statue* (Ithaca: Cornell University Press, 1995), 100, 101.

26. Bishop also marks this moment as the play's key transformation, but he locates the pivotal figure in the bear and not Antigonus's dream (152–53). See also Palfrey, 111.

27. Paster, *The Body Embarrassed: Drama and the Disciplines of Shame in Early Modern England* (Ithaca: Cornell University Press, 1993), 25. See too her essay "The Body and Its Passions," in which Paster notes that the early modern period was "a moment in the history of bodies, minds, and souls when bodily fluids could still carry the full weight of a character's destiny, a moment when dense causal networks linked body, mind, culture, and the physical world" and that "If bodily fluids were the stuff of emotions, then to alter the character and quantity of a body's fluids was to alter that body's passions and thus that body's state of mind and soul" (*Shakespeare Studies* 29 [2000]: 46).

28. Paster, *The Body Embarrassed*, 273.

29. Pafford, ed. *The Winter's Tale* (London: Routledge, 1993), lxxxvii.

30. Adelman, 192.

31. *The Winter's Tale*, ed. Stephen Orgel (Oxford: Oxford University Press, 1996), 62.

32. Lynn Enterline has persuasively linked the play, and this scene in particular, to its Ovidian and Petrarchan heritages as well as to literary theorists' critiques of J. L. Austin's speech-act theory. Of Paulina's lines, she comments: "her command represents an *idea* about language as performance" rather than being "literally a performative utterance"; the idea, Enterline explains, is Ovidian: "the dream of a voice so persuasive that it can effect the changes of which it speaks" (*The Rhetoric of the Body from Ovid to Shakespeare* [Cambridge: Cambridge University Press, 2000], 222).

33. For another reading of Paulina's words that is concerned with Renaissance theology, see Walter S. Lim, "Knowledge and Belief in *The Winter's Tale*," *Studies in English Literature* 41 (2001): 317–34.

34. As Harold Bloom remarks, in act 5 "Prospero's abjuration sounds more like a great assertion of power than like a withdrawal from efficacy"; he is "an uncanny magician whose art has become so internalized that it cannot be abandoned, even though he insists it will be" (*Shakespeare*, 683). The boatswain's speech, then, brings the play to where it first began, because it reminds us of his role in both act 1 and act 5, through which we are able to witness the bewildering effects of Prospero's powers. For a discussion of the play that also emphasizes Prospero's desire for control throughout the play and especially in act 5, see Orgel, "New Uses of Adversity," 129–32. Orgel writes, "His tone is that of a character with a full comprehension of the experience of the drama; and the sense it gives us is of a mind achieving full control of itself" (114). When he fears relinquishing that control, sleep provides instrument and metaphor for power over others and the threat of of oblivion.

REVIEWS

Writings by Early Modern Women
Edited by Peter Beal and Margaret J. M. Ezell
English Manuscript Studies 1100–1700, Volume 9
London: The British Library, 2000

Reviewer: Sara Jayne Steen

Writings by Early Modern Women continues the English Manuscript Studies tradition of providing first-rate essays about manuscripts and manuscript culture in books that are both well edited and beautifully produced. The editors of volume 9 are among the most respected scholars in manuscript studies, and their work necessarily underlies this collection. Peter Beal's volumes of *Index of English Literary Manuscripts* and his *In Praise of Scribes: Manuscripts and Their Makers in Seventeenth-Century England* (1998) have provided invaluable information about resources and about the previously overlooked participants in manuscript culture: its scriveners. Margaret J. M. Ezell's *The Patriarch's Wife: Literary Evidence and the History of the Family* (1987), *Writing Women's Literary History* (1992), and *Social Authorship and the Advent of Print* (1999) have transformed our understanding of manuscript culture and women's place in a world where literary reputation could be established through manuscript circulation. With Harold Love (a member of the editorial board for the series), they have led early modern literary studies to a new interest in manuscripts and materiality and set high standards for the use of manuscript evidence.

For this volume, Beal and Ezell have chosen essays written by a number of scholars who are well known in the fields of manuscript studies and women writers; the majority of authors have been associated with the Perdita Project and the allied Renaissance MS colloquia or with the Brown University Women Writers Project. The result is an informed and engaging collection treating writings by many sixteenth- and seventeenth-century women in a broad range of genres:

poems, translations, illustrated books, letters, mothers' advice books, meditations, commonplace books, biographies, and diaries. The essays consider manuscript evidence—handwriting, calligraphy, paper, dating—but the authors' concerns also extend to theoretical questions of public versus private writing, the complex social, biographical, and political contexts in which these works were produced, and the collaborative nature of some of the manuscripts.

The volume opens with a treatment of wider issues in Jane Stevenson's "Women, Writing and Scribal Publication in the Sixteenth Century." Fifty English and Scottish women wrote verse before 1600 that is extant, and Stevenson asks what these pieces reveal. Half of the women printed some of their work, and half did not, suggesting that we should not place women completely within the manuscript culture: "women and print in the sixteenth century is at least as important a topic as women and manuscripts" (1). Like a number of recent scholars, Stevenson also argues that the notion of writing as either private (handwritten) or public (printed) should be reconsidered. For gentlewomen and aristocrats, verse composition could be a social skill; in verse exchanges, women flirted or wooed and enjoyed the wit. Women compiled manuscript miscellanies such as the Devonshire Manuscript, circulated among a group of female friends, and women's verse was included in women's and men's manuscript miscellanies. Women also served as patrons and dedicatees and as employers of poets and scribes. Stevenson concludes that the distinction between manuscript and print is not the distinction between private and public, that women's use of manuscript and print was, like men's, dependent on audience and situation.

In "Princess Elizabeth's Hand in *The Glass of the Sinful Soul,*" Frances Teague reads not the text of the eleven-year-old Elizabeth's translation of Marguerite de Navarre's *Miroir de l'ame pecheresse,* but the manuscript book as a material object and in relation to its potential use and cultural symbolism. The volume was one of several given as gifts to family members at about the same time, and Teague argues that they "provide an interesting synecdoche for their creator, the Princess Elizabeth, as a commodity, a marriageable princess" (36). If the manuscript of *Glass of the Sinful Soul* was occasioned by marriage negotiations (and Teague notes that three spouses were proposed for Elizabeth during this period), how would it present her as a potential royal bride? Through its handwriting and embroidery, Teague contends, the book would fulfill its goals: to demonstrate to potential suitors the princess's chastity, piety, education, and worthinesss.

Two essays examine the works of calligrapher Esther Inglis. Anneke Tjan-Bakker, in "Dame Flora's Blossoms: Esther Inglis's Flower-Illustrated Manuscripts," notes that Inglis focused on complex flower illustrations for only a short time during her career. Tjan-Bakker argues that serious financial need led Inglis during this period to create many gift books demonstrating her skill as a calligrapher in hopes of acquiring patrons and improving her situation. Georgianna Ziegler offers a modern parallel to Inglis's work in "Hand-Ma[i]de Books: The Manuscripts of Esther Inglis, Early-Modern Precursors of the Artists' Book." To Ziegler, Inglis was an artist who was conscious of the form of her manuscript books, creatively incorporating into them diverse elements to create unique works with her own identity. In their variety and innovation, then, Inglis's works can be seen as precursors of the modern "artist's book," a form that in turn offers another perspective from which to understand Inglis's achievement.

Several essays treat women's manuscript materials of which few people have been aware. In "Two Unpublished Letters by Mary Herbert, Countess of Pembroke," Steven W. May augments the twenty letters collected in Hannay, Kinnamon, and Brennan's edition of Pembroke's *Collected Works* (1998) with two new letters to neighbor John Thynne that show Pembroke as a patron. Victoria E. Burke, in "Elizabeth Ashburnham Richardson's 'Motherlie Endeauors' in Manuscript," adds two new manuscripts to the corpus of Richardson's writing. These manuscripts indicate that Richardson "treated both her manuscript and printed texts . . . as sites for continual revision" (98), never considering either her print or manuscript versions fixed and finished. Moreover, these texts demonstrate that Richardson was engaged in mother's advice writing much earlier than previously believed. Margaret P. Hannay brings Pembroke and Richardson together in "Elizabeth Ashburnham Richardson's Meditation on the Countess of Pembroke's *Discourse.*" In one of the manuscripts described by Burke above is a "précis of and meditation on the Countess of Pembroke's *A Discourse of Life and Death* (1592)," a meditation that was either "composed, or supervised" (114) by Richardson, with corrections in her hand. This text expands Pembroke's reception history, providing an unusual example of one early modern woman writer commenting on the work of another, and also demonstrates Richardson as a reader and a scribe rewriting Pembroke, sometimes quoting and sometimes composing independently, reshaping Pembroke's translation to make it suit Richardson and her experiences. A transcription of Richardson's meditation appears in an appendix.

Other essays focus on the collaborations between women and men in the production of texts. Sylvia Brown, in "The Approbation of Elizabeth Jocelin," compares the manuscript of Elizabeth Jocelin's *Mother's Legacy to Her Unborn Child* with the printed version supervised by chaplain Thomas Goad. Although there is no authenticated sample of Jocelin's handwriting, Brown argues that the evidence indicates this manuscript was Jocelin's autograph fair copy, used as the copytext for the print version. Brown analyzes the significant changes made by Goad, focusing on his "editorial interference" (130) with Jocelin's words, and argues that Goad appropriated Jocelin's work for his own "religious and political agenda" (134), toning her down, making her more orthodox and less reformist, more acceptable as a woman. Similarly, Brown contends, Jocelin censored herself, and her changes indicate that Jocelin imagined a wider readership than her unborn child as she edited. Jean Klene strikes a cheerier note with regard to gender relations in "'Monument of an Endless Affection': Folger MS V.b.198 and Lady Anne Southwell." Klene maintains that the commonplace book illustrates "a lively domestic and textual collaboration" (165) between Southwell and her second husband, Captain Henry Sibthorpe. The manuscript demonstrates that they had a strong working relationship; they were, Klene says, aware of the gender system and employ it in a way that expands our sense of the possibilities that were available.

In a thoughtful and careful analysis of manuscript evidence, Heather Wolfe, in "The Scribal Hands and Dating of *Lady Falkland: Her Life*," considers the four different hands in the manuscript biography of Elizabeth Cary and argues persuasively that the main scribe likely was daughter Lucy and that the manuscript was annotated by Mary and Patrick Cary. Wolfe dates the writing of the manuscript to February through August of 1645 (not 1655 as has been accepted) and notes that the manuscript was bound by approximately 1650. The essay concludes with a postscript on English Nuns' Manuscripts, with locations and a bibliography of published transcriptions, also a boon to scholars.

Three essays treat texts associated with seventeenth-century English politics. Elizabeth Clarke's "Elizabeth Jekyll's Spiritual Diary: Private Manuscript or Political Document?" examines MS Osborn b 221 in the Beinecke Library at Yale and argues that it is not an autograph commonplace book: the final entry, in the same hand as the rest of the manuscript, is a copy of a printed text from over thirty years after Elizabeth Jekyll's death. Clarke suggests that this diary was a scribal publication written for political reasons, perhaps as a vindication of Jekyll's husband John, who was prosecuted in the 1680s as a political activist. Her diary emphasizes his good motives and his piety, in a work by an exemplary woman, and no one could be prosecuted because the copy was a scribal rather than a print publication. Mark Robson turns to a royalist poet in "Swansongs: Reading Voice in the Poetry of Lady Hester Pulter." Drawing on a manuscript collection of one prose romance and one hundred and twenty poems ranging from pastorals to polemics, Robson distinguishes three categories of poetry: political, including responses to the Civil War, devotional, and domestic. He explores the concept of voice through readings of two elegies, one political (on Robert Devereux, 3rd Earl of Essex) and the other personal (on a daughter, Jane). David Norbrook, in "Lucy Hutchinson and *Order and Disorder*: The Manuscript Evidence," argues that the Yale University Library's manuscript book containing an eighty-five-hundred-word poem of the book of Genesis is by Hutchinson and is an earlier version of the text later published anonymously in 1679 under the title *Order and Disorder: Or; The World Made and Undone. Being Meditations upon the Creation and the Fall; as it is recorded in the beginning of GENESIS* (a poem Norbrook has attributed to Hutchinson, rather than her brother Sir Allen Apsley). Norbrook maintains that there were political reasons not to put her name on the printed text, but also suggests that more of her work probably circulated in manuscript than has been known. In an appendix, Norbrook provides major substantive variants between the Yale manuscript and the 1679 printed text.

The final entry is A. S. G. Edwards's "Manuscripts at Auction: January 1999 to December 1999," a brief summary of literary manuscripts owned in the British Isles between 1100 and 1700 that have been sold in major auction houses in London and New York. The list is incomplete by definition, especially with regard to women's writing, since it excludes items traditionally classified as historical, such as letters and recipe collections. The list does, however, serve as a reminder to those not regularly monitoring Sotheby's that manuscripts from this era regularly emerge and change hands, with renewed possibilities for scholarship.

In short, the collection fulfills its promise. One could always cavil about individual points or wish for even more illustrations and greater clarity in reproduction, but this volume is a useful and elegant contribution to the fields of manuscript studies and early modern women's writing.

Shakespeare and the Poets' War
By James P. Bednarz
New York: Columbia University Press, 2001

Reviewer: Heather Hirschfeld

In his *Shakespeare and the Poets' War*, James Bednarz shows himself as feisty as the dueling writers—Ben Jonson, John Marston, Thomas Dekker, and William Shakespeare—whose combative relations he paints. Bednarz pulls no punches in his introduction, where he submits that the "Poetomachia" (a term coined by Dekker to describe a series of plays in which a set of dramatists mocked one another in various caricatures) was a real phenomenon, the "most important theatrical controversy of the late Elizabethan stage" (1), despite recent scholarship that has portrayed it as either an early modern advertising stunt or an invention of mid twentieth-century critics. As he says, "The first great dramatic criticism in England begins with this public dialogue—at once philosophical and personal—among Shakespeare, Jonson, Marston, and Dekker" (2). Bednarz makes good on his conviction by positing a fresh chronology of "phases" for the plays associated with the war, by explaining the playwrights' dissensions as the result of commercial and ideological as well as personal motives, and by measuring the dramatists' adversarial engagements not only in terms of their "impersonations" of one another but also in terms of their plays' generic affiliations. Whether or not one ends up agreeing with this thesis, that "it was during the Poets' War that drama became the definitive site for the struggle to articulate a new mode of unauthorized representation that examined the very process of legitimation with a new skepticism that would permanently alter the canon of Western literature" (17), Bednarz's readings of the dramatists' uses of romantic comedy and comical satire reinforce the value of this moment of intertextual debate for understanding the playwrights' investments in generic convention.

Bednarz distinguishes himself from earlier scholars of the Poets' War from the outset of the book with two particular arguments. First, he claims that during the Poetomachia Elizabethan playwrights themselves, and not their Restoration or Romantic heirs, generated what has become the almost mythic distinction between a scholarly Jonson and an inspired Shakespeare. As he writes, "the double portrait of a slow, learned Jonson and a quick-witted Shakespeare that [Thomas] Fuller and [John] Dryden popularized and passed on to Coleridge . . . was thus ultimately derived from their own criticism of each other during the Poets' War, not invented during the Restoration" (45). Bednarz returns to this refrain repeatedly, and in so doing he develops, in another hallmark of the book, a theory of rivalry-induced Shakespearean "self-construction." Second, he recasts the development of the Poets' War into three discrete phases, which he maps out at the start of the book and explicates in an appendix. (The book might have been better served if the explication had been up front, especially since some of its assertions are likely to be contested.) By grouping the texts in this way Bednarz provides a new perspective on their referential relationships, and he thus offers provocative interpretive pairings (like *Cynthia's Revels* and *Twelfth Night*) while making especially convincing the notion that the plays were in direct conversation with one another.

Oddly, although the bulk of the book moves in chronological order, Bednarz *starts* with the *last* of the Poetomachia plays, *Troilus and Cressida*, a distracting choice that forces him on multiple occasions either to supply plot summaries or to invoke later chapters. The point is to use the reading of *Troilus* to foreshadow the book's governing methodologies and central concerns, and Bednarz does demonstrate effectively his intention to interweave theater history with literary theory in his construction of institutional as well as personal frameworks for the Poets' War. Here Bednarz discusses *Troilus* as Shakespeare's effort, on behalf of the Chamberlain's Men, to challenge Ben Jonson and the Chapel Children for an educated, elite audience. Bednarz makes the connection, as he acknowledges others have before him, between the man Jonson and the character Ajax, but he is unique in reading the caricature as an exposure of Jonson's vulnerability to the sophisticated audience he believed, ironically, that he could train. By giving such a concrete context to *Troilus*, Bednarz sheds fresh light on the play's deconstruction of honor and value; for Bednarz, its deep skepticism is a specific response to Jonson's inflated humanism, and it reveals Shakespeare's "paradoxical destiny to both participate in the Poets' War and to confute the fundamental assumptions that brought it into existence" (51).

The remaining eight chapters of the book, which are divided into three sections that correspond to the phases of the Poets' War, rely similarly on this melding of the institutional contexts and aesthetic commitments of the playwrights. In the first of these sections, Bednarz submits that Jonson's *Every Man Out of His Humour* was the first sally in the wit-combat (though revised later in response to *Histriomastix*), and he is eloquent in his explanation of Jonson's reliance on Aristophanic comical satire to replace Shakespeare's Plautine sensibilities. *Every Man Out*, Bednarz argues, represents Jonson's humanist commitment to the perfectability of man, to the "idea that consciousness could indeed be radically changed for the better by great theater" (60). The following three chapters of this section discuss Marston's and Shakespeare's replies to this kind of dramatic hubris, which Bednarz asserts they found both formally and philosophically unsupportable.

Bednarz argues that *Histriomastix*, while offering praise as well as blame of Jonson through the pompous character of Chrisoganus, is nevertheless an attempt at "symbolic domination" that is ironically undercut by Marston's own suspicion of such ascendancy: "The paradox of Marston's participation in the Poets' War is that he sought to obtain the rewards of glory—intellectual mastery and cultural predominance over Jonson—by philosophically questioning the redemptive value of poetry" (103). Bednarz places *As You Like It* in this first stage of the Poetomachia, reading it against the opening of the Globe in 1599, the appearance of Robert Armin as the Chamberlain's Men's fool, and the possible cameo of the author himself as the hapless country bumpkin William, Audrey's ousted lover. These contextual details are supplied to undergird Bednarz's interpretation of Shakespeare's larger philosophical argument against Jonsonian "self-righteous satire" that neglects or even purges the role of desire in human change. As Bednarz explains, "*Every Man Out* upholds the moral power of an art that Shakespeare supposedly lacked, while *As You Like It* meditates on the primal opposition between the intellectual categories of nature and art that Jonson's comical satire presupposes" (129). In the final chapter in the section, he reads Marston's *Jack Drum's Entertainment* as more punitive than his earlier work, as it features, in a kind of *mise en abyme*, a caricature of Jonson caricaturing Marston himself. Bednarz is especially good here at cataloguing Marston's debts to Shakespeare (he says that "Marston imitated Shakespearean themes, characterization, plot, and diction *in every play he wrote for Paul's*" [176]), and he portrays convincingly Marston as a writer of festive as well as caustic comedy who mined the child actors for their romantic as well as satiric impulses.

Such an image of Marston as a romantic "poet-gallant" is central to the opening chapter of the book's next section, where it stands in opposition to Jonson as the "poet-scholar" of *Cynthia's Revels* whose role it is to supplant human desire with reason. Bednarz then pursues Shakespeare's approach in *Twelfth Night* to this dichotomy, what he calls "a struggle over the reinvention of coterie drama staged for a privileged audience involved in reassessing its philosophical and theatrical allegiances" (157). Here Bednarz has to backtrack a bit, since he introduced *What You Will* in the preceding chapter but now invokes it as a follow-up to *Twelfth Night* and extends the analysis he has already begun. This may be a small quibble, since the readings, which rely on distinctions between London's public and private theaters, are deft and engaging: he posits the "radicality" of Shakespeare's view of desire as both potentially selfless and a path toward, rather than away from, self-knowledge. As a critique of Jonson, *Twelfth Night* reaches its apogee in the character of Malvolio, whose "rhetoric of self-restraint only conceals sublimated desire" (189). Bednarz sees *What You Will* as the disaffected kin of Shakespeare's play; while Marston is similarly suspicious of Jonsonian rationality, he cannot sustain a genuine romantic impulse and thus turns "his sarcasm against festive comedy to secure a new, more alienated dramatic position that mapped Paul's distance from both Blackfriars and the Globe" (195).

The final section culminates with provocative readings of *Poetaster*, Jonson's most explicit challenge to Dekker and Marston and what Bednarz sees as a renunciation of the reforming potential of the theater, and *Hamlet*. It also includes speculations on Dekker's *Satiromastix*, which Bednarz believes is the work of Dekker alone (rather than a collaboration with Marston), and he perceptively interprets Dekker's work as an assault on Jonson, which nevertheless reinforces the latter's poetic standards. *Hamlet*, on the other hand, is portrayed by Bednarz as a thorough critique of these standards. He begins his discussion of the play by addressing textual questions associated with the "little eyases" passage, which he asserts was composed in 1601 in response to *Poetaster* and was represented in a corrupt form in Q1, cut from Q2, and portrayed correctly in F1. Bednarz's discussion of the relations between these versions seems thin; he insists, for instance, that "it is more plausible that [the eyases passage] . . . was cut from Q2 than that it was added to Q1 and F1" (248) without explaining, even in a lengthy footnote that addresses recent scholarship, *why* he is so persuaded. But his overall reading of *Hamlet* in the context of the Poets' War is illuminating. Bednarz reconsiders in original ways conventional observations about the play's extreme self-consciousness, explaining it as a response to "trenchant indictments of the public stage" that came "not . . . from Puritans or city authorities but from *within* the theater itself" (252), an important reframing of the antitheatrical debate. Bednarz thus reads *Hamlet*'s metatheatrics as a "defense" of the "common stages not by emphasizing the didactic power of poetry to transform its audience or the status of its performers, but by insisting that theatricality was the fundamental condition of human experience" (253). As a concluding statement on the stakes of the Poets' War, this is a wonderful observation, especially when combined with Bednarz's final remarks in the epilogue about *Troilus*'s corrosive skepticism and Jonson's "manipulative idealism" (263).

Despite such strong observations, however, there remain some gaps or loose ends in Bednarz's achievement. There are the aforementioned organizational issues—invoking plays not yet explained, referring back repeatedly to plays already covered—as well as the possibility that in his effort to reconsider the origins of the Shakespeare-Jonson dichotomy, he only reinforces the binary itself. Nor does he give a definitive sense of whether Shakespeare, even if he was responsive to the issues of the Poetomachia, was really in the thick of the fray or whether he simply remained a serene commentator. (Both models are available from this book.) But these are relatively small concerns. More substantial is Bednarz's handling of competing frameworks for understanding the Poets' War. Ironically, what makes his book compelling—its effort to assimilate the aesthetic, commercial, and philosophical components of dramatic composition—also provokes methodological inconsistencies. Bednarz has no systematic way for relating these components, and while it would be unfair to demand from him a unifying theory of the impact of the personal versus the professional on creative work, the lack here makes the emphasis of the chapters uneven, often resulting in a sense that issues of theater history—venue, audience—seem like late additions, inorganic to the argument. Readers may also find it disappointing that Bednarz does not pursue some of his fascinating observations about levels of impersonation provoked by the Poets' War—the concept, that is, that a playwright could present a caricature of another dramatist caricaturing him. Such insights cry out for further reflections on the nature and meaning of "identification" in the Poets' War, and yet Bednarz lets these opportunities slip by. And, in this era of critical interest in the literary politics of "negotiation," some readers may find the overall emphasis on writers' hostility and fractiousness misleading.

Nonetheless, these criticisms also reflect the strength and interest of the book, particularly the ways it approaches Shakespeare as an active participant in the Poets' War, traces the development of theatrical genres from a materialist perspective, and rejuvenates non-canonical plays for their aesthetic as well as topical meanings.

Fictions of the Pose: Rembrandt against the Italian Renaissance
Stanford: Stanford University Press, 2000; and

The Absence of Grace: Sprezzatura and Suspicion in Two Renaissance Courtesy Books
Stanford: Stanford University Press, 2000
By Harry Berger Jr.

Reviewer: Timothy Hampton

Montaigne prefaces his *Essays* with an address to his reader which insists on the private nature of what is about to be read. His book, he says, is for the use of his family and friends, so that they might

remember him after he is gone. Were he interested in public glory,
he notes, via Florio's translation, "I would surely have adorned my
selfe more quaintly, or kept a more grave and solemne march. I desire therein to be delineated in mine owne genuine, simple and or-
dinarie fashion, without contention, art or study; for it is myself I
pourtray." He goes on to say that the book will show his imperfections, "so farre-forth as publike reverence hath permitted me." Had
he been born among those nations which live under the law of Nature (presumably, the Americas), he concludes, "I would most will-
ingly have pourtrayed my selfe fully and naked." Montaigne's
formulation nicely captures a certain paradox that animates the
gesture of self-representation. On the one hand, there is an impulse
to individuality, if not sincerity. He wants to be seen as he is, without artifice. On the other hand, "publicke reverence," the strictures
of social decorum, or what we might call facticity, dictate that only
certain aspects of his identity may be made visible. Because he is a
European, for example, he keeps his clothes on. And yet, as Montaigne knows very well and notes repeatedly throughout the book,
clothes are precisely one of the most powerful bearers of "contention, art [and] study," the very things he disdains. In other words,
contingency shapes representation in such a way as to unmask sincerity as pose. Yet the possibility of escaping pose (through the
dream of complete expression or nakedness) remains nothing but
fantasy. In Montaigne's case the sense that self-representation is
threatened by posing may be seen as well in the cumulative power
of Florio's text, where Montaigne desires "therein to be delineated
. . . without contention, art, or study" juxtaposed with the original
French, where he says, "I want to be seen" [je veux qu'on m'y
voye]. The two versions together suggest that wanting to be seen
and being delineated may be inseparable.

Though his concern is not with Montaigne, this kind of representational paradox animates much of these two remarkable books by
Harry Berger Jr. *Fictions of the Pose* is a lengthy and dense elabora-
tion of an approach to reading Renaissance portraiture. Part of its
argument, which unwinds through some twenty-six chapters, involves a cogent and suggestive rereading of Castiglione's *Cortegiano*. *The Absence of Grace* develops the implications of Berger's
take on Castiglione, expanding it to include a reading of what is
probably the second most influential Italian courtesy book after
Castiglione's, Della Casa's *Galateo*. In the process, moreover, *The
Absence of Grace* literally incorporates the reading of Castiglione

from *Fictions of the Pose*; it simply reprints, almost verbatim (as the author announces in the preface), several chapters from the book on portraiture. The reasoning behind this uncommon publishing strategy may simply be that Berger has too much to say about this material, and that someone decided that six hundred pages was quite enough for the portraiture book. Or, it may be the equally pragmatic thought that perennially underpaid literary scholars might hesitate to shell out the necessary funds for a big book on the arts, whereas they might be tempted by less pricy readings of the courtesy book tradition (which hereby emerges as the poor cousin to portraiture). Either way, I would recommend purchasing both books. *The Absence of Grace* marks a stimulating contribution to our study of courtesy literature. It sparkles in its discussions of both Castiglione and Della Casa and links the problem of representation at court to the problem of narrative authority (unreliable, it turns out). But the portraiture book is even more powerful. It is, I think, a remarkable piece of criticism and a suggestive reimagining of certain influential features of early modern European culture. It is a work of immense intellectual energy, which inspires admiration, even when it sparks disagreement. In what follows, I will try to offer an account of *Fictions of the Pose* (with occasional side glances at *The Absence of Grace*), which intimates the range of Berger's passions, while suggesting both the interest of the book for scholars who might not necessarily be art historians and some of the problems I think it raises.

Fictions of the Pose sets forth a fairly simple, if elaborately argued, thesis. This thesis is that the representations one sees in the canonical tradition of European portraiture from the middle of the fifteenth century to the end of the seventeenth century are not representations of people, personalities, selves, or interiorities. They are representations of subjects posing as ideal images, as versions of what they'd like to seem. That is, they are representations of posturings, of people "performing" certain types of images of themselves. What are these images? They are fictions that the sitters believe they must produce in order to achieve social success. These fictions are the products of what Berger calls the regime of "mimetic idealism," the term he uses to indicate a particular form of representation underpinned by the culture of courtly (or, later, bourgeois) ambition. Berger argues that "mimetic idealism" is what makes Renaissance portraiture work, in all of its paradoxical power. The "mimetism" of portraiture involves the ways in which it partakes of new technologies of representation (perspective, certain approaches to line and color, etc.) which allow for innovatively precise and expressive forms of depiction in Renaissance painting. But Berger calls this mimesis "idealist" since those whom it portrays are struggling to represent themselves as "exemplars," as ideal instances of larger collective identities such as gracious aristocrats or newly empowered burghers. In the case of female sitters, the portrait stages the attempt to construct an image acceptable to the scopic economy of conjugal negotiation (and the consideration of gender in *Fictions* dovetails nicely with an extended meditation on the gender politics of courtly representation in *Absence*). Thus the "content" of the sitter's image is not psychological, in any banal sense of that word. It is not produced by some type of interiority that is expressed; rather, it is impressed on the sitter by external forces, inscribed on the body—or "delineated," to recall Montaigne's term—by the social regime. For Berger every poser is a *poseur*, a subject struggling to put on, if not a happy face, at least a face that is recognizable as belonging to a particular social or economic subgroup. In consequence—and this is the necessary and more striking corollary argument—the dramas played out in the pictures he explicates are not dramas of personality or character. Rather, they involve the ways in which the posing subject struggles with the role she or he aims to perform. Berger is interested in aspects of portraits that seem to show the sitter in positions of discomfort, straining to bear up under the weight of props or positionings that stress the body. Or, in the case of Rembrandt, he focuses on the ways in which the artist represents himself mocking the very patronage system that produces courtiers and courtly painters to begin with.

Berger's target is an entire tradition of art historical scholarship that has relied upon accounts of how this or that portrait reveals the "character" or "temperament" of the sitter. His presupposition, obviously enough, is that such readings are projections of the viewer or interpreter, and he is amusingly merciless in his unmasking of the simple-minded psychologizing that underpins much art historical interpretation. Yet Berger takes the point a step further to argue that it is folly to seek some sort of "personality" in the sitter to begin with. Interiority can only be read through external signs on the body that seem to point toward it. One may presume that those signs are nothing but by products of new technologies of looking, new social dynamics, new regimes of bodily control (here Berger is drawing on the work of Judith Butler). In this regard, the "personality" of the sitter is not something inherent, which needs to be portrayed or dragged forth ("pour-traire" = to pull out). It is simply an excess thrown off from the strain of social ambition and courtly competition. It is mere supplement, a holographic or shadowing effect.

This is heady stuff. But then, the stakes are high. Berger is up against some of the toughest cases in the art world, from Pope-Hennessey to Kenneth Clark. And in order to make his case as powerfully and persuasively as possible, he fixes a number of necessary points of reference as he goes, both theoretically and historically. Thus, much of the book consists of setting up contexts, working out models, and demolishing sacred cows—pretexts to his discussions of the paintings. And it is these pretexts that may be of greatest interest to students of Renaissance culture who are not specialists in the history of art. First off, he defines a vocabulary, via the semiotics of Peirce, for talking about certain pictorial effects and techniques which he might read as signs of the types of social and ideological problems that interest him. Then he tries to show that these problems have a specific historical dimension. He argues that they only emerge in fifteenth-century Italy, at the moment of the conjunction of the rise of court society, on the one hand, and the development of new "technologies" for defining the subject in public view, on the other. These technologies involve the shifts in the nature of visual culture mentioned earlier (perspective, new ways of using paint, etc.), as well as new forms of record keeping, and the new regimes of bodily control explored by Norbert Elias (with whom he engages critically and at length). In other words, he argues, it is no coincidence that portraiture emerges at the same moment that Europeans begin cleaning up their bodies and manners, since in both cases they are placing themselves under the gaze of others in new ways. He then focuses on the ways in which these new strategies of self-control and self-presentation are destined to fail—not least because one is never certain that one's self-policing is producing anything but a parody of manners (and parody is one of the aspects of Della Casa which he explicates in *Absence*). This failure of the self to present itself is theorized through a consideration of certain aspects of Lacan's discussions of the subject as "thrown under" its own representations. From this we learn that the act of self-representation is always haunted by its own failure, and that that failure—and the often painful struggles of men and women to overcome their "orthoscopic anxiety"—shapes the rise of portraiture.

In the second half of the book, he argues that a similar conjunction of factors pertains, with some changes, in seventeenth-century Holland, and that the jolly soldiers and coy ladies of Dutch portraiture are caught in the paradoxes of a culture tormented by its own success and vulgarity, longing for central authority and prey to vicious social competition. Berger's burghers are all dressed up with nowhere to go but up the corporate ladder—provided they can mimic their own ideals of how they want to be seen. And Berger is expert at pointing out moments of orthoscopic failure: Mantegna's Ludovico Trevisan is grimacing, not because he's dour or heroic, but because his neck and chin are straining to look like those of a noble Roman (he is mimicking a bust of Nero used by the artist to lend dignity to the painting); Titian's Francesco Maria della Rovere is weighed down with the effort of exploiting "not the mind's construction in the face, but the mind's construction of the face" (215); Hals's Willem van Heythuyzen shows his knuckles white with the effort of propping himself up on an immense sword which he has no experience carrying around; and the three figures at the center of Rembrandt's "Anatomy Lesson" are each striving to "outdo the others in pretending to be as strenuously observant as he can" (343). Berger is a master of nuance, and once these details are pointed out, it is difficult to reject his main thesis that these pictures are, at least in some measure, about posing.

This is art history as social history as historical sociology as critique of ideology as psychoanalysis. It's great fun. There are, to be sure, moments of tough sledding. Given the ambition of the book, Berger is obliged to take on dozens of other scholars on topics ranging from the possible historicity of Lacan to the proper interpretation of Alberti. Still, his engagement with the details of arguments by other scholars are models of intellectual seriousness, and, despite its size, *Fictions of the Pose* is generally a pleasure to read. Berger carefully shepherds his readers across the terrain of his enquiry, generously recalling earlier moments in his own argument and pointing us onward. His own self-representation (for this book is, like Montaigne's, a portrait of its author) displays the erudition and wit that readers familiar with his work have come to expect. Simply at the level of critical style there are many delights here: a digressive footnote listing interesting hats in Renaissance paintings; a steamroller-like pulverization of Francis Barker's pompous reading of Rembrandt's "Anatomy Lesson"; a fashionably irreverent rechristening of Lotto's "Portrait of a Man" as "The Dyspeptic"; an appropriation of the phrase "to beam up" for expository prose (as in "He beams up another example"). The reproductions of the paintings, moreover, are of excellent quality.

*

Berger's notion that the subjects of early modern portraiture are struggling with their own inability to construct themselves as ideals or exemplars of their social group places the portrait in the generic register of what one might call mock, or burlesque, epic. Like Falstaff or Panurge Berger's sitters puff themselves up for the heroic construction of ideal images, only to be shown up as inadequate to the task at hand. Like Don Quixote, they twist their bodies into what Berger calls "the armor of an alienating exemplarity" (172), only to find that the paunch doesn't quite fit behind the rusty breastplate. The tradition of the portrait depicts a series of failures, in which the idealizing impulse of Renaissance culture crashes against the fragile facticity of the flesh.

And yet this very mock heroic dimension suggests both the historical specificity and theoretical interest of Berger's conception of the portrait sitter as social climber, caught in a web of negotiations and desires that she cannot master. For it stands in contrast with a slightly different tradition of reading and looking, in which the subject's encounter with ideal images of the self (saints' lives, classical biographies, etc.) may well be understood as a form of momentary liberation from the pressure of the present on identity formation—something like the emancipatory "tiger's leap into the past," of which Walter Benjamin spoke as the ground of post-historicist historical understanding. Think of Machiavelli taking refuge in his classical reading (recounted in the famous letter to Vettori), or, perhaps, even of Montaigne's fantasy of a naked, "natural," self. Indeed Berger's vision of the sitter framing himself for success locates group identity as the determining factor in self-presentation. Yet it also frames portraiture off from most of the multifarious ways in which we know that representations of the self (texts, images, miniatures, etc.) were used in early modern culture.

Berger's focus on sitters as failed types of social grouphood may be a methodological necessity, but it brings both benefits and costs.

Every history of portraiture must also be, on some level, a history of the face. And in order to root his sitters in the burlesque regime of clumsy posturing, Berger shapes a particular theory of the face in its relationship to the "soul" or "self" imagined to lie behind it. For Berger the contrast between appearance and essence that portraiture presumes to bring out is itself a logocentric illusion—an illusion which depends on an "inside" that is signified by a visible "outside." This illusion gounds both aristocratic ideology and the interpretive practices of over-zealous art historians: "The basic formula of physiognomy, 'the face is the index of the mind,' confers on the word 'index' its active, Peircian sense of a dynamic—and in this case, causal—relation (the face is the index of the mind as smoke is an index of fire). As a general theory and discourse, physiognomy supplies an intellectual rationale for social formations legitimized by and dependent on the ascriptive categories—blood, lineage, gender, seniority—that naturalize customary rules and roles and thus tend to perpetuate their inertial givenness" (122).

Berger is at pains to deconstruct this logocentric vision of the face. Yet it is difficult to discern here where methodological exigency ends and ideology begins. We should note that it is in fact Berger who beams up the formula "the face is the index of the mind," and claims it as "basic," with the term "index" neatly producing the link with Peirce. And while his claim about the ideological function of fictions woven around the discourse of physiognomy is right, his claim that "interiority" is a kind of after effect of the inscription of meaning on the body raises the question of why it should be social ambition that should provide the key to reading the visages of these striving sitters. Why not, say, the discourse of Renaissance medicine, which has its own strategies of inscription and which sees (à la Panofsky) the face as an indication of the (dis)-equilibrium of the humors? Perhaps Lotto's "Dyspeptic" (as Dr. Berger calls him), just needs a good bleeding. In other words, we might wonder why, of all the various discourses which interpellate the subject and locate her in the regime of power, it should be a particular form of ambition which carries the interpretive key to bodies in portraiture.

At one level, both the rhetorical power of Berger's argument and the limitations of his theory of facehood may stem from the necessity to speak about the frozen moment of the pose. Still, a large part of early modern writing about the body as a signifier concerns itself as much with action as it does with pose. Recall, for example, this counsel by the Spanish courtier Baltasar Gracián, who thought as much about surfaces and power as anyone did during the period: "The passionate man speaks with a language different from that of normal things. . . . Know how to decipher a face and spell out the letters of the soul in its signals. . . . He who always laughs is a fool, and he who never laughs is false" (*Oráculo manual*, #273). Even Cassius's "lean and hungry look," noted by Julius Caesar, comes from the fact that "he thinks too much" (1.2.194), and follows hard on Cassius's own lengthy conversation with Brutus about how his friend's eyes lack the "show of love as I was wont to have" (5. 35). In these instances, character is defined through action, passion, or habit of mind read as signs on the body. Such signs are hard to read, and Renaissance discourses of the body generally accept the ambiguity of corporeal signs without either assuming that the face is a causative "index" of essential character, or that it is no index at all. In response to that ambiguity, they produce their own strategies for reading corporeal indices—as, say, marks of virtue, or traces of humoral imbalance (to take the most obvious approaches).

By looking for counter examples in literature, instead of painting, of course, I'm reading against Berger's project. He is certainly right to argue that historians are wrong to read "inside" the minds of the sitters or portraits a "character" that has in fact been written on them by power. Yet his claims in *Fictions* about faces unfold to include a reading of humanist court culture itself (echoed in *Absence*). Deconstruction of the discourse of physiognomy wavers between the *methodological* restraints of a particular medium (he has reasons to focus on faces as "only" surfaces, since he's talking about canvases, and his sitters are necessarily not active), and a more general *ideological* argument about the nature of personhood in humanist court culture. Thus, he writes in a consideration of Renaissance schooling, "The sociopolitical subtext of whatever gets taught—whether Latin or vernacular, Cicero or Ariosto, Euclid or the abbaco, composition for *orationes* or for *ricordi*—is instruction in the performative skills of self-representation, instruction in mastering the know-how needed to fashion the equivalent of what Aristotle in Book 2 of the *Rhetoric* called the ethos of the speaker. The ethos in this context would be the person of speaker or writer as notary, merchant, magnate, statesman, father, schoolmaster, clergyman, prince, or courtier" (*Fictions*, 135; *Absence*, 23).

Now, just how could the same "subtext" teach comportment to such radically different social roles as those listed above—which if anything seem a lineup of the types in Shakespearean comedy (and which, by the way, he has multiplied from Aristotle, who speaks only of "young men" and "old men")? What is at issue here is not whether or not portraits project psychological "depth," as traditional art historians claim they do, but whether the surface of paint performs anything beyond the pantomime of social ceremony. In other words, there is a certain tension between methodological exigency (analysis as determined by the object of study—"they're only images") and historical description ("but they're also images of certain types of people"). And this tension haunts any analysis that seeks to move between the study of a specific genre or mode of representation (in this case, portraiture) and a broader synchronic or cultural studies approach.

It is in this context that Castiglione, and the notion of "sprezzatura," are made to carry a heavy load as the mediating mechanism between the representation of sitters in a specific generic register and the representation of personhoods more generally. For the invention of "sprezzatura" marks nothing less than a revolution in personhood, which in turn lends itself perfectly to a revolution in the representation of personhood. In Berger's formulation, "sprezzatura" is precisely a strategy for dealing with a world in which there are too many ideal images, too many representations in circulation, all struggling for domination. In this regard, Mantegna's portrait of Trevisan mimicking a bust of Nero marks a kind of allegory of the shift from a nostalgic "Renaissance" vision of classical ideality to a viciously competitive "early modern" world of circulating *poseurs*. The sitter strains to imitate a Roman bust as a way of exuding some type of virtue, while "cooperating with the painter, and discernibly conscious of being beheld" (199). He's trying to look ancient in order to look modern.

For Berger what is important about "sprezzatura" is not merely that it defines the courtier as actor or dissimulator. In a context of vicious competition, where courtiers do the dirty work of very nasty princelings, being able to "represent the ability to deceive" (98) is as important as being able to deceive. By showing the prince that he might possibly be able to trick others, the courtier takes the trope of self-representation to an extreme, self-referential level; he represents representing. This dynamic is set forth in what, for Berger, is the crucial passage of the *Cortegiano*. In book 1, chapter 26, Castiglione relegates the idea of any kind of innate noble virtue or "grazia" to a zone beyond attainment. He does so at the very moment he introduces the concept of sprezzatura: "to reiterate that grazia is a grace beyond the reach of art just before the account of sprezzatura unfolds is to make deficiency in grazia the enabling condition of ideal courtiership. . . . The ideal courtier the interlocutors are in the process of constructing is not the absolute or inborn courtier, whose grazia is fully embodied, 'organic,' and inalienable. On the contrary, he is imagined as a simulacrum necessitated by failure to embody the fullness of being ascribed to aristocratic nature. In short, sprezzatura is treated as a behavorial prosthesis" (100–101). This means that the "absence of grace" underpins a culture of performance and posing which emerges in response to new forms of social mobility. This culture in turn produces subjects marked by performance anxiety, by a fear that they cannot perform in the ways required by the social context. Even the schoolboys, made famous by Elias, whom Erasmus encourages in his "On Good Manners for Boys" to bathe and wipe their noses are marked by a rift. For the moment the self is assaulted and formed by a "technology" designed to reform behavior, "then a new fissure opens up between the interiority one is socialized to represent and another interiority one is socialized to keep to oneself" (151). The awareness of this fissure is what produces the embarassment that Berger finds in Renaissance portraiture.

*

"You are stealing my face," wrote the Spanish poet Góngora to a certain Flemish painter who did his portrait. The panoptic dimension of court society which Berger stresses—and links, via Lacan, to modern subjectivity more generally—means that there is no escape from being seen, or from being embarassed about being seen. Humanist retreat is mere pastoral fiction, and such disruptive moments as Montaigne's imagination of himself naked, living in a society under the first rules of Nature, is mere momentary fantasy. Or, to be more precise, the only escape from performance anxiety is through parody of performance. Like all genres, portraiture has its late, elegiac phase. And this is where the arguments of *Fictions of the Pose* and *The Absence of Grace* form two halves of a diptych. Berger's fascinating discussions of Rembrandt's portraits and self-portraits argue that Rembrandt is out to show the stage of portraiture as what it is, mere artifice. He shows how the extravagant poses and costumes in Rembrandt, the remarkable applications of pigment in the self-portraits are all involved in an elaborate unmasking of the patronage system and a questioning of the stage of representation. Rembrandt is identified by Berger as the Joker, as the clown who resists being interpellated through his own capacity to mock interpellation itself. Similarly, though more darkly, in *Absence*, Berger shows Castiglione and Della Casa as unreliable authorities whose depictions of the technics of self-improvement inevitably mock the very processes of self-control they seem to advocate. They leave us caught between an ideal of innate aristocratic "grace"—always receding into an unreachable past—and a world of suckers painfully mimicking what they think is the formula for worldly success. And in a world of simulacra—then as now—art's only hope seems to lie in the activity of media critique. Mock epic satire of idealized forms of representation gives way to post-modern parody of representation itself. The post-Renaissance burlesque of Rembrandt unmasks the strenuous heroics of Titian and Mantegna—just as Berger's Borgesian post-modernism turns back on the ponderous Joyce-like modernisms of Panofsky and Clark. The final paradox of this situation may be that it is precisely such an art as Rembrandt's, endlessly obsessed with pointing to its own theatricality, which has most powerfully created the illusion that something may lie behind the face after all.

These are both fascinating books which will, I predict, become touchstones for our study of the ways humans represented themselves in early modern Europe.

The Rhetoric of the Body from Ovid to Shakespeare
Cambridge: Cambridge University Press, 2000

Reviewer: Ann Rosalind Jones

Lynn Enterline begins this book with an exhilaratingly intelligent and subtle reading of what she calls "misfirings" in Ovid's treatment of bodily violence, voice, and poetic composition in the *Metamorphoses*. Looking at what happens to figures such as Actaeon,

Orpheus, and Philomela, whose experience of physical attack leads to a shattering loss of identity and speech, she argues that such episodes reveal the instability of any speaking self: we speak languages already given; our words fail to capture our states of mind; we can be only what other people see and hear us as being. Starting from this deconstructive and psychoanalytic assumption about the instability of any speaking subject, Enterline analyzes the ways that Ovid and later writers, including the Shakespeare of *Lucrece* and *The Winter's Tale*, identify with characters silenced by bodily trauma. She argues that poets, by speaking for and through female victims of violence and rape and through violated male figures such as Actaeon and Orpheus, reveal the fragility of their own gendered identity and the undependability of public eloquence.

According to Enterline's focus on wordlessness as the theme and situation linking Ovid to his followers, Petrarch provides obvious analogies to Ovid. Invoking Echo and Philomela, dramatizing his own frightening metamorphoses and paralyzed speech, he speaks through Laura even as he represents her silencing him. Enterline offers vivid readings of Petrarch as Actaeon, Pygmalion, and Orpheus, and argues that his fascination with Medea reveals an unconscious recognition of the feminine and maternal energies repressed but not finally contained in language. In contrast, she uses John Marston's *Metamorphosis of Pygmalion's Image* to exemplify a familiar and less complex shoring up of masculinity: Marston, silencing Pygmalion's statue by denying her even the name Ovid gives her, identifies with the manipulations and triumph of the sculptor as much as he satirizes them. And he establishes a homoerotic intimacy with his readers, inviting them to side with him against women in general from a rhetorical position structurally identical to the one Freud identifies as enabling the dirty joke: a male-male exchange excluding the woman at whose expense the story is told. Marston's satire of Pygmalion-like love poets, then, misfires because he is unconsciously and professionally implicated in the language and gender-affirming processes he shares with such writers.

Turning to Shakespeare's *Lucrece*, Enterline takes issue with critics who have argued that the poet, as narrator of the rape, occupies a position similar to Tarquin's. Rather, she argues, the poet shares Lucrece's lack of a language adequate to prevent or describe her rape. Like Lucrece and Petrarch, exiled from language as is Actaeon, Shakespeare can represent such suffering only by naming the inadequacy of language to express it ("sorrow . . . blown with wind of words") and by calling, through Lucrece, upon heroines given voice by Ovid (Hecuba, Philomela). Enterline pursues this line in a strikingly original reading of *The Winter's Tale*, linking Hermione to Lucrece through her silencing by Leontes and her final address not to men at court but, Demeter-like, to her refound daughter Persephone/Perdita. However briefly, women call to women in a solidarity unavailable to male poets and heroes isolated by bodily and linguistic trauma.

Enterline's argument is sustained through persuasive close reading as well as a wide range of references to contemporary theorists such as Kristeva, Felman, and Žižek, as well as Derrida and Lacan. Shakespeareans will learn much that is new from her radically pessimistic view of "the English Ovid's" sense of language as repressive training ground and threat to autonomy in *Lucrece* and *The Winter's Tale*. Though her interpretations are complex, she presents them in clear, forceful prose, enlivened by a sense of discovery. And though the split subject central to poststructuralist theory seems to have no history (we are all always already exiled from any possible selfhood by the gendered strictures of language), Enterline glances in interesting ways at the training of schoolboys and poets in Shakespeare's England, siting her commentary on *Lucrece* and *The Winter's Tale* in a specific time and place.

One might take issue with her claim that these poets can be read in a feminist way: a male poet who ventriloquizes women may speak less in sympathy with them than with himself, and the dramatization of speechlessness can produce powerful alternative forms of speech. Enterline overuses the pedagogical imperative: she commands her readers to "notice," "recall," and "consider" to a degree surprising in a study so attentive to the coercive force of language. But her study breaks new ground in many ways. By challenging readers to recognize the misfirings of poetic intent as an inevitable consequence of writing in a culturally gendered body, *The Rhetoric of the Body* rewrites Ovidian literary history in an original and stimulating way.

Generation and Degeneration: Tropes of Reproduction in Literature and History from Antiquity to Early Modern Europe
Edited by Valeria Finucci and Kevin Brownlee
Durham and London: Duke University Press, 2001

Reviewer: Tanya Pollard

Generation and Degeneration undertakes an ambitious, wide-ranging, and deeply comparative project. The essays in this collection explore discourses of genealogy and procreation, both literal and metaphorical, in a range of texts including literary, medical, and religious writings; countries including Egypt, Greece, Italy, France, Spain, and England; and historical moments ranging from the ancient world through to the nineteenth century (though with an emphasis on the early modern period). Although this sprawling scope at times threatens the book's cohesiveness, its expansiveness is for the most part a source of great strength. In its juxtaposition of multiple discourses, disciplines, places, and time frames, the collection thoughtfully challenges the boundaries that habitually limit our fields of inquiry, and demonstrates many of the rewards of exploring a wider intellectual landscape. The book offers a number of extremely intelligent, original, and rigorous researched essays; it will be of interest to a wide range of scholars and critics, particularly those with interests in the history of gender, medicine, and the body.

The collection is divided into four sections. In the first, "Theories of Reproduction," essays by Elizabeth A. Clark and Valeria Finucci meditate explicitly on debates surrounding insemination, conception, genetic transmission, and birth. In the second, "Boundaries of Sex and Gender," Dale B. Martin, Gianna Pomata, and Valerie Traub examine constructions of gender in medical, moral, and travel writings, with attention (for the most part) to issues related to reproduction. The third section, "Female Genealogies," features Marina Scordilis Brownlee and Maureen Quilligan on women's literary uses of family structures as responses to contemporary political concerns. The fourth, "The Politics of Inheritance," contains essays by Nancy G. Siraisi, Kevin Brownlee, and Peter Stallybrass that analyze medical and literary confrontations with the legacies of the past.

The volume begins on a strong note. Valeria Finucci's introduction adeptly comments on, and ties together, the various aspects of generation that the essays explore. In doing so, she also points to the volume's theoretical foundations, which, to a great extent, ally feminist and psychoanalytical inquiries with a rigorously historicist methodology. One of the great strengths of the book is that so many of its essays not only demonstrate the compatibility of these often warring approaches, but offer models for their responsible and powerful cross-fertilization. In this, it joins recent works such as Carla Mazzio and Douglas Trevor's *Historicism, Psychoanalysis, and Early Modern Culture,* in building and legitimizing a valuable new critical space for asking questions about the history of the body, the mind, and their relationship to each other. Finucci's own essay is a good example of this methodological hybridity. Her fascinating examination of monstrous births, focusing on the figure of Clorinda—a white daughter of black Ethiopian parents—in Tasso's *Gerusalemme liberata,* opens a conversation between Freud's discussions of daydreams and early modern writings about the dangerous effects of the maternal imagination on conception. Valerie Traub's analysis of anxieties about the clitoris and the tribade in early modern England similarly draws together these two modes, finding in early modern anatomies and travel writings a means of critiquing Freudian narratives about the nature and development of homoeroticism. Traub's essay—which was previously published elsewhere—offers a lively and intelligent account of early responses to what were perceived as female sexual perversions, but never explicitly engages with the book's emphasis on generation. This is a pity, as her material suggests interesting possibilities for reflecting on the relationship between female eroticism and reproduction in the early modern period.

Psychoanalytic readings do not feature in all of this collection's essays, but feminist critiques of genealogical discourses are pervasive. In fact, all but three essays (those in the last section, "The Politics of Inheritance") take gender as a central focus of their arguments. At times, this emphasis runs the risk of becoming slightly uniform and predictable; how many contemporary scholars and critics will be surprised to learn that constructions of male and female bodies, and beliefs about conception, were informed by patriarchal ideologies? Luckily many of these essays go beyond this claim, in some cases even questioning and complicating it. Gianna Pomata, for instance, persuasively demonstrates that early modern doctors saw male periodic bleeding as a version of menstruation, and that far from carrying stigma, this was widely seen as a good thing. Drawing on a wide array of medical writings, she argues that in the Galenic tradition "menstruation was the paradigm of critical evacuation, the clearest instance of nature's healing endeavor. Thus, notwithstanding the asserted superiority of the male, it was in fact the female that was exemplary from a therapeutic point of view" (138). This observation, she points out, contradicts Thomas Laqueur's argument that the male body served as the prototype for both genders in the early modern period. It also discredits the received wisdom that European medicine has historically been hostile to menstruation, a development that Pomata traces to the nineteenth-century identification of menstruation with ovulation and reproduction rather than purgation.

Dale B. Martin's essay also touches on the phemonenon of menstruating men, but as part of a broader set of examples of contradictions in classical models of masculinity. Martin shows that to aspire to manliness in the ancient world was to negotiate with not only confusing, but directly conflicting, requirements. To inseminate was manly, but so was sexual asceticism; to be a man meant not menstruating, but, as Pomata points out as well, male menstruation could be a sign of health and potency. Martin establishes his claims through a compelling and entertaining survey of classical medical authorities before speculating on the reason for these contradictions, which, he argues, both lent power to the medical establishment (often the source of final judgment), and added to the mystique of masculinity by making it a precarious commodity. His discussion of the powerful link between manliness and procreation ties in nicely with Elizabeth A. Clark's analysis of debates between Augustine and Julian of Eclanum about the transmission of original sin. Clark shows that important theological arguments hinged fundamentally on claims about the nature of reproduction. Augustine, like Aristotle earlier, argued that men alone generated seed, while women merely provided material vessels; accordingly, Jesus was born free of original sin because his progenitor was God. Besides the strength of their intellectual contributions, Clark's and Martin's essays are valuable in offering glimpses into some of the classical and medieval intellectual traditions that provide a foundation for the early modern theories of generation discussed elsewhere in the volume.

The essays in the book's third and fourth sections are less physiological and more literary in their topics than those in the first half. The third section, "Female Genealogies," continues the book's feminist emphasis by examining women who turn to fictional genealogies to critique the status quo and construct their own forms of authority. Marina Scordilis Brownlee argues that the writings of María de Zayas undermine established familial and political structures by imagining alternative, ungenerative models of social relations. Maureen Quilligan's essay examines Elizabeth I's translation of a poem by Marguerite de Navarre that portrays the soul as both sister, mother, wife, and daughter of God. Quilligan suggests that this implicitly incestuous structure, which caused the poem to be banned in France, resonated with accusations of incest in Elizabeth's immediate family—her father attempted to repeal a marriage to his brother's widow on the basis that it was an incestuous liaison, and her mother was accused of having slept with her brother— and, furthermore, that just as Henry VIII made political use of these problems of incest, Elizabeth turned to the incestuous vocabulary offered by this poem in order to establish her own female authority, unfettered by family ties, as a figurative wife, mother, and sister to the English people.

The final section, "The Politics of Inheritance," moves the discussion of genealogies to an even more abstract plane. Nancy G. Siraisi's essay examines the desire of many Renaissance physicians to trace the roots of their medical traditions to ancient Egypt, offering an alternative intellectual ancestry to the standard forebearers, Aristotle and Galen. Kevin Brownlee studies a similar attempt at forging distant ancestors in order to bypass more recent ones, but in a literary rather than medical context. His essay examines how three medieval Italian texts—Brunetto Latini's *Il Tesoretto,* the anonymous *Il Fiore,* and Dante's *Commedia*—attempt to erase their cultural dependency on French literary culture (and in particular, the *Roman de la Rose*) by self-consciously identifying themselves with ancient Roman texts. This is a classically Bloomian argument about the anxiety of influence, with an emphasis on the complexity and competitiveness of family relations within the early Romance vernacular literature. The book's closing essay, by Peter Stallybrass, also examines a literary genealogy, though in this case one within a text rather than between texts. Addressing a quintessentially canonical text, *Hamlet,* Stallybrass considers the haunting nature of paternal legacies through a study of the ghost of Hamlet's father, with particular attention to the material markers of identity represented by the armor, drapery, or clothing the ghost wears in different productions.

As may be evident by my account of the book's essay clusters, this collection divides into two halves, whose links to each other are slightly strained. The first two sections, amply annotated with medical texts, engage questions of generation at a literal and corporeal level, while the third and fourth sections emphasize more abstract forms of family legacies. Although both of these modes arguably fit within the larger frame of the volume, and complement each other in intriguing ways, their aims and methodologies differ considerably, and the move from one to the other feels a bit abrupt. More attention to the connections between the two halves would help to demonstrate what the conversations share. One way to go about this might be more explicit emphasis on the ways that figurative genealogies engage (or ignore) the corporeal vocabulary they implicitly invoke. Another might be more attention to the relationships between literary representations of generation and their medical counterparts. Finucci does this elegantly in her essay on the maternal imagination, in which she turns to medical writings on monstrous births to illuminate the status of Tasso's fictional creation. In general, the essays in the first half of the book fit together more tightly than those in the second half. The shared medical tradition, as well as the immediacy of the corporeal focus, ties their individual interests together, while the more abstract essays have less common ground to balance against their disparate national and disciplinary areas of inquiry.

As a final quibble, the title *Generation and Degeneration* suggests attention to the relationship between birth and its opposite: death, decay, corruption. Although Finucci also discusses this pairing in her introduction, the latter theme is in fact far from an equal partner in the volume; very few of the essays even touch on it, and none makes it a major focus. While the opposition lends itself to a neatly parallel title, it suggests directions that the book does not really fulfill, and readers looking for discussions of the relationship between birth and death will be disappointed. Beyond the relatively superficial matter of labelling, though, and limits to its overall cohesiveness, this book is an impressive achievement. It offers provocative

perspectives both on the individual topics it examines, and on
larger questions of how we define the scope of early modern studies. If it encourages more scholars and critics to expand the frames
within which we conceptualize our temporal, geographic, and dis-
cplinary arenas, it will have performed an important service.

Reading Shakespeare's Will: The Theology of Figure from Augustine to the Sonnets
By Lisa Freinkel
New York: Columbia University Press, 2002

Reviewer: *Julia Reinhard Lupton*

Reading Shakespeare's Will heralds a new approach to Shakespeare and religion, one that refuses to reduce Shakespeare's theological imagination either to his immediate historical context and
biography or to a set of scriptural stories or images, but rather
places his dramas in a hermeneutic horizon that reaches back to
biblical and patristic habits of thought and forward to include modern traditions of critical reading. This new approach neither pi-
ously recapitulates Christian belief patterns nor exposes religion as
sheer ideology. Instead, by taking seriously the infinite variety of
Christian doctrine as well as Christianity's difficult dialectic with
its religious others (especially Judaism and Islam), critics such as
Lars Engle, Lowell Gallagher, Richard Halpern, Graham Hammill,
and now Lisa Freinkel effectively link religion to problems of race,
economy, sovereignty and empire without ceding their solution to
the historicists.

Freinkel states the project of her book: "*Reading Shakespeare's
Will* offers the first systematic account, in theological terms, of the
construction of Shakespeare as author. It is in this light that I examine the 'I' of the Sonnets: instead of describing the secular subject,
my study offers readings of the theological author" (xix). Freinkel's
critical engagement with the scriptural dimension of Shakespeare's

writing does not focus on the content of works so much as shuttle between the evolving functions of author and reader in the drama of Western literature. Following Auerbach, Freinkel finds in the theology of *figura*, the exegetical technique of converting Old Testament stories and tropes into New Testament truths, not only a poetics and hermeneutics of writing and reading, but also a philosophy and economy of history built on the supercession of one epoch (Judaism) by another (Christianity). Already nascent in Paul's ambivalent inheritance of Jewish exegesis, the theology of figure was perfected by Augustine as both a mode of reading and a principle of composition, forced into the fullest flower of secular lyric in the sonnets of Petrarch, and drawn into permanent crisis in the theology of Luther. It is this vexed history, Freinkel argues, cut off in the blossom of its promises, that Shakespeare "wills" to us, marking his world of crossed temporalities as our legacy and forever shaping our vision of authorial intentionality (or "will").

Freinkel weaves her careful argument around a recurrent set of figures from and for the scene of hermeneutics, including Moses as originary author and the Pauline image of Christianity as a wild olive (*oleaster*) grafted onto the domestic olive (*oliva*) of Judaism (Romans 11:13–21). In a stunning reading of a passage from the *Confessions*, Freinkel listens to Augustine as he yearns for Moses to appear before him and speak the meaning of his text directly into the saint's ear, only to realize that even the physical presence of the author would not guarantee knowledge of his intentions, since the true meaning of the Hebrew text depends on the Christian community that now receives it. Freinkel concludes, "Ultimately, then, the truth-bearing intersubjective contact that counts for Augustine is that connection most fundamentally structured by *figura*: the connection not between a reader and an author but between a reader and a text" (38).

In a lovely coinage, Freinkel calls this readerly vector of Augustine's figural hermeneutics "addressivity" (60), a word that both captures the ethics of reader response and, by rhyming with "aggressivity," evokes the losses and even violences that occur when authors give way to readers, past is displaced by present, and the Old Testament cedes to the New. Freinkel reflects on these two faces of typological reading: "To read *for our sake* is to take responsibility for the meaning of the text—a responsibility that is infinitely precious and infinitely sweet. . . . At the same time, this responsibility comes at a likewise infinite cost: the present, in all its nontranscendent empirical density . . . is what the infinite meaning of the infinite text gives up" (xviii). Elsewhere she writes, "A loss is incurred in the production of figural meaning. . . . Since *figura* has always been about promises—i.e., the Old as promise of the New—we might then want to say that its promises can be kept only by being broken" (23). Freinkel describes here the losses entailed by any act of reading, but, writing from the position of what she calls "holocemia," "a kind of poisoning of the world's blood, a lingering symptom of the Holocaust" (xxvii), she clearly also aims to redress the aggressivity peculiar to Christian forms of hermeneutic address.

In the unfolding drama of her own book, Freinkel is stronger on figure than on fulfillment, on the exegetical and economic structure of the promise than on the delivery of its promised end. After stunning readings of Paul, Origen, Augustine, and Luther, Freinkel's final couplet of chapters on the Sonnets and *The Merchant of Venice* feels more like coda than climax. To find in the Sonnets, as Freinkel proposes to do, "a new poetics, one grounded in a sense of *figura*'s failure" (203) is bold, suggestive, and very likely right. But Freinkel avoids sustained study of the poems' theological impulses and substructures, relying instead on weak analogies between Shakespeare's rhetoric and Luther's. Above all, the Sonnets chapter is haunted by the critical genius of Joel Fineman. Freinkel's attempt to displace Fineman's "chiasmus" with Lutheran "catachresis" feels weakly supercessionist, oddly out of tune with her critique of typology (for example, "*Will,* like Luther's catachrestic flesh, is a supplement, but it departs significantly from the [post-] structuralist logic of supplement that Fineman employs" [233]). Indeed, the book's preface, itself a moving synthesis of critical and autobiographical writing, ends with Freinkel's statement that Fineman died in the same year as her father, as if to acknowledge without exorcising the ghost in her criticism (xxvi–xxviii).

Thankfully, the chapter on *Merchant* is stronger. Even more than the Sonnets this play calls for a hermeneutic rapprochement with theology that resists recapitulating a Christian logic of conversion while also refraining from a post-Holocaust misprision of the play's rough music. Freinkel sets herself the project of breaking down the distinction, now common among literary critics and historians alike, between *anti-Judaism* (a medieval discourse based on theology and animated by the millenial dream of the conversion of the Jews) and *anti-Semitism* (a modern discourse of racial essentialism that led most notoriously to the "eliminationist" policies of the Nazis). The theology of *figura*, Freinkel argues, is not displaced by the science of race so much as it lays the ground for the very super-cessionist narrative of secularization that the faith/race opposition presupposes. Glossing Paul as a founding moment in the Western binding of race and theology, Freinkel writes, "the dichotomy used to distinguish a theological anti-Judaism from a modern anti-Semi-tism . . . is ultimately . . . the very dichotomy by means of which Christianity from the start determines its difference from—and its supercession of—the Jews" (242).

This is a strong and supple thesis, one which could be amply de-fended by unlocking Shylock's bonds to his exegetical avatars be-fore and after the Renaissance. Yet Freinkel shies away from Shylock, preferring to tease competing models of allegoresis out of the theme of the three caskets. Freinkel's Belmont musings show ingenuity and insight, yet they don't bolster the stronger claims that she wants to make concerning race and religion in the Renais-sance and post-Holocaust contexts. The Lutheran legacy to anti-Semitism, for example, remains a barely opened casket on the stage she has set for us with such originality and care. Yet Freinkel's com-mitment to Portia bears weightier fruit at the end, when she links Portia's legal offices to Luther's infinitization of the Law as a neces-sary moment in the passage to grace: "Like the Laws of Moses, be-wildering (as Luther tells us) in their number and complexity, the Law proliferates wildy in Portia's hands, branching out in every di-rection, its reach ever more extensive, its satisfaction ever more patently impossible" (289). Here Freinkel breaks through truisms concerning Portia's legalism or Venetian cynicism to grasp the theo-logical integrity of Portia's performance, without relinquishing any ethical ground to the conversionary forces that Portia mobilizes in the name of mercy. (In a brilliant move, Freinkel links Portia's mercy to Luther's *scharffe barmherzigkeit*, "the sharp or harsh mercy that Luther recommends against the Jews in his late writ-ings" [286].)

Although Freinkel may not keep all her promises, she has in best hermeneutic fashion opened up a field for further analysis—a re-turn to Hamlet's Wittenberg after Greenblatt's journey through Pur-gatory, for example, or a re-audit of *Measure for Measure*'s typological economy. At every turn, *Reading Shakespeare's Will* serves as an urgent invitation to listen, like Augustine to Moses, with exegetical ears to the words and worlds of Shakespeare's plays. *Tolle, lege.*

The Cambridge Companion to Shakespeare on Film
Edited by Russell Jackson
Cambridge: Cambridge University Press, 2000

A History of Shakespeare on Screen: A Century of Film and Television
By Kenneth S. Rothwell
Cambridge: Cambridge University Press, 1999

Reviewer: Peter S. Donaldson

Filmed Shakespeare began in 1899 with Sir Herbert Beerbohm Tree in the death scene from *King John*, closely followed in 1900 by Sarah Bernhardt's performance of the duel scene in *Hamlet*. Literally hundreds of Shakespeare films were made in the silent era, many of which are now lost. In the age of the talking picture, the pace of Shakespeare film production actually diminished and became more erratic, with periods of relative drought interrupted by films by Olivier, Kozintsev, Kurosawa, Welles, and Zeffirelli as well as by lesser artists. We are now in the midst of (or, on a pessimistic estimate, at the end of) a great revival initaited by Kenneth Branagh's *Henry V* in 1989. Since then, more major Shakespeare films have been made than in any period since the advent of sound. Branagh himself directed *Much Ado About Nothing* (1993), *Hamlet* (1996, a "full," four hour *Hamlet*), *In the Bleak Midwinter* (1995, a "backstage" *Hamlet* film which tells the story of a low-budget provincial production of the play), *Love's Labour's Lost* (2000), and a television production of *Twelfth Night* (1988). Branagh also appears as Iago in the Oliver Parker *Othello* (1995). Other recent work includes Franco Zeffirelli's *Hamlet* (1990), Baz Luhrmann's *William Shakespeare's Romeo and Juliet* (1996), Richard Loncraine's *Richard III* with Ian McKellen in the title role (1995), Julie Taymor's *Titus* (1999), Michael Almereyda's *Hamlet* (2000), and such "spin-offs" or "offshoots" as *Shakespeare in Love* (1998), *Ten Things I Hate about You* (1999, loosely based on *Taming of the Shrew*), *O* (2001, more closely based on *Othello*), and Al Pacino's *Looking for Richard* (1996, a documentary-style film about Pacino's search for an approach to the role of Richard III). The boom may not last; as Russell Jackson shows in the introduction to the *Cambridge Companion to Shakespeare on Film* (xx), Shakespeare films have tended to come in waves, establishing themselves as a genre for only so long as major productions avoid financial disaster. According to this view, developed further in Samuel Crowl's essay on Kenneth Branagh in the *Companion*, Polanski's *Macbeth* (1971), now a critical success, was such a film, inhibiting investment in Shakespeare films for nearly two decades. The disappointing box office performance of Julie Taymor's artistically ambitious *Titus* and of Branagh's eclectic *Love's Labor's Lost* may mark another such turning point. The "new wave" of Shakespeare films may have crested.

If so, the same cannot be said of scholarly production. In the same period, roughly from 1988 to the present, Shakespeare on film has firmly established itself as a field for serious academic work, and there is no sign of abatement or retrenchment. Until the late 1980s there was only a tiny handful of books on the subject, most notably Jack Jorgens's *Shakespeare on Film* (1977) and Robert Hamilton Ball's *Shakespeare on Silent Film* (1969). Now there are excellent filmographies including Annabelle Henkin Melzer and Kenneth Rothwell's *Shakespeare on Screen* (1990) and Luke McKernan and Olwen Terris's *Walking Shadows* (1994) and close to a hundred monographs and collections, the most recent including *Spectacular Shakespeare* (2002) and *The Reel Shakespeare* (2002) both edited by Lisa Starks and Courtney Lehmann, Courtney Lehmann's *Shakespeare Remains* (2002), *Shakespeare after Mass Media*, edited by Richard Burt (2002), Stephen Buhler's *Shakespeare in the Cinema* (2002), Herbert Coursen's *Shakespeare in Space* (2002, one of three recent Coursen books that deal with Shakespeare films), and a second edition of *Shakespeare: The Movie*, edited by Richard Burt and Lynda Boose (forthcoming 2003). Shakespeare on film had its first international conference in Malaga in 1999 with over one hundred participants. Well attended sessions and lectures on filmed Shakespeare at the meetings of the Shakespeare Association of America, the International Shakespeare Conference, and the World Shakespeare Congress are now the rule rather than the exception. The flood of publication should not be mistaken for an abandonment of standards: the quality of the emerging secondary literature is high and with a few exceptions compares very favorably with "traditional" Shakespeare studies produced in the same period. The material for such study will continue to be plentiful, for even if the pace of major film production should prove to be declining, filmed records of theatrical productions are now appearing on tape and DVD (e.g., the Kevin Kline *Hamlet* and the Joseph Papp *King Lear* with James Earl Jones in the lead), and these, along with television and low-budget video versions of the plays will fill in the gaps until the next wave gathers strength.

Russell Jackson's *Companion to Shakespeare on Film* (2000) and Kenneth Rothwell's *A History of Shakespeare on Screen: A Century of Film and Television* (1999) are among the best books to come out of the renewal of academic interest in Shakespeare films. Both are resolutely visual as well as textual, finding ways to honor Shakespeare film as the double thing that it is, inevitably part of the world of film as well as the world of Shakespeare production and interpretation. Both are scholarly, well written, and accessible in the best sense, inviting the reader into dialogue with the methods of a new field of study in the making, rather than presenting simplified conclusions. The world of academic periodicals and monographs often seems somewhat removed from the needs of undergraduates and the interested public. These books help to bridge that gap, narrowing the distance between expert and novice interpretation by offering lucid prose and transparently deployed methodologies. These books are landmarks in the field; their influence on scholars, teachers, and students will be long lasting, as will the pleasures they afford the non-specialist reader.

The Cambridge Companion is divided into sections on adaptation, genre, the work of major directors, and "critical issues" (a loose designation that makes room for feminism, nation and race, Shakespeare and illusion, and Shakespearean "offshoots"). The first of these categories—adaptation—gives the book its special character, for many of the essays in the other sections also focus on process, problem solving and the vicissitudes of media transition and translation. The editor, Russell Jackson, is director of the

Shakespeare Institute and has served as text advisor on several of the Branagh's films. His introduction and opening essay on how a play text becomes screenplay set the tone of scholarly, sophisticated pragmatism for the volume. The introduction is a highly useful overview of how Shakespeare on film has found a niche in the extraordinarily finance and audience dependent story of film production in the twentieth century. Jackson reminds us of how shaky the foothold has been, and how modest, by industry standards, the results. Jackson's take is counter-hyperbolic: rather than celebrating the lost hundreds of silents, for example, he makes the less exciting but illuminating point that only about forty major Shakespeare films have been made in the sound era, a very small fraction of film production in the period. Jackson is realistic and practical without being deflating as he brilliantly sketches how films get made and guides us through the details of finance and market, such as the industry rule of thumb that films need to recover two and a half times their "negative cost" (this term does not mean cost that somehow magically appears as credit, but the cost of producing the master negative) to be considered profitable. Rejecting the idea that such necessities are automatically corrupting, and drawing on his own experience in production, Jackson points out commonalities of interest linking the artistic and commercial sides of the business: "the makers of films want to have their work seen by as many people as possible, and the producers may have artistically valid suggestions to make." Side swipes contrast Jackson's approach with "deconstruction," undefined here and used, as is now the custom, as a blanket term for ivory-tower speculation, and support the valid point that interpretation ought, more often, to begin with understanding how films are actually made. With the essay on the adaptation of play texts for the screen that follows, also shrewdly grounded in the realm of the possible, Jackson makes a distinctive contribution by providing essential information and by setting up an implicit challenge to kinds of interpretation that cut themselves adrift from the realities of film making. Discussions by others of the significance of cuts and textual transpositions, for example, often treat those made in a specific film without a sense of general practice or of the recurring, thorny problems that confront any would-be adaptor. Jackson's work is uniformly energetic, witty, and powerful, condensing a wealth of experience and good sense into brief compass. These fine essays should be required reading for students and scholars alike.

The adaptation section also includes Michèle Willems's very thoughtful exploration of video, emphasizing its role as a carrier for other media, including film. To use the term Jay Bolter and Richard Grusin coined as title of their recent book on the subject, video inevitably "remediates" film as well as theatrical peformance, altering expectations, enabling different scenarios of use and study. According to Willems, video can open texts and performances to new meanings and new audiences, while also "sealing" meaning simply by providing, in the case of theater, a stable copy of record and reference for what is in its essence and in principle an ephemeral art form. Paradoxically, video contributes powerfully to an appreciation of the great variety of forms a Shakespeare play can take while at the same time creating a new kind of canonicity. Willems's central insights into this medium, which transports and reframes other media and is so seldom only itself, made me think of digital media and wish that the essay had continued further into this new territory, for digitality has made media convergence and remediation ubiquitous and protean, raising the question of whether any medium will ever again seem separate and self-sufficing. If not, the Shakespeare film may soon become the study of Shakespeare adaptation across a wider range of media. Current studies of Shakespeare popular culture references such as those of Richard Burt, or of Shakespeare animation, game, theatrical trailer, and video clip (Laurie Osborne) suggest that such a shift is in progress.

Barbara Freedman's piece on *Richard III* at moments of media transition (stage to silent film, film to television, and film to digitally inflected cinema) enters these waters brilliantly and is a fine example of what cross-media scholarship and interpretation can be. Film is at the center of her concerns, but film is always seen in the context of a changing spectrum of media forms. Her major texts are the 1912/13 Frederick Warde production, unsuccessfully struggling to merge stage tradition and cinema; Olivier's *Richard III*, shot in huge Todd-AO format but with its near-simultaneous release on the small screen in mind; and Loncraine's hyperreal, computer-enhanced 1996 film, also at odds, but in a different way from Warde or Olivier, with the text and the stage production that inspired it. Freedman is explicitly concerned with the awkwardness of these transitions, the mix of styles, motives, processes, audiences, and meanings that can result when one medium "remediates" another, and with the insight that may be gained from a systematic exploration of media hybridity at "critical junctures in media history, when the use of emerging, competing, and dormant technologies reflects situations of crisis, defense, reciprocal influence, commercial interdependency and realignments among various branches of the entertainment industry" (47).

Harry Keyishian's essay on the role of filmic genres in adapting Shakespeare contrasts three versions of *Hamlet*: Olivier's *film noir*, Zeffirelli's action-adventure, and Branagh's epic. Keyishian shows how systematic attention to film genre offers a needed corrective to text-centered literary analysis. There is a touch of the mandatory syllabus in the piece: "*only* by placing them in the cinematic traditions . . . can we engage the actual film product" (73; emphasis mine). Surely there are other ways of engaging, but the case for a generic approach is persuasively made and economically presented in ways that will be especially helpful in teaching.

Keyishian's essay might as easily have been placed in the next group, "genres and plays"—except that genres, in this section, refers to the dramatic genres of comedy, tragedy and history named in the full title of the 1623 Folio, rather than to cinematic genres. Shakespeare films often have both kinds, a filmic genre like epic or *film noir* and a second (remediated) dramatic genre. In this group, Michael Hattaway writes on the comedies on film, Herbert Coursen on three *Richard III* films, Patricia Tatspaugh on the tragedies of love, and Laurence Guntner on *Hamlet, Lear,* and *Macbeth*. These are all fine essays, but apart from Coursen's they don't focus on the translation of the early modern genres systematically, for the most part, but on individual films or on more general and not quite generic issues. For example, Patricia Tatspaugh's contribution launches a shrewd and interesting discussion of how the *Romeo and Juliet* and *Antony and Cleopatra* films "open out" the text to provide more meetings between the lovers, in keeping with the expectations of film romance, but does not write directly about what a tragedy of love might have been in Shakespeare's time or how its defining features might be reworked (or ignored) on film. Hattaway's chapter on the comedies deals with problems of translating theatrical space and place into filmic terms, emphasizing film's "masking" rather than "framing" effects, and problems opposed by the expectations of contemporary audiences and by the differences between Elizabethan and contemporary acting. Many of the problems discussed, however, are not unique to the comedies, and so the essay's contribution is more general than generic. This may be so because, as Hattaway suggests, no great Shakespeare film com-

edy has yet been made, and because success in Shakespeare film
comedy may depend on "formal difference" from the source rather
than fidelity to it, in the manner of *Prospero's Books* or *Chimes at
Midnight*. This view is plausible, and it would be good to have a bit
more of Hattaway's views on such formal divergences and how
they work in these intriguing films. But the collection, perhaps as a
whole, shies away slightly from the idea of difference as structure.

Coursen's work on *Richard III* comes closer than the others to engaging the question of how the Folio *genres* (rather than the specific
plays that comprise them) cross time and media, how they speak or
do not speak to our times. His assumptions about the genre of the
historical play are somewhat traditional, with a heavy emphasis on
Richard's violation of the sacred cosmic order and the providential
restoration of that order. That such generic expectations had been
created for Elizabethan audiences by the Tudor Homilies and prose
histories is likely, and there is energy and illumination in
Coursen's systematic inquiry into why contemporary versions—
Loncraine's and Pacino's especially—differ from what an Elizabethan playgoer might have expected. Coursen always "puts the
question" to performances and films in his work, and when he
doesn't find what he is looking for, he keeps looking. So, for example, when he writes of the Loncraine film that it fails to be either
providential (as Shakespeare's play is) or realistic (as epic film
ought to be) he is specific and dogged in his listing of failures of
realistic portrayal of 1930s Britain—down to details of Nazi rallies
and types of aircraft. Coursen knows that Loncraine is trying for
something more postmodern, jarring and eclectic than this and he
doesn't want to like it. But his exercise in historical "matching,"
which seems at first to miss the point, actually illuminates how
Loncraine's postmodern *Richard* works by making its dissonances
and jarring historical overlays visible. (This is difference as structure.) Coursen's reading of Pacino's even more fragmented *Looking
for Richard* is compelling, again, not because Coursen is necessarily right, but because he has a strong interpretive hypothesis which
he pursues with vigor, namely that Pacino's fractured film, part *cinema verité*, part *faux* documentary, engages with the dimension of
the sacred more powerfully than the other *Richard* films, even the
overtly more traditional Olivier version. I think this is true, but I
would never have seen it without reading this essay. When Coursen
says of Pacino that "he holds our culture up to another until gradually an infinite regress develops," we see how an un- or anti-theo-

retical critical practice, such as Coursen's, can lead to theoretically interesting results. For Coursen, Loncraine is the bad postmodernist, Pacino the good. Perhaps this is a sound judgment, but it is easy to imagine an opposite conclusion. Coursen invites dialogue, and makes one grateful for the chance to disagree.

J. Lawrence Guntner's essay on *Lear*, *Hamlet*, and *Macbeth* adaptations stresses contemporary relevance, the ways these film adaptations allegorize aspects of the modern world. He emphasizes the work of non-Anglophone directors, Kozintsev, Gade, Kurosawa, and others, tracking "how Shakespearean tragedy has been able to transcend the temporal, national, ideological and cultural boundaries of Elizabethan England, even without Shakespeare's language" (117). "Transcendence" of anything is not now in fashion, but Guntner's approach is in fact more contemporary, immanent, and localized than his terminology, and the chapter illuminates some of the most interesting Shakespeare films by placing them firmly in the context of national traditions and issues that shaped them. In the section on the work of specific directors, Anthony Davies argues persuasively, following and revising Hapgood, for a shifting, in Olivier's work, between theatrical and cinematic modes that is intentional and conscious, part of the design of the films. His essay also makes liberal use of film reviews and published criticism. The essay is sound, but I prefer Davies's more focused emphasis on cinematic space in his *Filming Shakespeare's Plays* (1988).

Pamela Mason's approach to Welles through attention to narrative logic and coherence runs if not counter to then at least in a separate stream from most commentary on Welles, which stresses his creative divergence from source and his cinematic style. (Welles is the only one of Andrew Sarris's "Pantheon" *auteurs* to have worked in Shakespeare film.) Mason doesn't ignore the visual dimension, but she does believe Welles's style is subordinated to narrative, and that Welles follows Shakespeare's own emphasis on the need to tell and retell stories, especially tragic stories. In his *Macbeth*, according to Mason, Welles "acknowledges that the narrative imperative is both the play's method and its message" (193). This chapter is a gem, and an important reminder not to ignore narrative in the face of a virtuoso display of film style. Mason's approach is one good example among many in the *Companion* of how a slight shift in the terms in which we look for fidelity to Shakespeare can enliven questions of the relation between film and text, liberating one from arid noting of textual cuts, failures to live up to the standard of Gielgud or Olivier in the speaking of "the verse" and other woeful distractions of attention from the work of creative adaptation and response.

Mark Sokolyansky's excellent, too brief essay on Kozintsev locates the work of this major director in the context of Soviet film culture. His work is detailed and brings a rich knowledge of Russian sources and Russian history to bear on Kozintsev's work. This chapter merits expansion, perhaps in book form. Deborah Cartmell's short essay on Zeffirelli is an excellent introduction to the films, and also to a major topic in film study, the workings of "the gaze." The mechanics of the cinematic gaze, first connected to Shakespeare studies in Barbara Freedman's *Staging the Gaze: Psychoanalysis, Postmodernism and Shakespearean Comedy* (1991), is made possible by combining close-ups and cutting between looker and looked-at in ways that the stage can only weakly emulate. Since the 1960s, the apparently simple dynamics of this cinematic technique have played an important role in feminist film theory and in work on cinema influenced by the revisionist psychoanalytic theories of Lacan. Laura Mulvey's "Visual Pleasure and Narrative Cinema" is still the classic, indispensable text for the first phase of the feminist theory of the gaze in cinema. Cartmell revises and applies Mulvey's theories to Zeffirelli, showing how manipulation of the gaze "adds another layer to Shakespeare's narrative—a layer that can subvert the actual words of the text" (216). Thus Zeffirelli can construct, for *Taming*, a "feminist version of the play" that may not be there in the script. And thus the Shakespearean text, with its associations of high culture, propriety, etc. can function in Zeffirelli's art as the conscious level of narrative, while cinematic style constructs an unconscious, partly hidden alternative. This approach is especially productive in the case of Zeffirelli, in whose work revelation and disavowal play shifting roles.

Samuel Crowl's essay on Branagh is the stand-out in the "directors" group. In a way that does not seem to be the case in literary study, access to the *auteurs* themselves actually improves the work of commentators on Shakespeare film directors. Crowl, an amiable and probing interviewer, is the second example of this phenomenon in the book, Jackson being the first. Crowl's is a subtle, balanced, and brilliant reading of Branagh's development as a Shakespeare film director. The spine of that story is Branagh's gradual emancipation from the theater, his increasing willingness to trust himself to purely cinematic means. The cinema is not merely a newer craft than theater for Branagh; becoming more fully cinematic in his art brings with it a surfacing of his early infatuation with the populism and emotional expansivness of Hollywood movies. This line of analysis leads up to a brilliant reading of the *Hamlet* film and its stylistic and psychological dynamics as the culmination of Branagh's liberation from filmic and theatrical predecessors, which Crowl reads in Bloomian terms as anxiety of influence. At the conclusion of the film, which evokes Errol Flynn as well as Olivier's soaring leap from the parapet at the end of his *Hamlet*, "actor and director and movie tradition all converge in evoking and finally getting rid of all the dominating fathers who haunt Branagh's keen awareness of the Shakespearean tradition on stage and film" (235). But do such pointedly outward gestures really express an achieved resolution? Branagh's likeness to Olivier here is that both try, consciously or not, to imitate Hamlet's *sprezzatura* in the fifth act. Olivier balanced the bravado of his dangerous leap onto Claudius with an unequalled performance of the meditative, inward-looking, forgiving side of a Hamlet who recognizes, as Branagh's Hamlet does not, that there are conflicts that may not be capable of resolution at all and that certainly cannot be resolved through *panache* alone. I read Branagh's *Hamlet* as less, not more, mature than Olivier's, and *Henry V*, his first Shakespeare film, as Branagh's best work. Branagh becomes more inventive, more cinematic, more postmodern over time, yes. But in *Henry V* he was not only brilliant but lucky in the conjunction of the stars and in the convergence of his own story as upstart artist with Shakespeare's take on the story of a king who had much to prove.

In the section on "critical issues" we have a superb piece by Carol Rutter on "Looking at Shakespeare's Women." Rutter's essay is unusual in the degree to which the emphasis on the visual is systematic: she refers, on principle, only occasionally to *words*. Rutter develops, at a more complex level, the kind of "gaze" criticism we see in Cartmell's essay on Zeffirelli but amplifies that approach with her own strong gifts as a critic of theatrical performance. In the Shakespeare films—looked at all at once as a phenomenological unit—women are constantly framed, confined, corsetted. But film's "historic interest in female bodies" also dictates that women's roles "multiply, filling in the *mise-en-scène* with supplementary extra-texts that are there to be read with—or against—the dominant narrative" (243). One such moment is Mary Pickford's complex wink at the end of the 1929 *Shrew*. Rutter is brilliant not only on the moment but on how it encapsulates a tract of Shakespeare film history yet to come in which gender functions in similar ways. Another such moment is the role of Anne as spectator of the coronation of Richard in the Loncraine film. Her analysis of this magnificent and complex sequence is one of the best passages in the *Companion*.

Neil Taylor on national and racial sterotypes in the Shakespeare film corpus and Neil Forsyth on the supernatural continue the section on critical issues; both essays are good reviews of the relevant material and are fine contributions to the *Companion*. "Stereotypes," however, may be too limiting a framework for how Shakespeare film engages or evades constructions of race and ethnicity, and sticking to the topic of "the supernatural" similarly seems to limit Forsyth's scope— the chapter suggests a broader ambition to locate cinematic Shakespeare more precisely in the context of the uncanniness of the cinematic image and the history of cinematic ghosts and vampires than space permits. An expanded version might draw on psychoanalytic and media studies approaches like those of Marjorie Garber (*Shakespeare's Ghost Writers*) or Avital Ronel (*The Telephone Book*), or on Angela Lant's work on the intersection the role of "Egypt," mummification, and the trope of the living dead in the discourse of silent cinema.

Tony Howard's long chapter on Shakespearean "Offshoots" is a most welcome conclusion to the *Companion*. For the Shakespeare film scholar or fan, this essay, like Jackson's opening chapters, is likeliest to provide information we simply did not have in convenient form before. Howard's discussion is far more comprehensive than the comparable section in Rothwell's *History*, discussed below. Howard begins with the interesting idea that the offshoots are, as he puts it, "*in* history" in a way that differs from "orthodox" Shakespeare films. Neither kind can, of course, escape from history, but the films that follow the text or in other ways present themselves as versions of the plays they are based on typically strain either to "recreate history" or to "evoke timelessness," while such Shakespeare-derivative films as *West Side Story* or Mazursky's *Tempest* engage with the contemporary world more directly. The distinction needs some refinement, but serves the essay well. Howard covers an enormous number of offshoots, attempts a typology, and provides valuable generalizations about how films in a given decade or period make use of Shakespeare to allegorize current issues. For example, Howard suggests that "post-war Elsinore became the capitalist status-quo," a general statement that manifestly invites testing, but which nevertheless allows us to understand affinities among such disparate works as Kurosawa's *The Bad Sleep Well*, the Finnish *Hamlet Goes Business*, Chabrol's *Ophelia*, and Helmut Kaulner's *The Rest Is Silence*. With this context in mind, one sees the Zeffirelli and Branagh *Hamlets* as departures from the norm, or as marking a period shift away from corporate critique. Michael Almereyda's corporate neo-*noir* vision of the play appeared too late for Forsyth to include it, but seems to belong to the *Hamlet* film tradition he identifies. *Macbeth* and *Othello*, in contrast, "have been seen as studies of the relationship between marriage, eroticism . . . and violence" (302).

Any collection of this kind is bound to suggest demarcations of the field in regard to subject matter and method. The *Companion*'s suggestions are for the most part good ones, especially its emphasis on process, its finding of multiple ways to approach adaptation, its attention to visual strategy and form, its pragmatism, and its broad inclusiveness. As is inevitable, some important kinds of work on Shakespeare films do not appear in the collection, or are not represented in sufficient strength to matter. Most of the contributors are Shakespeareans. That is hardly a disqualification, and is offset by the truly impressive labors these Shakespeareans have made to encounter film as film and not as a muddy mirror of text or stage—but film historians and cultural studies scholars might be better represented. Ideological and theoretical approaches (except for feminist ones) are almost entirely absent. There is a slight distortion or skew in how the field is represented. But at the same time it must be said that the book is genuinely multivocal and diverse. The view of the field it offers is open, at its edges, to expansion and revision. In the *Companion* there is no one best approach, any more than there is one text or authoritative performance of *Hamlet*.

Perhaps no other scholar has done as much as Kenneth Rothwell to establish Shakespeare on film as a field of academic study. He co-founded and co-edited the *Shakespeare on Film Newsletter* (1976–92). He was the primary editor of *Shakespeare on Screen: An International Filmography and Videography* (1990) and has published many articles on specific films, directors, and trends in Shakespeare film. *A History of Shakespeare on Screen: A Century of Film and Television* draws on Rothwell's long and distinguished career as editor, filmographer, and critic, and goes beyond what he has done in the past by bringing into active play his prodigiously extensive knowledge of film reviews and of the now immense secondary literature on Shakespeare film.

Rothwell's encyclopedic scope enables him to make connections between early and recent films, between minor films and well known ones, and between forgotten literary scholarship (particularly at the fringes of the discipline) and the interpretive work of specific directors in surprising and illuminating ways. He notes the precedent for *Shakespeare in Love* in *Shakespeare Writing "Julius Caesar"*; he compares King Lear's falling out of the cinematic frame in the Brook *Lear* (1970) to a very similar moment in the Warde production of 1913 (21); he notes, the well-known relationship between Svend Gade's gender-bending interpetation of Hamlet's "femininity," and the nineteenth-century theories of Arthur Vining, and also the far lesser known resonance between Polanski's unusual and influential interpretation of the role of Rosse as betrayer and M. F. Libby's "Some New Notes on *Macbeth*" (1893) through the latter's influence on Kenneth Tynan's co-authored screenplay for the film (158). These connections are not always original discoveries made by Rothwell, but they are among the fruits of his mastery of the field.

In addition to its success in distilling a large secondary literature and in weaving together an extraordinary number of skilled close readings of films, *The History of Shakespeare on Screen* is engagingly written; it is at least as companionate a volume as the Jackson collection. Rothwell's significant gifts as a storyteller enable him to create a shrewd and scholarly history of a complex field that is also a book that can be read for pleasure.

In part, the readability, even fascination of the book is a function of Rothwell's strong narrative voice and presence. Though hundreds of films are discussed, Rothwell writes as if he had just seen each one and is ready to share his first reactions. Yet, as the author weaves together production history and context, early reviews, his own readings of the films, and the views of other critics and scholars, judiciously sifted and generously acknowledged, those reactions seem to have been informed, as indeed they are, by a lifetime of learning and active participation in the creation of the academic discourse of the field. The prose affects something like a sequencing of camera distance in film, integrating very close range and the long, considered view, refined by time, reflection, and multiple viewings. When at close range, Rothwell is even willing to share those moments in his viewing of these films in which the experience becomes fragmented, and failures of craft and coherence intrude: extras wandering out of frame, silent actors whose gestures seem exaggerated by contmporary standards, alternative cinema techniques or costumes that seem silly if measured only by realist expectations, etc. At first, I was mildly alarmed by this, remembering how hard it can be at times to invite students to "see through" such moments—especially in silent Shakespeare—to the artfulness behind them. But acknowledging such failures of continuity or illusion is part of a complex and effective strategy of exposition here. Shifting perspective in such ways, *A History* not only holds attention through its century-long story, but also negotiates the distance between a beginning student or ordinary filmgoer and the modes of close analysis characteristic of an academic approach to the films. Like the *Cambridge Companion*, Rothwell's book potentially opens the world of the academic study of Shakespeare on film to a wider readership.

The *History* is organized roughly chronologically, but the individual chapters usually also focus on the work of a director or group of directors (Olivier, Welles, Castellani, Zeffirelli) or on a theme (there are chapters on "other Shakespeares," Shakespeare and the cinema of transgression, Shakespeare from television to the web), but even in the thematic ones Rothwell's tendency to group films by director as well as by period is strong. Though this bias toward the director as *auteur* is one I share, it has consequences, both good and mixed, the most important of which is that Rothwell writes the history of Shakespeare on film largely, though by no means entirely, as a series of readings of individual films and as the story of the tension between the artistic agendas of individual directors and the constraints of the marketplace, or, to use Rothwell's terms, between "art" and "tickling commodity." Rothwell borrows this vivid expression from *King John* (2.1.574), which was also the first Shakespeare play to be filmed, so the opposition gets introduced early on. Recurring attention to the struggle between art and commerce enlivens the account of the silent era, helps to explain the long periods of drought in Shakespeare film's history, lends a poignant dimension to Rothwell's chapter on Welles (perhaps the finest in the book), and plays an important role in the chapter on Branagh. "Tickling commodity" is never forgotten for long in Rothwell's *History*. As theme, this opposition provides one of the ways in which a massive amount of material may be unified and contextualized, yet, as analytic tools these terms can be somewhat limiting, tending to produce a universalizing narrative in which art and commodity are always in struggle. One might contrast *A History*, in this respect, with the work of Wiliam Uricchio and Roberta Pearson in *Reframing Culture: The Case of the Vitagraph Quality Films* (1993). The authors show, for one studio in the silent era, how complex, multidimensional, and sometimes paradoxical the push toward "art" could be, involving shifting alliances among many interest groups including clerical and educational reformers, exhibitors, civic authorities, as well as those involved in making and financing films.

No large-scale history could be as detailed as Uricchio and Pearson are for Vitagraph, but Rothwell's book could do more to foreground the complexity of the problem. Not doing so means risking having the opposition play out as a more or less eternal and unchanging one that takes only superficially different forms for each director or in each period. Another kind of simplification that results is a certain naiveté about fully funded work—such as early television productions in England (1937–39) or the state supported Soviet films of the period of the thaw (Kozintsev, Yutkevich, Fried). Rothwell acknowledges that such arrangements are not utopian, but his overall model doesn't offer enough scope to discuss how such mechanisms of support also engage with broader issues in their respective social systems. If the category of "commodity" were expanded to include something like ideology, by that name or another, this framing device could generate, for many of the films discussed, more searching questions.

Rothwell's discussion of the Branagh *Henry V* offers an example of how this limitation in the book works, as well as how it can be partly made up for through generous acknowledgment of the work of others, a hallmark of Rothwell's approach. In one place, Rothwell appears to dismiss "the mantra of British cultural materialists that Kenneth Branagh is somehow darkly complicit with agents of capitalist imperialism" (251); yet, in probing the film's complexities, he draws graciously on studies by Donald K. Hedrick and Dympna Callahan, critics whose work engages directly with the place of Branagh's work in late capitalism, in analyzing the film's "ability to appear anti-war while employing pro-war codes" (248). Branagh, as Rothwell says, has the ability to have his cake and eat it too. But it is precisely in this duality, noted by Rabkin and much analyzed by New Historicists in regard to the play and by Hedrick, Callaghan, and others for the film, that the workings of iedeology (and complicity) can be seen and need to be addressed. In the recently published *Shakespeare Remains* (2002), Courtney Lehmann's chapter on the film "There ain't no 'Mac' in the Union Jack" continues the ideological critique of the film that began almost as soon as it was released. Lehmann expores the ideological implications of the contrast, on and off camera, between Branagh, the assimilated Irishman who plays the king, and John Sessions, an Irish classmate of Branagh's at RADA who, in contrast to Branagh was thought not quite right for Shakespearean tragic roles and who plays Macmorris in the film. She discovers visual allusions to "King Billy" in Northern Irish iconography in Branagh's *tableaux* of rearing horse and warrior king at Harfleur. Lehmann, of course, does not settle the question; the debate on the question of Branagh's complicity with "capitalist, imperialist ideology" will no doubt continue. My point here is that Rothwell in fact takes the specifics of that debate very seriously, as is clear in his explicit debts to Hedrick and Callaghan, but he also seems to disavow ideological criticism if it is named as such.

A second major theme which is also introduced with *King John* in the first pages and runs through the book as a whole is the tension between the Shakespeare text and its realization in a visual medium. As in Crowl's essay on Kenneth Branagh and other contributions to the *Companion*, this story is told as an emergence or emancipation of cinematic Shakespeare from its textual and theatrical antecedents. The shape of this narrative is complicated by the fact that film was at first largely wordless, except for intertitles and by the early habit of filming actors reciting whole speeches the film audience could not hear, so that visual storytelling had to (and did) get off to a relatively quick start in the new medium, producing visually sophisticated films by the mid teens. But, Rothwell's account suggests, visual Shakespeare needs to be reinvented as each director finds ways to make the transition from page to screen, often against the resistance (somewhat abated now) from textual "purists" among scholars, critics, and reviewers, which continued in surprising force throughout the twentieth century. (Rothwell sometimes calls the opponents in this long struggle "bardolaters" and "cinéastes.") Shakespearean cinematic art, then, struggles against commodity and against textual or theatrical bias, succeeding brilliantly in some cases, gaining respectability, and even making money. But, even if the long term trend is positive, there is an interesting, slightly sad intermittency to the story of Shakespeare on film as Rothwell tells it that makes Orson Welles, for this reader, the central figure in the book.

The Welles chapter is an example of Rothwell's usual practice as well as of his best writing. Welles's Shakespeare films, demonstrably "uncommodified" on the record of their box office performance, owe their existence, paradoxically, to Welles's failures—the controversies over *Citizen Kane,* and the "production turmoil" connected with *The Magnificent Ambersons* relegated Welles to B-movie budgets. Yet, out of the necessities of constrained budgets and other limitations, Welles produces the most impressive Shakespeare films of all, perhaps precisely because they bear the impress of his struggles with "tickling commodity" and thematize them. *Chimes at Midnight* is, of course, the central text in such an account, and Rothwell's analysis of it is brilliant, drawing the work of many others into a sharply focused intepretation of the film as an allegory of the embattled *auteur* in a commercial age.

What Rothwell chronicles in his attention to the conflict between the textual "purists" and the cinematic adaptors (with the eventual but shakily held victory of the latter group at century's end) is what Barbara Hodgdon refers to as the gradual diminishing of the "discourse of loss" about Shakespeare on film ("From the editor," *Shakespeare Quarterly* 53 no. 2 [summer 2002]: iv–v; and Hodgdon, "Two *King Lears*: Uncovering the Film Text," *Literature/Film Quarterly* 2 no. 3 [1983]: 143). Long after the idea that only the full text of a play could give performance authority, "what lingered was the sense that transforming print text—and actors' performances—into cinematic conventions diminishes performative force" (v). Critics and scholars no longer regarded film as an illegitimate or unworthy medium for Shakespeare, but continued to lament the failure of specific films to find cinematic equivalences for details, tropes, and patterns of imagery in ways that would have confirmed the critics' own reading of the text. Rothwell's *History* itself would be, in these terms, a post-discourse of loss text, in which "reading through the lens of *literary* criticism" takes "second place to foregrounding elements of *film* language—mise-en-scène, editing, and sound" (Hodgdon, 2002: v). This is clear not only in the book's brilliant analyses of specific films, but in his celebration of directors as *auteurs* in their own right. For example, Rothwell says of Polanski: "he didn't need to borrow Shakespeare's robes when he had so many of his own" (160). However, there is a note of lament and loss in Rothwell's book, different from Hodgdon's "discourse of loss," that comes through most clearly (once again) in the Welles chapter. After *Chimes at Midnight*, Rothwell writes, "like Falstaff, Welles still hoped to 'be sent for,' yet fresh betrayals and disappointments lay ahead as he dickered to make more Shakespeare movies" (93). This tone, of course, suits the Welles story best, but it is present through much of the *History*, most often, as here, in conjunction with the major theme of the conflict between art and commodity. But "loss" in the *History* also has to do with the fact that, even when financing is not a major barrier, Shakespeare films fail for other reasons, and not in textual terms but in purely cinematic terms. Rothwell's account includes the failures—bad early films, the failed Charlton Heston *Antony and Cleopatra*, and others. There is also the loss associated with the waning of Shakespeare film as art cinema (though Rothwell is extremely open to the more popular, or more experimental Shakespeare films of the last decade). There may be something to regret, as well, in the ongoing history of "electronic Shakespeare: from television to the web," since, as I have suggested above in discussing Michèle Willems's chapter on video in the *Companion*, the period of "film" as an entity and an art form distinct from its many media analogues and avatars may be ending. But in the *History*, the sense of loss, intermittency, and precarious success is balanced by nuanced celebration of what has been achieved, and by a willingness to redefine and reconfigure the story of Shakespeare on film in response to new work and changing boundaries.

What counts as a Shakespeare film, and why? Rothwell's book is attentive to the range and variation in kind of adaptations, and especially to the spectrum from theatrical to more fully cinematic adaptations:

> The history of Shakespeare in the movies has, after all, been the search for the best available means to replace the verbal with the visual imagination, an inevitable development deplored by some but interpreted by others as not so much a limitation on, as an extension of, Shakespeare's genius into uncharted seas. (5)

Like the *Cambridge Companion*, Rothwell includes a section that deals explicitly with films that are even further removed from Shakespeare's verbal art—films which Tony Howard calls "offshoots" and Rothwell calls "derivatives." While Rothwell covers fewer films than Howard does, he constructs a useful typology of

such works (219 ff.)—his categories of "mirror movies," backstage
and related dramas like *A Double Life* and *The Dresser* in which
the lives of Shakespearean performers mirror and/or reverse their
on-stage roles, recontextualizations, "parasitical" Shakespeare
films and others that are thought-provoking and interesting. More
importantly, Rothwell finely articulates the priciple of the moving
boundary, whereby what is "outside" the pale of what we construct
as a valid adaptation may move inside the boundary in ways one
cannot foresee—after all, works that have become canonical within
the domain of Shakespeare on film—*Chimes at Midnight, Throne
of Blood*, and others, have already shifted status. It is easy to recall
why they were outside; it is more difficult, as custom legitimates
them, to reawaken the passionate resistances that they encountered
on first release. And that is why it is good to have Rothwell's ex-
cerpts from the reviews—they help to estrange, again, what has
comfortably found entry under the capacious umbrella of the
Shakespearean. However, as Rothwell notes, there is always a further boundary to cross or violate. In the current scholarly landscape, the "outside" includes Shakespeare-based pornography and
cult films like *Hamlet for the Love of Ophelia, Tromeo and Juliet*.
After the publication of *A History of Shakespeare on Screen*,
boundaries were extended even further, perhaps, by *Hotel O*, a
hardcore porn film starring Nina Hartley and Lexington Steele with
a screenplay by Richard Burt, who is also the major scholarly voice
calling for a reconsideration of the categories we use to extend high
culture status to popular culture but not to schlock, amateur, or
porn versions. Rothwell's closing remarks in the chapter on
"Shakespeare in the cinema of transgression and beyond" could be
applied to this project:

> At this point the distance from the Shakespearean vision is so vast that
> the label must be something like Shakespeare movies of no kind what-
> soever. And yet no kind may turn out to be some kind after all. (229)

This is not a lax or easy agnosticism; the history Rothwell writes
is one in which scandalous appropriations of Shakespeare in new
modes and media have become naturalized and accepted in unexpected ways. Rothwell's engaging way of telling this story, while
himself furthering the process by advancing the state of the art of
scholarly study of Shakespeare on film, is a distinguished contribution not only to this emerging field but also to our understanding of

the increasingly cross-media, unpredictable, and eclectic cultural world in which we live.

Pure Resistance: Queer Virginity in Early Modern English Drama
By Theodora A. Jankowski
Philadelphia: University of Pennsylvania Press, 2000

Reviewer: Jyotsna G. Singh

"The possession of biological virginity—an unperforated hymen— has consistently set certain women apart from others throughout history. Some cultures may validate the virgin and highly fetishize the intact hymen; others may demonize the intact female and denigrate her uncommon status. But whether validated or denigrated, the virgin woman does differ from (usually the majority of) women who are not virgins, whether that difference is physically located in biology or culturally/socially located in lack of 'alliance' with a man" (4). Theodora Jankowski's book sets itself to the task of addressing why and how such a "virgin/not virgin binary" for women has been deployed in early modern English culture and literature. What are the society's investments in culturally managing the biological virginity of women?

Jankowski addresses this provocative question to a variety of cultural and literary texts via the mediations of contemporary gender and "queer" theory. Drawing in theorists ranging from Theresa De Lauretis, Judith Butler, and Marilyn Frye, Jankowski is interested in exploring a multitude of gender and/or erotic positionings to show how virginity represented a queer space within a constraining early modern sex/gender system. Where she departs from Butler and others is by considering celibacy and chastity as a category of sexuality—and more importantly, as "a specific choice and manifestation of sexuality" rather than simply a rejection of it (8). Thus, she makes an important political claim for virginity as "a queer space within the otherwise restrictive and binary early modern sex/gender system" (8).

While Jankowski usefully points to instabilities in the discursive and material productions of virginity, the strength of her argument lies more in its historical underpinnings than in its ideological aim of "disrupting the regime of heterosexuality." A strange dissonance runs through a highly original work that skillfully explores the material and discursive formations of virginity. While the author carefully charts the shifts and turns in the shifting attitudes and deployments of the notion of virginity, she seems curiously fixed in her definition of "patriarchy." At the outset, she states her aim of demonstrating "how implicated in patriarchy and male need is the traditional definition of the biological virgin" (5). While Jankowski does consider specific patriarchal versions of inheritance laws, among other practices, she seems to imply an unchanging male/patriarchal need to dominate and oppress, underpinning the sex/gender arrangements. Having said this, I would nonetheless like to stress the historical and literary significance of the book. What I take issue with is more a question of style and tone than substance.

To get a sense of the substance of the book, let us first turn to its historical contribution. Giving considerable evidence, Jankowski demonstrates how Catholic medieval Europe afforded a "plurality of sexual/erotic arrangements" in contrast to the "more limited, and therefore restrictive, sex/gender arrangements of early modern Protestant England" (11). Buttressing these claims, the author offers a compelling narrative of the two trends in chapters 2 and 3. In the first account (the strongest chapter of the book), she explores the early ascetic Christian movements and the importance of virginity and celibacy for both men and women. Here, the author demonstrates how the Roman Catholic discourse of sexuality organized gender relations not only around the traditional "man/woman binary," but also around the "theological virgin/non-virgin one as well" (10). The monastic traditions articulated by the early Church fathers, and affording both men and women the choice of celibacy and virginity, resulted in many religious houses for women being founded from the sixth to the twelfth century, specifically as retreats of aristocratic widows and daughters. Initially, Jankowski explains, the women's monasteries were centers of power and learning, but after 800, the women's abbeys were also caught up in the struggles resulting from "the Church's attempts in the eleventh, twelfth, and thirteenth centuries, to take control over all religious houses" (67). Clearly, as Jankowski demonstrates, the history of how these discourses of sexuality and virginity operated from the sixth to the twelfth century is complex and unstable. Overall, she shows us how this period was one "of intense and continual negotiation of the virgin's power both within the Roman Catholic Church and within the monarchal system" (66).

To understand why women's monasteries and religious communities were stripped of their power in Catholic Europe, Jankowski offers a credible historical explanation in the development of the cult of the Virgin Mary, namely Mariolatry. By the twelfth century, restrictions on the power of consecrated virgins in monasteries were enabled and promoted by the image of the humble and obedient virgin. Here Jankowski notes that the cult of Marioltary enabled edicts such as the "Fourth Lateran Council's mandate that no new orders be established," which was "used to restrict women to [existing orders] that demanded claustration" (73). This was reinforced by the Papal bull, Periculoso. The power of virgins was well on its way to being restricted by the time of the Reformation promotion of marriage.

Jankowski also offers a complex and nuanced account of the gradual devaluation of the spiritual benefits of virginity and the valorization of marriage and the family in Protestant England (in chapter 3), drawing on the commonly accepted connection between the emergence of the bourgeois family structure under a nascent capitalism and the privileging of marriage over virginity for women. But in an unusual move, Jankowski shows us how two Catholic theorists and humanists of the early sixteenth century, Juan Luis Vives and Desiderius Erasmus, also come out in favor of the "necessity and inevitability of marriage for women," and the "importance of virginity only as a transitory, premarital condition" (90). In doing so she demonstrates the resilience of patriarchal traditions—both Catholic and Protestant—regarding the role of women, though she does make clear the doctrinal distinctions between the two camps in the shifting meanings of terms like "virginity" and "chastity."

Jankowski's description of Protestant discourses ranging from the doctrine laid down by Luther and Calvin to popular marriage manuals also makes some important observations regarding these semantic and substantive shifts in social attitudes toward women's sexuality. While it is a commonplace assumption that Luther and

Calvin discounted vowed celibacy in order to repudiate Catholic monastic vows and validate a companionate marriage, Jankowski adds to this discussion by showing how the word "virginity" is eliminated as a term of discourse in Protestant marriage manuals. Instead " 'chastity' is used equally to describe the unmarried (virgin) daughter and the sexually active, faithful wife" (96). As a result, Protestant discourses of marriage viewed virginity as a "transitory, solely premarital condition for women" (114).

Part 2 Jankowski's book applies this historical account to a new reading of the women characters in several Renaissance dramatic texts. These works, as the author approaches them, can be viewed as sites of ideological struggle relating to cultural attitudes toward women's roles as virgins and wives. In the three chapters of this section, somewhat predictably, Jankowski examines the roles of virgins in terms of their varying degrees of resistance to patriarchal authority, specifically in terms of marriage. She describes under three labels: dutiful virgins who see their virginity as a transitional state to marriage; "challenging virgins" who marry but question the institution itself; and "resistant virgins who completely repudiate marriage and the patriarchal sexual economy" (115). Within these categories, Jankowski makes a further distinction between "queer" virgins and "nonqueer" ones—whose resistance to marriage is nominal or temporary. Furthermore, in recognizing the relation between "textual women and real ones" as a complex one, Jankowski offers illuminating readings of a large number of plays, ranging from comedies like *The Merchant of Venice, Twelfth Night,* and *The Roaring Girl* to more problematic plays like *Measure for Measure* and *The Convent of Pleasure.*

In these accounts of the plays, we look afresh at the roles of the women characters specifically as virgins, ranging from the "dutiful," "nonqueer" virgins like Hero, Viola, and Perdita to the "nonmarrying queer virgins" like Isabella in *Measure for Measure* and Happy in *The Convent of Pleasure.* In fact, one of the most compelling chapters of the book is one that deals with the situations of these two "cloistered characters" who demonstrate that "lives lived in isolation from men provide a space within which traditional notions of gender and gender-marked pleasure can be challenged, redefined, and reinvented" (172). Jankowski's historicized reading of Isabella's role as a nun is particularly illuminating in the way it shows how Roman Catholic discourses about virginity intrude into the Protestant ideology of the play. Jankowski also notes

Isabella's reference to flagellation in erotic terms ("keen whips I'd wear as rubies") as signifying a range of possibilities for "queer sexual practices open to virgins."

According to the author, "the possibility that she maintains an erotic life without male contact—and outside the patriarchal sexual economy—makes her doubly threatening by suggesting that queer virgins could live with sexual pleasure and without men" (177).

If one of the aims of *Pure Resistance* is to explore the "correlation between textual women and real ones," representations of Elizabeth the Virgin Queen in Lyly's *Gallathea and Endymion* (in the introduction and conclusion respectively) obviously offer great examples for such a study. In these readings of the allegorical aspects of these plays, Jankowski shows us how their engagement with the idea of virginity "has the potential to question dominant social constructions of virginity" (27). Yet ultimately Jankowski does not consider Elizabeth a "queer virgin," since Elizabeth's iconic construction inevitably stresses her unique and anomalous nature. Were other women " 'allowed' to be perpetual virgins, Elizabeth's position would not have been unique" (198). Conclusively, Jankowski argues, her aggrandizement does little to challenge the restrictive Protestant sex/gender system, and thus, the Virgin Queen could never be a "queer virgin" in the terms set up by this book. Overall, this is a useful book for early modern historians and literary critics, and especially feminist scholars. Despite its ideologically fixed reading of patriarchy, this is a book worth reading.

Shakespeare's Tribe: Church, Nation, and Theater in Renaissance England
Chicago: University of Chicago Press, 2002

Reviewer: Michael Schoenfeldt

Shakespeare's Tribe is an important book, which will be required reading for all who are interested in the period, in religion, and in the stage. Its central claim—that there is a profound assonance among the apparently disparate communities of church-goers, theater audiences, and members of a single nation—promises to refashion our sense of the ways that politics, religion, and literature interacted in the period. Early modern historicist literary studies are turning, somewhat belatedly, to the critical importance of religion in the period; *Shakespeare's Tribe* will assume a central role in this reorientation. The book is immensely learned, and written with clarity and energy. Throughout, Knapp illuminates forgotten corners of familiar texts even as he sheds light on texts and materials that are rarely discussed. *Shakespeare's Tribe* deliberately challenges a series of truisms that have inhibited our understanding of the period. Particularly striking in this regard is Knapp's examination of the overly simplistic orthodoxy that links the period's marked antitheatricalism to a particularly Puritan pathology about performance. Knapp demonstrates that many Renaissance English dramatists, including Shakespeare, believed deeply in the religious potential of the theater to save wayward souls. Knapp, moreover, carefully cross-examines standard assumptions about England's burgeoning nationalism in this period, demonstrating the contradictions that early English Protestants experienced between the claims of an endemic nationalist Protestant tradition and the ideals of the Pauline body of all true believers that transcended nationalist boundaries. Knapp's capacity to interrogate prevailing assumptions through a blend of original scholarship and breathtaking insight will have a widespread and salutary effect on the field.

Knapp deftly avoids the two primary models available for interpreting texts from the Renaissance stage amid religious contexts: either ferreting out hidden Christian allegories, or claiming that the stage serves only as a secular compensation for the emptying out of meaning of religious rituals at the Reformation. Knapp demonstrates convincingly that writers in the period envisioned their plays as religious enterprises, and deliberately assimilated religious materials to their performances. What emerges is a fascinating sense of the competition between stage and pulpit for the attention and communitarian identifications of the populace. Focusing on the genres of history plays and comedies, Knapp explores in detail how the stage represented preachers and religious extremists, and also describes how preachers characterized stageplays. Knapp, moreover, shows how preachers frequently portrayed their own pulpit activities as theatrical performances. It is

thrilling to watch Knapp reclaim a sense of performative adaptabil-
ity for a religious evangelism founded on a Pauline rhetorical care
for the audiences, since such self-fashioning has tended to become
the exclusive province of the widespread thesis about secular indi-
vidualism at court. Likewise, it is refreshing to see Knapp's emphasis on the importance of identity that emerges from a sense of
community in the period, particularly since so much recent work
in early modern studies has been devoted to the concept of a self
isolated from community involvement.

Knapp is an excellent close reader, and has a particular talent for
rendering the overarching significance of the odd detail. The various chapters are rife with illuminating readings of familiar and unfamiliar texts. The discussions in chapter 1 of Jonson's revelry, and
of the relations between good fellowship and religious communion, are refreshingly original. The next chapter, "Rogue Nationalism," analyzes the imagined community of vagabonds that
Elizabethan England's paranoia about the homeless seems to have
produced. This phenomenon is strikingly seen as progenitor of
other forms of community—the community of the theatrical experience, the community of religious believers, and the community of
the nation.

The next chapter, "This Blessed Plot," develops a provocative argument about Shakespeare's internationalism, one that challenges
assumptions about Shakespeare's endemic Englishness. "Preachers
and Players," the following chapter, portrays the stage as a spiritu-
ally valuable institution, and explores the ways that the stage and
the pulpit competed as a site of community. I particularly liked the
ways that Knapp was able to place interpretive pressure on the
punishment of Bardolph in *Henry V*. The final chapter, "Pseudo-
Christianity," offers a fascinating reading of the play *Sir Thomas
More* amid a particularly resonant question about the relationship
between the outward conformity demanded by the Elizabethan
compromise and the theatricality celebrated by the Elizabethan
stage. The suggestive epilogue proffers a reading of *Twelfth Night*
amid the potentially opposed discourses of merriment and religious doctrine.

It is a remarkable testimony to the contagious exuberance of
Knapp's argument that the book left me longing for the opportunity
to query some of his claims. I would have liked to see a discussion
of magic in this context, particularly since magic and religion are
inseparable in this period. Plays like Marlowe's *Dr. Faustus* and

Shakespeare's *The Tempest* might be enriched by Knapp's claims even as they ruffle some of the edges of these claims. I also would have liked to see more about the tensions between good fellowship and good kingship that *Henry V* seems deliberately to stage. King Henry's cold-hearted if necessary farewell to Falstaff certainly suggests that the good fellowship of the tavern may be incommensurate with the demands of the nation. Furthermore, I sometimes felt that Knapp tends to take at face value the claims of playwrights for the moral efficacy of their productions; these claims, though, may have just been frantic attempts to justify a questionable enterprise in terms borrowed from the very morality that would condemn it. But all fine books produce the impulse to extend and challenge their insights, and critics will be doing this frequently with Knapp's provocative work for years. This is a remarkable and substantial book that will hold a signal place in the critical conversation about religion and the early modern stage for many years to come.

The Reign of Elizabeth I
By Carole Levin
New York: Palgrave, 2002

Extraordinary Women of the Medieval and Renaissance World: A Biographical Dictionary
Edited by Carol Levin et al.
Westport, Connecticut: Greenwood Press, 2000

Reviewer: Susan Frye

Because Elizabeth I was a powerful, highly visible woman in a patriarchal society, she continues to generate popular attention, in the films *Shakespeare in Love* and *Elizabeth*, as well as in computer games like "Civilization III," in which—according to my daughter—the player may opt to become Elizabeth and preside over an Age of Enterprise. In a college setting, this attention spurs departments to offer courses on the Tudors, on Elizabeth herself, and on the literature of the early modern period. Designed for such courses, Carole Levin's *The Reign of Elizabeth I* will appeal to many teachers and students. The author of *The Heart and Stomach of a King: Elizabeth I and the Politics of Sex and Power* (1994), Levin is a prominent historian of Elizabeth. As her title promises, *The Reign of Elizabeth I* is a survey of English history during the second half of the sixteenth century. At 122 pages of text and fourteen pages of notes, the book comprises a good summary with few surprises for the scholar, but is geared more toward the undergraduate or graduate student who needs an introduction. Classes might well read *The Reign of Elizabeth I* alongside *Elizabeth I: Collected Works* (2000), edited by Leah Marcus, Janel Mueller, and Mary Beth Rose. In fact, as I reread *The Reign of Elizabeth I*, I hoped that students would read this book in connection with primary documents of some kind (as Levin doubtless hopes as well), precisely because its summary—with the exception of the final chapter on culture and difference that is more of an original essay—moves so easily over the rough terrain of the sixteenth century.

Chapter 1's title, "Overview of Elizabeth's Life and Reign" announces the book's purpose. In this first chapter comprising seventeen pages, Levin covers the ground from Elizabeth's birth and the world of Tudor politics in which she was born and grew to womanhood, moving from her birth to accession as queen to the principle problems and issues that she faced until her death in 1603. This chapter by itself would make a useful summary for students of the notable events of the queen's life and reign.

The emphasis in chapter 2, "Religious Divides and the Religious Settlement," is on how Elizabeth and her government managed to return the country to Protestantism, while maintaining a discreet ambiguity that officially brooked no discussion. Chapters 3 and 4 deal with England's foreign relations; chapter 3 is titled "England's Relations with Others in the First Part of the Reign" and chapter 4, "England's Relations with Others in the Last Part of the Reign." In addition to a lucid overview of the foreign policy questions with which Elizabeth and her government had to deal, Levin in the third chapter raises one of the most frequently asked questions about the queen and her reign: Just how responsible was Elizabeth for England's foreign policy? As Levin points out, historians have often concluded that the queen was responsible for a great deal of England's foreign policy, especially since foreign policy was tied to her marriage proposals. Levin's follow-up question is, Were Elizabeth's reactions to other countries then reactive or active? Did she "simply drift" (39)? Was she, in D. M. Loades's phrase, "reactive rather than proactive" (D. M. Loades, *John Dudley, Duke of Northumberland, 1504–1553* [Oxford: Oxford University Press, 1996], 224; cited in Levin, 39)? After raising these interesting questions— but not questioning the assumption that in foreign policy to react is bad, and to act is good—Levin proceeds to discuss whether or not Elizabeth ever meant to marry—another classic question about her life, and one about which Levin voices a clear opinion backed by reference to *The Heart and Stomach of a King*, that Elizabeth was not psychologically equipped to marry.

But Levin never answers the questions that she raises about Elizabeth's role in English foreign policy. This omission seems to reveal a problem with Levin's accomplished summarization. In such a book, is it best simply to point out where a few of the historical questions lie, answering one or two, leaving some in the air, and never mentioning others? Certainly, in a book of this type it would be impossible to delve into the complexities of even half of the recurring questions about Elizabeth and her reign. But Levin might well take a stand, however brief, on this question among others, to couple her knowledge of the period with a willingness to state clear answers, even if they are necessarily speculative.

In chapters 5 and 6, Levin's always readable prose gains energy, and her wealth of historical detail drives her argument forward. Chapter 5, "Plots, Conspiracies, and the Succession," continues to summarize, but with a willingness to interpret her material that recalls the energy of Levin's chapter, "Wanton and Whore," from *Heart and Stomach of a King*. Chapter 6, "Culture and Difference at the End of the Reign," departs even further from the summary approach to move to discuss the marginalized peoples living in Elizabeth's England, especially the poor, those accused of witchcraft, Jews, and Africans. Although this chapter approaches areas of increasing interest for scholars and students alike, here Levin might have spent more time researching the first-rate work that has been done on the poor and on witches and witchcraft. She has read David S. Katz and James Shapiro on the Jews in England, but not Kim Hall or Margo Hendricks on race and blackness. Nevertheless,

Levin's willingness to bring her overview to a close with a discussion of these groups, and especially with the Elizabethans' involvement in the slave trade is admirable, while the book as a whole is both useful and readable.

Extraordinary Women of the Medieval and Renaissance World: A Biographical Dictionary, for which Carole Levin was coordinating author, offers a very different kind of overview. Levin, Debra Barrett-Graves, Jo Eldridge Carney, W. M. Spellman, Gwynne Kennedy, and Stephanie Witham have together produced a remarkable biographical dictionary, in that it provides three- to four-page biographies of such English women as Eleanor de Montfort, Anne Askew, and Arbella Stuart, alongside those of continental women like Katherine Luther, Louise Labé, and Vittoria Colonna—and, most impressively, alongside Hürrem Sultan (Roxelana) of Turkey; Melisende, queen of Jerusalem; Malinche (Doña Marina) of Mexico, interpreter for Hernando Cortés; Nzinga, queen of Angola; poet and Śaivite Akka Mahādēvī of India; as well as poets Ono No Komachi and Izumi Shikibu of Japan. While the entries are summaries of existing scholarship (at least on the women I know most about), each entry is clear and readable, including discussion of non-Western forms of verse and religion. Each entry is followed by a brief but exemplary bibliography, while one of the chief delights of the volume is its copious and well-selected illustrations.

Levin's introduction recalls how, when she first began teaching women's history twenty years ago, she asked her students to list "famous European women of the medieval and Renaissance period" (xiii). During the first few years, there were few if any names to write; then as the years went by the blackboard began to fill with the names of "queens, religious leaders, warriors, and writers such as Elizabeth I, Isabella of Castile, Joan of Arc, Lady Jane Grey, Eleanor of Aquitaine, Hildegard of Bingen, Heloise, Margery Kempe, Julian of Norwich, and Christine de Pizan" (xiii). This biographical dictionary deliberately moves beyond these women about whom information is now readily available, to include courtesans as well as royal figures, women who lived more in the public sphere, and women "who as wives, mothers, daughters, and friends demonstrated the courage to live their lives in ways that went beyond the ordinary expectations of the times" (xv–xvi). I welcomed the chance to read about lesser-known European women and especially women from around the world. In this way the volume is in tune with our increasing desire to turn our scholarly lens toward Africa, Asia, and the New World, while not forgetting Britain and continental Europe.

At least thirty-seven of the seventy entries are devoted to women who were writers, poets, dramatists, or scholars, while six of the women were artists—Sofonisba Anguissola, Lavinia Fontan, Artemisia Gentileschi, Esther Inglis, and Levina Teerlinc—and twenty-one were religious figures of some kind. The biographical dictionary also includes one physician, Jacqueline Félice; three martyrs: Anne Askew, Elizabeth Barton, and Marguerite Porete; and six diarists. Deviating slightly from the count helpfully provided in "Appendix A: Notable Women by Title, Occupation, or Main Area of Interest," I count at least twenty-four women who were political figures of some kind—rebels, queens, and activists. *Extraordinary Women* also includes an appendix listing the countries of origin of the seventy women, a basic timeline of historical events, and an up-to-date selected bibliography. Reading these seventy remarkable biographies serves as a reminder that all these "extraordinary women" lived political lives. Although they encountered the limits placed on women by their very different cultures, they still managed to lead active, often outspoken or expressive lives. Grouping these women together in a single volume expands our sense of women on several continents during the period known in Europe as the Middle Ages and Renaissance.

Elizabeth I: Collected Works
Edited by Leah S. Marcus, Janel Mueller,
and Mary Beth Rose
Chicago and London: University of Chicago Press,
2000

Reviewer: Valerie Wayne

In her Latin oration at Cambridge University in 1564, Elizabeth I announced her intention of doing "some famous and noteworthy work" and observed that even if she were unable to complete it fully, "yet will I leave an exceptional work after my death, by which not only may my memory be renowned in the future, but others may be inspired by my example, and I may make you all more eager for your studies" (88–89). The kind of "work" she refers to is never specified; her mention of it is prompted by seeing the "sumptuous edifices" of Cambridge and reflecting on Alexander's response to viewing monuments erected by princes, after which he turned "to his counselor and said, 'I have done no such thing.'" She diminishes her "grief" for a comparable lack of achievement—the comparison with Alexander constituting all the while a claim to the most exemplary form of leadership—by promising to produce her "work." Although Elizabeth's extraordinary accomplishments have been acknowledged for many generations, this volume of *Collected Works* as edited by Marcus, Mueller, and Rose brilliantly fulfills her earlier promise by providing within one place those speeches, selected letters, poems, and prayers that the editors judge to be most reliably attributed to her. Unlike the slim volumes of previous editions, this four hundred page book provides ample and authoritative evidence of her achievements as a rhetorician, speaker, politician, poet, correspondent, counselor, religious writer, and woman. Elizabeth's "work" is here realized as it has never been before.

The extent and diversity of the material made the task of creating this edition especially challenging. In addition to gathering, authenticating, transcribing, translating, dating, and annotating these texts, the editors had to develop some form of organizing them that would convey their generic variety while putting related texts within proximity of one another. The choice to divide the book into four sections, within which would appear the speeches, letters, poems, and prayers of each period, seems to me especially shrewd. It has the effect, for example, of positioning some of Elizabeth's letters on Mary, Queen of Scots and the Northern Rebellion close to her poem prompted by the threat they posed, "The Doubt of Future Foes," and of grouping other related materials together, while foregrounding the different genres in which she wrote. Section I provides a sense of Elizabeth's exceptional abilities as a writer and thinker from the age of eleven. Her subtlety, diplomacy, and skillful use of ambiguity appear as she communicates in Italian and French with a stepmother who could influence her own father, in Latin with her father and her younger sibling who had become king, and in English with her older sister whose power as queen put her in the Tower. The event that takes on the most importance in this section is related to Thomas Seymour's trial for treason due to his relations with Elizabeth, and the edition presents four additional documents on the testimony of Elizabeth's governess, Katherine Ashley, concerning her role in encouraging a potential marriage. Here as elsewhere the additional documents are well chosen to provide fuller information on the issue at hand without becoming a distraction or making the book too cumbersome.

Section II begins with Elizabeth's accession in 1558 and includes her addresses to Parliament over marriage and the succession; her conversations with William Maitland, the Scottish ambassador; and letters to and about Mary, Queen of Scots and the Northern Rebellion. This section also presents for the first time since the sixteenth century Elizabeth's devotional materials drawn from two printed collections of the 1560s. In the third section, two issues become especially compelling: Elizabeth's marriage negotiations with the duke of Alençon, and her fascinating correspondence with James VI of Scotland during the time his mother was charged with treason and then put to death. The edition reprints James's answers to Elizabeth's letters and corrects the dating of "On Monsieur's Departure" so that it applies to Alençon rather than Essex. That section also includes multiple versions of Elizabeth's two replies to parliamentary petitions regarding the execution of Mary, Queen of Scots; two versions of the extraordinary poem "When I was Fair and Young"; and all of her two inch by three inch prayer book dating from 1579–82 surrounded by miniatures of Elizabeth and Alençon. The fourth section, which begins with the Armada speech at Tilbury that the editors affirm was actually delivered, also offers her Latin rebuke to the Polish ambassador and the exchange about it between Lord Burghley's son, Robert Cecil, and the earl of Essex; three versions of the Golden speech of 1601; letters to Essex while he was in Ireland; and the editors' verse translation of her twenty-seven stanzas in French on the progress of the soul.

By including these and many more texts in the edition, the editors have resisted others' doubts about Elizabeth's competence and authorship. Leicester Bradner, who prepared a 1963 edition of the poetry, questioned whether she wrote "When I was Fair and Young" on the grounds of "manuscript attribution and provenance" as well as Elizabeth's ability.[1] But the editors have located further attributions of the poem to Elizabeth, and they judge her poetic range sufficient by citing Puttenham's praise of her as a lyric poet and pointing to her accomplished verse exchange with Sir

Walter Ralegh. They include "Now Leave and Let Me Rest," another poem that Bradner excludes, and the verses between Elizabeth and Ralegh discovered after his edition. Steven May also made these attributions to Elizabeth in his book, *The Elizabethan Courtier Poets*, and identified the twenty-seven stanzas in French as "almost certainly her original composition."[2] He later published a transcription and prose translation with Anne Lake Prescott, in which they describe the poem as Elizabeth's translation "from an unidentified verse meditation of unknown composition."[3] Barring the discovery of that original, the editors of the *Collected Works* "find no features of the manuscript to invalidate our assumption that this poem is a complete, original composition by Elizabeth" (413), a conclusion to which they are entitled given their extensive work with her writing. The untitled poem is haunting, enigmatic, and deserves further study.

The most strenuous objections against Elizabeth's authorship concern her speeches, many of which are memorial reconstructions, but here the editors emphasize the "complex coproduction" associated with those materials and the likelihood that "a significant portion of her writing was produced in collaboration or after consultation with officials of her government" (xii). They develop a new paradigm for the speeches by arguing that she most often spoke extemporaneously or from memory "and only wrote the speech down afterward or had it transcribed from her dictation" (xxi). When they compare these recorded versions with later manuscript or printed versions of the same speech, they sometimes find the earlier texts more vivid and vigorous, while the later ones moderate their observations with a wider audience in mind. So the edition prints multiple versions of the speeches to allow readers to see the development from spontaneous rhetoric to more considered "—and often less inflammatory—language" (xxi). This seems to me an intelligent adaptation of the revised editorial theory that led to the multiple editions of playtexts beginning with *King Lear* two decades ago. By moving beyond the goals of sole authorship and a single text, the editors allow students and scholars to explore the relations between different textual versions for themselves. I would welcome the application of similarly progressive editorial thinking to the texts of other early modern women writers, who also deserve the degree of careful editing that Elizabeth I receives here.

The decision to modernize all of the texts was, as Leah Marcus has described it, the "most difficult decision" that the editors had to make, since "to modernize is necessarily to interpret,"[4] but it was a crucial one given the variety of readers that this book solicits and deserves. It required that Marcus herself, as the one who determined editorial policy, revise the position she had articulated in *Unediting the Renaissance*, yet in doing so she exhibits the kind of flexibility and the desire to "undo rigidities inherited from the past" that had informed her previous study.[5] She is also acknowledging the potentially wide readership of the *Collected Works*, for unediting is an editorial approach that, in my opinion, is most valuable for more advanced students and scholars. For those who prefer to read Elizabeth's work in their original spelling and punctuation and to consult the foreign language texts in their originals, Marcus and Mueller are publishing another volume, *Elizabeth I: Autograph Compositions and Foreign Language Originals*, in early 2003. All of the texts in Elizabeth's hand included in the *Collected Works* will be transcribed there, together with those translated from foreign languages. The important translations that Elizabeth herself prepared from other writers are excluded from both books and "would constitute a large volume in themselves" (xv). Although others have objected to their exclusion, that decision seems to me appropriate given the aims and audience of this book. Add to those translations the many letters that the editors could not include in this edition, which "would run to several volumes" (xiv), and one gets a fuller sense of Elizabeth's prodigious output. This is a collection of many of her works, but it makes no claims to completeness. It will enable much further work on the queen.

The selective recording of textual variants, which is yet another departure from standard editorial practice, is a further way in which this edition accommodates itself to a wide reading audience, and in this instance we are asked to trust the judgment of the editors when they record only what they determine to be "significant differences" between texts, because full annotations would become "impossibly unwieldy" (xx). The textual notes are combined with commentary notes as a way of calling attention to "the historicity of all elements of Elizabeth's texts" (xx), rather than implying a timeless or objective editorial authority. Yet this procedure effaces editorial interventions in ways that more traditional editions do not, for the decision to modernize without presenting a full textual apparatus means that readers cannot see or assess the changes made to the early texts. That is a questionable choice, since even

the most diligent editors are fully fallible. Yet the approach seems
to me understandable because the edition combines scrupulous
scholarship with a highly accessible textual presentation, because
the forthcoming volume will supply some material that allows for
further comparisons, and because this is a first attempt to produce
a scholarly edition of many of Elizabeth's works. Fuller textual an-
notation might have prevented our seeing this edition for many
years to come, and the editors are certainly justified in asking that
the collection be judged "in light of the magnitude of the task"
(xxiv). *Elizabeth I: Collected Works* nonetheless exhibits many of
the features of an "unedited" text: it has a preface but no formal
introduction, no headnotes, no list of texts consulted, no textual
apparatus, no extended commentary, no subject or general index.
Its appealing simplicity belies an extensive exercise of editorial authority.

A primary delight of this edition is the opportunity to see Elizabeth's rhetorical skills at work in a wide variety of difficult political
and personal circumstances: her urgent lucidity to Mary, Queen of
Scots when she learns of Darnley's murder: "O madame, I would
not do the office of faithful cousin or affectionate friend if I studied
rather to please your ears than employed myself in preserving your
honor" (116); her affection for the Duke of Alençon in 1580: "I con-
fess that there is no prince in the world to whom I would more will-
ingly yield to be his, than to yourself, nor to whom I think myself
more obliged, nor with whom I would pass the years of my life,
both for your rare virtues and sweet nature" (243), followed by her
very sharp words in 1582 when he wants more money for his campaign in the Netherlands: "My God, Monsieur, how unfortunate
you are to believe that this is the way to preserve your friends, by
always debilitating them!" (259); and the momentary plainness of
her argument to James about executing his mother: "By saving of
her life they would have had mine" (293). Although she could be
self-effacing when she chose, she could also display her intelligence and learning with a brilliance that convinced Essex she had
a "mind of gold" (335). In one of her less modest moments, she remarked to Parliament in 1585 that "I am supposed to have many
studies, but most philosophical. I must yield this to be true: that I
suppose few (that be no professors) have read more" (182). As a
result of this extraordinary edition even the professors, who only
may have read more than she, can now read more, much more, of
her.

Notes

1. *The Poems of Queen Elizabeth I,* ed. Leicester Bradner (Providence: Brown University Press, 1964), xii–xiii.

2. Steven W. May, *The Elizabethan Courtier Poets: The Poems and Their Contexts* (Columbia: University of Missouri Press), 317–18.

3. Steven W. May and Anne Lake Prescott, "The French Verses of Elizabeth I (Text)," *English Literary Renaissance* 24, no. 1 (1994): 9–43, quote on 9.

4. Leah S. Marcus, "Confessions of a Reformed Uneditor (II)," *PMLA* 115, no. 5 (2000): 1072–77, quote on 1075.

5. Leah S. Marcus, *Unediting the Renaissance: Shakespeare, Marlowe, Milton* (London and New York: Routledge, 1996), 37.

Gender and Heroism in Early Modern English Literature
By Mary Beth Rose
Chicago: The University of Chicago Press, 2002

Reviewer: Phyllis Rackin

Living in what is often called a post-feminist age, those of us who still identify ourselves as feminists have learned that women's progress cannot be plotted on the kind of clean upward trajectory of increasing opportunity and power that meliorist narratives have often attempted to construct. Advances are often followed (and even accompanied) by setbacks, gains in some areas of experience offset by losses in others. Women still have to run very hard just to stay in place—or even to keep from losing too much ground.

Feminist historians are still debating the answer to Joan Kelly's famous question, "Did Women Have a Renaissance," but the answer increasingly seems to be "No." During the course of the seventeenth century, English women lost ground in a number of fields. Excluded from many trades in which their predecessors had been active, they were also confined by the rising barriers that defined the household as a private world, separate from the public arenas of economic and political action. Or so it has seemed to many feminist scholars. Mary Beth Rose complicates the picture by arguing that the feminization of the household can be seen in many ways as an advance for women, since this was a period when the private world itself acquired increased prestige and importance in the cultural imagination. Within this context, she believes, heroism itself was regendered from masculine to feminine, as passive suffering and endurance—virtues traditionally regarded as appropriate to women—came to replace warlike action in the public sphere as the proof of heroic status. The stakes in this argument are high because, as Rose points out, conceptions of heroism reveal the fundamental ways a culture assigns value.

Gender and Heroism in Early Modern English Literature draws on Rose's impressive previous work, both as editor of the recent edition of the *Collected Works* of Elizabeth I, and as writer of the influential book, *The Expense of Spirit: Love and Sexuality in English Renaissance Drama*, where she argued that the Protestant idealization of holy matrimony produced a "heroics of marriage," which enabled private life to become the arena for heroic action and women to become its protagonists. In *Gender and Heroism*, she finds traces of a related progression in a selection of sixteenth- and seventeenth-century texts, beginning with Christopher Marlowe's *Tamburlaine* and ending with Mary Astell's *Some Reflections upon Marriage.* The analysis is restricted to a relatively limited selection of texts, but it sheds new light on many others because, as Rose points out, the historical trajectory they suggest is also visible in a variety of other work produced during the period, such as the representation of Christ's heroism in *Paradise Regained.*

In chapter 1, Rose identifies the beginning of this trajectory in four plays—*Tamburlaine, Dr. Faustus, Volpone,* and *Macbeth*—all of which feature active, hypermasculine heroes. In subtle and provocative readings, she argues that all four plays reveal the instability of a warlike, masculine heroic ideal which was already becoming outdated as technological innovations transformed the practice of warfare and an increasingly centralized state claimed its own monopoly on violence. In the first three of these plays, the male protagonists' drive to omnipotence requires that they attempt to monopolize every possible subject position, female as well as male, even as they insist on male dominance and female submission. In *Macbeth*, by contrast, women and the female are eliminated, leaving the hero with a purely male heroic identity, but because that identity is defined as criminal the play implies a devastating critique of the masculine heroic ideal.

Chapter 2 turns to the public speeches of Elizabeth I to show how subtly the queen constructed her heroic royal identity. This chapter provides a much-needed and convincing rebuttal to recent studies that focus on the references to virginity and motherhood in Elizabeth's early speeches and emphasize the disabilities she suffered as a female monarch. Rose examines speeches written throughout Elizabeth's reign to show that she actually exploited and transformed a full range of gendered subject positions, appropriating both a male heroics of action and a female heroics of endurance and survival. In addition to its important contributions to our understanding of Elizabeth's achievement, this chapter also suggests that we may need to rethink our beliefs about the positions of her female subjects. As Rose suggests, Elizabeth both understood and exploited "the fact that gender roles and distinctions in Elizabethan England are more malleable and unstable than has been suggested previously" (30).

Chapter 3 focuses on a very different type of women's writing, the autobiographies produced by four upper-class seventeenth-century women—Margaret Cavendish, Ann Fanshawe, Anne Halkett, and Alice Thornton. Their experiences of the civil war, Rose argues, placed all of these women in situations that relaxed some of the constraints on female action and self-expression. In the final chapter, Rose assembles an intriguing variety of texts—Milton's *Samson Agonistes*, Aphra Behn's *Oroonoko*, and Mary Astell's *Some Reflections upon Marriage*—to argue that by the end of the seventeenth century all heroism was problematically conceived in terms that were gendered female. For both Samson and Oroonoko, the defining condition of heroism is slavery. For Astell, marriage itself is a kind of slavery, but "she . . . who can be so truly mortify'd as to lay aside her own Will and Desires, to pay such an entire Submission for Life, to one whom she cannot be sure will always deserve it, does certainly perform a more Heroic Action than all the famous Masculine Heroes can boast of" (qtd. on 111).

For women, the advantages of a heroics of endurance are mixed at best. Although patient suffering in adversity is a comforting ideal for both men and women oppressed by conditions they have no hope of changing, the political interests served by that ideal are inevitably those of the oppressors, since it discredits the impulse to protest or rebel against injustice. In this connection, as Rose points out, it is noteworthy that all four of the women writers examined in chapter 3 were Royalists and that none of them consciously rejected the restrictions that defined their roles as wives and mothers. Nonetheless, Rose sees her study as being in some ways "recuperative," since it allows "evidence for female heroism, much of which has been invisible, to become legible and articulate" (xxii). If, as she argues, the dominant mode of heroism represented in the literary texts at the end of the seventeenth century was patient suffering and endurance, then heroism itself was gendered female, and heroic behavior was clearly possible for women as well as men. However, Rose acknowledges the problematic consequences of both terms in the binary opposition she constructs: just as the older, masculine heroics of action privileges violence and domination, the feminine heroics of endurance tends to glorify slavery and unwanted death; "the differences between the heroics of action and the heroics of endurance," she observes, "frequently come down to a choice between killing and dying" (xxii). Even the humane alternative she proposes—a celebration of "the human capacity and desire to survive"—speaks to a world of severely diminished expectations—post-feminist indeed, and also post-heroic.

Tough Love: Amazon Encounters in the English Renaissance
By Kathryn Schwarz
Durham, NC: Duke University Press, 2000

Reviewer: Maureen Quilligan

In *Tough Love,* Katheryn Schwarz tracks the presence of Amazons as a means for understanding how heterosexual desire, far from normative or natural in English Renaissance culture, is a social construct of the most fragile and problematic sort. Situated at a crucial cynosure of multiple discourses, and far from merely rewriting colonial encounters with racial others in the New World into rehearsals of ancient classical encounters with barbarian others, the figure of the Amazon allowed Renaissance culture to contemplate its own unstable domestic arrangements. Relying on Derrida's notion of the supplement as something which not only adds to but also supplants, Schwarz argues that the figure of the Amazon in diverse texts by Ralegh, Shakespeare, Jonson, Spenser, Daniel, and Sidney reveals heteroerotic desire to be a social invention which is always haunted by the possibility of female same-sex bonding. Thus, rather than being as insignificant as Valerie Traub would have it, female homoeroticism however much these texts attempt to patrol it, poses a distinct and early threat to patriarchal domestic arrangements.

Beginning with the notion that Amazons do not exist and are therefore purely "fantasmatic," Schwarz proposes a psychoanalytic study of the processes of gender construction which reads its canonical texts in such energetic and often playful ways that the literature is made to say things it has never said before. Schwarz recognizes that the texts aim to "reinforce male homosocial power and to make female homosociality invisible" (41), but her interest is always in tracking the point in the text at which this project fails to achieve any stable triumph but works, often, in the opposite direction.

Schwarz is at her most interesting when she is dealing with figures who are not actual Amazons, but something close. Her analyses of Britomart in Spenser's *Faerie Queene,* Cleophila in Sidney's *Old Arcadia,* or Hippolyta in Shakespeare's *Midsummer Night's Dream* allow her to interrogate the means by which the suggestion of an Amazon figure works to reveal the instability of gender categories. Schwarz, for instance, does not deal in detail with Radegund, who is an Amazon, in book 5 of *The Faerie Queene,* but rather with Britomart, whose Amazon-like qualities (she is "dressed to kill" in the chapter title) effectively domesticate Artegall, as the actual Amazon Radigund does. "Amazon myth does not oppose the normative to the monstrous—Britomart to Radigund, male to female power, marriage to ungoverned sexuality, heroism to emasculation—but makes it impossible to tell the difference" (157). Shakespeare's Hippolyta, who has so little to say in the play, becomes a means for analyzing the "traffic in women" in *Midsummer Night's Dream.* Choosing not to tell the story of Hippolyta's having been given as a gift by Hercules to Theseus, Hippolyta's marital Amazon history, powerfully recalled in the play, underwrites the same-sex bonding of the girl lovers and poses female separatism as a real choice. One of the more fascinating suggestions she makes is why Hippolyta has her specific name—recalling the mythological character's son's name, Hippolytus, whose tragic-son status Schwarz hears in the story of the changling boy. Schwarz, however, ignores the problem of incest at the heart of Hippolytus's story, a problem which may have helped us to see Hippolyta as a theoretically significant exception to the rule of the traffic in women, the traffic being specifically designed to avoid incest.

Schwarz's discussion of Sidney's *Arcadia* seems most problematical, if in part because the argument never registers the role that Sidney's sister may have played in the various guises in which the text appears. Schwarz reads the comic *Old Arcadia* more than the new and thus takes Pyrochles actually to be the Amazon Cleophila—specifically because the pronouns the narrator uses to refer to "him" are always in the feminine. Because such pronouns are excised from the *New Arcadia* at the same time that we are told that Mary Sidney Herbert, the countess of Pembroke, becomes something like its coauthor rather than privileged reader, it seems that their presence has something to do with the auditor who turns author. Some comment on this fact would have been useful. Female agency is exercised here in a context to which Schwarz does not attend. Most importantly for Schwarz, at the moment when Dametas discovers the naked Cleophila and Philoclea locked in an embrace, we are supposed to see Pyrocles as a "tribade" rather than a fully fleshed male. While one can follow the Derridean logic of the supplement and see Pryocles as a girl, to do so is to lose some of the fun there is in the scene—rather as if the girl in "The Crying Game" was really just a girl and not a boy in very good disguise. I think Valerie Traub's history—which does not allow the tribade to threaten the "chaste femme" of female friendship until the close of the seventeenth century—is a little more persuasive than Schwarz's history here. Sidney can have as much fun as he does because Pyrocles remains a prince. If Pyrocles is a girl, the patriarchal threat exercised by Euarchus also loses its shocking oedipal power. It is, however, deeply interesting to entertain the possibilities—and Schwarz does an elegant job of conjuring them up. If finally we opt for a more stable set of texts and genders than Schwarz wants to give us, that does not mean the book does not provide some very amazing encounters.

Sovereign Amity: Figures of Friendship in Shakespearean Contexts
By Laurie Shannon
Chicago and London:
University of Chicago Press, 2002

Reviewer: Rosemary Kegl

Sovereign Amity: Figures of Friendship in Shakespearean Contexts is a resolutely utopian project. Laurie Shannon sees in the rhetoric and logic of English Renaissance friendship a model of "likeness, parity, equality, and consent" that would have offered contemporaries a "thoroughgoing antidote to hierarchies and tyrannies now (seemingly) obsolete; the likeness between friends radically cancels vertical difference" (11). *Sovereign Amity* specifies the distinctiveness of Renaissance "affectivity and its representations" and outlines the "broader implications [of friendship's 'sovereign amity'] for English culture, subjects and political thought," including its tentative aspirations toward an anti-absolutist, pre-liberal "mode of self-governance that, within each gender or status, may be parlayed into consensual governance, a governing with or by someone else in a state of parity" (1, 2, 125). Our ability to comprehend the very particular Renaissance manifestation of friendship turns on Shannon's second utopian premise—that the rhetoric and logic of Renaissance friendship provides if not a thoroughgoing antidote to, then, at the very least, an unsettling of our tendency to rely on methodological norms that derive largely from nineteenth- and twentieth-century phenomena. Renaissance friendship serves as both *Sovereign Amity*'s object of analysis and its methodological conscience.

The book divides into two sections—"The Sovereign Subject" and "The Subjected Sovereign." The first examines the Renaissance ideal of a private friendship that is, as the second section explains, inevitably impossible for the monarch to attain. In the first of the three chapters that comprise "The Sovereign Subject," Shannon establishes the cultural pervasiveness of a Tudor and Jacobean emphasis on "figures of friendship and the rhetorical tropes of like-ness around which they cluster" (19). The material she considers (writing in a number of genres on friendship, counsel, and tyranny) and its typical protagonists ("sovereign, private selves who exer-cise virtually utopian powers of autonomy," "counselors whose liberty of speech is enshrined," and "kings who listen to that speech and also heed the examples that the 'figures of perfet amitie' provide" [53]) will be quite familiar to Renaissance scholars and students. Entirely compelling and much less familiar are Shan-non's observation that the marvelous sameness depicted in narra-tives of "perfet amitie" is "not a matter of philosophical identity. . . . Metaphorical, approximated, comparative, and, as it were, vir-tual: likeness remains an imaginative process or poesis," and her assertion that friendship's " 'politics of likeness' voices—in radical ways for the sixteenth century—an alternative politics in which the sovereignty of the private self was speculative, rather than ortho-dox or normative" (21, 22).

The second and third chapters bring these general observations about the utopian possibilities of Renaissance friendship to bear on Elizabeth Cary's *The Tragedy of Mariam*, Shakespeare and Fletch-er's *The Two Noble Kinsmen*, and, much more glancingly, Donne's elegies to the ladies Markham and Bedford. Cary's play is of inter-est because it grapples with the fundamental irreconcilability of two cherished Renaissance norms—the "powerfully homonorma-tive bias in Renaissance thought [that] favors both self-likeness (constancy) and same-sex affects" and the "heterosexual organiza-tion of love and marriage" that "proves contradictory to the like-ness topos at the center of positive ideas about union"—and because it structures female chastity as a counterpart to an ideal-ized male friendship (55, 56). Both idealized male friendship and female chastity model an autonomous, self-sufficient, private sov-ereignty resistant to the subordination that is, at the very least, al-ways potential in absolutism's hierarchy between ruler and subject and, by analogy, in the hierarchy between husband and wife. Cary's associative female chastity enables, in the shadow of a capricious tyranny, a matrix of affiliations among women. If Donne's elegies specify the potential didactic force of those female friendships, *The Two Noble Kinsmen* reminds us why likeness—male or female—remained an "imaginative process" and why its alternative politics of the sovereign subject remained speculative. Shannon concludes her analysis of *The Two Noble Kinsmen* and of "The Sovereign Subject" by emphasizing that "even the strongest conventions regarding gender, sexuality, and friendship could rewrite themselves when governed by a stronger urgency: the frightening blend of personal and political power embodied in the Renaissance conception of authority" (122).

With this somewhat forbidding formulation Shannon shifts her attention to "The Subjected Sovereign," where utopia inheres in the unfriendly guise of the monarch. In the first of this section's three chapters, Shannon outlines the protocols of sixteenth-century *mignonnerie*—the civic crisis occasioned by a monarch's attempt to enter into the private friendships that are denied to public officials. It is not simply that the hierarchical "relation of 'degree' between sovereign and subject" precludes friendship's volitional and consensual relation between equals, or that the Renaissance monarch who underestimates either the "special fixity" of that hierarchical relation or the special parity between friends calls "his sovereign condition into question" (98, 128). It is that, during the sixteenth century, the monarch becomes in person and in theory an increasingly untenable vessel for civic rule. The monarch's "body natural" desires the pleasures of autonomy and self-sufficiency that his "body politic" cannot allow: "The sovereign's exclusion from the range of private pleasures and powers Montaigne calls friendship's jouissance so indicates what is being sought in the protobureaucratic theorization of public power: a 'body' without any residual affective interests or imperatives of its own" (154). The increasing subjection of the monarch, his sovereign status as the least sovereign of individuals, is registered most familiarly in the Renaissance ruler's almost formulaic yearning for the pleasures of a private life.

In the two chapters that follow, Shannon considers the price of sovereign friendship in *Edward II*, *The Henriad*, and *The Winter's Tale*. Marlowe stages the incompatibility of "soveraigne amitie" and ethical monarchy that costs Edward II his estate and his life. In *Henry IV*, Shakespeare stages the exile not simply of Falstaff but of private friendship's affective bonds—the "diminution of *both* sovereign and subject"—as the "founding moment of [a] polity or commonweal" that is "impersonal, neutral, procedural, and bureaucratic" (184; my emphasis). In *The Winter's Tale*, the figure of the friendly counselor rewrites the commonweal's "diminution of both sovereign and subject" as a regenerative "happy confusion" between private friendship and public statecraft (188).

This is a remarkable book—original in its argument that friend ship modeled likeness and equality to a culture otherwise permeated by models of difference and hierarchy; persuasive in its speculations about friendship's far-reaching affective and political implications in Tudor and Jacobean England; and enormously exacting in its analyses of English Renaissance writing, the work of contemporary Renaissance literary critics, and the more general formulations about friendship and difference by Jacques Derrida, friendship and sexuality by Michel Foucault, and homosociality by Eve Kosofsky Sedgwick. Like most compelling scholarship, Shannon's book tends to draw us up short—to trace the contours of what is often fairly familiar interpretive territory (the imperfect analogies between state and household hierarchies in prescriptive writings on marriage, the emphasis on regulating female heterosexuality and the relative inattention to female homoeroticism, the limited success of royal efforts to establish absolute rule in England, the stress lines that develop in the notion of the sovereign's two bodies, the monarch's yearning for the pleasures of private life, and the humanist's doubts about the effectiveness of good counsel), and then to shift our orientation so that it becomes impossible to return to Renaissance culture with our old perceptions comfortably in place.

At times, the structure of *Sovereign Amity* does seem to be slightly off-balance. For instance, in her first chapter, Shannon catalogues at some length Tudor and Jacobean figures of friendship in order to demonstrate, as I suspect most Renaissance scholars would readily agree, that those figures were culturally pervasive. And yet Shannon's remarks about the modern polity toward which Renaissance sovereign amity inclines and against which its myth making is defined are generally relegated to the prologue and epilogue and, even there, tend to be largely allusive—assuming on the part of her readers a shared conception of modern bureaucracy, its civic and corporate institutional forms, and our contemporary division between public and private space.

I mention this not because it is a crippling flaw in Shannon's analysis, but because it is one effect of her attempt to make visible to us the "preliminary and different" (11) character of Renaissance discourses of friendship—which is to say, the place of sovereign amity in a pre-history of modern affect and polity and, at the same time, the absolute alterity of its pre-liberal mythography from our modern world. Working under the imperatives of this double impulse, Shannon is less concerned that we will find unconvincing her argument that Renaissance friendship is akin to modern affect and polity than that, in spite of our interpretive good will, Renaissance friendship will remain illegible to us as we persist in underestimating the distance of its protocols from our own. Counteracting her readers' modernizing tendencies requires an unyielding interpretive vigilance. Shannon tells us that "instead of judging early modern likeness from a post-liberal perspective," she will track "its rhetorical patternings to assess them for the specific opportunities they afforded sixteenth-century subjects and selves" (21); that the "sense of love as something one might greet with lamentation seems historically very distant to twenty-first-century readers trained to consider it the most real thing" (65); that "our modern conflation of chastity with celibacy only approximates one of a variety of Renaissance senses" (68); that the "classificatory significance of the Renaissance's own nomenclatures" is obscured by our tendency to invoke "eroticism as an organizing principle" (91); that Renaissance "categories of relation and their transgression derive less from erotic designations and more from the status of the parties as like or unlike" (94); that Renaissance friendship adds to Derrida's "dilemmas of autonomy and heteronomy" a "third term . . . homonomy, or rule by an other who is like" (125); and that the "lens of contemporary heterosexuality and the notions of 'family drama' from which it stems have occluded our view of Shakespeare's least gender exclusive rejoinder [in *The Winter's Tale*] to what he seems to have seen as a deterministic biologism" (219).

Of course, the chapter in which Shannon catalogues Tudor and Stuart figures of friendship is meant to demonstrate not simply that those figures were pervasive but that they were pervasive across a variety of cultural forms—an emphasis in keeping with Shannon's claim that *Sovereign Amity* "establishes a broad discursive context and ranges widely across the generically mixed, networked array of Tudor and Jacobean texts construing friendship's political and affective dispensations" (11). In this respect, the chapter is quite successful, drawing on "classical texts and their Renaissance dissemination through pedagogy and translation, redactions, popular pamphlets, commonplace books, and emblem collections . . . Renaissance translations of Cicero, humanist advice-to-princes texts, Elyot, Ascham, Montaigne's 'Of Friendship,' and Donne's 'Sir, more than kisses.' " (11). Yet the chapter is also an early indication of a potentially misleading turn in Shannon's argument. In spite of Shannon's prefatory emphasis on the "generically mixed, networked array of Tudor and Jacobean texts," *Sovereign Amity* is relatively inattentive to the local Renaissance contexts—of genre or form, for instance, or of production, circulation, or reception—that would help us to see even more precisely how these disparate texts, and their figures of friendship, were linked to one another. *Sovereign Amity*'s broad discursive context and its significance are never in doubt; the principles of networking are a bit murkier.

I also mention the slight mismatch between the tenor of Shannon's prefatory comments and her eventual interpretive emphases so that readers of *Shakespeare Studies* will know what to expect from *Sovereign Amity*'s subtitle—*Figures of Friendship in Shakespearean Contexts*. The subtitle's reference to Shakespearean contexts is presumably a way of identifying for literary scholars Shannon's focus on Tudor and Jacobean England, indicating her preference for analyzing Shakespeare's texts, and signaling the usefulness of her larger argument about sovereign amity for Shakespeare scholars. Those contexts do include some discrete observations about the genres of individual plays—most perceptively, the mixture of genres that critics have associated with *Henry IV*, and the character of romance in *The Winter's Tale*. And yet, in keeping with Shannon's interpretive emphases, although her chapter headings and the bulk of her analysis focus on plays (*Edward II, The Henriad, The Tragedy of Mariam, The Two Noble Kinsmen*, and *The Winter's Tale*), *Sovereign Amity* is not concerned with theater, with drama, or with the links among various forms of dramatic and nondramatic writing. Shannon has cast her utopian vision in a very different direction.

*Reading Revolutions: The Politics of Reading
in Early Modern England*
New Haven and London:
Yale University Press, 2000; and

*Remapping Early Modern England: The Culture of
Seventeenth-Century Politics*
Cambridge: Cambridge University Press, 2000
By Kevin Sharpe

Reviewer: Cynthia Herrup

Kevin Sharpe is among the most important scholars currently writing in the field of early modern British studies. He has helped lead
the way in refashioning how we see politics, antiquarianism, Cava-
lier poets, monarchial authors, and the interdisciplinary possibilities for history.[1] Sharpe was one of the first "revisionist" scholars;
he co-edited two of the earliest and still influential interdisciplinary collections on political culture; he has long been and remains a
tireless advocate for reintegrating the visual and the literary with
more conventional forms of historical archives.[2] Because they contain work done throughout the 1990s, the books reviewed here provide an exceptionally good introduction to both Sharpe's ideas and
his style. *Remapping Early Modern England* reprints a selection of
lectures, articles, and reviews, and *Reading Revolutions* is the first
monographic fruit of Sharpe's current preoccupations. Although
only one of the pieces (an intellectual autobiography of sorts) in
Remapping Early Modern England is unavailable elsewhere, the
collection's thematic organization allows even those already familiar with Sharpe's work to read it profitably. The result is a coherent
volume that sets out Sharpe's most recent re-visioning of the field.[3]
    Having once believed that the most likely route to explaining the
collapse of government in the early 1640s was an approach separat-
ing politics from ideology, Sharpe here rejects what he now sees as

the superficiality of that characterization. Having once been interested primarily in royal courts and parliaments, Sharpe now emphasizes the importance of working on a broader canvas. He argues that in order to understand political events, we must first understand political culture: how seventeenth-century public figures fashioned their credibility; how rulers and subjects reciprocally created meaning; and how acts and values reflexively transformed each other. He calls for a "reconfigured political history that takes as its materials language and literature, prints and emblems, . . . a move not only from the austerities of revisionism but from the constraints of most political history as it is currently written" (*Rewriting,* 37). For Sharpe himself, this means abandoning 1640 as a stopping point; adding images, graphics, and the use of space to his historical kitbag; and raising questions that explore the making and morphing of political views well beyond Whitehall and Westminster.

As he explains in the title essay to this collection, Sharpe is pursuing his interest along three complementary tracks: the performance of royalty in writing and speech, the imagery of power, and the political activity in styles of reading. Most of *Remapping*'s essays originated from one or the other of these three projects and the organization of the essays accords with this tripartite strategy. Dividing writing from reading from representations may have helped Sharpe organize his own research and writing, but it at times allows for unnecessary repetition. Moreover, dividing text and image seems at odds with the author's plea for a holistic approach to the culture of politics. Not surprisingly, then, in the strongest of these pieces ("A commonwealth of meanings," "An image doting rabble," and "Re-writing Sir Robert Cotton"), Sharpe moves easily among his questions rather than serially through them.

Sharpe is doing much more here than outlining his own schedule for scholarship. As he argues in the collection's opening essays, he is laying out an agenda for the field. If we are to understand early modern politics, he contends, we need a new definition of politics, one that pays as much attention to the workings of language as to the workings of parliament. For early modern people, the key text of politics was man. The key problem was that a common willfulness alienated humans from nature's harmonies. Good governance was a repeated lesson encouraging people to see the value in communal interests or at least the danger in ignoring them. Language, symbol, and gesture were as political as were debates and statutes. Analogy and metaphor allowed government to be taught in fables and husbandry manuals and histories as easily as in treatises and in sermons. Historians need to pay more attention to these issues if we are properly to understand politics within a providential universe.

The crisis of mid seventeenth-century politics, Sharpe argues, was ultimately a crisis in meaning and language. Neither the Republic nor the Protectorate found a means for teaching harmony effectively without reference to a king. The monarchy's return in 1660 addressed that need, but however familiar its rituals and expression, political culture in the Restoration began from radically new assumptions. Harmony had come to mean a balancing of distinct interests, not the realization of a communal likeness. A sovereign created concord rather than merely facilitating it. And after a decade of non-monarchial governments, which, whatever their failures, had not destroyed society, even Royalism became one political stance among several possibilities, no longer the one "natural" affiliation. The essay in which Sharpe presents these ideas most fully ("A commonwealth of meanings") should be read by anyone interested in the workings of early modern English society. Some readers might not find the conclusions fully persuasive, but all will be delighted by its elegance, erudition, and provocativeness.

The three essays grouped together as studies of "Texts and Power" take us back to the first Stuart decades to detail Sharpe's case for royal writing as a critical tool of monarchy. Tudor and Stuart monarchs, Sharpe tells us, took very seriously the need to perform sovereignty in demeanor, speech, and printed representations. However often their behavior fell short of the ideal, these rulers accepted a responsibility to teach moderation and order by example. In early Stuart England, there was a special urgency to such attempts. The godly emphasis on reading scripture and on private conscience made James I in particular eager to make use of writing. He produced poetry, political treatises, and scriptural exegeses, as well as a stream of older didactic instruments such as proclamations. The attention of both James VI/I and Charles I to the use of private libraries and public records reflected their recognition of writing's political authority. The epitome of this power, ironically, came not from the loquacious father, but from his considerably more taciturn son. Sharpe returns several times in this collection to the impact of *Eikon Basilike,* the posthumously published spiritual meditations allegedly written by Charles I. The popularity of the king's text and of his claim to have died for the integrity of royal conscience, Sharpe convincingly argues, helped to deny the Republicans' full victory in 1649 and (despite the best efforts of John Milton) to deny the Commonwealth the cultural credibility essential for its success.

The section called "Visions of Power" contains a superb survey of this process. In "An image doting rabble" Sharpe shows how the Commonwealth tried and failed to construct new cultural loyalties. The contrast between the means available to monarchs for establishing authority (surveyed here in "Stuart monarchy and political culture") and those that might be easily adapted by Cromwell's government is striking. Political language was suffused with reminders of monarchy, and, in any case, depending extensively on images conflicted with the Puritans' fundamental iconoclasm. The royal ghost survived 1649—not only in works such as *Eikon* but also in still circulating coins, recycled royal furnishings, architectural signs, and the like. In a culture that used symbols as shorthand for deeper truths, the turn back to monarchial forms through the 1650s was a critical capitulation. The Commonwealth deprived the later Stuarts of what had once been unthinking dedication to monarchy, but a regime that accepted the idea that trappings of kingship bestowed political authority could never be Republican enough for radicals or kingly enough for Royalists.

Sharpe introduces the arguments of his third preoccupation, the politics of reading, in "Re-writing Sir Robert Cotton" and develops them more fully in *Reading Revolutions: The Politics of Reading in Early Modern England.* Sharpe details the many ways that the uses of antiquarian libraries such as Cotton's belie our definitions of antiquarianism. Cotton and others like him, he argues convincingly, were politicians whose tools were documents. The distinctions that we might make between past and present, scholarly and pragmatic, reflect modern rather than early modern views of human nature. To early modern readers, Sharpe explains, history was a claim on ownership of the past, and its value was in the lessons that it provided to contemporaries. If ideals of governance reflected the difficulties of taming human nature, then early modern readers could reasonably draw current wisdom from past events. As long as human nature remained the same, so too would the qualities best suited to realizing order. That common humanity outweighed the contingencies of place and time.

Yet, if we want to understand what men and women took from reading, we must rigorously examine not only what they read, but also how they read. Most importantly, Sharpe contends, we have overlooked the historicity of the act of reading. For early modern people, for example, reading was often neither solitary nor passive. It was often (and perhaps more often than we know) communal: people were often read to by others, and they regularly discussed their reading with others as well. Some gentlemen employed a scholar specifically as a companion with whom to read and discuss ideas. Sharpe explains how commonplace books, by favoring the clustering of passages by theme rather than by text, allowed readers to become authors themselves. He points out how little we know about such things as the political uses of fables, emblems, library cataloguing, and annotations. The records of private libraries show how such active reading meant that in sharing texts, readers created interpretative communities.

Reading Revolutions uses the notebooks of a seventeenth-century Buckinghamshire gentleman, Sir William Drake, to solidify Sharpe's case. Sharpe provides a first-rate introduction to the critical study of language. He then continues the analysis begun in the Cotton essay. Sir William was a religiously moderate member of the Long Parliament whose most overtly political activity seems to have been his extensive reading. *Reading Revolutions* explores that reading in three discrete but not always differentiated stories: how early modern English people read; how Sir William Drake read; and how reading overlapped with the crisis of the mid century. Following the important example of Anthony Grafton and Lisa Jardine's essay on Gabriel Harvey, as well as the largely still unpublished work on marginalia by Steven Zwicker, Sharpe discusses Sir William's reading as a physical engagement with multiple texts simultaneously.[4] Contemporary concerns about identity and indeterminacy made seventeenth-century reading in many ways fundamentally postmodern. Reading allowed Sir William to create new texts that could be visited and then revisited for different purposes at different times. His reading was always contextual, always working from and back toward an idealized picture of moral behavior in an immoral world. And it was always pragmatic, a means of self-fashioning, never an amusement or a haven from the contemporary world. For Sir William and those like him, reading was less background for politics than political activity in itself. Placing and replacing passages individualized what began as communal texts; organizing the passages thematically made them into guides for action; annotating, underlining, and shifting examples from one association to another became political analyses.

The book's central chapters tell Sharpe's second story, of how Sir William Drake read. Sir William left the largest extant collection of reading notebooks from this period, close to sixty known volumes with perhaps others still unidentified. He read widely and ecumenically; his notes included works from the Continent as well as England, Catholic texts as well as Protestant, classical as well as very recent history. For him reading could reveal the essentials of human nature, and, as such, the means for material advancement. Since all social intercourse followed the same rules of engagement, all writing became a species of self-help for realizing one's own ambitions. The world Sir William understood was one of strategic dissimulation, more resonant of Machiavelli (whom he valued highly) than of Christian precepts. It was a world of endless ambition and endless striving, one in which both men and words were suspect. Sir William feared any encouragement to difference and disorder, including the encouragement offered by too much or too random reading. As Sharpe observes, in many ways this was Hobbes's world before Hobbes claimed it.

Sharpe's final objective is to tie Drake's labors to the times in which he lived. If Drake fashioned himself through reading, how did what he experienced fashion what he read? Sharpe has some astute things to say here about reading's impact. He points out how relatively easily Sir William seems to have turned away from the values of his humanist education and the prescriptions of his religious learning. Sharpe notes the absence of references to the courtesy books, devotional literature, and how-to manuals that we have taken to be so popular (although he says little about the apparent unimportance for Sir William of the *Eikon Basilike*). Pace John Pocock, Sharpe effectively argues that men such as Drake understood themselves as political actors and nourished an explicitly political consciousness.

Sharpe is less convincing, however, in his claims for what difference reading made in Sir William, what he would have been without his notebooks. By 1660, Sir William clung more than ever to the belief that unity was critical for a peaceful commonwealth. He had concluded that peace was more important than either his disdain for ambitious clerics or his disapproval of the elaborate rituals of monarchy. But these were popular views among the gentry after

1660. Sir William gave more attention to work about revolutions in history and about church government in the 1650s than in prior decades, but living through years of dramatic change seems reason enough for that. Sharpe never manages successfully to reconcile the importance he wants reading to have and the fact that Sir William avoided direct involvement with war and politics as much as possible, spent much of the 1650s on the Continent, and virtually never commented explicitly on current events.

Sharpe acknowledges the chicken-and-egg dilemma of Sir William and his reading. Yet the author's difficulty here calls attention to some inconsistencies in his own reading practices. Like his subject, Sharpe is the referent center of his own reading universe. Combined with his desire to influence the ways that historians study seventeenth-century England, he tends too often to merge the field's biography with his own. Sharpe's work has always been original enough to defy simple characterizations, yet he retains a distressing attachment to labels such as "revisionist" and "post-revisionist" and to revisiting his own position in now worn out controversies. His conviction about the centrality of, first, revisionism, and now, the somewhat nonsensically-named post-revisionism underpins a view of history that leaves little place for historians of other than central politics and ideas. This creates exactly the sort of blinders that Sharpe otherwise so eloquently condemns.

To produce the history that he properly desires, Sharpe needs to be as ecumenical within history as he has long been about other disciplines. What if, for example, he had taken his questions not from traditional political history but from his own broader definition of political culture? Might he have benefited from what appear to be similarities between the ways that men and women read politics and the ways that they were taught to read the scriptures? What if he had understood Sir William's fondness for the law courts in the context of the need for understanding conflicts that did not end in chaos? Might it have sent him to materials about the influence of law and legal concepts in the provinces? And what if he had approached Sir William's views on women as yet another form of political expression? Or seen Sir William in the light of his experiences in the shires? These angles of vision might have led Sharpe to the most recent work of younger scholars; it might also have modified his sense of what remains unexplored in the history of seventeenth-century England.[5] It also might have allowed Sharpe to say more about some of the subjects that he does explore: the experience of provincial life in the 1650s, for example, the means through which the Revolution did inspire change, and the ways that print culture spread within the provinces.[6] Even more eloquently than Sharpe's own words, these lapses confirm the need for us to consider the repercussions of a narrow conception of what counts as politics.

Remapping Early Modern England would be worth reading alone for the valuable research ideas that Sharpe generously offers, and *Reading Revolutions* will provide an important starting point for anyone interested in how seventeenth-century men and women read and thought. Once again, Kevin Sharpe has prepared a path that others should and undoubtedly will follow. These books provide a summary of where traditional political history has been and of what it can become, cutting back restrictive disciplinary and chronological hedgerows. If Sharpe does not see every passage or seem willing to follow every trail himself, that is simply a measure of the richness of the vista he has cleared before us.

Notes

1. See, for example, *Sir Robert Cotton, 1586–1631: History and Politics in Early Modern England* (Oxford: Oxford University Press, 1979); *Criticism and Compliment* (Cambridge: Cambridge University Press, 1987); and the essays collected in *Politics and Ideas in Early Stuart England* (London: Pinter, 1989).

2. On Sharpe's revisionism, see his *Faction and Parliament: Essays on Early Stuart History* (Oxford: Clarendon Press, 1978); and *The Personal Rule of Charles I* (1992). On his interest in redefining political culture, *Politics of Discourse: The Literature and History of Seventeenth-Century England* (Berkeley: University of California Press, 1987), edited with Steven Zwicker; *Culture and Politics in Early Stuart England* (Stanford: Stanford University Press, 1994), edited with Peter Lake; and most recently, *Refiguring Revolutions: Aesthetic and Politics from the English Revolution to the Romantic Revolution* (Berkeley: University of Califronia Press, 1998), edited again with Zwicker.

3. The new essay is "Remapping early modern England: From revisionism to the culture of politics."

4. "Studied for action: How Gabriel Harvey read his Livy," *Past and Present* 129 (1990): 30–78.

5. My own incomplete list of those whose work Sharpe might have made more of would include Mike Braddick, Laura Gowing, Steve Hindle, and Andy Wood, as well as the literary critic Fran Dolan.

6. And here, see the work of Alastair Bellany, Sean Kelsey, and among more senior scholars, Martin Ingram, John Walter, and Keith Wrightson.

Demon Lovers: Witchcraft, Sex, and the Crisis of Belief
By Walter Stephens
Chicago: University of Chicago Press, 2002

Reviewer: Stuart Clark

As witches were being questioned in hundreds of early modern courtrooms, so their crimes were being interrogated in as many texts. It is as if the trial took place of theories of witchcraft, as well as those actually charged with it, with the latter ceasing to be merely the objects of other people's accusations and becoming expert witnesses in another kind of proceeding, in which arguments were prosecuted, not human beings. From the Council of Basle to the publication of the *Encyclopédie*, intellectuals argued in print about the nature and the reality of witchcraft, all the while unraveling the complexities of the subject and its implications for their lives and culture. Legal and criminological questions were undoubtedly of central importance in this long literature, but witchcraft raised issues across a much wider terrain, making demonology an unusually revealing guide to early modern intellectual and cultural values in general.

For this reason, no doubt, it is currently the focus of fresh attention after a long period of relative neglect—one thinks, in particular, of the recent studies of Sophie Houdard, Gerhild Scholz Williams, Jonathan Pearl, Marianne Closson, Martine Ostorero, Armando Maggi, and, above all, Ian Bostridge, whose *Witchcraft and Its Transformations c.1650-c.1750* (1997) surely counts as the most sophisticated and original of all recent histories of early modern demonology. The balance of interest seems to be shifting away from witch hunting to witch hating, from patterns of prosecution to styles of thought. It is no longer automatically assumed that witchcraft belief was intellectually incoherent or merely a justification for what happened in the courts. On the contrary, demonology is turning into one of the most important thoroughfares into key debates in early modern science, historiography, religion, and politics, where witchcraft often had a decisive conceptual role.

Walter Stephens's *Demon Lovers,* an analysis of the theological and philosophical issues that dominated the first century of demonology (from the 1430s to the 1530s) is part of this scholarly sea-change. It loosens yet further the causal connection between witchcraft trials and witchcraft theory in order to stress that what witchcraft meant for intellectuals involved much broader vocabularies—much broader trials, indeed. Seemingly gone is the idea that demonology must be treated pathologically, attributable to something *else,* like social dysfunction, irrationality, or misogyny. "Witchcraft persecution was a complex phenomenon," says Stephens, "but the motives of its defenders were comprehensible, familiar, and *rational"* (9; author's emphasis). The result is the closest and most absorbing reading ever attempted of the early (mainly Latin) literature of witchcraft.

*

Demon Lovers is a self-conscious application to early witchcraft theory of the issue of interest: *cui bono.* This was defined in its legal sense by Thomas Hobbes as the presumption that "there is none that so evidently declareth the Author, as doth the Benefit of the Action," and was applied by him too to the "doctrines" of churchmen, including their demonology (designed, said Hobbes, to keep the people "more in awe of their Power"). At the head of Stephens's book stands a quotation from John Wagstaffe, the late seventeenth-century English free-thinker who, more Hobbesian than Hobbes, demolished the entire history of witchcraft belief by asking of its "sayings and actions" the simple question, "for what end or advantage they were said and done." Stephens leaves out the "actions," as well as any benefit accruing to individuals or institutions, and concentrates entirely on what kind of *argument* was best served by the "sayings" of fifteenth- and early sixteenth-century witchcraft writers. His striking and original conclusion is that it lay deep in their theological anxieties about the central components of Christian belief. The intellectuals who wrote about witchcraft hoped to gain from it various kinds of proofs that would warrant their faith— especially proofs having to do with the reality and corporeality of demons, the miracle of transubstantiation, and the spiritual and physical efficacies of baptism and the other sacraments. Far from being smug or credulous or even dogmatic about witchcraft, they were preoccupied by the contradictions and implausibilities that

appeared to threaten the very credibility of Christianity itself. Demonology, therefore, was not so much a question of confident belief
as of worrying doubt, with witches and their testimony serving to
make believable aspects of Christianity that intellectuals feared
were too vulnerable to sceptical attack—and, indeed, to their own
misgivings. Witchcraft theory, Stephens repeatedly argues, was
"theological damage control"—a kind of resistance to scepticism.
In one of the book's many telling remarks, he says that this was not
so much belief, as make-believe.

Stephens proceeds by looking at all the various aspects of early
witchcraft theory—from sex with devils and flying to sabbats to
host desecration, infanticide, and penis stealing—and asking what
broader metaphysical purposes they fulfilled. For example, copulation between demons and witches proved, in the most concrete and
experiential manner, that demons were real and corporeal, not
imaginary, that they regularly interacted with human beings, and
that they were therefore a fundamental part of Christian theodicy;
verisimilitude, puns Stephens, was a matter of virisimilitude. So
too, by definition, did the assumption by demons of the virtual bodies required for sex and their ability to convey witches to sabbats
physically, not just in their dreams. The reality of *maleficium* confirmed the equal but opposite power of *beneficium*, theologically
present in those energies and effects of the church's sacraments
which, because they were imperceptible, ran the danger of being
thought imaginary. Desecration by witchcraft gave credence to the,
again, invisible reality of transubstantiation, while infanticide and
the witches' cauldron (with its broths and unguents) maintained
the sacrificial efficacy of baptism and its powers to protect, as well
as a general sense of God's justice.

To support these and the other *cui bono* arguments in his book
Stephens offers a (rather scattered) historical case for the particular
vulnerability of Christianity to doubt in the decades of early demonology. "The crises that led to witchcraft theory in the early fifteenth century emerged," he says, "from a long, uneasy debate
between lived experience and doctrinal theory about God, the efficacy of his sacraments, and the demons." He cites the strains of incorporating Aristotelian empiricism into the spirit world of
medieval Christianity (highlighted, eventually, in the writings of
Pietro Pomponazzi), doubts about God's providence and presence
in the world, the threat posed by theories of the imagination, proto-
Protestant (and Reformation) attacks on the sacraments, and, above

all, the famous Canon *Episcopi,* with its claim that witchcraft was essentially a dream experience. In the light of these various challenges, witchcraft writers *needed* their witches and the sexual and other transgressions they committed. Far from fearing witchcraft, they hoped that it was real. They needed in particular the first-hand testimony that witchcraft confessions provided and were prepared to justify any methods for obtaining them. Although Stephens is not altogether clear about the relationship between witchcraft theory and the general motivations for witchcraft trials (many of which had nothing at all to do with theory, of course), he nonetheless implies that much of the enthusiasm for witch hunting shown by intellectuals stemmed from their dawning conviction that witchcraft offered a unique opportunity for the experimental verification of metaphysical truths.

Stephens makes his case with a series of brilliant readings of individual witchcraft theorists, from Nicholas Jacquier, Jean Vineti, Heinrich Kramer, and Alonso Tostado in the mid to late fifteenth century, to Bartolomeo Spina and Gianfrancesco Pico della Mirandola in the early sixteenth, all set into the context of late scholastic theology and philosophy. This may not seem like promising material. Stephens rightly complains that it has all too often been neglected or misread, and he has considerable fun with our ignorance of even the famous *Malleus maleficarum.* Working out how late medieval theologians thought it was possible for demons to copulate with humans or possess their bodies or steal penises (more of a joke, surely, than "one of the most important passages in all witchcraft theory" [303]) can be no more exciting than working out how many they thought might stand on a pin. But Stephens brings it off in great style, never failing to entertain or write engagingly, and all the while retrieving for his obscure topics the major intellectual significance they undoubtedly once had. Great linguistic and philological skill and a clear eye for the niceties of philosophy and logic allow him not only to clarify the abstruse Latin arguments of the past but also to make them intelligible and engrossing to readers now. No one will ever be able to consider the ingredients of a witch cauldron in the same way again.

The overall argument is certainly of enormous scope and ambition, amounting to nothing less than a reconfiguration of the direction in which late medieval and early modern theology was moving, together with a reassessment of its whole intellectual mood. Witchcraft theory emerges as Christianity's final effort to maintain its credibility before the onset of rationalism, scepticism, secularity, and modernism. Scholars of witchcraft in particular cannot possibly disregard the idea that witchcraft theorists needed demonology not, as we have all tended to assume, because it was a straightforward component of religious beliefs they were absolutely convinced of, but because without it they could not sustain those religious beliefs at all. We have recently become accustomed to talking about the intellectual functions of demonology, but the urgency with which Stephens applies this concept to the very essence of late medieval Christianity is new and important—so, too, his ability to see this kind of function in the smallest details of witchcraft lore. Of course, as time went by, many early modern intellectuals came to appreciate Stephens's argument *themselves*—in England after the Restoration, for example, it became simply a cliché to say that the reality of demons and spirits and the existence of credible spirit testimony went to the very heart of Christian belief. But Stephens reads this idea back into an era when outright atheism seemed less of a problem than Christianity's own internal contradictions. In effect, he is saying that witchcraft was argued over not simply because of hostility to witches, nor, especially, hostility to women (or through prurience or pornography) but because showing its reality was a way of showing the reality of the devil and, thus, of God, the sacraments, and other crucial components of orthodox religion. What is reaffirmed in *Demon Lovers* is that, right from the start, an *intellectual* problem lay at the center of early modern witchcraft, not a social problem and certainly not a war on women.

Stephens goes out of his way at several points to challenge the idea that demonology and witchcraft prosecutions were ultimately based on misogyny. He acknowledges the misogyny present, but always insists that, deeper still, demonologists were motivated by theological fears to do with maintaining their faith. This argument is conducted, moreover, over exactly the same ground as that chosen by those who stress the themes of women-hating in demonology—the issue of sex between devils and humans. Stephens's point is that, although the theologians talked a great deal about sexual matters, to treat them as driven solely by misogyny is to see them through modern eyes. They were driven instead, by the intellectual paradoxes internal to Christianity and through fear of the theological doubts that would destroy their faith if these paradoxes were

not resolved. It has to be said that this is an approach that will surprise and antagonize many witchcraft historians.

*

In any case, bold, imaginative, and highly readable as it is, this
book does encounter other difficulties. One of Stephens's principle
claims, and the implication of his somewhat arch title, is that the
sexual aspects of witchcraft preoccupied and even obsessed his authors (but precisely because of their crucial *theological*, not psychological or social implications) and that they constituted the very
heart of witchcraft theory. This must surely remain debatable. If
one tries to read through the longer output of demonological texts,
through the seventeenth and into the eighteenth century, or simply
pay attention to the entirety of each single text, it soon becomes
clear that witchcraft theory was about many other topics (some of
which Stephens himself discusses, in any case) and mattered in
many other areas—often for the same *cui bono* reasons. One thinks
of the numerous non-sexual aspects of witchcraft's reality and possibility that served the intellectual interests of natural philosophers, of witchcraft's marked ability (as in Hobbes's case, but also
in Bodin's) to focus on issues having to do with rulership and "the
Peaceable Societies of Mankind," and of its capacity to prove the
reliability and predictability of an entire philosophy of history—
each of these in highly contested areas of early modern intellectual
life. There seems to be no overwhelming reason, therefore, to insist
that the sexual aspects of witchcraft were the preoccupation of authors writing on demonology between 1400 *and 1800*, or even of
those writing down to the 1520s. They have to be for Stephens because he chooses demonic corporeality as *the* theological paradox
of the era, and sexual contact as *the* main proof of corporeality. Others may make different choices. Bearing the whole literature of
witchcraft in mind, therefore, one has to question whether or not
the modern obsession with sexuality has been foisted on texts that
talked about many other things with equal enthusiasm.

The question of what to do with demonology after the 1530s
clearly interests Stephens but is nevertheless threatening to his thesis and not fully confronted. *Demon Lovers* begins with two witchcraft cases from 1587 (Walpurga Hausmännin) and 1628 (Johannes
Junius), from which most of the book's principal themes are said to
spring. We have to assume from this that demonology before the

302 Reviews

1530s is being asked to illuminate the entire witch hunting era of European history, and that Stephens's insights into its intellectual functions hold good for this longer period too. Occasionally, they are applied into the future. He argues, for example (101), that after 1570 the sexual aspects of witchcraft were exaggerated yet more, and rendered more violent and lurid—an impression gained from texts like Pierre De Lancre's and not properly substantiated from elsewhere. But even if the level of interest and detail had merely stayed the same, we would still have to ask why an element of witchcraft theory that lasted for two hundred more years should be regarded as an obsessive piece of make-believe, located at a particular moment in later medieval theology, and not a matter of perennial intellectual routine. There is, too, the issue of what to make of *Protestant* demonology, which did not find the sexuality of witches or their sabbat particularly interesting. Stephens makes only a half-hearted stab at "English witchcraft" (102–6), where the witches' "teat" and their animal familiars are said to be Protestant substitutes for confessions of demonic copulation in the business of proving the corporeality of demons.

A further problem arises from the emergence after the 1530s of whole areas of demonological debate, like the one about apparitions, where the issue of how demons assumed visible corporeality was raised at least as much as, if not very much more than, in the texts chosen by Stephens. Both Protestants and Catholics were active in this controversy, which was still lively in the mid eighteenth century. If *Demon Lovers* is to be read only as an account of how late medieval Catholic scholastic demonology developed over one century, then perhaps none of these problems are relevant. But that is not the impression given at its outset. And even so, the trajectories which the same or similar arguments took over two further centuries do seem to impinge on the kinds of claims Stephens makes for the distinctiveness and force of those he chooses to concentrate on. Again, can we really say that after three centuries of intense cerebral activity, intellectuals were *still* trying (and presumably still failing) to convince themselves—nobody else (124)—of what they truly believed?

This brings us to the question of belief. Stephens is absolutely right to say that we can be too simplistic about what it meant to believe in witchcraft—or in anything, for that matter. Amongst the apparent sureties and dogmatic pronouncements of the texts lay doubts and uncertainties. There were always aspects of witchcraft that intellectuals found impossible to believe or difficult to rationalise or hard to match with their religion, their politics, their natural philosophy, or just their common sense. From the outset demonology was a debate, with scepticism co-existing with conviction and plenty of things struggling for credibility in between. Moreover, this remained true throughout its history. Over and over again, its exponents insisted that neither too much nor too little should be believed about witchcraft. To realize this is, in itself, not novel; the question is, what do we do with the realization? For Stephens there was uncertainty not just about this or that feature of the demonic but about Christianity itself—a religion built on the contradictions of incorporeality and therefore inherently difficult to square with Aristotelian empiricism. More than uncertainty, however, there was also deep "anxiety"—a word that appears many times in *Demon Lovers*.

There are two difficulties with this application of "anxiety" to arguments. One concern is how we identify such a thing. Ultimately, it will always be an interpretative leap to speak of anxiety in an argument, since the psychological state being invoked can never be recovered or evidenced. But this is a leap which Stephens makes many times. Expertly unpicking a line of reasoning or a piece of logic that the rest of us would imagine to be designed to persuade someone else, he seizes on it as an indication of deep intellectual insecurity on the part of the writer, who hopes thereby to be persuaded himself. This can only be a matter of conjecture, yielding statements that affirm the existence of a negative (lack of belief) in something expressed as a positive (belief). It is as if the general field of force of an argument is to be reversed and turned back on itself, so as to reveal something other than (in fact, quite opposite to) what it appears to be saying. Partly, Stephens defends this kind of reading by adopting Umberto Eco's notion of "textual intention"; partly, he looks out for tell-tale signs of discursive stress—moving arguments around in a text without paying attention to the rewording that this may require, saying things in a convoluted manner, constantly reaffirming something, and, above all, considering every possible objection to an argument before going on to substantiate it.

This makes for dense exposition but also high rewards; over and over again, *Demon Lovers* brings to exciting and sometimes hilarious life the apparently driest details of remote Latin texts. But none of the discursive traits it looks out for is ever historicized. We are

never asked to think how later medieval and early modern intellectuals argued *anyway*—that is to say, most of the time and on all subjects. What counted as correct or incorrect wording, or clear or
convoluted logic at the time? What did *non*-demonologists think
of the way their intellectual colleagues argued? As many modern
scholars know to their cost, constant reaffirmation (the "rhetoric of
overstatement" [143]) is a stylistic hazard encountered throughout
the intellectual world of Renaissance and (especially) Reformation
Europe, and yet no one has suggested that this meant universal anxiety or doubt. As a result of scholastic education and the logic of
scholastic argument, later medieval theological debates were invariably conducted as question and answer exercises, in which the
opposing case was put first and its doubts and questions were then
handled one by one. Later in the history of demonology one finds
the same discursive style transmuted into dialogue form, with
sceptical participants planted in fictional conversation in order to
put all the objections to what was being asserted. It is especially
worrying, therefore, to find "the influence of the Scholastic method
of exposition itself" and "the classroom methods on which it was
based" being relegated to a brief mention in a brief footnote (385,
note 97). The footnote is appended to the statement (86) that because the *Malleus maleficarum* had said all there was to be said on
the subject of demonic copulation with witches, subsequent theorists needed only to discuss it very briefly "as a fact of common
knowledge." Instead, "[e]ach new treatise reviewed the same basic
collection of authorities and sources; each usually added some new
detail, a bit of bibliography or a fanciful explanation. And each
treatise had its own characteristic touches of doubt, hesitation, and
exaggeration." This kind of remark seems to miss what sort of motives there may have been, or what sort of discursive habits made,
for writing repetitively about subjects throughout the book culture
of the period. In this case and in others, Stephens is perhaps ex-
pecting his writers to behave more like him in the construction of
new and original arguments. Disappointed by their lack of conformity to the stylistic and discursive standards he has set for them,
he attributes it to the destabilizing influence of radical doubt.

   The second difficulty with the idea of anxiety is that the more it
is insisted upon—and it is insisted upon a great deal—the greater
the danger of returning to the kinds of explanations for witchcraft
belief that most commentators now wish to avoid. It is not all that
far into *Demon Lovers* before we encounter the language of Freud-

ian psychology in an account of the way the religious strife of the mid sixteenth century took over, temporarily, from witch hating as a way of dealing with doubts and anxieties about the validity of Christianity by bringing them out into the open and acting them out. Metaphysical, like sexual, anxieties, we are reminded, demand attention; otherwise, their repression finds expression "in bizarre form as symptoms." For a while, Reformation polemic dealt with the same sort of anxieties "that Western Christian intellectuals had *acted out* symptomatically over the previous century when they constructed witchcraft through trials, torture, and treatises." (100; author's emphasis). Later still, Europe "relapsed," and witchcraft theory returned, almost inevitably, as a way of repressing doubt, just as witch hunting revived after 1580 as a "comfortably camouflaged way of exploring doubts about the validity of one's Christianity" (101). Here we are back with an old temptation—that of accounting for witchcraft beliefs in terms of something that doesn't sound like a belief (even a doubted belief) at all. In *Demon Lovers*, it is "anxiety" that usually performs this role—but there is worse. Shortly after his Freudian analogy, Stephens remarks that Jean Bodin and De Lancre were writers who needed to believe and couldn't quite manage it. They were addicted to "fantasies" about witches, and unless they kept on increasing the dose the fantasies "lost their ability to satisfy the underlying compulsion, even temporarily." Hence the message of Stephens's entire book: "The less one believed in the verifiable presence of the Devil, the more exaggerated claims one made for his being everywhere, at all times, in all forms" (102).

Clearly, Stephens's distaste for the arguments he writes about has, after all, got the better of his intention to find them comprehensible and even rational. Instead, they are in danger of being reduced to emotional needs, although what such needs might have meant in the fifteenth or sixteenth centuries or how one arrives at them historically are never explained. Nobody should be expected to *like* demonology; that would be absurd. But symmetry—the kind of symmetry applied in Bostridge's *Witchcraft and Its Transformations* (which *Demon Lovers* does not cite)—requires us to pay attention to the maximum, not the minimum, comprehensibility of arguments that either lost out historically to opposing ones or strike us as being faulty or just plain wrong. And this, of course, is the problem with *cui bono*. Admirable as a way of alerting us to the positioning behind every historical utterance and action, it can nevertheless lead to neglect of the sense they nevertheless made—hesitations, contradictions, and self-delusions notwithstanding. Hobbes and Wagstaffe used *cui bono* arguments to attack doctrines *they* could see no sense in, and what they said about witchcraft beliefs is, thus, invaluable as a guide to seventeenth-century scepticism. What is not clear is why they should act as models for us to follow now.

*

Demon Lovers is an exciting and spirited book, and hugely effective in showing what can be done with witchcraft texts—most of which emerge unrecognizable from the kinds of pallid and inaccurate readings they usually receive, if they receive any at all. Walter Stephens has demonstrated once and for all how ideas about witchcraft—even about its strangest and seemingly most ridiculous manifestations—were deeply entangled with issues of the greatest contemporary significance. He has also captured, as no one else has, two other important truths about witchcraft theory. One is that it consisted of a mixture of doubts as well as convictions; for him, the convictions turn into doubts as well, but that may turn out to be an over-extension of the case. The other is that demonology ran into fundamental difficulties whenever it confronted questions having to do with the reliability of sensory perception and empirical verification, precisely because it drew on two paradoxical ideas—that incorporeality could be made visible (and so real) and that demons had powers to create complete sensory delusion. In this respect, demonology—despite the hopes and intentions that *Demon Lovers* surveys—may have been the least, rather than the most, assimilable aspect of the great late medieval project to combine Aristotle with patristic and conciliar Christianity.

Common Prayer: The Language of Public Devotion in Early Modern England
By Ramie Targoff
Chicago: University of Chicago Press, 2001

Reviewer: Reid Barbour

Ramie Targoff takes as her focus a chief tenet held by early modern defenders of decency and prescription in public worship, namely, the conviction that liturgical norms or paradigms serve to shape and enhance the private spiritual life of a parishioner. In tracing the reformation of liturgical practice from the early days of English Protestantism through the 1630s and 40s, Targoff ends up in pursuit of the thesis that the Protestant institution of common prayer greatly helped to produce the brilliant flowering of devotional poetry in the seventeenth century, especially the poetry of Herbert. Underlying this study is the often repeated irony that Protestantism was far less conducive to private worship than was the Catholicism that it replaced. In sustaining these provocative claims, Targoff's is a good but an uneven book, and ultimately a book divided against itself.

Even though the book is divided into two groups of chapters— one dealing with public prayer, the other with poetry as common prayer—there is no formal division between sections in the make-up of the book, and the trajectory of the argument is essentially chronological. Chapter 1 commences with the 1549 *Book of Common Prayer*, "the first vernacular liturgy used in the Church of England" (16), then studies the liturgical thought of Thomas Cranmer and the several revisions of the prayer book over the next few years. Chapter 2 centers on the Elizabethan debate over whether prescribed conformity or extemporaneous worship were more conducive to true and godly devotion, with a section on Richard Hooker's defense of the "devotional efficacy" of common prayer. Chapter 3 stays with the theme of "devotional efficacy," but it shifts attention to the value placed on verse Psalters as against the prose formulae of the *Book of Common Prayer*. This chapter takes as its main subjects Philip Sidney and Mary Sidney Herbert. The fourth chapter offers a reading of George Herbert, while the conclusion shifts ground to the New World and to the defense of liturgical poetry in Massachusetts Bay. Over the course of these chapters, Targoff contributes many insightful readings and formulations to the study of religious culture. But there are some serious problems with her argument, too.

No small part of the book's problems arises from the fact that the introduction is its weakest segment. Only thirteen pages long, it devotes four of those pages to reading a scene in *Hamlet,* which would be more agreeable if the other nine pages were satisfactory. But they are not. Targoff is perhaps right to maintain that recent literary critics have privileged the individualistic over the normative in their studies of English Protestantism, but the same can not really be said for church historians, and her engagement with church history is far too sketchy. Targoff wants to combat the Collinson thesis of a Puritan mainstream in the English church, but she pays far too little attention to the vast material of church history from Horton Davies to Kenneth Fincham and Judith Maltby, a few occasional citations notwithstanding. At a smaller level, the language of the opening suffers from a New Historicist hangover; I put the point that way for the simple reason that the critical language of the book astonishingly changes by the conclusion, indeed, even when some of the key words (especially "powerfully") remain the same. The introduction likes to talk about the English Protestant "establishment," thereby lumping together countless thinkers and writers whose differences matter as much as their similarities. It likes to imagine that this "establishment" seeks to "subsume" private devotion (as we shall see, the way in which this argument is put crucially changes over the course of the book) so as to produce uniformity. When Targoff seeks to concretize this establishment with its "overarching desire" for uniformity, she quotes Lancelot Andrewes, Robert Shelford, Foulke Robarts, John Browning, and Thomas Browne—all early Stuart writers, and by and large on the "Laudian" or neo-ceremonialist side of church debates. Early on, Targoff adopts a New Historicist suspicion of this "establishment," the one with which she would supplant Collinson's "Puritans." By the end of the book, she is offering up virtual paeans to their "powerful" enhancement of worship in religious poetry, with her critical models such sympathetic close readers of Herbert's poetry as Joseph H. Summers. The introduction then ends with a little blurb on the execution of Charles I, a point without payoff in the book itself.

Chapter 1 stresses what Targoff considers a key paradox: the Catholic church allowed more space and time for private worship during the service (since the priest essentially had his back turned during the Mass) than did the Protestant church, which fully engaged the attention of the congregation in the exercise of common prayer. With this feature as her only evidence for reversing the critical consensus, Targoff is largely satisfied with repeating this paradox rather than pursuing it or modifying it in a systematic way. At times this means that she writes as though (repeating a charge leveled against one of her subjects) she "seem[ed] almost entirely indifferent to what transpires outside the walls of the church" (51). At other times, she either ignores or contradictorily considers the Protestant fear of those anarchical "fancies" unleashed by the Reformation. Set on keeping the "establishment" high and on asserting the paradox that historians and critics have gotten the private-public divide backwards in considering differences between Reformed and Catholic, Targoff at still other times allows the diacritical language of her argument to slip and slide from one state of liturgical affairs to another. Early on, then, the "establishment" has a "strategy" for "transforming" and "shaping" the potentially wild but largely malleable individual soul, a "powerful" strategy, I should add. "English Protestants"—all of them, presumably—are committed to controlling and confining the extemporaneous prayer. Over the course of chapter 1, however, Targoff insists that she is interested in devotional efficacy rather than political strategy, and in her notes we begin to read about such church historians as Judith Maltby, whose work on the prayer book ought to have been foregrounded in Targoff's argument.

Once she has shifted from the language of strategy to the language of devotional efficacy (see 18: "the invention of common prayer was not strictly part of a political strategy"), her argument becomes richer—in its characterization of liturgical reform, in its sense of developing Protestant notions of community, in its reading of particular writers, and in its understanding of a spectrum of views in English Protestantism itself. As a consequence, it is not too long before Targoff's characterization of the way in which common prayer was thought to work in the sixteenth century has left behind the static and simplistic model of establishmentarian confinement. On page 26, we come at last to the Protestant critique of how the Catholic church has "eliminated the laity's essential role in the service." Common prayer is said, quite rightly, to involve the serious and complex question of how authority is delegated in religion, with the Protestants believing that the laity plays a major part in authenticating that delegation, a part that considers the matter of how well they have understood, digested, and consented to the priest's words. Thus, "to 'answer . . . in your own person' is not to assent to whatever the priest may or may not have said, but instead to affirm that your personal voice has been justly represented" (27). The Elizabethan chapter on reading prayer finds Targoff doing a much better job with capturing the contentiousness within Protestantism; she is much less prone to lump everyone under the "establishment." The chapter covers familiar territory, but her discussion of the Admonition controversy is concise and cogent, and she isolates what is extraordinary about Hooker's defense of the spiritual benefits of common prayer in a convincing and compelling manner.

If Targoff's argument begins in the land of establishmentarian strategy then moves to a more dynamic and rational lay worship, it has one further shift to make. As she moves toward the Sidneys, Donne, Wither, Herbert, and early modern Protestant poetics, Targoff begins once again to stress what is "powerful" (rather than historically accurate) about her subject. Only now a suspect strategic power gives way in her rhetoric to a celebrated kind of appropriate fusion between Christian paradigms and creative selves.

Having offered a useful background on the development of metrical Psalms, Targoff turns her attention to Philip Sidney and his sister Mary, showing how, in theory and practice, they contributed to the emergence of "poetry as a legitimate devotional practice" (74). In this section, she resumes the language of power ("powerfully" is used twice in a row on page 78), but now this terminology serves to corroborate Targoff's new critical assessment of what she considers an "inherent" suitability connecting liturgical norm to poetic form. Targoff leaves no doubt about this program and sees it as repudiating a critical consensus that links private selfhood to good poetry. It is doubtful that there has been a critical consensus in this matter, especially if one considers such slightly older critics as Rosemund Tuve and Joseph Summers. But whether or not Targoff is alone in her recovery of a liturgical poetics, her language is unmistakably that of a critic's organic unity, a move accompanied by the repetition of the word "seems" in her sentences. It is true that she continues to press home a historical thesis about the reformation of devotional practice as well as the emergence of devotional poetry as a form of common prayer. But history runs cheek by jowl with what can only be called prayer appreciation, especially once Targoff turns to Herbert.

Targoff's thesis about Herbert is that his volume of poetry parodies the *Book of Common Prayer,* and she is especially convincing when discussing the provenance (Cambridge University Press) and the physical composition (especially the use of the "pilcrow") of the *Temple.* Textually, however, the reader might expect a detailed treatment of how Herbert's poetry appropriates motifs from the prayer book, but this is not what the reader gets. The chapter commences with a slight critique of Louis Martz and Barbara Lewalski; offers a dubious dismissal of the Puritans as proto-Romantics with an antagonism toward poetry (this, despite the last chapter's argument that the Puritans in the New World prized devotional poetry); offers a paragraph-long paean to liturgical poetry, which she equates with the "power of eloquent verse" and with the "possibility for a new form of poetry . . . released into the world" (87); and persists in deploying the language of "inherent" suitability, of "seeming," "affective force" (105), and "perfect yoking" (110, elsewhere, an "interweaving of the personal and the universal" that defies "critical binaries" [107], or "the perfect fusion of personal and universal voice" that a reader might experience [117]). Her seventeenth-century heroes are Izaak Walton's: Hooker, Donne, and Herbert. In short, we get close readings with generalized connections between the characteristics of liturgy and the assets of Herbert's poetry. Targoff is on better ground when she asserts something historical, when she discusses what Herbert "hopes" for or "aims" at, or what his like-minded churchmen also seek in a unity between liturgy and devotional efficacy. But the historical assertions are pretty familiar (e.g., "Herbert firmly believed that no opposition ought to exist between outward worship and the cultivation of inwardness" [100]), and even when Targoff turns to "The Forerunners" in order to complicate such statements, there is little that has not been offered up by previous Herbert scholars. And even in that final analysis of "The Forerunners," Targoff emphasizes the power of poetry's suitable fusion with liturgy over and above any kind of complicating historical or literary factor.

Despite the fact that her book begins with a reversal of the commonplace that the Protestants cared more about private worship than did the Catholics, Targoff ends with the admission that those Protestants going off to the New World shared in an "antiliturgical spirit" (119) that embraced spiritual spontaneity and "the individual voice of the minister over the collective voice of the congregation" (120). Even so, her two concluding points are well worth making: that in Massachusetts as in England, Protestants sought out bold new ways to devise community and that poetry came to play a major role in the reformation of devotional practice. Much of the slender *Common Prayer* is interesting, provocative, and useful. But the critical voice and method of the book are too divided and haphazard for the argument to develop with sufficient complexity or rigor. The book moves from one critical terrain to another, one antipathetic to her subject and the other highly sympathetic, and in between these two affective registers lies the solid yet original historical work that Targoff is clearly capable of doing very well.

Staging Domesticity: Household Work and English Identity in Early Modern Drama
by Wendy Wall
Cambridge: Cambridge University Press, 2002

Reviewer: Jean E. Howard

Who would have thought the Early Modern domestic sphere could be so fascinating and so strange? It is the enormous accomplishment of Wendy Wall's new book to make the Early Modern household the pulsing heart of the nation, the crucible where gendered and sexed subjects took shape, and the locus for powerful fantasies of abjection, empowerment, nurturance, and violence. In conception and in style, Wall challenges old stereotypes about the household as the sober seat where lessons of obedience and self-discipline were instilled and patriarchal order affirmed. There is nothing staid about the domestic sphere Wall describes. Rather, it is the vibrant and sometimes dangerous center of middle class life where women, in particular, exercise considerable authority and creativity as cooks, medical practitioners, butchers, and instillers of culture, starting with the English tongue itself. Written with verve and wit (the book is peppered with subheadings such as "A Cow Is Being Milked"), *Staging Domesticity* is a major achievement.

The book can serve as a partial index of what has changed over the last ten years in Early Modern studies. If much early New Historicism focused on the Court, the aristocracy, and "the people," Wall focuses on an emergent social group, the middling sort, and on the household relations and everyday practices that formed the backbone of their conception of themselves and their place in the nation. Wall is not alone in this focus. Richard Helgerson, Patricia Fumerton, Lena Orlin, Mario DiGangi, Natasha Korda, Gail Paster, Fran Dolan, and Juliet Fleming are among those who have helped to direct attention to the importance of the domestic realm and practices of everyday life as they bear on subject formation and national identity in this period. Together, these scholars invite us to see, for example, what the housewife's application of the glister-pipe might have to do with the erotic lives of Early Modern subjects; and they invite us to look beyond monarch-based discourses to see how the domestic realm could become the locus for powerful fantasies of national belonging. Wall's work is both a consolidation of much of this scholarship and a sophisticated extension of it.

Wall's texts, moreover, indicate the new directions in which scholarship has turned. There are no analyses of *King Lear* or *Richard III* in *Staging Domesticity*. Instead, cookbooks and household guides figure prominently, and Wall does an excellent job of distinguishing Markham and Tusser and Plat and allowing them to upset our anachronistic or universalizing ideas of what constitutes Early Modern domesticity. Wall clearly enjoys these books, and a delightful aspect of her treatment of them is her inclusion of brief passages of whimsical writing in which Wall addresses the housewife at her work and enters into the thoughts and fantasies that might have accompanied her molding of marzipan, her slaughtering of a capon, or her preparation of an eyewash made from breast milk. Besides these household manuals, Wall also foregrounds comedy: city comedies such as *The Shoemaker's Holiday* and *The Knight of the Burning Pestle*, romantic comedies such as *Midsummer Night's Dream*, early comedies such as *Gammar Gurton's Needle*, and Shakespeare's "suburban" comedy, *The Merry Wives of Windsor*. The latter is a text that for years no one found particularly interesting. Suddenly, it is at the heart of a number of monographs, including Wall's, that deal with housewifery, household property, and women's place in the Early Modern nation.

Wall occupies a distinctive niche in this burgeoning field of work. The most striking aspect of her book, in my view, is its historicization of domesticity. Criticizing scholars who anachronistically conceive of the Early Modern domestic realm as a private sphere where nuclear families were set off from the realm of production, Wall underscores what was *different* about Early Modern households. Servants, for example, were integral parts of household units; the household was often the site of production for the market; breastfeeding was not always a mother's job; the household was routinely the site of homoerotic or queer sexualities as well as of male-female unions; mistresses of households had considerable power over many aspects of domestic life including care of the body, diet, market production, and early education. In fact, in stressing how central a role women played in Early Modern household life, especially among the middling sort, Wall criticizes feminists who have focused on women's oppression within the domestic sphere or who imply that households actually followed prescriptive injunctions for wives to obey husbands as subjects obeyed their monarch. Wall wants, she says, to suspend the metaphor of patriarchalism to see how else one might describe the practices of domestic life evident in her texts. Wall succeeds, I feel, in renewing our sense of just how much power women were perceived to have within the domestic realm and how, consequently, they figure both prominently and ambivalently in the fantasy life of Early Modern subjects. Wall does particularly fine readings, for example, of the way a play like *Friar Bacon and Friar Bungay* links male erotic desire to the sight of a woman performing the household chore of making cheese, or the way a a play like *Gammar Gurton's Needle* reveals the household realm, symbolized by Gammar Gurton's lost needle, as a site of male abjection and also as the male subject's true home.

Wall relies heavily on the concept of fantasy throughout her study. Here, again, her work is markedly different from earlier historicist work. In employing the term "fantasy," Wall explicitly distances herself from the anachronistic use of concepts arising from nineteenth-century family formations or ideas of the volitional individual. Rather, drawing on Žižek, she wants to get at *social fantasies* that arise from specific historical circumstances and are signalled by "scenes that depict curiously heightened emotional

expressions" (11). Such fantasy structures, she argues, allow subjects to experience contradictory and provisional identifications.
Repeatedly, Wall is drawn to moments in her texts which elicit
"both/and" reactions. For example, Prince Edward in *Friar Bacon
and Friar Bungay* is powerfully drawn by the erotic lure of the
milkmaid *and also* must separate from this low realm to marry a
Castillian princess. Desire *and also* disgust lie at the heart of the
play's fleeting vision of the union of a prince and a dairymaid. At
her best, Wall points us to the messy and multivalent responses that
the shaping fantasies of Early Modern domestic texts could elicit.

In a book this rich in sensitive readings, one will always disagree
with particular points of interpretation and emphasis. I could list
some of those places where I make something different of a particular text than Wall does. But that is really beside the point and is
primarily a testament to how thoroughly Wall's book engaged my
attention. I would like, for example, in regard to *The Shoemaker's
Holiday* to discuss the implications of Simon Eyre's repeated deni-
grations of Margery's person and his challenges to her authority
over the workers in the shop: to what extent do they undermine
Margery's status as Eyre's "co-manager" in the domestic production unit? Where my conclusions on this matter might diverge from
Wall's points to the one substantive critique I have of her argument.
I think that in "suspending patriarchalism" Wall has somewhat un-
derplayed the ways in which the domestic realm not only gave
women scope for creativity, authority, and control over bodies,
things, and psyches, but also hemmed them in, subjected them to
regimes of surveillance and discipline, bridled their tongues, and
made them the objects of degrading and violent fantasies. Both aspects of domestic life deserve attention. If we have overemphasized
one (regimes of oppression), it may be no more true to overstress
the other (domains of female power). If one took a slightly different
sample of Early Modern domestic texts such as *The Taming of the
Shrew, The Fair Maid of the Exchange, Othello,* or Isabella Whitney's London poems—or even if one read a play like *The Shoemaker's Holiday* with a slightly different emphasis—one's picture of
women's role in domestic life might be somewhat different from
Wall's construction of it. Wall is well aware that women's power in
the domestic realm could make them the target of anger and aggression, but her book takes little account of the systematic ways in
which structures of gender inequality constrained female subjects
even in the domestic realm where their authority was perhaps most

extensive. Wall has done a wonderful job in moving beyond tired
critical paradigms that simply emphasize women's oppression; it
is important to embrace the new directions she maps and also, in
my view, to be mindful that in a hierarchical society, gender hierarchies were real, if complex, and had important consequences for
women's lives.

In the future, I think it will also be necessary more fully to integrate women's writing into our accounts of domestic life in the period. The drama is a great source for domestic fictions and
fantasies, and I learned a great deal from Wall's treatment of her
playtexts. But we now also have a whole array of scholarship on
women's diaries, wills, poetic productions, closet dramas, and letters. At some point this material needs to be integrated into our accounts of domesticity and the household, especially if we are fully
to understand how relations among women figured in that domain.

But that is only to point to what is left to do in what is emerging
as a sophisticated and vital new area of Early Modern studies.
Wall's book is an extremely important contribution to this field, de-
familiarizing the very concept of the domestic and providing evidence of the many kinds of fantasies that domesticity generated
and of the centrality of the household and of women to the life of
the middling sort. It would be a great blessing if all critical books
delivered pleasure and insight in such generous portions.

English Professional Theatre 1530–1660
Edited by Glynne Wickham, Herbert Berry,
and William Ingram
Cambridge: Cambridge University Press, 2001

Reviewer: Sally-Beth MacLean

English Professional Theatre, 1530–1660 is the sixth volume in an
anticipated sixteen-volume series of documents essential for the
study of European theater history. A volume on *Restoration and*

Georgian England, 1660–1788 was the first published so a reader tracing the story of the Red Bull Theater, extensively represented in the new volume, will find it picked up by Samuel Pepys in 1661 in the Restoration documentary history.

These compilations are generous acts of scholarship, intended to provide "comprehensive collections of primary source materials for teachers and students" while serving as major reference works for theatrical and dramatic literary studies. The selection of materials is wide in its range: official statutes and proclamations, account books, legal contracts, and lawsuits, as well as informal correspondence, eyewitness accounts, and literary allusions. Standard editorial features include introductions with social background and relevant context for each major section, briefer linking narrative passages with notes, the precise source and location details for every original document used, as well as complementary lists of similar documents or principal secondary sources printing reputable previous (often fuller) transcripts of documents, substantial bibliographies, and an index.

The general editor's preface (xli) indicates that unfamiliar documents are preferred, short ones chosen over long ones, "excerpting for inclusion all passages which either oblige quotation by right of their own intrinsic importance or lead directly to a clearer understanding of other documents." The documents transcribed are mostly modernized for accessibility.

Some volumes are more fortunate than others in the illustrations available for selection: the editors of the present volume have chosen to limit their images stringently to pictures that supplement documents printed in the text (e.g., portraits of Edward Alleyn, the actor who transcended "common player" status, and his wife, Joan) or those, like the photo of Edmund Tilney's tomb in St. Leonard's Church, Streatham, not already reproduced in R. A. Foakes's *Illustrations of the English Stage, 1580–1642* (1985).

A strong sense of the restrictions imposed on editorial selection by modern publication costs pervades both the preface and the introduction (see, for example, page 8, where the process of compromise achieved with sacrifice is described with some feeling). The focus of the collection has been necessarily narrowed to English professional theater. Excluded are amateur and occasional academic or courtly dramatic entertainments other than those charting the gradual suppression of overtly religious plays between 1530 and the 1580s (a decision that can hardly be faulted, given the ongoing enterprise to publish such documents in the Records of Early English Drama series). Tempting though the splendid resources might be, a separate volume or volumes would have been needed for the documents of Stuart courtly drama and so they too had to be discarded.

The editors of this volume are three of the most distinguished senior scholars in the field. We are fortunate that the depth of their collective knowledge of original sources from 1530–1660 has been brought to bear on the selections for this volume. The division of responsibility is as follows: documents of control, 1530–1660 (Glynne Wickham); players and playing (William Ingram); and playhouses, 1560–1660 (Herbert Berry). Unlike the Restoration and Georgian volume, which had two compilers, with one taking the lead as editor, there seems to have been no presiding editor for this volume to ensure continuity in approach. The result is three distinct sections with varying applications of the general directives for the series.

Part One is a compendium of documents of control for London and the provinces issued under the Tudor and early Stuart governments up to 1647. The editorial approach is to embed narrative passages amongst and sometimes within the selected document extracts, in a layout which I found confusing and infelicitous at times. An early example should suffice. The introduction to the section on Henry VIII's reign concludes at the top of page 18, followed immediately by its footnotes in a smaller type size, after which the narrative picks up again for a paragraph, followed immediately by its footnote, then a larger boldface heading, the location details for the document, and the first record, a heavily damaged proclamation, quoted from the REED *Chester* volume in a rare— and daunting—example of semi-diplomatic transcription. Strong stuff for a student unfamiliar with such material!

Yet the problems with layout cannot undermine the value of this useful collection of central records hitherto scattered across diverse printed sources, now brought together with some newly offered to illuminate the course of official response and eventual repression of professional theater in England. Among the engaging additions is a letter of the utmost urgency—"haste post haste, haste, haste"— from the Privy Council to the Lord President of the North, ordering the arrest of Sir Francis Leek's players, for presenting plays in 1557 "containing very naughty and seditious matter touching the King and Queen's Majesties," a document not known to Chambers and newly transcribed from its present location at Lambeth (42–43).

Part Two, on players and playing, is the most accessible—elegant and economical in its editorial style, with clear and consistent layout. The linking narrative passages are concise and less obtrusive, allowing the documents to speak for themselves. From varied and less familiar sources we find passages to illustrate the popular image of the stage player; biographical sources for a representative player's life (Augustine Phillips); relations between patrons and their playing companies; the sometimes contentious relations between players and their playing places; costumes, properties, and playbooks; provincial travels; children's companies; and illustrative instances of professional theatrical life and practice.

All of the topics are stimulating and important; if anything we might wish for more. There are, for instance, no documents relating to professional players at court, even though the goal of many Elizabethan companies would have been to perform before the queen at Christmas or Shrovetide. The section on the representative life of a player, compiling typical fragments of evidence for biographical study, is illuminating; a similar section for a sample professional troupe would have been equally worthwhile. Leicester's men, one of the most active of the troupes, might have been a good choice: several key documents are already in place in the text (Dudley's letter interceding for his new troupe, the players' 1572 petition to be his household servants, the 1574 royal patent). Samples from the patron's household books, some town accounts, evidence of their repertoire, and more could have been instructive additions.

Those interested in the provincial experience that featured in so many players' careers will be disappointed that the emphasis here is largely on the negative aspects of touring that characterize older scholarship on the subject. Ingram includes none of the most typical sources, i.e., the numerous civic and private household accounts from the 1530s through 1642 that recorded the details of an extensive tradition of touring by London-based as well as provincial troupes. Eyewitness accounts of particularly successful performances such as the outdoor performance by the Queen's Men at Shrewsbury in 1590 would have provided welcome variety and a less distorted view of professional players' experiences in the provinces (see, for example, *Somerset*, ed. J. Alan B. Somerset, REED 1:247 [1994]). And why not print the full text of Willis's nostalgic account of his childhood experience at a professional play before the mayor in Gloucester (243)? There are no ellipsis dots to indicate omission here, but the passage has been severely truncated.

If the reader has cause to regret the evident sacrifice of fuller transcriptions in the first two parts of the book, he or she may wonder at the contrasting length of the final part, devoted to playhouses, which accounts for more pages than the first two combined. Admittedly, Berry has here gathered the most complete collection yet of rich source materials to chronicle the rise and fall of public playhouses in the period, but the book is somewhat unbalanced as a result. The editorial style here is more luxurious, with longer introductions and narrative sequences, not merely supplementing but often summarizing the content of the documents included. There are a number of entries repeated in full or in part here, probably unnecessarily. For example, number 411 repeats extracts from the renewal of the Blackfriars' leases which have already been more fully presented as number 162. Why not simply cross-reference to this entry in Ingram's section on players and their playing places and save some space? And where the transcripts of the same entry differ in two sections, one wonders what the careful student, wanting to cite an entry like the 1580 Privy Council minute rebuking the Surrey JPs will make of the editorial variations in Wickham's number 37 and Berry's number 244.

The proportion of documents per playhouse could also be questioned. Although numerous sources relating to the Rose are available and have been printed, not all the relevant publications (e.g., Carol Chillington Rutter's recently updated *Documents of the Rose Theatre*, 2nd ed. (1999) appear in the bibliography nor is there an attempt to represent the records more fully here as an alternative. The Rose section, in which there would likely be considerable interest, given the ongoing story of its excavation, is notably short compared with the Boar's Head or Red Bull.

On a more positive note, Berry has assembled here an authoritative collection of historical and literary sources for the study of private and public playhouses in London from 1560 to 1660, starting with the Red Lion and the four London inns first known to have been used by professional companies. Among the less familiar entries are foreign eyewitness accounts from Dutch, German, and Swiss travellers (e.g., numbers 352, 353, 396), a court record relating to a playgoer's injury by an actor's sword from Middlesex County Records (number 445); the trial of wit at the Hope (number 461); and evocative selections from several plays characterizing individual theaters, for example, Shirley's scathing reference to the vulgar appetites of the public theater audience at the second Globe (number 472d).

Playhouses in the provinces are less well served, despite the general coverage indicated by the title of Part Three. Berry, unlike Wickham and Ingram, does not attempt to represent the development of playhouses or their alternatives beyond the capitol. Ingram gives details of the children of the queen's chamber of Bristol; Berry might have provided complementary evidence for the early seventeenth-century theaters in Bristol, the second city in the land, but they rate only the briefest mention in passing in his introduction. The statement, in fact, is misleading: "a scattering of permanent theatres began to appear in such places as Liverpool, Bristol and Manchester" (288–89). There is no documentary evidence, to my knowledge, of theaters in the two northern towns before 1642 at least, although there was an abortive attempt to establish one in the larger city of York in the early seventeenth century. The term "makeshift" for the numerous other provincial spaces used by players across the country (288) is somewhat derogatory and one wonders what the mayor of Coventry would have thought of this expression used for the splendid space provided at St. Mary's Guildhall. Alan Nelson's pioneering work on *Early Cambridge Theatres: College, University and Town Stages, 1464–1720* (1994) is one of the notable omissions in the bibliography, an indication perhaps of residual London-centered assumptions that are rapidly becoming dated. A resulting oversight is the evident parallels between the design and use of private halls belonging to the nobility and gentry in the provinces and the development of private playhouses in London (the introduction to Part Three mentions only parish halls, innyards, and "even town halls" [287], but see also p. 11, where the "spacious rectangular yards" of coaching-inns are cited as a major influence on London playhouses while other rectangular indoor halls , public and private, are elided).

A general editorial decision does seem to have affected Berry's heavy use of ellipsis dots: "[The compilers] in order to conserve space, have only quoted that part (or parts) of particular documents which serve to confirm or advance knowledge of the topic under discussion with reliable, supportive evidence . . . especially desirable where protracted lawsuits, bureaucratically worded parliamentary Statutes, and Decrees issued (and frequently reissued as occasion demanded) by provincial town clerks were concerned"

(9). Compare here the lease of the first Blackfriars playhouse property to Farrant by Sir William More in 1576, an important document previously printed in the *Malone Society Collections* 2, no. 1 (1913): 28–35. Berry's selection (390–93) of an extract from a record that runs almost seven pages in *MSC* may make sense, given the restrictions of the present publication, but his transcription is plagued by ellipsis dots every few lines, and comparison reveals that many are of so little consequence as space-saving devices that it would be less distracting for the reader simply to include the elided phrases. A unique document such as this one, deemed essential to reprint, could justifiably be quoted in its entirety. Overuse of ellipsis dots can create either unease or curiosity in the reader while undermining the integrity of the original.

A final quibble. The volume on *French Theatre in the Neo-classical Era, 1550–1789*, edited by William Howarth (and associates) in the same series (1997), lists all source references at the start of the bibliography, with archival documents indexed by their (boldface) number in the main text, followed by other print sources similarly indexed and further supplementary references. Such an indexing approach would have been welcome in this volume's bibliography as well, given the number and variety of manuscript sources.

To conclude, while I wished for more integration and balance in the editorial style and a more current approach to the provincial extension of professional theater in the period, *English Professional Theatre, 1530–1660* must be recognized as a substantial contribution to the field. The editors have assembled an important and fascinating collection of materials for the study of Tudor and Stuart theater history which is assured its status as a major reference work for the period.

Vagrancy, Homelessness, and English Renaissance Literature
By Linda Woodbridge
Urbana and Chicago:
University of Illinois Press, 2001

Reviewer: Lawrence Manley

Christopher Hill once remarked that early modern English people lived in fear of the tramp. Evidence of this fear can be found in official policies that criminalized vagrancy and in the many works of popular literature—extending from John Awdeley's *Fraternity of Vagabonds* (ca. 1561) and Thomas Harman's *Caveat for Common Cursetors, Vulgarly Called Vagabonds* (1566–67) to the cony-catching pamphlets of Robert Greene and beyond—that associated the wandering homeless and the transient working poor with the deviant activities of the criminal underworld. This association was unfortunately enshrined for twentieth-century scholarship by the title of Frank Aydelotte's foundational study of the subject, *Elizabethan Rogues and Vagabonds* (1913).

In her marvelous study of *Vagrancy, Homelessness, and English Renaissance Literature*, Linda Woodbridge takes a fresh and systematic look at literary representations of the homeless poor. Drawing on a range of resources, including early modern social history, studies of poverty by leading political scientists, and recent literary scholarship on vagabondage by (among others) William Carroll, Heather Dubrow, and Patricia Fumerton, Woodbridge arrives at a perspective so broad and coherent as to put the subject on a whole new footing. The key to her approach is the disparity between the representation of homelessness and the facts, so far as they can be determined. This disparity has perhaps not been as obvious as it ought to be—Woodbridge cites an alarming number of fairly recent historians who have credited literary treatments of the poor as one or another kind of historical evidence. Still, it is not altogether surprising to learn from her reading of social historians like A. L. Beier and Paul Slack that court records and other archival sources indi-

cate that the homeless poor were not, as they were reputed to be in
so much of Renaissance literature and in the rhetoric of the Tudor
poor laws, an organized subculture of criminal specialists who
spoke an incomprehensible dialect of thieves' cant while pursuing
seditious designs and sexual mayhem.

To the actual conditions of sixteenth-century poverty, its causes
and its effects, Woodbridge devotes an informative Appendix and
a usefully up-to-date bibliographical survey. Her real subject,
however, is the misrepresentation of poverty in the Renaissance
imagination. Her purpose in treating homelessness as a literary
phenomenon is not to make it unhistorical but to offer an historical
explanation for its three most striking features: (1) the topic's per-
sistence over time and its pervasiveness in so many discursive contexts (Woodbridge points out that while it was never the age's most
pressing concern, the subject of "houseless poverty" crops up
everywhere; if the vagabond was seldom the age's worst villain, he
nevertheless was, as she says, "everyone's bogeyman," [13]); (2) the
discursive tendency to dissociate the homeless from the virtuous
"settled" poor and to link them instead with criminal deviance;
and (3) the tendency to frame the abject realities of poverty in the
literary decorum of comic merriment.

In order to shift the terms of discussion toward literature, Woodbridge, who alerts readers to the dangers in our very ideas of a "culture of poverty," devotes an opening chapter showing that Thomas
Harman's influential *Caveat of Common Cursetors* was not (as it is
sometimes taken to be) a work of "protosociology" based on Harman's experience as a J.P. in Kent but a jestbook that draws its material from literary sources such as the earlier *Liber Vagatorum*
(1509). Harman's taxonomical rubric, Woodbridge argues, is merely
a modified staple of late medieval estates satire serving as a framing
device to the anecdotes that Harman calls his "tales." For Woodbridge, however, to shift the discussion from protosociology to literary genre is not to eliminate an historical problem but to identify
one. In Harman's transformation of homeless poverty into jestbook
knavery Woodbridge reads the anxieties of the mid Tudor age, as a
Kentish gentleman living along the main highway to London registers his uneasiness about his changing society in a text that ambivalently mixes jest with earnest, prurience with moralizing, and the
comfort of cataloguing with the fear of chaos.

In the chapters that follow, Woodbridge demonstrates how ridicule and comic fantasies about homelessness figured into many

cultural developments of the sixteenth century—the Protestant Reformation and its new attitudes toward poverty, the humanist agenda of shaping human virtue, the creation of a state apparatus and a sense of nationhood, and the development of the ideas of domesticity, hygiene, and civility that were so essential in to the shaping of early modern society. The historical process on which Woodbridge places the greatest emphasis is the use of laughter for purposes of ridicule, in order to laugh people "into corners from which they could not escape" (50). The literary transformation of the homeless poor into comic rogues was thus a form of "othering," by means of which social identities were defined and rendered functional through the disowning of undesirable attributes as foreign, uncouth, or monstrous. "The crucial building blocks of Renaissance culture," Woodbridge argues, "the Reformation, the new humanism, the political patriarchalism and centralizing tendencies of English government, the new sense of English nationhood, the valorization of domesticity— . . . all involved disclaiming and penalizing vagrancy" (175).

Woodbridge is more convincing on some of these developments than on others. Most successful is her splendid account of the ways in which pre-Reformation anticlerical literature, with its ridicule of medicants and roguish friars, was adapted to the purposes of Reformation propaganda in works like Simon Fish's *Supplication for the Beggars* (ca. 1529) and John Bale's *Acts of the English Votaries* (1548). The "fraters" and "patricos" of Harman's canting beggar underworld, she shows, were latter-day literary descendents of the idle wandering clergy, filtered through religious developments that simultaneously dismantled the charitable institutions of the medieval church, desanctified poverty, and replaced the theology of religious works with one of faith alone. Also persuasive are the fine account of the vagabond underworld as the "other" of Tudor domesticity and the discussions of hygiene and civility.

One shortcoming of Woodbridge's approach is a rhetorical side effect of her way of modeling the "othering process," her tendency to ascribe conscious intention and moral attributes to abstract agencies. It is evident, for example, in her claim that "the Crown had its own reasons for disliking vagrancy: it threatened to derail the Tudor bureaucratic juggernaut" (153), or that "unwillingness to face squarely the disturbing consequences of their theology . . . led Protestant theologians to demonize . . . beggary" (100). In statements like these, Woodbridge's fine sense of how ideological misrecognition actually operates, as well as her desire that people should, as Kent says, "see better," leads to an extravagance of statement that undermines the valuable truth of what she is saying: fears of disorder led to Poor Laws that enhanced the state bureaucracy, and Protestant theology encompassed views that would seem to us contradictory.

But ridicule and "othering" are not in any case the whole story in Woodbridge's account of the comic treatment of vagabonds. Though less explicitly formulated than her arguments about ridicule, there is throughout the book an implicit recognition that comic ambivalence provides the opportunity for identification as well as alienation. The two possibilities are perhaps summed up in Woodbridge's widely separated discussions of the abject Widow Edith, the much persecuted subject of a particularly mean-spirited "humanist" jestbook, and the roguish jestbook hero "Howlglas," whose unflagging resistance to conformity takes the form of "mooning" all types of respectability. This ambivalence is remarked as well in Woodbridge's astute connection of crime fiction to the sense of domesticity: the place to enjoy a good crime novel, she notes, is by the cozy fireside, where the pleasure of domestic security is enhanced by the secret thrill of unhomey outrage.

The urban sociologist Robert Park once observed that complex and socially unstable environments like that of the modern metropolis (or Woodbridge's deracinated Tudor England) provide the ideal setting for the criminal, the detective, and the genius. It was the genius of the cony-catching author Robert Greene to have discovered, with the author *Oedipus* and many authors of detective fiction, that reader and writer are positioned alike in sharing the perspectives of both policeman and crook. This being so, it may then be asking the wrong thing of the literary imagination to expect a less sensational representation of the poor: much of literature is about people (including the rich man Dives in his many Renaissance guises) who are bad. This is the point behind an argument Woodbridge does not cite, Empson's account of *The Beggars' Opera* as "rogue pastoral," but it is also an implicit point in her own discussion of the "merry beggar" tradition in works like *Bartholomew Fair*, Fletcher and Massinger's *Beggar's Bush*, and Brome's *A Jovial Crew.*

For the most part Woodbridge prefers to treat comic ambivalence as an unconscious effect, as representations of homeless poverty deconstruct themselves in their (finally unsuccessful) attempts to construct legitimacy by disowning the undesirable attributes they project onto beggars. As Woodbridge would have it, the note of sympathy that slips through "othering" is only for *us* to hear. The one great exception is her treatment of *King Lear*, which—in violation of her professional stance against exempting Shakespeare "from the rigorous historicizing to which we subject his contemporaries" (206)—she regards not only as "politically and socially radical" in its non-comic treatment of homelessness but as "head and shoulders above his culture and . . . centuries ahead of his time" (206–7). Throughout the book Woodbridge notes the many ways in which the Tudor preoccupation with homeless beggars touches Shakespeare's works—in *As You Like It* and the romances, in the tricks of the masterless Autolycus, in Falstaff's ragamuffin regiment and in his roguishly self-inflicted nosebleed, in Pistol's exploitation of his scars, in the comic discomfiture of the malingering Simon Simpcox, and in the menace of Jack Cade's invasion of Alexander Iden's garden. But in *King Lear* she tracks the many signs of the deeper process Rosalie Colie called unmetaphoring, as the rich, privileged, and "legitimate" are forced literally to become what they, both materially and ideologically, have made of the poor.

In her reading of the play Woodbridge does honorable battle with many recent critical arguments that would set bounds to *King Lear's* economic radicalism—Naomi Liebler's claim that the play "takes no view of the large population of Jacobean poor" (224), Margreta de Grazia's view that no compassionate redistribution of the superflux takes place, Annabel Patterson's view that Lear unfortunately recovers from the mad wisdom of his sermon on injustice, Richard Halpern's view that the loyalties the play affirms are regressively feudalistic. Her responses to these objections vary, but the substance of her case is consistent with her own approach throughout the book, which is to trace the ways in which attitudes are culturally engrained in the very language from which stereotypes are formed. Seen in these terms, the play's ultimate significance lies not so much in the outcome of its fable as in the way that its fable transforms attitudes and language, as the word "poor," for example, loses its sting as a term of denigration and instead becomes a means of extending compassion.

If there is a reason to pause over the idea of making an exception of Shakespeare, it is not so much because this is one more step in his hyper-canonization, or because historicizing methods have not in fact been rigorously applied (they have, and in ways that are cru-

cial to Woodbridge's reading). Rather, it is because the methods
have been applied differently, in ways that allow for the conscious
perception of ironies and complexities as an historical phenomenon. The fruits of this different application lead to the question of
whether similar treatment might have been extended to at least
some of the other works and authors covered in the book. Perhaps
not to the author of the *The Twelve Merry Jests of the.Widow Edith*,
or to Judge Harman, to whom the voices of vagrant women were
never as audible as they are to Woodbridge's acutely trained ear,
but perhaps to more complicated figures like Erasmus and More,
who often make their ambivalences the conscious subject of their
writing and whose capacities for thoughtfulness and irony on the
subject of poverty seem greater than Woodbridge allows.

Index